THE COMPARATIVE HERMENEUTICS OF RABBINIC JUDAISM

VOLUME SIX

SEDER TOHOROT

TOHOROT THROUGH UQSIN

THE COMPARATIVE HERMENEUTICS OF RABBINIC JUDAISM

VOLUME SIX

SEDER TOHOROT

TOHOROT THROUGH UQSIN

JACOB NEUSNER

Academic Studies in the History of Judaism
Global Publications, Binghamton University
2000

Library of Congress Cataloging-in-Publication Data

Jacob Neusner
The Comparative Hermeneutics of Rabbinic Judaism. Volume VI. Seder Tohorot. Tohorot Through Uqsin

1. Hermeneutics 2. Judaic Studies 3. Religious Studies
4. Tohorot 5. Zabim and Niddah 6. Uqsin

ISBN 1-586840-14-2

Published by Academic Studies in the History of Judaism
Distributed by Global Publications, ICGS
Binghamton University, State University of New York
Binghamton, New York, USA 13902-6000
Phone: (607) 777-4495. Fax: 777-6132
E-mail: pmorewed@binghamton.edu
http://ssips.binghamton.edu

ACADEMIC STUDIES IN THE HISTORY OF JUDAISM

TABLE OF CONTENTS

PREFACE

Precisely what is at stake in an account of the hermeneutics of the Halakhah of Judaism begins in a reliasble definition of hermeneutics, that of K. M. Newton:

> The central concern of hermeneutics as it relates to the study of literature is the problem created by the fact that texts written in the past continue to exist and to be read while their authors and the historical context which produced them have passed away in time. Reading such texts, therefore, becomes inseparable from the question of interpretation. Before the modern period hermeneutics was concerned primarily with how scriptural texts such as the Bible should be read. Should the Bible, for example, be seen as a text which exists in its own terms and read accordingly or should any understanding of it be mediated by an acceptance of the doctrines of the church?[1]

It follows that, by hermeneutics is meant "the rules of reading a text and interpreting it." Then precisely what constitutes the understanding of a text, which is what I mean by, the rules for defining and reading a document — text, context, matrix of meaning? Newton cites Wilhelm Dilthey's dictum, "an act of understanding constitutes what he called a 'lived experience.'" Dilthey states:

> The methodological understanding of permanently fixed life-expressions we call explication. As the life of the mind only finds its complete, exhaustive, and therefore, objectively comprehensible expression in language, explication culminates in the interpretation of the written records of human existence. This art is the basis of philology. The science of this art is hermeneutics.[2]

The hermeneutics that conveyed the rules of proper reading of the Halakhah formed out of occasional rules and conceptions a single, demonstrably cogent statement, one of entire integrity: a category-formation. The hermeneutics of all Halakhic texts of Rabbinic Judaism commences with the respective category-formations, seen whole. These constitute the coherent texts of the living religion of the dual Torah, the building blocks out of which that religion constructs its social order and intellectual system. Any other approach takes data

---

[1]K. M. Newton, *Interpreting the Text. A Critical Introduction to the Theory and Practice of Literary Interpretation* (N.Y., 1990:Harvester/Wheatsheaf), pp. 40-41.

[2]Cited by K. M. Newton, *Interpreting the Text,* p. 42.

— sentences — out of context or treats them as having no context, yielding only philology, not religion.

Hermeneutics, thus conventionally defined as "theory of interpretation," in Rabbinic Judaism finds its data in the modes of analytical thought that produce useful knowledge out of the facts deriving from three sources. These sources are [1] the Torah, Scripture and tradition, [2] nature, and [3] the social order constituted by holy Israel, the latter two as contemplated and classified to begin with by the Torah. These data require structure, proportion, order, balance, rationalization. What theory of interpretation identifies among those data points of likeness and contrast that define category-formations of cogency and proportion? That is the question I systematically answer, following the sequence of the Halakhic category-formations of the Mishnah-Tosefta-Yerushalmi-Bavli. Hermeneutics then articulates the results of a distinctive mode of thought, and, in the Halakhah, it is the analogical-contrastive kind. That is to say, analytical thought defining the category-formations that are subject to hermeneutical reflection proceeds in accord with the rules of analogical-contrastive thinking.

These rules are simply stated. Things are alike and fall into the same classification, all arrayed in conformity with that classification's governing rule, its cogent data, and its range of consequent exegetical problems.[3] Or they are unlike and fall into contrasting, opposite classifications, with contrary governing rules. Each of these generative rules applies the logic of the hermeneutical principle to the cogent data that are selected for interpretation by the governing hermeneutics. And each within that same overriding logic produces its urgent exegetical problems. Then the issue of hermeneutics — again, defined conventionally and publicly as "theory of interpretation" — is, [1] what modes of analytical thought have generated a given category-formation, [2] with what result, and [3] to what end? What is at stake here is to explain how the Rabbinic sages have created, time and again, category-formations that transform and transcend the data that are interpreted. For the hermeneutics of Judaism produces a single result time and again, and that is, the formation of wholes that add up to more than the sums of the parts. In the language used here, category-formations yielded by the theory of interpretation impart to the selected data meaning and consequence that vastly transcend the qualities of the data viewed out of categorical context.

---

[3] That exegesis is the effect of hermeneutics, its program defined thereby, forms a rule well-established by the history of the exegesis of any classical document. On analogical-contrastive thought, see especially G. E. R. Lloyd, *Polarity and Analogy. Two Types of Argumentation in Early Greek Thought*. Cambridge, 1966: Cambridge University Press.

Part of my lifelong inquiry into the definition of Judaism in its classical documents, this project addresses the hermeneutics of the Halakhic documents, within the very particular framework defined by the native category-formations of the Halakhah. Those category-formations embody the results of a theory of interpretation of the normative rules of the Pentateuch and associated laws of tradition, of nature and of Israel's social order. Each component of the work contributes to our knowledge of that theory: the way the Rabbinic sages read the diverse texts of the law, their rules for the formation of molecules out of atoms, active knowledge out of raw data. Here, therefore, I analyze the topical framework within which the Halakhic compilations conduct their discourse, the entire Halakhah being organized by subject-matter and within a logic comprised by two components:

First, the organizing logic imputes coherence to the requirements of topical exposition.

Second, the logic insists, within the concrete case, abstract principles are to be encapsulated. The case embodies the rule.

Specifically, in this protracted exercise I identify the theory of how a given topic is defined out of the data of the Torah, nature and society and is to be interpreted. That requires, specifically, moving backward from exegesis of cases to hermeneutics of topics, that is, from the evidence of the (consequent) exegesis that gives actuality to that theory backward to the (causative) theory of interpretation itself. What modes of analogical-contrastive thinking are in play in the hermeneutics of interpreting data in one way, rather than in some other. What I mean, concretely, is, organizing data within one category-formation, rather than some other.

The category-formations of Rabbinic Judaism in its normative, Halakhic component form the building blocks of that Judaism, its organizing and rationalizing constructions. And we everywhere encounter their definitive status: they dictate the character of the tractates of the Halakhah, Mishnah-Tosefta-Yerushalmi-Bavli. That is to say, Rabbinic Judaism in its normative corpus of Halakhah comes to us in four documents, the Mishnah, the Tosefta, the Yerushalmi (Talmud of the Land of Israel), and the Bavli (Talmud of Babylonia). All appeal to the same category-formations, that is definitions of data deemed to cohere. So a huge testimony to the hermeneutics of Rabbinic Judaism comes to us in the definitive documents. It follows that, in a routine way, documentary hermeneutics also enters in. Therefore I further compare and contrast the theory of presenting a given topic that dictated the character of the one document with the theory that governed in another of the cognate writings of Judaism. The results of that comparison are mostly, but not entirely negative. Having completed my preliminary account of the hermeneutics of the

Aggadah, at certain points here I further take up the task to come: the comparison of the Halakhic and the Aggadic hermeneutics of Rabbinic Judaism.

With these principles in mind, readers will follow as I parse the title of the project as a whole, which allows a simple definition of the project.

HERMENEUTICS: First comes the key-word, "hermeneutics." What issue falls into the category of hermeneutics, within the conventional and accepted definition, "the theory of interpretation of a received document"? The hermeneutics of a religion of a textual community such as is represented by the Halakhic documents governs how a given topic is going to be defined ("category-formation") and expounded by the cognate texts of that community. To begin with, the hermeneutics determines the category-formations of that textual community, by which I mean, how random data fall into common classifications and thereby form coherent compositions. Hermeneutics in guiding the formation of organizing categories thereby defines the rules of coherence — how one and one equal two — and the conclusions to be drawn for further cases from that fact — how one apple and one apple equal two apples. It guides reading the facts received from holy Scriptures and (in the case of Rabbinic Judaism, with its tri-partite sources of a single truth) the organizing of the data set forth by nature and by society as well. The hermeneutics brought to bear upon the data of Scripture, society, and nature dictates questions that will be raised and those that will not be raised. It further predetermines the entire exegetical program, so allowing a system to extend and amplify itself to the outer boundaries of imagination. Hermeneutics here, in the context of Rabbinic Judaism, forms the theory that guides the formulation and transmission of tradition from generation to generation. To use the language of the present project, hermeneutics guides the identification of systemic categories and their agglutination in category-formations; hermeneutics states the theory that produces paradigms and identifies problems of detailed exegesis thereof — whether in the raw data of Scripture, the social and historical order, or nature.

HERMENEUTICS AND EXEGESIS: How do I conceive hermeneutics to relate to the detailed work of exegesis (in which, in this context, I am not engaged)? Common usage suffices: hermeneutics forms the governing process of interpreting data, mediating chaos into order, and exegesis takes up the consequent, episodic challenges to harmonious reason, coherence, cogency. First therefore in logic comes the theory of interpretation, then follows its application to specific problems. Hermeneutics then predetermines the program of exegesis, the rules for not only solving, but to begin with identifying, ad hoc problems. Accordingly, hermeneutics defines the exegetical task, that is, the work of dealing with detail in a consistent, rational manner. That is because hermeneutics identifies what, within a received piece of writing, requires attention, framing problems for exegetical inquiry in a particular setting. Defining rationality, hermeneutics explains the coherence of the bits and pieces of the writing.

COMPARATIVE HERMENEUTICS: as briefly indicated at the outset, to identify the governing rationality I progress from detail to generalization, from the results of a process of exegetics to what I conceive to form the generative hermeneutics, from the manner of the exegesis of details to the guiding hermeneutics of the whole. This I do in an encompassing framework, reading first the documents — the Mishnah, Tosefta, Yerushalmi, and Bavli — in sequence, then the entire corpus of authoritative writings viewed whole. In due course, comparative hermeneutics of Rabbinic Judaism extends from the Halakhah to the Aggadah, from norms of behavior to norms of belief. And that brings us to the second key word of the title: what of the "comparative" exercise? Here, if "hermeneutics" derives from the theory of exposition of a given topic by their category-formations, "comparative hermeneutics" concerns itself with the logical next step. That is, the comparison and contrast of the respective theories of the exposition of a single program of topics in cognate documents, for the Halakhah, and ultimately for the cognate genres of writing, the Halakhah and the Aggadah, as well. How a given topic is expounded, the issues people deem to inhere therein and to require exposition — description, analysis, and interpretation — these rules of interpretation in particular terms embody the general theory of how to make sense of a received, determinate tradition, that is, the Torah or "Judaism." In this part of the larger project, I deal with the comparative hermeneutics of the Halakhic category-formations, producing a negative result (so I anticipate). In the next part, I return to the comparison of the hermeneutics of the Halakhah and the Aggadah, which I have already defined in more than a preliminary way.

But how productive is the comparison of the Halakhic hermeneutics of the four Halakhic documents? Alas, readers will quickly note that comparing the several documents' reading of a common topic or problem repeatedly yields a severely limited range of results. These are two. First, the two Talmuds take up secondary and derivative problems. Second, the Tosefta sometimes clarifies the Mishnah and sometimes makes a statement of its own. So the upshot of the comparison of the hermeneutics of the Halakhic documents in dealing with a common range of data is negative. I do not discern among the successor-documents even significant variations in the Mishnah's Halakhic hermeneutics. That negative result is important, to be sure, but reaching it induces a certain tedium. As the project unfolds, I shall comment only when I note in a successor-document a fundamentally new theory of interpreting Halakhic data. But, compensating for that disappointment, at specific points we find that the Aggadah contributes its distinctive perspective, and the comparison of the hermeneutics of the Halakhah of a given topic and the hermeneutics of the Aggadah of that same topic, as set forth by the Bavli in particular, yields more than routine results.

RABBINIC JUDAISM: What of "Rabbinic Judaism"? That language refers to the Judaic religious system — way of life, world view, realized by a determinate "Israel" — portrayed, for the present purpose, solely by the Rabbinic documents of the classical age, the first six centuries of the Common Era: the Mishnah, Tosefta, Yerushalmi, Bavli, and Midrash-compilations produced by authorities of the Rabbinic tradition in particular. Now, as a matter of fact, these documents not only come to us with a vast exegetical literature. They themselves constitute an exercise of exegesis as well: they systematically mediate between a corpus of information, deriving from various sources but encompassing Scripture in particular, and the formulation of law in expository, not exegetical, form by the Mishnah and the Tosefta. So far as the history of religions is the exegesis of exegesis, this is a project at the very heart of the history of religions as that discipline takes up the Judaic problematic in its larger enterprise.

PRACTICING COMPARISON: I present a systematic comparison of Mishnah-Tosefta-Yerushalmi-Bavli on how each document determines what it wants to know, and say, about a shared agendum of specified subjects. What may we expect the Mishnah to do with its topic? What then does the Tosefta want to accomplish in the presentation of the same topic, whether in dialogue with the Mishnah or not (that is an autonomous question)? When the Yerushalmi takes up the same topic, what interests its framers? Finally, how does the Bavli recapitulate the subject, and what are the traits of its mind in addressing a common heritage? I do not know a systematic account of these matters, and that is what I am trying to achieve. For the mighty labor may produce modest results, but very solid ones: we know how Rabbinic Judaism in the Halakhah worked out its theory of interpreting the topical program, the corpus of native category-formations, that encompass and impose rationality upon the vast corpus of details that all together comprise the norms of that Judaism: the hermeneutics of the Halakhic sector.

WHAT IS AT STAKE IN THIS PROJECT? A distinguished historian of religion once said, "The history of religions is the exegesis of exegesis." In a profound sense, that judgment animates an entire field of learning, and here, within my approach to matters, always from the bottom, the raw data, upward, hermeneutics is the exegesis of exegesis. In this project in the history of religions, I undertake an inductive account, through systematic inquiry into data, of the hermeneutics of the principal documents of Rabbinic Judaism. At issue is the theory of interpretation that guides the sages in their exposition of the topics that they define and expound. That theory is realized in the category-formations, of Rabbinic Judaism in the documents that expound those formations. These documents fall into two classes, Halakhic, normative for behavior, and Aggadic, normative — if in a different way — for belief. I have dealt with the latter and here continue my study of the former. I aim at an account of how the two classes of writing fuse, the Halakhic and the Aggadic, and for that purpose require a systematic account of the native category-formations that govern in each class — hence the present project. I use the word "hermeneutics" to refer to the process of interpretation — embodied in the results in systematization, rationalization, configuration and representation — that guides thought the data of the Halakhah, their configuration and their articulation.[4] I undertake the comparison and contrast of the rules of interpretation realized in the respective documents (so far as these vary, as they do occasionally). That is what I mean, in the present context, by the comparative hermeneutics of the Rabbinic Judaism: the rules for interpreting the topics that all together comprise the Halakhah, the norms of actuality, of that Judaism.

The goal of this study is to define the main lines of that process, the hermeneutics of the Halakhah, as that hermeneutics governs the formation and articulation of native category-formations out of a mass of data, some deriving from Scripture, some from natural reason, and further guides the interpretation and articulation of each of those native category-formations. A subsidiary goal is comparative, namely, an effort to identify evidence of variation within the hermeneutics of the native category-formations as these categories are set forth in the successive documents of the Halakhah, from the Mishnah, ca. 200, which is primary, to the Tosefta, ca. 300, Yerushalmi, ca. 400, and Bavli, ca. 600.

RECAPITULATING THE INTRODUCTION: The Introduction to the entire project, in Volume I, provides a systematic account of the theoretical framework. But readers will want to have in hand a brief picture of the procedures that, in the shank of the book, I follow to elicit the information that I seek. Here are the issues and how I investigate the data pertinent to them.

[1] THE DEFINITION OF A CATEGORY-FORMATION: what topics are covered within an established category-formation, corresponding to a tractate of Mishnah-Tosefta-Yerushalmi-Bavli? How is the encompassing formation defined, and what principles of selection govern the selection of data that are encompassed? Here the character of Rabbinic Judaism, defined by its dialogue with Scripture and (in some measure) the dialectics of its relationship therewith, defines the logically-consequent question: the hermeneutical stimu-

---

[4] That in various philosophical settings, for other purposes altogether, the word has been defined very differently need not prevent us from using it in its conventional sense. I do not enter into the philosophers' debate of "hermeneutics versus epistemology" or pretend even to follow it.

lus, Scripture or some logic perceived internal to the native-category itself. And that leads to the second issue.

[2] THE FOUNDATIONS OF THE HALAKHIC CATEGORY-FORMATIONS: Two sources for category-formations present themselves: Scripture and some kind of autonomous logic, e.g., the organization of data through the identification of species of a common genus. In the former case these questions emerge: Does a category-formation correspond to one of Scripture, e.g., a passage of Scripture that systematically expounds a topic? An example of an affirmative case is the category-formation Negaim, which corresponds to Leviticus 13-14. An instance of a negative case is the category-formation Berakhot, which occasionally utilizes data supplied by the Written Torah but entirely on its own identifies a large category of activity and defines, divides, and organizes the pertinent data. In the later case — the working of autonomous logic — can we specify the workings of that logic? An instance of an affirmative answer comes to us from Berakhot, which organizes around the classification of data within the genus, the individual's obligations to Heaven, a variety of species, carefully limited to those that share common traits dictated by the genus.

[3] THE EXPOSITION OF THE COMPONENTS OF A GIVEN CATEGORY-FORMATION BY THE MISHNAH-TOSEFTA-YERUSHALMI-BAVLI: This brings us to the heart of the matter. That is, the hermeneutical core of the category-formation. Here I systematically ask, how is the topic expounded in the successive documents, and what traits of mind, what theory of consequence and significance, in those documents dictate the course of exposition? Here I have to present the Halakhah, in abbreviated form, but in a comprehensive manner. I undertake to describe what each document contributes to the exposition of the Halakhic category-formation. That is where I find the data that tell me what hermeneutical principles are in play, how successive sets of sages represented by the four documents of the Halakhah mediate the category-formation in their literary labor.

I did exactly that — a presentation of the successive documentary treatments of one and the same topic — for a different purpose in my *The Halakhah. An Encyclopaedia of the Law of Judaism.* There I constructed a précis of the Halakhah. articulated in detail in the four successive documents of the halakhah. These are signaled in the following type-faces: **the Mishnah**, the Tosefta, *the Talmud of the Land of Israel,* and THE TALMUD OF BABYLONIA. Here I draw upon, but have revised, that presentation

I cite, from the Tosefta, Yerushalmi, and Bavli, those passages that represent fresh initiatives, but not those that merely take up and amplify what has already been said. This requires a labor of selection, sorting through the types of Halakhic expositions in the Tosefta, Yerushalmi, and Bavli, with special interest in the approach to Halakhic presentation, analysis, and reconstruction particular to the successive documents in sequence. The outcome is to specify a documentary hermeneutics, e.g., the Bavli's characteristic way of analyzing a problem, the Yerushalmi's typical manner of disposing not of a passage of the Mishnah (which does not concern us here) but of a native-category received from the Mishnah.

In my repertoire for the Tosefta, Yerushalmi, and Bavli, therefore, I omit glosses and clarifications of the Mishnah's initial presentation of the Halakhah. I stipulate in advance that the successor-documents have made integral to their hermeneutics a theory of tradition that encompasses a labor of clarification. I find no need to give a great many demonstrations of that established fact. So I make no reference to what merely recapitulates the received formulation of the Halakhah in the Mishnah. I lay stress, rather, upon what is not only characteristic of the successor-compilations in sequence but original to each of them, again in sequence. Here I do not elaborately cite what the documents say, but rather describe their contribution in a few words, based on an abstract of the text.

It follows that, since the successor-documents undertake to amplify the received statement of the Halakhah that the Mishnah sets forth, my portrayal of matters omits reference to that fact. Where the Tosefta pursues its own program, where the Yerushalmi and the Bavli raise fresh questions of Halakhic description, analysis, and interpretation, there I cite, in as brief a form as possible, what is said. In general, therefore, I cite just so much of the texts as is absolutely necessary in order to make the point at hand. So while I start with already-completed work, the articulation of the project requires a very different presentation of the Halakhah from the one that served in the *Religious Commentary*.

[4] DOCUMENTARY TRAITS: For each category-formation I conclude with some remarks upon the traits of the respective documents' expositions, seeking to generalize out of the particularities we shall have examined. That is the point at which results pertinent to the purpose of this project will emerge. I aim at laying a very, very solid foundation in data for the generalizations that I shall systematically set forth in the category-formations and then recapitulate at the end. These summary-remarks will prove fairly succinct, but well-founded. My initial experiment told me that I should work in pairs of documents, each set bearing its own distinctive task: the Mishnah and the Tosefta, then the two Talmuds.

[5] HERMENEUTICS OF A GIVEN CATEGORY-FORMATION: The hermeneutics of each category-formation is identified in the answers to the basic question that altogether account for the character and function of a category-formation: what forms the center of interest, fusing the halakhic data into

a well-delineated and lucidly articulated classification (genus, species)? Once I raise the issue of a category-formation, I invoke the three criteria that I identified for the study of the Aggadic counterpart in my *Native Category-Formation of the Aggadah*.[5] These are the traits of [1] activity, meaning, a category-formation has the capacity to accommodate data in diverse settings, pertinent to a variety of issues, to form a whole that transcends the sum of the parts; [2] consistency, meaning, a category-formation exhibits uniform results, its principles of interpreting data repeatedly producing a coherent and cogent outcome; and [3] generativity, meaning, a category-formation has the power to extend its boundaries to new territory, to generate new problems and to solve them.

These then represent the five rubrics that serve to describe the hermeneutics of the Halakhic component of Rabbinic Judaism. I can think of no others. Future inquiry will surely lead to refinements, but I am confident that here I lay solid foundations for further description, analysis, and interpretation of the Halakhic construction, its structure and its system, and how that construction joins with its Aggadic counterpart, where and when it does.

ANALYTICAL VOCABULARY: I make use of the established, technical vocabulary of the field in which I work, that of history of religion, which may not be entirely familiar to readers not in that field. That analytical vocabulary, standard in history of religion in North America and in no way my invention, contains within itself the issues I pursue and the methods that I follow in addressing them. It is not idiosyncratic (though I may conduct the research in a way other historians of religion will find unfamiliar, with my focus on the distinctive documents at hand and my sustained interest in large-scale constructions of religious thought into systemic formations, e.g., theology). It is an established approach, and the purpose and goals of this project will elude readers who have not reflected for a moment on that well-established approach. Let me then briefly refer to the more frequently-used language.

CATEGORY, CATEGORY-FORMATION: These two words are easily confused, but in this study each bears its own meaning.[6] By category I mean,

---

[5] *The Native Category-Formations of the Aggadah*. I. *The Later Midrash-Compilations*. Atlanta, 1999: Scholars Press for South Florida Studies in the History of Judaism; *The Native Category-Formations of the Aggadah*. II. *The Earlier Midrash-Compilations*. Atlanta, 1999: Scholars Press for South Florida Studies in the History of Judaism.

[6] Hence the requirement to distinguish "category" from "category-formation." The former is fully worked out for the Rabbinic writings in Volume One of the trilogy: *The Theological Grammar of the Oral Torah*. Binghamton, 1999: Dowling College Press/Global Publications of Binghamton University [SUNY]. I. *Vocabulary: Native Categories; The Theological Grammar of the Oral Torah*. Binghamton, 1999: Dowling College Press/Global Publications of Binghamton University [SUNY]. II. *Syntax: Con-*

that part of a proposition that allows the meanings of other words to be determined by virtue of its presence. In linguistics such terms are called collectively "the head noun." In descriptive theology these categories govern classification of data concerning what God has said and done, now recorded in the Torah. The single word of a statement that determines the meaning and properties of the whole, out of linguistics, here corresponds to those categories that govern — dictate what fits with what, and how things hold together — everywhere. In that context, a category gives way to a category-formation, that is, a large construction that functions in expository contexts the way a category functions in the smallest whole sense-unit.

A CATEGORY-FORMATION forms a principal building block of a theory of the social- or world-order. It is a main component of the structure and a principal part of the operating system, of that coherent account of the social order put forth by a set of cogent ideas in a corpus of authoritative writings that I have called "a system." From "category" we proceed to category-formation, the analogy to which in grammar is syntax. The rules of correct syntax — sentence-construction, in familiar terms — are to vocabulary as the rules of making connections and building constructions are to the native categories of a theological structure and system. Each dictates how the smallest whole units join to form clusters of meaning. The coherent phrases and even cogent sentences of a language correspond to the conceptual composites, the building blocks and even propositions of a theological system. Certain words in a language, as certain native categories in the documents of the Oral Torah, properly join together, forming intelligible clusters of meaning and even complete thoughts. Other words or native categories, when joined, jar. They yield gibberish. When we know which words may join with which others, and which not, formulating the theological counterpart to the rules of syntax of a language, we know the inner logic of the system: how to set forth statements that make sense. We may even explain why in context they make sense. Native categories such as "God," "Israel," "Sinai," "Torah," for example, combine and recombine. While meanings may well shift in context, within a prescribed range of possibilities, "God," "gentiles," "idolatry" and "love," rarely join, and when "Sinai," "Torah, and "gentiles do, the negative (e.g., "why did the gentiles *not* accept...?") must make its appearance early and promi-

---

nections and Constructions; The Theological Grammar of the Oral Torah. Binghamton, 1999: Dowling College Press/Global Publications of Binghamton University [SUNY]. III. *Semantics: Models of Analysis, Explanation and Anticipation*. I realize that "category-formation": is an awkward phrase, but the distinction between category and composition of categories is exceedingly critical to all thought about the Halakhic literature, as the difficulties not fully resolved by Max Kadushin show.

nently. The distinction between category and category-formation is fully spelled out in my *Native Category-Formations of the Oral Torah.*[7]

What tells us that we deal with a category-formation of a system? As explained in the Introduction to this project, Volume One Part A, I discern three indicative traits: those of a generative, active, coherence-imparting paradigm, to wit:

A PARADIGM GENERATIVE OF LOGIC OR RATIONALITY OF COHERENCE AND PROPORTION: A category-formation is defined, out of the vast range of data that comprise the system, by an active paradigm or pattern, one that may pertain to an event, person, idea, symbol or image that typifies and rationalizes events, persons, ideas, symbols (visual or verbal) or images (narrative or static).

ACTIVITY: Such a formation is one that plays an active role in holding together and organizing, rationalizing the discrete details of thought.

CONSISTENCY: And, most important, it is one that does so in a consistent manner, with predictable and regular, orderly results. I cannot overstate this point, which is the centerpiece of the entire composition.

In this context, then, I invoke the criteria of generativity, activity, and consistency. A category-formation in the Halakhah imposes a coherent logic upon the data that it draws together and forms of the whole a clear picture, an orderly statement. The category-formation can accommodate new problems and generate new propositions, dealing with time and with change. The source of the data that requires the categorical rationalization — Scripture, tradition, logic — makes no difference. The category-formation encompasses all and forms the whole into a cogent construction. Let me briefly point to concrete examples to instantiate this abstract definition of what a category-formation is and does.

DEFINING SOME SPECIALIZED VOCABULARY, E.G., LOCATIVE, UTOPIAN, ENLANDISED: Since Rabbinic Judaism recapitulates the Scriptural theology of the possession of the Land of Israel as a critical component of Israel's covenant with God and of the Temple and its cult as central medium for the divine service and relationship, I invoke three words in fixed, particular meanings. These are the binary opposites, utopian and locative, meaning, everywhere in general as against here in particular, and enlandised, a subset of locative, meaning the particularization of place by its identification with a distinctive geographical construction (fabrication, really), in the case of Rabbinic Judaism in the heritage of Scripture, the Land of Israel, Jerusalem, the Temple, and the like.

---

[7] *The Native Category-Formations of the Aggadah,* cited above.

HIERARCHICAL CLASSIFICATION, ANALOGICAL-CONTRASTIVE REASONING: A fair part of the analytical vocabulary also derives from my *Judaism as Philosophy. The Method and Message of the Mishnah*[8] and the corpus of research that is summarized there, e.g., issues of hierarchical classification, analogical-contrastive reasoning, and the like. The analytical vocabulary is meant to turn cases into rules, rules into generalizations, generalizations into knowledge useful for analysis of other cases of religion altogether — the equivalent of mathematics for the physical sciences, I suppose.

MODES OF THOUGHT: Analogical-contrastive reasoning at the service of hierarchical classification represents a species of the genus, modes of thought. Let me conclude by briefly explaining the more general considerations that engage my interest. The documents of the Oral Torah appeal to a system of thought that everywhere defines matters and appeals to a self-evident logic of order, proportion, and balance that we can readily comprehend Its inner logic is always presupposed. Its modes of thought and even specific propositions dictate the identification of data that await analysis, the character of problems that require explanation, and the implications that define what is to be anticipated. Semantics is to grammar as models of analysis, explanation, and anticipation are to theology. The one identifies what is implicit in intelligible discourse and therefore intuitive or presupposed, the other, what is implicit in the particulars of religious discourse and therefore definitive of the a priori theological system — one that makes possible an immediate understanding of a range of statements that have never been made before but once made make sense. The specifics of cogent discourse turn out to derive from a generative structure, encompassing both modes of thought and massive conceptions of a concrete order. These modes we uncover by noting regularities of analytical procedure and repeated appeals to a finite corpus of explanations of a very particular character. It is at the point of anticipation that the specificities of the generative system come to the surface — but these turn out fully to embody the givens of the intellectual disciplines that govern: find the counterpart, establish the balance, take the measure of appropriate proportion.

PARTICULAR, GENERIC HERMENEUTICS: These terms are critical. By "particular hermeneutics of a category-formation," I mean, the theory of interpretation — selection of data, interpretation thereof — that concerns the topic of a given category-formation. By generic hermeneutics I mean the body of interpretative issues common to the entire Halakhah.

PARTICULAR HERMENEUTICS OF A CATEGORY-FORMATION: PRINCIPLES OF SELECTING DATA, ORGANIZING AND INTERPRETING

---

[8] Columbia, 1991: University of South Carolina Press. Paperback edition: Baltimore, 1999: The Johns Hopkins University Press.

THEM: This I claim to discern through the hypothetical reconstruction of the process of reasoning that I think defined for said topic the governing theory of matters: what do we want to know and why? This hypothetical reconstruction of mine rests on the theory that a process of analogical-contrastive analysis engaged with a given topic and treated said topic as a species to be compared with, and contrasted against, a counterpart species (or more), the pair then forming a common genus. This process of analogical-contrastive analysis established the like-traits in a taxonomic labor of hierarchical classification — classification of the species of a genus, hierarchization of the species within the genus — and then defined the unlike traits. Examples of how I reconstruct this process abound through volumes I-IV. In general, I have found that the presentation of the Halakhic category-formations presents the particular hermeneutics first, then proceeds to problems of generic hermeneutics.

GENERIC HERMENEUTICS: Everyone who has studied more than a few passages of the Mishnah-Tosefta-Yerushalmi-Bavli recognizes the activity of a hermeneutical program that transcends the topics and the category-formations of the Halakhah. Each of the documents in succession works up all topics in the same way, a manner distinctive to its compilers, so that we can readily differentiate a passage of the Bavli from a passage of the Yerushalmi, not only in rhetoric but also in modes of thought and inquiry. Experience in presenting the Halakhah the way I have done in this project has also shown me how ordinarily, though not invariably, to differentiate the Tosefta's from the Mishnah's treatment of the same subject. So we may say that there is a corpus of documentary hermeneutics to be defined in some detail. But overall, permeating all Halakhic documents, is a generic hermeneutics, a hermeneutics that pertains everywhere and that dictates the course of exposition, the exegesis, of any category-formation. I have defined a fair portion of that hermeneutics, thinking it was particular to the Mishnah, in my *The Philosophical Mishnah.*[9]

This work stands at the beginning of inquiry. Enough has been said, however, in explaining the utilization of an analytical vocabulary in the service of research to indicate that, so far as I know, a new inquiry commences. True, much has been written under the rubric "hermeneutics," but by "hermeneutics"

---

[9] I refer to *The Philosophical Mishnah.* Volume I. *The Initial Probe.* Atlanta, 1989: Scholars Press for Brown Judaic Studies; *The Philosophical Mishnah.* Volume II. *The Tractates' Agenda. From Abodah Zarah to Moed Qatan.* Atlanta, 1989: Scholars Press for Brown Judaic Studies; *The Philosophical Mishnah.* Volume III. *The Tractates' Agenda. From Nazir to Zebahim.* Atlanta, 1989: Scholars Press for Brown Judaic Studies; *The Philosophical Mishnah.* Volume IV. *The Repertoire.* Atlanta, 1989: Scholars Press for Brown Judaic Studies. The results of the foregoing form the foundation of my *Judaism as Philosophy. The Method and Message of the Mishnah.*

people seem to have in mind "theory of exegesis," generalizations about the mechanisms by which conclusions are reached for episodic cases. I have in mind a much broader problem, as I have already explained. That is why so far as I have found, this project has no antecedents in prior research on the history of Rabbinic Judaism in its formative centuries and documents. Every document, every detail we consider has been studied for many centuries and under diverse auspices. But apart from topical studies of severely limited use and even relevance, e.g., collections and arrangements of sayings on this and that, I could find no bibliography of any weight or substance to attach to this project and its companions. Only a few others, represented by the name of Max Kadushin, have ever pursued the inquiries followed here, and my systematic, already-published critique of prior works on "Judaism," whether theological or historical in intent, explains why I find no bibliography of any interest that pertains to this exercise.

THE FUTURE: In general terms, I mean to contribute to the opening up of the problem of the similarities and differences between different types of knowledge, mediated by different modes of discourse, a formulation I owe to the esteemed G. E. R. Lloyd. What I can explain is the character of the category-formations we have — how they treat their topics, the modes of thought that guided them in choosing data and interpreting them. In that sense I claim to account for the types of knowledge produced by the given, the category-formations of the Halakhah set forth by the Mishnah-Tosefta-Yerushalmi-Bavli. These, all together, in proportion and in balance, define Judaism.

WHAT HAVE I NOT ACCOMPLISHED? I cannot account for the category-formations themselves: why these particular ones and no others? The definition of this project — a demonstration of the intellectual processes of analogical-contrastive analysis that I maintain account for the character of the category-formations of the Halakhah — treats those category-formations as the given, requiring description, analysis, and interpretation. But how to account for that "given," the "givenness" of which surely cannot be gainsaid? — that I do not know. But I know how to find out. A process of comparison and contrast awaits. It is in two parts.

The first is internal to the Mishnah-Tosefta-Yerushalmi-Bavli examining the ways not taken, composites that by the criteria of the established category-formations can have undergone articulation and extension as fully-realized category-formations on their own. These are large-scale, free-standing topical constructions of a Halakhic character, which signal possibilities of category-formation both by reason of their sheer volume and by reason of their cogency and even generative promise. The results — ways not taken — should provide the materials for answering the question, why this, not that? What traits do the Halakhic category-formations exhibit that the Halakhic composites not developed into category-formations do not exhibit, and vice versa? With the "not that" in hand, at least in a sizable sample, the "why this?" — the actual choices carried out by the framers of the categorical structure in hand — will represent decisions sages made. In the contrast with possibilities that they did not choose to explore, for which they did not shape a particular hermeneutics and consequent exegetical program, with the facts in hand, I should hope to find guidance on the possibilities they did determine fully to realize and the reasons therefor.

The second is external to the Mishnah-Tosefta-Yerushalmi-Bavli: the character of other congeries of category-formations altogether, the comparison of the Halakhah of formative Judaism with the category-formations that, later on, the Geonim or Maimonides or Joseph Karo or even the modern and contemporary Rabbinic codifiers chose for the structure and system of the Halakhah as they wished to portray it.

After I complete Volume VII of this project, *A Handbook of the Generic Hermeneutics of the Halakhah*, I take the former of the two steps forward, *Why This, Not That? Ways Not Taken in the Category-Formations of the Halakhah of the Mishnah-Tosefta-Yerushalmi-Bavli*. But the latter lies beyond my ken at this time.

For the volumes, Seder Tohorot, on the Halakhic category-formations of the Mishnah-Tosefta-Yerushalmi-Bavli I have made minor changes in procedure. In the prior volumes I compare the various documents' definition of the category-formation for a given topic, Mishnah-Tosefta-Yerushalmi-Bavli. For two reasons I suspend that exercise here. First, we have no Yerushalmi or Bavli for the sixth division of the Halakhah, except for Niddah. Second, the results to date have hardly proved commensurate to the effort. I never found that a later Halakhic document revised in any material way the definition, proportions, or presentation of a given category-formation. Each document that continues the Mishnah's presentation of the Halakhah followed its own, distinctive exegetical program. But the Tosefta ordinarily depends for its hermeneutics, and even for the organization of its presentation of its program, on the Mishnah, all the more so the two Talmuds. Comparing documents yielded familiar propositions on the exegetical proclivities of each, but overall I have discerned no fresh thinking about fundamental questions of hermeneutics in any of the continuator-writings.

It remains to acknowledge the support, for my research, of the University of South Florida, where I had the honor of holding a Distinguished Research Professorship in Religious Studies. Further support comes from Bard College, where, in the first semester of the academic year, I additionally held the position of Professor of Religion. Both at USF through the year and at Bard during fall semesters, I enjoy the friendship and collegiality in learning of many, with whom I undertake common projects in teaching and in writing. These truly professional and accomplished people define the norm for scholarship in the American academy.

In this project of reconstructing thought processes, I am inspired by the example of Harry A. Wolfson. I found much theoretical guidance and criticism in correspondence with Robert Segal, Lancaster University, Guenter Stemberger, University of Vienna, and Ithamar Gruenwald, Tel Aviv University. Prof. G. E. R. Lloyd, Cambridge University, presented me with some stimulating questions. Professor William Scott Green, University of Rochester, remains a principal conversation-partner in all that I do.

I have been impressed by the elegance and effectiveness of Global Publications and am grateful to its editor, Professor Parviz Morewedge, that he has undertaken to publish these rather sizable, short-run monographs.

JACOB NEUSNER
BARD COLLEGE
NEUSNER@BARD.EDU

1.
TRACTATE TOHOROT

I. THE DEFINITION OF THE CATEGORY-FORMATION

Four large topics comprise the category-formation, Tohorot, devoted to the uncleanness of food and drink, secular and sacred:

I. PRINCIPLES OF UNCLEANNESS OF FOOD: MEAT. FATHERS AND OFFSPRING OF UNCLEANNESS. THE MATTER OF REMOVES
II. SUSCEPTIBILITY TO UNCLEANNESS OF HOLY THINGS, HEAVE-OFFERING, AND UNCONSECRATED FOOD, AT THE SEVERAL REMOVES OF UNCLEANNESS THAT PERTAIN
III. DOUBT IN MATTERS OF UNCLEANNESS
IV. THE *HABER* AND THE *'AM HA'ARES*
V. CONCLUDING MISCELLANIES AND REPRISE. THE UNCLEANNESS OF FOODS, LIQUIDS; ISSUES OF CONNECTION

Called "purities," generically, the Halakhah of Tohorot covers four topics that correlate, tacking on a reprise at the end:

[1] Fathers and Offspring of uncleanness;
[2] removes of uncleanness, from the original source through successive points of contamination, e.g., contact, and the affect of what is made unclean at one or more removes upon food in various degrees of sanctification; thus the interplay of removes of uncleanness with levels of sanctification of food and drink;
[3] matters of doubt in connection with the uncleanness of food and utensils and a repertoire of principles for their resolution;
[4] relationships between those who keep the purity laws within the domestic household (the *Haber*) and those who do not (the *'am ha'ares*), and how ambiguities are resolved in that connection.

On the very surface, therefore, the category-formation is comprised by two components,

[A] a topical exposition that responds to what we shall see as a particular hermeneutics (1, 2), followed by

[B] a topical exposition that takes up what will present itself as the generic hermeneutics (3,4,5) of doubt and mixtures and connection, pertaining whether to classes of food or to classes of persons (unclean/clean, unobservant/observant, respectively.

I propose to explain the category-formation not by appeal to its topical program but by an account of its inner coherence, the logic that explains why this, not that. And that requires an account of the particular hermeneutics: the theory of selection and interpretation of the data that are assembled. Then to devise a hypothesis on how the particular hermeneutics of the category-formation has come about, the processes of thought that produced it, we focus on the first two units.

Our procedure for a hypothetical reconstruction of the thought-process that yielded the category-formation is now familiar. We treat the present category-formation as a species of a genus, then extrapolate a counterpart species of a common genus: two species that are alike to form a genus, but unlike to sustain speciation. With such an exercise of analogical-contrastive analysis in hand, we gain perspective on the category-formation subject to study.

The category-formation before us takes as its topic uncleanness affecting food and drink. If, then, the tangible species is, food and drink, susceptible of becoming unclean, the hypothetical counterpart-species of a common genus is, food and drink, unsusceptible of becoming unclean. These represent in gross, undifferentiated species, the components of the common genus, food and drink, that is, the genus of "media for sustaining life." Then the speciation takes place where, within this theory of the Halakhah, it always takes place, at the point of speciation. What principle distinguishes the susceptible from the unsusceptible? Drawing on the known, supplied at Kelim and at Ohalot, we identify the governing variable in the matter of man's evaluation of what serves as food and drink, his intentionality in that regard. The variable is readily stated. What is unsusceptible to uncleanness in food and drink is a volume too negligible to register on man's consciousness, and what is susceptible is that to which man pays attention. Not only so, but when it comes to susceptibility to uncleanness by reason of sanctification of food or drink, it is man's act of intentionality in consecrating the food or drink (or other objects) that to begin with precipitates the working of the entire system of sanctification.

The variable of intentionality applies to susceptibility to uncleanness as much as to status as to sanctification, to utensils as much as to food and drink. We have already established that what man deems nourishing enters the system of uncleanness, and what he intends to treat as holy at some level of sanctification will be differentiated within that system. But we need not rely upon generalities that emerge in other category-formations to validate the claim that the critical variable to differentiate the genus into the species before us and its theoretical counterpart is the matter of intentionality. If we examine the four large composites of which the category-formation is comprised, each laying out its own principles, we see that all address the same basic issue. That issue, in one form or another, is the matter of intentionality. At each point we deal with a problem of taxonomy, which is resolved by appeal to the attitude or the will of the Israelite who effects the taxonomy. To understand how this is so, we have to pay attention to the details of the large composites of the Halakhah.

Viewed from one perspective, it is how to differentiate the species of a given genus: on the side of contamination, source of uncleanness from removes, Father from Offspring; on the side of sanctification, what is subject to uncleanness of one virulence, what to another; what food or drink may or may not have contracted uncleanness; what Israelites may or may not have imparted uncleanness under specified circumstances of indeterminacy.

Viewed from another perspective, we deal with a variety of persons and objects that have had each its own "history." That history encompasses the initial act of imparting susceptibility to food, drink, or objects (in Kelim) and subsequent "events," points of contact with other objects, e.g., through touching, or with persons in various conditions, e.g., a gentile or a Zab, or — more to the point — contact with other objects that have touched objects or persons in various conditions of uncleanness, at one or two or three removes from a corpse, for example. Each must tell its own story, but the chapters are the same: is the person or object, food or drink, to be classified as unclean or clean? To answer that question, I need to know the following:

1. The level of sanctification for which the cleanness is required (how the person, object, food or drink has been subject to surveillance over time), which dictates the number of successive contacts to which the food, drink, or utensil will be affected by that original point of contamination;
2. The character of the uncleanness to which the person or food may or may not have been exposed, primary or secondary, and the number of removes from exposure to that source at which the person or food stands: immediate contact, once-removed, and so on outward;
3. In what location (public, private domain), in what season (dry or rainy), and within what sort of transaction, the exposure is supposed to have taken place or not taken place;
4. What sort of instructions, conditions, and rules were articulated to the parties who may or may not have imparted uncleanness by touching the food or drink or utensils that are subject to doubt.

In reaching a decision on how to classify a person, object, food or drink, each of these questions requires an answer, and at every stage in the process of interrogation, we have to reconstruct the story of what has happened to this person, object, food or drink in the context established by the inquiry into the status that pertains. And that brings us back to our starting point. For, having come this far, we realize what holds the whole together: the four principal parts of the Halakhah before us contribute to the single, sustained narrative that encompasses the person or object, the food or drink, and that determines the taxonomic outcome of the process. The narrative tells us what things the person or object has touched, what things those things have touched, and so on through a sequence of removes; and it further tells us the status imputed to the food or drink (or, in line with Mishnah-tractate Hagigah, the person) *by the attitude and intentionality of the principal player in the drama*, the person affected by the considerations at hand: uncleanness at the one side, sanctification at the other. All of this, amplified by the consideration of removes, forms a small narrative of a cosmic transaction.

Each component turns out to appeal, in the end, to a consideration that operates for them all, intentionality. In this unseen world the impalpable force of the attitude of responsible actors makes its impact everywhere. Uncleanness is relative to that which it affects, and the sensitivity to uncleanness of that which is affected by uncleanness depends upon the status imputed by man's will. To that which is affected by uncleanness, it is man's attitude toward the food, drink, or utensil that [1] renders the object susceptible or unsusceptible; [2] and determines the sensitivity to uncleanness — that is, as a Holy Thing, as in the status of Priestly Rations ("heave-offering"), or as in the status of ordinary food to be preserved in a condition of cleanness.

Stated simply, the proposition that validates invoking intentionality throughout is simple. If man assigns food or drink to the status of Holy Things and so acts as to preserve the cleanness of what is sanctified in that status, then the sources of uncleanness affect the food or drink through successive removes, as many as three (Parah will add yet another, as we have already noticed). If man's intentionality does not impart to the food or drink the standing of Holy Things but of ordinary, secular food or drink, then fewer removes from the source of uncleanness produce effects. So man's plan for the food dictates the susceptibility of that food to various removes of uncleanness. It is the initial decision and attitude of man that makes the difference. If man is alert and capable of forming intentionality, if man can be interrogated in the assumption that he cares about contamination, then the rules of contamination are strictly enforced; if not, then they are null. A child cannot form an intention to preserve cleanness and, therefore, in a case of doubt, he also cannot be assumed to have imparted uncleanness. The *'am ha'ares* is assumed to touch whatever he can reach — unless he is instructed not to. Then his intentionality, to respect the wishes of the householder, is assumed to pertain and therefore to protect from uncleanness what the *'am ha'ares* can have touched but probably did not contaminate at all. At the critical turnings in the decision-making process, the taxonomic question finds its answer in the relativities of attitude and intention.

But along with the principal variable of the category-formation, we identify what is excluded by that variable from a place in the same category-formation. That is to say, one matter is not subject to the decision-making process of man, and one component of the system, one chapter of the narrative, does not find its dynamics in human will. That is the sources of uncleanness. These function *ex opere operato* and do not depend upon man's will for them to bring about contamination. On the contrary, the corpse contaminates whatever is in the tent that overshadows it, and the contaminating power of flux (zob) depends upon its emerging naturally and not by artificial stimulus. That same insistence on the inexorability of the workings of sources of contamination emerges in the consideration of the distinction between Fathers and Offspring of uncleanness; at no point in that corpus of Halakhah do considerations of attitude intervene.

So we may define the particular hermeneutics of Tohorot, that is, those first two of the category-formation's four constitutive components. The web of relationships between warp, sanctification and uncleanness, and woof, removes of uncleanness from a primary source of uncleanness, spins itself out into every corner of the Israelite household, where the system makes a difference. And it is the will of the householder that determines the difference — warp and woof of the whole fabric — that the distinction between clean and unclean is going to make. Everything is relative to the householder's will; he has it in his power to draw the household table into alignment with the altar in the Temple, that is to say, to place the table and the food set thereon into relationship, onto a continuum, with the altar and the Holy Things of the cult. This he can accomplish through an act of will that motivates an attitude of constant watchfulness for those very same sources of contamination that Scripture identifies as danger to the Lord's altar in the Jerusalem Temple. Such an attitude of watchfulness then comes to realization in actions that confirm the attitude and embody the intentionality: take note, avoid, watch out for this, that, and the other thing. That is because the faithful of the Halakhah think of themselves as Temple priests but situate themselves in the ordinary world.

In the actual Temple avoiding sources of uncleanness, e.g., corpses, menstruating women, people suffering a flux, posed no enormous problems; most of the virulent sources of uncleanness were walled out to begin with. But in the household and in the marketplace no one and nothing can be safely excluded, and who knows what can happen — and commonly does? And bumping into someone or something quite inadvertently, sitting down or standing up, still or in motion, at home or in the piazza, who can trace the history of each person, his or her encounter with a corpse, her period, for instance, or with someone who has had such an encounter or sat on a chair on whom a menstruating woman or a man with flux has sat? The possibilities for cultic contamination, controlled in the cult, prove limitless outside. But then, the Halakhah aims at imposing order and a certain rationality, a well-construed assessment of probabilities, upon that chaos of the unclean and the profane that altogether comprises the everyday world. That is what is at stake in the particular hermeneutics of this category-formation.

What about the generic hermeneutics? Here we have a text-book case of its working: theories of probability for the resolution of doubts, e.g., cases of mixtures, connections, and the like. The category-formation provides the occasion to offer some large-scale generalizations and — for the shank of the topic — a set of guidelines on how to resolve cases in which the status of food as to uncleanness is subject to doubt. The matter of doubt further encompasses relationships between those who at home for the domestic table keep the cleanness-laws and Israelites who do not keep those laws and hence are subject to cultic uncleanness. Since day-to-day relationships are assumed to be close and constant, the issue arises: how to sort out cases in which such an outsider, called in Hebrew *'am ha'ares,* has had access to the things belonging to an observant person and in the status of a person afflicted with flux (zab) imparts uncleanness to what he touches, called in Hebrew *haber,* and therefore may or may not have imparted to them cultic uncleanness.

Addressing cases of doubt, how to sort out and resolve cases of doubt affecting food, invites sages to lay forth their judgments on matters of probability. The first principle governs: confirm the status quo: unclean things are adjudged in accord with their condition at the moment that they are found. When an unclean thing has a place, a matter of doubt affecting that place is resolved as unclean; when not, not. The second is, where one may find grounds for a ruling in favor of cleanness, the decision should rest on those grounds. Where there are grounds to assume something is unclean, e.g., proximity to a grave area, to dirt that comes from abroad, to clothing of an Israelite who does not keep the purity laws, and the like, we treat what is subject to doubt as having been contaminated, and so, if that is food in the status of heave offering, we burn the food. On the other hand, sages resolve as clean conditions of doubt concerning a variety of less weighty matters, e.g., unconsecrated food (not heave offering), matters of doubt concerning the hands, matters of doubt concerning rulings of the scribes (at a lower level of authority than those of the Torah itself), and the like. We rely on the most likely outcome; we assign a doubtful case to the condition of the majority of pertinent cases or persons; where one doubt piles up upon another, we resolve doubt in favor of cleanness when public domain is involved, uncleanness when private domain is involved.

But we take full account of peoples' sensibility, meaning, they are assumed to pay attention to what they touch and where they walk or sit. If they can be interrogated and cannot give a reason to assume something has not been contaminated, that testimony to thoughtlessness suffices to rule unclean the matter subject to doubt. They must be prepared to state in positive terms that they have grounds for maintaining food has not been contaminated, as in the following exemplary instance: A person went into an alley and made dough, and afterward a creeping thing was found — and the person said, "If it were here, I would have seen it" — it is unclean, until he will state, "It is clear to me that it was not here beforehand." Here again, what intervenes is the householder's own attitude toward these matters: is he alert and careful, or mindless and careless? Now attitude and intentionality form the foundation for assessing probabilities on what might have happened.

The principal focus upon the relationship of the Israelite who observes purity in connection with ordinary food and the one who does not takes up the generic hermeneutics of mixtures, this time, mixtures of classifications of Israelites. That area of the law allows sages to spell out their deepest convictions about how to live in a diverse society. Essentially we deal with sages' estimate of how people concern themselves with issues of cultic contamination, and that in the end testifies to the intentionality of the concerned parties. If they want to preserve the cultic cleanness of their food and utensils, we translate that intention into fact: we assume they have accomplished their goal. If they do not form such an intentionality, then we dismiss the possibility that purity has been maintained.

The upshot may be stated very simply. The category-formation, Tohorot, forms a large and sustained exercise in the exposition of the particular hermeneutics of intentionality and the generic hermeneutics of doubt and probability as these together pertain to the topic, food and drink. The data selected, the problems formulated and solved — all come together to realize that coherent hermeneutical program for the designated category-formation.

II. THE SCRIPTURAL FOUNDATIONS OF THE HALAKHIC CATEGORY-FORMATION

No verses of Scripture figure in the presentation of the Halakhah by the Oral Torah (cf. H. Albeck, *Seder Tohorot* [Tel Aviv, 1958], pp. 297-298). But sages found in the Torah foundations for most, though not all, of the principles of the removes of uncleanness, the distinction of Fathers and Offspring of uncleanness, and other governing premises.[1] The judgments contained within the Halakhah on probabilities and likely behavior of one or another classification of persons, by contrast, derive entirely from sages' own assessments of matters. Here the operative principles tend to derive from a theory of probabilities applied to cases, as we shall see.

III. THE EXPOSITION OF THE COMPONENTS OF THE GIVEN CATEGORY-FORMATION BY THE MISHNAH-TOSEFTA

I. PRINCIPLES OF UNCLEANNESS OF FOOD: MEAT. FATHERS AND OFFSPRING OF UNCLEANNESS. THE MATTER OF REMOVES

M. 1:1 Thirteen matters regarding the carrion of the clean bird: (1) [to impart uncleanness as food] it requires intention and does not require preparation. And (2) it renders unclean with food uncleanness when it is the size of an egg, and (3) [it conveys food uncleanness] when it is the size of an olive in the [eater's] gullet. And (4) he who eats it requires waiting until sunset. And (5) they are liable on its account for entering the sanctuary. And (6) they burn food in the status of heave offering on its account. And (7) he who eats a limb from the living [bird] from it is smitten with forty stripes.

M. 1:2 (9) The large feathers and the down are susceptible to uncleanness and convey uncleanness, and they do not join together. (10) The beak and the claws are susceptible to uncleanness and convey uncleanness and join together.

M. 1:3 The carrion of the unclean bird (1) requires intention and preparation; and (2) renders unclean with food uncleanness when it is the size of an egg; and (3) in the size of a half-loaf's bulk of it to render the body unfit. And [the rule of] an olive's bulk in the gullet does not apply to it. And (4) the one who eats it does not require waiting for sunset. And (5) they are not liable on

---

[1] The principal location for that discussion is Mishnah-tractate Sotah 5:1-5, carried forward in the continuator-documents, Tosefta-Yerushalmi-Bavli.

account of it for coming to the sanctuary. But (6) on its account they burn food in the status of heave offering. And (7) he who eats a limb from the living [bird] from it does not receive the forty stripes. And (8) slaughtering it does not render it clean. The (9) large feathers and the down are susceptible to uncleanness and convey uncleanness and join together [to form the egg's bulk or the half-loaf's bulk]. The (10) beak and the claws convey uncleanness and are susceptible to uncleanness and join together.

M. 1:4 And with regard to cattle: (1) The hide, (2) the fat, (3) the sediment, (4) the flesh, (5) the bones, (6) the tendons, (7) and horns, and (8) the hoofs join together to convey the uncleanness of foods but not the uncleanness of carrion. And similarly: He who slaughters an unclean beast for a gentile, and it jerks — it conveys the uncleanness of foods but not the uncleanness of carrion until it will die, or until one will cut off its head. [The law] has prescribed more [conditions] to convey uncleanness of foods than to convey uncleanness of carrion.

M. 1:5 The food which is made unclean by a Father of Uncleanness and that which is made unclean by an Offspring of Uncleanness join together with one another to convey the lighter remove of uncleanness of the two. How so? A half-egg's bulk of food which is unclean in the first remove and a half-egg's bulk of food which is unclean in the second remove which one mixed with one another — [the consequent mixture is unclean in the] second [remove of uncleanness]. A half-egg's bulk of food unclean in the second remove of uncleanness and a half-egg's bulk of food unclean in the third remove of uncleanness which one mixed together with one another — [it is unclean in the] first [remove of uncleanness]. [But] an egg's bulk of food unclean in the first remove of uncleanness and an egg's bulk of food unclean in the second remove of uncleanness which one mixed together with one another — [it is unclean in the] first [remove of uncleanness.] [If] one divided them up — this is unclean in the second remove of uncleanness, and this is unclean in the second remove of uncleanness. This one fell by itself and this one by itself on a loaf of heave offering — they have rendered it unfit. [If] the two of them fell on it simultaneously — they have made it unclean in the second remove of uncleanness.

T. 1:1 Why did they say, 'Food which is made unclean by a Father of uncleanness and that which is made unclean by an Offspring of uncleanness join together with one another'? Because it is possible for that which is unclean in the third remove to be made unclean in the second remove. And it is possible for that which is unclean in the second remove to be made unclean in the first remove. And why did they say, 'The creeping thing and the carrion and the corpse do not join together with one another'? Because it is not possible for a creeping thing to become carrion, and carrion cannot become a corpse.

M. 1:6 An egg's bulk of food unclean in the second remove and an egg's bulk of food unclean in the third remove which one mixed with one another — it is unclean in the second remove. [If] one divided them — this one fell by itself and this by itself on a loaf of heave offering — they have not made it unfit. If the two of them fell simultaneously — they put it into the third remove. An egg's bulk of food unclean in the first remove and an egg's bulk of food unclean in the third remove which one mixed with one another — it is unclean in the first remove. [If] one divided them — this one is unclean in the second remove, and this is unclean in the second remove. For even that which is unclean in the third remove which touched something unclean in the first remove becomes unclean in the second remove. Two eggs' bulk of food unclean in the first remove, two eggs' bulk of food unclean in the second remove which one mixed with one another — it is unclean in the first remove. [If] one divided them — this is unclean in the first remove and this one is unclean in the first remove. [If one divided them into] three or four parts — lo, these are unclean in the second remove. Two eggs' bulk of food unclean in the second remove, two eggs' bulk of food unclean in the third remove, which one mixed together — it is unclean in the second remove. [If] one divided them — this one is unclean in the second remove, and this one is unclean in the second remove. [If one divided them into] three or four parts, lo, these all are in the third remove.

M. 1:7 Pieces of dough stuck together, and loaves stuck together — [if] one of them is made unclean by a dead creeping thing, they are all unclean in the first remove. [If] they were separated, they are all unclean in the first remove. [If they were made unclean by] liquid, they all are unclean in the second remove. [If] they separated, they all are unclean in the second remove. [If they were made unclean by] hands, they all are unclean in the third remove. [If] they separated, they all are unclean in the third remove.

M. 1:8 A piece of dough, which was unclean in the first remove, and one stuck others to it, they all are unclean in the first remove. [If] they separated, it is unclean in the first remove, but all [the rest] are unclean in the second remove. [If] it was unclean in the second remove and one stuck others to it, they all are unclean in the second remove. [If] they separated, it is unclean in the second remove, but all [the rest] are unclean in the third remove.

[If] it was unclean in the third remove, and one stuck others to it, it is unclean in the third remove, but all [the rest] are clean, whether they separated or whether they did not separate.

T. 1:2 A piece of dough which was unclean in the third remove, and one stuck others to it — they all are unclean in the third remove so far as Holy Things are concerned. [If] that which is unclean in the third remove separated, all [the others] are clean. And what is the one which sticks? (And) the one which removes anything at all from it. But if they were mashed together, for example, the ring of pressed figs and the dates and the figs and the raisins — lo, these are not connected. Why did they say concerning olives that it is a matter of connection? For in the first place one placed them only so that they should suck [draw moisture] from one another.

We start with a massive statement of the rules affecting food-uncleanness. The matter of intentionality enters in: a person must regard the carrion of the clean bird as food for the bird to impart uncleanness, but no further acts of preparation are required; the other considerations encompass both particular and generic issues. "The intention" of M. 1:1 is to regard the carrion of the clean bird as food; it does not require a confirming action, as does the carrion of an unclean bird. M. 1:5 reaches the point of generalization: food that is unclean joins together with other such food, whatever remove of uncleanness affects the two masses, respectively, to form the requisite volume to be unclean, or to convey uncleanness, as the case may be. This is spelled out in a clear way in the "how so" clause of M. 1:5. M. 1:6 then produces another problem of mixtures of food in different removes of uncleanness.

II. SUSCEPTIBILITY TO UNCLEANNESS OF HOLY THINGS, HEAVE-OFFERING, AND UNCONSECRATED FOOD

M. 1:9 Loaves of Holy Things, in the hollows of which is water preserved in cleanness fitting for Holy Things — [if] one of them was made unclean by a creeping thing, they all are unclean. In the case of heave offering, it [the creeping thing] renders unclean at two removes and renders unfit at one [third remove]. If there is between them dripping liquid, even in the case of heave offering, the whole is unclean.

T. 1:5 The creeping thing renders unclean at three removes and unfit at one [further remove] in connection with Holy Things; and renders unclean at two removes and unfit at one [further] remove in connection with heave-offering. It renders unclean at one remove and unfit at one remove in connection with unconsecrated food. Liquid renders unclean at two removes and unfit at one remove in connection with Holy Things. It renders unclean at one remove and unfit at one remove in connection with Heave-offering. And it spoils unconsecrated food.

T. 1:6 The hands convey uncleanness at one remove and render unfit at one remove in connection with Holy Things, and render heave-offering unfit, and [the rule governing the uncleanness of] hands [has] no [bearing upon] unconsecrated food. In respect to what sort of Holy Things did they speak? Concerning Holy Things of the sanctuary which are sanctified, for example, loaves of thanksgiving and the wafers of the Nazir over which the sacrifice has been slaughtered and meal-offerings which were mixed in a utensil. But loaves of thanksgiving and wafers of a Nazir over which the sacrifice was not slaughtered and meal-offerings which were not mixed in a utensil are like neither Holy Things nor unconsecrated food, but they are like heave-offering. And the dead creeping thing renders unclean at two removes and spoils at one remove in their case.

T. 1:7 The dough-offering and the first fruits and what is brought as restitution for heave-offering and its fifth, lo, they are like heave-offering. The edibles forbidden pending the separation of sacred gifts and the edibles with which heave-offering has been mixed and that which grows from heave-offering and second tithe, lo, they are in the status of unconsecrated food. Loaves of Holy Things — in their holes [is liquid] — and the [aforementioned] liquid of Holy Things is made unclean in the case of one of them by a dead creeping thing — they all are in the first remove of uncleanness. In the case of heave-offering, it imparts uncleanness at two removes and spoils [heave-offering] at one [further] remove. In the case of unconsecrated food, it imparts uncleanness at one remove and spoils [heave-offering] at one [further] remove. You have no liquid (of Holy Things) which touches something unclean in the third remove [and is] unclean except for Holy Things alone. But food which is unclean in the second remove which touched the liquid of the olive-press — it [the liquid] is unclean.

M. 2:1 The woman who was pickling vegetables in the pot and touched a leaf — outside of the pot, on a dry spot — even though it is an egg's bulk in size, it is unclean. But the whole is clean. [If] she touched a place on which there is liquid, if there is in it an egg's bulk, the whole is unclean. [If] there is not an egg's bulk in it, it is unclean. But the whole is clean. [If the wet leaf] returned to the pot, the whole is unclean. [If] she was [unclean because of] contact with [something unclean with] corpse uncleanness and touched, whether a place which is wet or a place which is dry, if there is in it an egg's bulk, the whole is unclean. [If] there is not an egg's bulk, it is unclean, but the whole is clean, [If] one

who had immersed on the self-same day was emptying the pot with unclean hands, and she saw liquid on her hands — there being doubt whether it [the liquid] had splashed from the pot, or whether the stalk had touched her hands — the vegetable is unfit, but the pot is clean.

T. 1:3 All the same is one who has immersed on the selfsame day on account of a stringent uncleanness and the one who has immersed on the selfsame day on account of a lenient uncleanness, and even one who has immersed on the selfsame day because of the Zab and because of the Zabah and because of the rest of the sources of uncleanness which are mentioned in the Torah — lo, they are like one who has immersed on the selfsame day on account of being made unclean by the dead creeping thing. One who has immersed on the selfsame day and one who is made unclean through a corpse and one who has had intercourse with a menstruant — he works at the olive press, except for one who is made unclean because of the Zab and because of the Zabah — (and even) on his seventh day [after being made unclean], lo, such a one should do nothing, and if he has done it, lo, this is suspended. And all the same is one who is clean, whose hands are unclean and one who has immersed on the selfsame day — he renders unclean liquid of unconsecrated produce and renders unfit heave-offering-foods.

T. 1:4 One who has immersed on the selfsame day just as he renders unfit liquid of heave-offering and foods of heave-offering, so he spoils liquid of Holy Things and foods of Holy Things.

M. 2:2 (1) He who eats food unclean in the first remove and food unclean in the second remove is unclean in the second remove. (2) [He who eats food] unclean in the third remove is unclean in the second remove so far as Holy Things are concerned, (3) and is not unclean in the second remove so far as heave offering is concerned — in the case of unconsecrated food which is prepared in conditions of cleanness appropriate to heave offering.

M. 2:3 Unconsecrated food in the first remove [from the source of uncleanness] is unclean and renders [heave offering] unclean. [Unconsecrated food] in the second remove is unfit but does not convey uncleanness. And [unconsecrated food] in the third remove is eaten in pottage of heave offering.

M. 2:4 Heave offering in the first and in the second removes is unclean and renders [Holy Things] unclean. [Heave offering] in the third remove is unfit and does not convey uncleanness. And [heave offering] at the fourth remove is eaten in a pottage of Holy Things.

M. 2:5 Holy Things: in the first and the second and the third removes are susceptible to uncleanness and convey unclean-

ness. And [Holy Things] in the fourth remove are unfit and do not convey uncleanness. And [Holy Things] in the fifth remove are eaten in a pottage of Holy Things.

M. 2:6 Unconsecrated food: in the second remove renders unconsecrated liquid unclean and renders unfit foods of heave offering. Heave offering: at the third remove renders unclean liquid of Holy Things and renders unfit foods of Holy Things, if it [the heave offering] was prepared in conditions of cleanness pertaining to Holy Things. But if it was prepared in conditions pertaining to heave offering, it renders unclean at two removes and renders unfit at one remove in reference to Holy Things.

M. 2:8 He who eats food unclean in the second remove should not work in the olive press. And unconsecrated food which is prepared in accord with the rules pertaining to Holy Things — lo, this is like unconsecrated food.

M. 3:1 Grease, bean mash and milk, when they are [in the form of] running liquid, lo, they are in the first remove of uncleanness. [If] they congealed, lo, they are in the second remove of uncleanness. [If] they became liquid [again], [if they are of the volume of] an egg, exactly — it is clean. [If they are of the volume of] more than an egg, it is unclean, for as soon as the first drop [of moisture] exuded, it was made unclean, [by the remainder which is] the bulk of an egg.

T. 2:2 Cress and bean mash, when one stirs them in the pot, receive uncleanness as food. [If] one put them into a dish and liquids exude from them, the liquid which exudes from them receives uncleanness as liquid.

T. 2:3 Oil is neither food nor liquid. In what context have they said, "Oil is always in the first remove of uncleanness"? For if it is wiped away and nothing remains of it but as much as a bean, that which exudes from it receives uncleanness as liquid.

T. 2:4 It comes out that one rules: There are three traits in respect to liquid. Grease and milk and bean mash, when liquid runs [from them], lo, they are in the first remove of uncleanness. [If] they congeal, they do not require intention [to receive uncleanness] as foods.

T. 3:1 Peat and grape-shells which were prepared in a state of cleanness and from which one squeezed liquids are clean. And those which were prepared in a state of uncleanness and from which one squeezed liquids are unclean.

T. 3:2 Grapes which are jammed in a wedge by the basket — they fell into the airspace of the clean oven — it is unclean. Olives which are jammed in a wedge by the press — and they fell into the airspace of a clean oven — it is clean. This and this [fell into the airspace of a clean oven], if there is on them running moisture — the oven is unclean.

M. 3:2 A clump of [unclean] olives which fell into the oven, and it was heated — [if it is the volume of] an egg exactly, it [the oven] is clean. [If it is the volume of] more than an egg, it [the oven] is unclean, for as soon as the first drop [of moisture] exuded, it was made unclean, [by the remainder which is] the bulk of an egg. [If] they were separate, even if they are a seah, it is clean.

T. 3:3 Unclean pots which fell into the airspace of the oven, whether whole or broken, even when it is heated up — it is unclean. When it is not heated up — it is clean. And [if] one made use of them in cleanness, and they are made unclean, and they fell into the airspace of the oven — when it is heated up, it is unclean. When it is not heated up, it is clean. And those which are broken, even when it is heated up — it is clean, for it does not contain liquids by which it will convey uncleanness.

T. 3:4 All the unclean things are adjudged as they are at the moment at which they are found, and in accord with every place [in which they are found]. [If] one lost a needle which is polished and came and found it full of rust, lo, this remains in its presumption [of being] polished, until one may say, "It is clear to me that it was full of rust." If it was lost when full of rust and one came and found it polished, lo, it remains in the presumption of being polished until one will say, "It is clear to me that it has put forth rust." And so in the case of a creeping thing. And so in the case of a rag. [If] one left it unclean in this corner and found it in another corner, the first corner is unclean, until one will state, "It is clear to me that it was uprooted from here." The second corner is unclean until one will state, "It is clear to me that it did not come here."

M. 3:3 One unclean with corpse uncleanness who pressed out olives and grapes — [if the olives or the grapes were of the volume of] an egg exactly, it is clean and on condition that he not touch the wet place. [If it was of the volume of] more than an egg, it is unclean, for as soon as the first drop [of moisture] exuded, it was made unclean, [by the remainder which is] the bulk of an egg. If it was a Zab or a Zabah, even [if only] an individual berry [was squeezed out], it is unclean, [for as soon as the first drop of moisture] exuded, it was made unclean through the carriage [of the Zab or Zabah]. A Zab who milked the goat — the milk is unclean, for as soon as the first drop [of moisture] exuded, it was made unclean through carriage.

M. 3:4 An egg's bulk of foodstuffs which one left in the sun and which shrank, and so (1) an olive's bulk of corpse matter,

(2) an olive's bulk of carrion and (3) a lentil's bulk of a creeping thing, (4) an olive's bulk of refuse, (5) an olive's bulk of remnant, and (6) an olive's bulk of prohibited fat — lo, they are clean. And they are not liable on their account because of refuse, remnant, and uncleanness. [If] one left them in the rain and they expanded, they are unclean, and they are liable on their account [for transgression of the laws of refuse, remnant, and uncleanness [Better: forbidden fat].

T. 2:5 Honey which oozes from the hive of bees receives uncleanness as liquid. [If] one gave thought to it as food, it receives uncleanness as food. Oil is neither food nor liquid. [If] one gave thought to it to make use of it as food and not as liquid his intention is of no effect. Blood which congealed is neither food nor liquid [If] one gave thought to it to make use of it as food, it receives uncleanness as food. And [if one gave thought to use it as] liquid his intention is null. The honey of palms is neither food nor liquid. [If] one gave thought to it to make use of it for food, it receives uncleanness as food. And [if one gave thought to it to use it] for liquid, his intention is null. And as to all other fruit juice, [it is] neither food nor liquid. [If] one gave thought to it, whether for liquid or for food, his intention is null. Snow is neither food nor liquid. If one gave thought to it for food, his intention is null. For liquid — it receives uncleanness as liquid. [If] part of it is made unclean, the liquid is made unclean. [If] part of it is made unclean, the whole of it is not made unclean. [If] part of it is clean, the whole of it is clean.

T. 2:6 Purification-water which froze over and does not contain running liquid is clean. [If] it melted, it has returned to its former uncleanness. An immersion pool of drawn water that froze over is clean in respect to drawn water. [If] it melted, it is fit to be added to.

T. 2:7 He who gives thought to the milk which is in the udder — it is clean. And [he who gives thought to the milk] which is in the maw — it is unclean. The hide and the placenta do not receive uncleanness as food. The hide which one boiled and the placenta to which one gave thought [for use as food] receive uncleanness as food.

The rule is, the higher the level of sanctification, the greater the sensitivity to uncleanness. That explains why in the case of Holy Things the dead creeping thing imparts uncleanness to what it touches, to what that touches, and to what that touches, and renders unfit (but not sufficiently unclean to impart uncleanness at a further remove) to what touches that; but in the lesser level, heave-offering, the same source of uncleanness affects only at two removes, and unfitness at a third, and in unconsecrated food, uncleanness is transmitted only at one remove from the original source, and unfitness at one further. Liquid that is unclean is affective at a diminished scale of removes as well. (We recall that that is the case for Holy Things, heave offering, and unconsecrated food; but in the case of purification water, we do not count removes for a stopping point, even at a hundred removes, contamination results!) The Tosefta provides the more systematic and orderly presentation of the matter, the Mishnah an episodic problem, at M. 1:9/T. 1:5-7. The composition, M. 2:3-7, by contrast, shows how the Mishnah's framers too can formulate a perfect statement, in the present case spelling out with great clarity the diverse levels of sensitivity to uncleanness that differentiate the diverse levels of sanctification, from what is unconsecrated upward to what is classified as Holy Things. The key language comes at M. 2:6: "if it [the heave offering] was prepared in conditions of cleanness pertaining to Holy Things. But if it was prepared in conditions pertaining to heave offering...." That is, if the householder's intentionality imposed the rules governing Holy Things, then one set of results applies, if heave offering, another. So all things are relative to the intentionality of the householder. So the entire system of removes responds to the attitude of the householder, specifically, to the rules of uncleanness that he has invoked in his mind, and observed in deed, for a given mass of food and drink: does he wish to preserve it as if it were Holy Things, as if it were heave-offering, as if it were unconsecrated food. His intentionality governs, and I cannot point to a more powerful statement of the matter than in the account before us. The Tosefta, for its part, contains nothing more remarkable in its proportion, lucidity, and comprehensiveness, than its presentation of this matter, which should be regarded as the Halakhah at its most elegant.

III. DOUBT IN MATTERS OF UNCLEANNESS

M. 3:5 All unclean things [are adjudged] in accord with [their condition] at the moment that they are found. (1) If they are unclean, they are unclean; and (2) if they are clean, they are clean; (3) if they are covered up, they are covered up; and (4) if they are uncovered, they are uncovered. A needle which is found full of rust or broken is clean. For all unclean things [are adjudged] in accord with [their condition] at the moment that they are found.

T. 3:5 If an olive's bulk of corpse-matter was lost in the house — they sought and did not find it — the house is clean. When it will be found, the house conveys uncleanness retroactively.

T. 3:6 The woman is raking stubble in the courtyard and a dead creeping thing is found inside the stubble — she is clean. [If it is found] on top of the stubble, she is unclean. [If] she was winnowing wheat in a sieve and a creeping thing is found in the sieve, she is clean. [If it is found] on top of the sieve, she is unclean.

M. 3:6 A deaf-mute, an imbecile, and a minor who are found in an alley in which is uncleanness, lo, these are assumed to be clean. But any person of sound sense is assumed to be unclean. And whoever lacks understanding to be interrogated — a matter of doubt concerning him is resolved in favor of cleanness.

T. 3:7 A child who was holding on to his father's hand or was riding on his father's shoulder — a matter of doubt concerning him is unclean, because his father may be interrogated about him. A deaf-mute, an imbecile, and a child — a matter of doubt concerning them is clean, because they do not have intelligence to be interrogated.

T. 3:11 A blind man and one who is sleeping and one who walks by night matters of doubt which concern them are resolved in favor of cleanness, because they have intelligence to be consulted. An ass which was standing in a clean place, and it is possible for him to pass over into an unclean place — utensils which are on him are clean.

M. 3:7 A child who is found on the side of a graveyard, and lilies are in his hand, and lilies are [located] only in the place of the uncleanness is clean, for I say, "Someone else gathered them and gave them to him." And so an ass among the graves — his utensils are clean.

M. 3:8 A. A child [who is unclean] who is found at the side of the dough and the dough is in his hand — it is declare unclean, for it is the way of the child to slap [dough]. Dough which had on it marks of hens' [beaks], and unclean liquids are in the house, if there is between the liquid and the loaves sufficient [space] for the hens to dry off their beaks in the ground, lo, these are clean. And in the case of the cow and in the case of the dog — sufficient space in which they may lick their tongue. And in reference to all other cattle, sufficient space in which they may dry themselves.

T. 3:12 A child who is found standing at the side of a basket of dough — [or] at the side of a jar of liquids — it is unclean, for it is the way of a child to slap [dough].

T. 3:8 Four [stages of] doubts have the sages stated in connection with the minor: [If] his mother left him and came and found him as he was, he is clean.

T. 3:9 [If] he began to go out and come in, his clothing is clean. But they do not prepare clean things depending upon his being clean. And Israelites did not refrain from this point [onward]. [If] he has intelligence to be consulted about his condition, a matter of doubt concerning him in private domain is resolved in favor of uncleanness; in the public domain, it is resolved in favor of cleanness.

T. 3:10 [If] he knew how to keep his body food which is on his body is clean. [If he knew how] to keep his hands, food which is on his hands is clean . And how do they examine him? They immerse him and give him unconsecrated food, saying that it is heave-offering. If he knows how to guard his body, food which is on his body is clean. [If he knows how] to guard his hands, food which is on his hands is clean.

M. 4:1 He who threw something unclean from place to place — a [clean] loaf of bread among [unclean] keys — an [unclean] key among the [clean] loaves of bread — it is clean.

T. 3:14 Whatever is suspended and whatever is dragged — matters of doubt concerning them are resolved in favor of uncleanness because they are [regarded] as if they were lying. And whatever is thrown — a matter of doubt concerning it is clean; except for an olive's bulk of corpse-matter, and whatever overshadows — they convey uncleanness from above as from below. But if something clean was thrown over an olive's bulk of corpse-matter — it is clean.

M. 4:2 The creeping thing is in the mouth of the weasel, and it [the weasel] walks on loaves of heave offering — there is doubt whether or not it [the creeping thing] touched [the loaves] — its matter of doubt is deemed clean.

M. 4:3 The creeping thing is in the mouth of the weasel — and a bit of carrion is in the mouth of the dog — and they passed among clean things, or clean things [or: people] passed between them, their matter of doubt is deemed clean, because the unclean thing has no place. [If] they were picking at them while [these lay] on the ground — and a person said, "I went to that place, but I do not know whether I touched or whether I did not touch" — his matter of doubt is deemed unclean, because the unclean thing has a place.

T. 4:1 [If a person] was wrapped in his cloak, with unclean things and clean things at his side, and unclean things and clean things above — there is doubt whether he touched or did not touch — his matter of doubt is deemed clean. And if it is not possible for him [not to come] into [contact] his matter of doubt is deemed unclean. (How so?) [If] there was a creeping thing suspended between the walls, and it is not possible to pass without touching — [if there] is doubt whether one touched or whether one did not touch his matter of doubt is deemed clean. And if it is not possible [to pass] there [without touching] — his matter of doubt is deemed unclean.

T. 4:3 [If] there was a [live] creeping thing suspended between the walls one rubbed against it, and it fell on his garments or on a loaf of heave-offering — it is clean. And if they found it dead before him, it is unclean. And if they saw it that it was alive between the walls, even though one found it dead before him, it is clean. [If the dead creeping thing] rested on his shoulder, lo, this one is unclean.

T. 4:4 A loaf of heave-offering which was placed on top of the board — something unclean with midras-uncleanness is set beneath it — and it is not possible for it [the loaf] to fall without touching that which is unclean with midras-uncleanness — and one came and found it on top of something else which is unclean with midras-uncleanness — it [the loaf] is clean. For I say, "Another person took it and placed it on that place." And if one said, "It is clear to me that no man has come here," it is unclean.

T. 4:5 A creeping thing in the mouth of the weasel and it walks on top of loaves of heave-offering — it touches it — there is a doubt whether it is alive or whether it is dead — it is clean. Under what circumstances? When it took it and went on its way. But if one found it dead in its mouth — if one saw it alive in its mouth — even though it [then] is found dead in its mouth — it is clean.

T. 4:7 The creeping thing is in the mouth of the chicken — and a bit of carrion is in the mouth of the dog — they pass through the courtyard — they do not convey uncleanness retroactively. For I say, "From some other place did they bring them." [If] they were pecking at them on the ground, they do convey uncleanness retroactively.

T. 4:8 A person went into an alley and made dough, and afterward a creeping thing was found — and the person said, "If it were here, I would have seen it" — it is unclean, until he will state, "It is clear to me that it was not here beforehand." Lo, he who immersed and went up, and afterward there was found on him something which interposes [between his flesh and the water], even though he was occupied with that very sort of thing after he immersed, lo, this one is unclean, until he will state, "It is clear to me that it was not on me before hand."

T. 4:9 A grave which is discovered conveys uncleanness retroactively. If a person came and said, "It is clear to me that it was not here twenty [years ago]," it is unclean only from the time that it was discovered and thereafter.

T. 4:10 An unclean olive-pit which was found inside a loaf on top of a boiling stew, even though flowing liquid is not on it [the pit], it [the loaf] is unclean. [If] it was discovered on top of a loaf inside of a cold broth, even though there is flowing liquid on it, it is clean. This is the general principle: Whatever is discovered in something which is boiling, even though there is running liquid on it, is unclean. Whatever is found in something which is boiling, even though there is no flowing liquid on it, is unclean. [If] it is found in a loaf in a cold broth, even though there is flowing liquid on it, it is clean. A pit which is in the house — they follow the majority.

M. 4:4 An olive's bulk of corpse matter is in the mouth of the raven— there is doubt whether it overshadowed the man and the utensils—in the private domain — the doubt concerning the man is deemed unclean; the doubt concerning the utensils is deemed clean. He who draws with ten buckets, and a creeping thing is found in one of them — it is unclean, and all [the rest of] them are clean. He who empties from utensil to utensil and a creeping thing is found in the lower one — the upper one is clean.

M. 4:5 On account of six matters of doubt do they burn heave offering: 1. concerning a doubt in regard to a grave area; 2. and concerning a doubt in regard to dirt which comes from abroad; 3. because of a doubt concerning the clothing of an *'am ha'ares*; 4. and because of a doubt concerning utensils which were found; 5. because of a doubt concerning drops of spit which were found; 6. because of a doubt concerning human urine that was nearby the urine of a beast — because of certainly touching them, which is a matter of doubt in respect to their [imparting] uncleanness, they burn the heave offering. [Because of a doubt about having touched them] in the private domain, they leave it in suspense. And in the public domain, it is clean.

T. 11:14 A dead creeping thing which is found floating on the rim of the cistern of a vat for heave-offering — its matter of doubt is deemed unclean. [If it is doubt as to] the workers, the matter of doubt is deemed clean, because it is a matter of doubt concerning that which floats.

M. 4:6 Two [drops of] spit — one unclean, and one clean — they suspend [a decision on the status of what as affected by them, in this wise: (1) on account of having touched them, and (2) on account of having carried them, and (3) on account of having moved them— in private property; and on account of having touched them — in public property — when they are moist; and on account of having carried them, whether they are moist or whether they are dry. [If] there was a single drop of spit and one touched it, and carried it, and moved it in public domain — they burn the heave offering on its account, and it is hardly necessary to rule, [if one did so] in private property.

T. 4:11 Flax which a menstruating woman has spun — he who moves it is clean. And if it was moist, he who moves it is unclean, because of the liquid which is in his [better: her] mouth.

T. 5:1 Unclean blood which was mixed with clean blood — they regard it as if it were wine in water. If its color is diluted, it is clean, and if not, it is unclean. Unclean spit which was mixed with clean spit — they regard it as if it were water. If its color is diluted, it is clean; and if not, it is unclean. [If] it fell into water, [if] it remains cohesive, it is unclean. [If] it dissolved, if its taste and its color are diluted, it is clean, and if not, it is unclean.

T. 5:2 Urine which was mixed with wine — they [do not] regard it as if it were water. [If] it was mixed with water, they regard it as if it were wine. If its color is diluted, it is clean, and if not, it is unclean. Urine of a gentile [mixed with other urine] — they follow the status of the majority [of the mixture].

T. 5:3 They purchase and borrow urine from any source, and they do not take account of the possibility that it derives from menstruating women, for the daughters of Israel are not suspected of collecting their urine when they are menstruating. The chamber pot of a Zab and of a Zabah — the [water of] the first and of the second [washings of the pot] convey uncleanness. The [water of the] third [rinsing] is clean. Under what circumstances? When he put water into it. But when he did not put water into it [but washed it with urine] — even up to the tenth [rinsing] — it is unclean.

T. 5:4 A Zab who put his mouth on the mouth of the cup and changed his mind and did not drink it — he who moves it is clean. [If] he drank from it any amount at all — whoever moves it is unclean, because of the spit of his mouth. [If] he bit from the bread or from the onion — he who moves it is clean. [If] he bit off a piece of gourd or cucumber, he who moves it is unclean, because of the spit of his mouth. And shells of beans and shells of beets which the gentile has shelled he who moves them is unclean. And as to those in the marketplaces — they follow the status of the majority.

T. 5:5 Two drops of spit, one unclean and one clean, and one touched one of them, or carried it on a shard — All the same is private and public domain: They suspend. [If] they were dried, or one moved them on a chip, in private property they suspend; and in public property they burn. [If there] is doubt whether he touched or did not touch, whether he moved or did not move, in private property they suspend, and in public property it is clean. [If] there was a single drop of spit — there is doubt whether one touched it or whether one did not touch it there is doubt whether one moved it or whether one did not move it in private property they suspend. In public property it is clean.

M. 4:7 These are [conditions of] doubt which sages have declared clean: 1. A doubt concerning drawn water [that falls

into] the immersion pool. 2. A doubt concerning uncleanness floating on the surface of the water. 3. A doubt concerning liquids, in respect to contracting uncleanness — it is unclean. [A doubt concerning liquids, in respect to] conveying uncleanness — it is clean. 4. A doubt concerning hands, either in respect to contracting uncleanness, or in respect to conveying uncleanness, or in respect to being made clean — it is clean. 5. A doubt concerning public domain. 6. A doubt concerning rulings of the scribes. 7. A doubt concerning the unconsecrated food. 8. A doubt concerning creeping things. 9. A doubt concerning *Nega'*- uncleanness. 10. A doubt concerning Naziriteship. 11. A doubt concerning firstlings. 12. A doubt concerning sacrifices.

T. 5:6 And just as they declared clean a matter of doubt concerning uncleanness floating on the surface of the water, whether it is in utensils or whether it is on the ground, so they have declared clean a matter of doubt concerning cleanness floating on the surface of the water, whether it is in utensils or on the ground — how so? A trough which is unclean with corpse-uncleanness — a loaf of heave-offering wrapped in bast or wrapped in paper is in it and the rains came and it was filled up, and it [the loaf-wrapper] is unfolded [by the flow's force] — lo, this [loaf] floats on the surface of the water — there is doubt whether it touched the sides of the trough or whether it did not touch — its matter of doubt is deemed clean, because it is a matter of doubt concerning something clean which was floating.

T. 5:8 And what is the doubt concerning creeping things which the sages declared clean? This is a matter of doubt concerning things which are thrown. And he who eats heave-offering which is suspended is clean. And any one whose matter of doubt is deemed clean — a matter of doubt concerning its offspring is clean. Anything the matter of doubt concerning which is unclean, a matter of doubt concerning its offspring likewise is unclean.

M. 4:9 A doubt concerning liquids to contract uncleanness is deemed unclean — how so? An unclean person who put out his foot among clean liquids — it is a matter of doubt whether he touched or did not touch — his matter of doubt is deemed unclean. [If] there was an unclean loaf of bread in his hand, and he threw it among clean liquids — it is a matter of doubt whether it touched or whether it did not touch — his matter of doubt is deemed unclean, And to convey uncleanness — it is clean — how so? [If] there was a staff in his hand, and on the end of it are unclean liquids, and he threw it among clean loaves — it is a matter of doubt whether it touched or whether it did not touch — its matter of doubt is deemed clean.

T. 5:9 And just as he who eats food unclean in the first remove and food unclean in the second remove and drinks unclean liquids, and he whose head and greater part enter into drawn water, and the clean person on whose head and the greater part of whose body three *logs* of drawn water are thrown — [as] a matter of doubt concerning his conveying uncleanness to others is deemed clean, so too: liquids which touch him — a matter of doubt concerning their rendering other things unclean is deemed clean.

M. 4:10 A matter of doubt in respect to liquids — in what concerns food, it is unclean, and in what concerns utensils, it is clean. How so? Two jars, one is unclean and one is clean — and one made dough [with water] from one of them — it is a matter of doubt whether he made it from the unclean or whether he made it from the clean — This is [the matter of which it is said]: "A matter of doubt concerning liquids — if it has to do with foods, it is deemed unclean, and if it has to do with utensils, it is deemed clean."

T. 5:11 A staff which is full of unclean liquids and one threw it among clean loaves — it is a matter of doubt whether it touched or whether it did not touch this is not the matter of doubt concerning liquids about which sages have disputed. But what is the matter of doubt concerning liquids about which sages have differed? Two jars — one unclean, and one clean — it is a matter of doubt whether he made the dough from the unclean water or whether he made the dough from the clean water — this is the matter of doubt concerning liquids: [if it concerns] foods, it is unclean. And [if it concerns] utensils, it is clean.

T. 5:12 [If] one went into an alley and prepared dough, and afterward a creeping thing was found there — it is a matter of doubt whether he touched or whether he did not touch it — a matter of doubt concerning foods and liquids is deemed unclean; and [a matter of doubt concerning] utensils is deemed clean. And one who had immersed on the selfsame day who put his hand into the airspace of a jar — it is a matter of doubt whether he touched or whether he did not touch — concerning foods and liquids, the doubt is deemed unclean, and concerning utensils, it is deemed clean.

M. 4:11 A matter of doubt concerning the hands, to contract uncleanness and to convey uncleanness and to be made clean — it is clean. A matter of doubt having to do with the public domain is deemed clean, A matter of doubt having to do with the rules of scribes — One ate unclean foods, drank unclean liquids — his head and the greater part of his body come into drawn water — or three logs of drawn water fell on his head and on the greater part of his body — a matter of doubt concerning him is deemed clean, But in respect to something which is a Father of Unclean-

ness, and it [the uncleanness at the level of the Father] derives from the rulings of scribes — its matter of doubt is deemed unclean.

T. 5:10 And just as that which is unclean in the first remove produces something unclean in the second remove, and something unclean in the second remove produces something unclean in the third, so a matter of doubt concerning something unclean in the first remove produces a matter of doubt concerning something unclean in the second remove, and a matter of doubt concerning something unclean in the second remove produces a matter of doubt concerning something unclean in the third remove.

M. 4:12 A matter of doubt concerning the unconsecrated food — this has to do with the cleanness of abstinence [Perishut]. A matter of doubt having to do with creeping things — it is adjudged in accord with their condition when they are found. A matter of doubt having to do with plagues — in the first instance, it is clean, before it has been subjected to a ruling of uncleanness. Once it has been subjected to a ruling of uncleanness, a matter of doubt concerning it is deemed unclean, A matter of doubt concerning Naziriteship — it is permitted. A matter of doubt concerning firstlings — all the same is the rule for the first-born of man and the first-born of cattle, whether unclean or clean, for: he who would take something away from his fellow, upon him is the burden of proof.

M. 4:13 A matter of doubt concerning sacrifices — a woman suffered five miscarriages that were in doubt — five fluxes that were in doubt — she brings a single offering, and eats sacrifices, and the remainder is not an obligation for her.

T. 5:13 Two jars, one unclean and one clean — and they were broken, and [the liquids therein] came onto clean things — it is a matter of doubt whether it is [liquid of the] unclean [jar] or whether it is [liquid of the] clean — a matter of doubt concerning foods and liquids is deemed unclean; [a matter of doubt concerning] utensils is deemed clean. A jar which is half filled with clean liquids and liquids fell into its airspace — it is a doubt whether they are clean or whether they are unclean — the liquids [in the jar] are clean, for they convey uncleanness only on account of the jar. [If] they fell on liquids [in the jar], the liquids are unclean, but the jars are clean.

T. 5:14 [If] one baked a loaf of bread in an oven, and liquids fell into its airspace — it is a matter of doubt whether they were unclean or whether they were clean — the bread is clean, because it is made unclean only on account of the oven. [If] they fell on the loaf of bread, the bread is unclean, and the oven is clean.

T. 5:15 He who sprinkles his house with unclean water, and there were clean things there — it is a matter of doubt whether it [the water] splashed or whether it did not splash — its matter of doubt is deemed clean. [If] it is not possible for him to [sprinkle unless the water does touch the clean things], its matter of doubt is deemed unclean.

T. 5:16 A person who launders his garment — and washes his hair — and boils his flax — and there were clean things there — it is a matter of doubt whether they are unclean or whether they are clean, their matter of doubt is deemed clean. [If] it is not possible for him [to do so without splashing] — its matter of doubt is deemed unclean.

T. 5:17 [If] a person splashed unclean and clean liquids in the house and afterward liquids were found on a loaf of heave-offering — and [if] one took it [forthwith] to inquire concerning it, lo, this is clean. [If] he waited for it until it dried off, lo, this is unclean.

T. 6:1 The bits of carrion and of properly slaughtered animals in a village they follow the status of the majority. Unclean and clean drops of blood in the house — they follow the status of the majority.

M. 5:1 The creeping thing and the frog in public domain — and so: an olive's bulk of corpse matter and an olive's bulk of carrion, and a bone from a corpse, and a bone from carrion, and a clod from clean earth and a clod from a grave area, a clod of clean earth and a clod of earth from abroad, two paths, one unclean and one clean — [if] one walked in one of them, and it is not known in which of them he has walked — [if] he has overshadowed one of them, and it is not known which of them he has overshadowed — he moved one of them, and it is not known which of them he has moved — it is clean.

T. 6:2 Nine creeping things and one frog are in the public domain — and one touched one of them — and it is not known which of them he has touched — his matter of doubt is deemed clean. One of them separated to private domain — its matter of doubt is deemed unclean. [One of them separated] to the public domain — its matter of doubt is deemed clean. And in the case of that which is found: they follow the status of the majority . Nine frogs and one creeping thing in the private domain — and one touched one of them, and it is not known which of them he touched — his matter of doubt is deemed unclean. One of them separated to the private domain — his matter of doubt is deemed unclean. To the public domain — his matter of doubt is deemed clean. Q. And in the case of that which is found: they follow the status of the majority.

M. 5:2 One who said, "I touched this, but I do not know whether it is unclean or whether it is clean" — "I touched, and I do not know which of the two of them I touched" — it is clean.

M. 5:3 Two paths, one unclean and one clean — one walked in one of them, and he prepared clean things, and they were eaten — he sprinkled and repeated and is clean — he walked in the second and prepared clean things — lo, these [second ones] are clean. If the first remained, these and these are suspended. If he did not become clean in the meanwhile, the first are suspended, and the second are burned.

M. 5:4 The creeping thing and the frog in public domain — he touched one of them and prepared clean things and they are eaten — he immersed, touched the second, and prepared clean things — lo, these are clean. If the first remain, these and these are suspended. If he did not immerse in the meanwhile, the first are suspended, and the second are burned.

T. 6:3 An unclean loaf which was mixed with nine clean loaves — and five people ate the five first ones — and afterward five ate the five latter ones — and one of them was made unclean — and it is not known [which one] — the first ones are unclean for they have no [mitigating factor] on which to depend, and [the ones who ate] the latter [loaves] are clean. This is the general principle: A man with a man, clean things with clean things, a man with clean things, M. and clean things with a man — lo, these prove [which must be unclean]. [If] the first ones are eaten [if] they were made unclean, or if they were lost before the second ones were made, the second are clean. S. [If this happened] once the second were made — the second are suspended.

M. 5:5 "Two paths, one unclean and one clean — [If] he walked in one of them and prepared clean things, and his fellow came and walked in the second and prepared clean things — If they are interrogated, this one by himself and this one by himself, they are clean. And if they are interrogated, the two of them at one time, they are unclean."

T. 6:4 Two paths, one unclean and one clean — and one walked in one of them and prepared clean things — [they are clean.] [One walked] in the second and prepared [clean things] — they are to be burned. In the first [did he walk], but he did not prepare [clean things], [then he walked] in the second, and he prepared [clean things] — they are to be burned. [He walked] in the first and [then] in the second and [then] prepared clean things — [if] these and these are lying before him, the first are clean, and the second are to be burned.

T. 6:5 Two paths, one unclean and one clean — and one walked in one of them and prepared clean things, and his fellow came and walked in the second and prepared — [if] these and these are lying [before them, still available] — lo, these prove [the condition of one another; the first is clean, the second burned]. [If] the first ones were eaten, [or] made unclean, or lost, before the second were prepared — the second are clean. [If this happened] after the second are prepared — the second are suspended.

T. 6:6 [If] both of them prepared a single [item in conditions of] cleanness — lo, this is unclean. [If] both of them prepared two clean things — "[If] this one comes and is interrogated by himself — one says to him, 'It is clean.'" "And [if] this one comes and is interrogated by himself, one says to him, 'It is clean.'" "[If] the two of them are interrogated together, one says to them, 'It is unclean'" — the words of R. Judah. R. Yosé says, "If both of them said, 'We were two, and we walked in two separate paths and we prepared two separate clean things,' one says to them, 'It is unclean,' "because even if one unclean thing is mixed together with a hundred clean things, they all are unclean.""

T. 6:7 Two paths, one unclean and one clean. and one walked in one of them, and entered the sanctuary — he is clear [of punishment]. [If he walked] in the second [and then entered the Temple], he is liable. [If he walked] in the first and did not enter [the sanctuary], and [then he walked] in the second and entered [the sanctuary], he is liable. [If he walked] in the first and entered, [then] was sprinkled and the sprinkling was repeated, and he immersed, then he walked in the second and entered the sanctuary — he is liable.

M. 5:6 "Two loaves, one unclean and one clean — one ate one of them and prepared clean things, and his fellow came and ate the second and prepared clean things — if they are interrogated, this by himself and the other by himself, they are clean. And if the two of them are interrogated at one time, they are unclean."

M. 5:7 He who sat down in public domain, and someone came and stepped on his garments — or someone spit, and he touched his spit — because of his spit, they burn the heave offering, and as to his garments, they follow the majority. [If] someone went to sleep in public domain and arose — [if] one touched someone at night, and it is not known whether he is alive or dead, and in the morning he arose and found him dead — it is unclean, for all the unclean things [are adjudged] as at the time that they are found.

T. 6:8 [If] one touched someone at night and did not know whether he was alive or dead, and at dawn he got up and found him dead — it is unclean, for all matters of uncleanness are adjudged in accord with their condition at the time they are found.

T. 6:9 [If] one fell asleep on a rock in public domain — at dawn (and) he found on it a creeping thing or a drop of spit — it is unclean, for all matters of uncleanness are adjudged in accord with their condition at the moment that they are found.

M. 5:8 [If there is] one [female] idiot in the village — or [one] gentile woman — or one Samaritan woman — all drops of spit which are in the village are unclean. He on whose garments a woman has stepped, or next to whom a woman sat down on a ship — if she knows him, that he eats heave offering — his utensils are clean. And if not, he will interrogate her.

T. 6:11 He who bumps against millstones in which a gentile is located — [or] in which a menstruating woman is located — his garments are unclean with midras-uncleanness. What are millstones? Any which one uproots and moves from its place. [If] one spit and tread, on account of his spit, they burn the heave-offering, and as to his garments, they follow the status of the majority.

T. 6:12 He on whose garments a woman has stepped — his garments are unclean with midras-uncleanness.

M. 5:9 A witness says, "He was made unclean," and he says, "I was not made unclean" — he is clean. Two say, "You were made unclean," and he says, "I was not made unclean" — he is believed concerning himself. A witness says, "He was made unclean," and two say, "He was not made unclean" — whether in private domain or public domain — he is clean. Two say, "He was made unclean," and one says, "He was not made unclean" — whether in private domain or in public domain — he is unclean. A witness says, "He was made unclean," and a witness says, "He was not made unclean" — a woman says, "He was made unclean," and a woman says, "He was not made unclean" — [if the case concerns] private domain, he is unclean. [If the case concerns] public domain, he is clean.

T. 6:13 Two say to him, "You were made unclean," and he says, "I was not made unclean" — he is clean. But they do not say to him, "You prepare clean things." But he should watch out for himself.

T. 6:14 A man brings an offering in behalf of his son and his adult daughter and his Hebrew slave and maid servant, and he contradicts them. He is believed concerning himself. How so? They said to him, "You have vowed," and he says, "It was subject to an unstated condition" — they accept his statement. "You have vowed," and he said to them, "I did not vow," and when they came, he said, "It was subject to an unstated condition" — they do not accept his statement. "Your wife has vowed," and he says to them, "She did not vow," and when they came, he said, "I intended to annul her vow for her" —

they do not listen to him.

T. 6:15 One is believed to say, "This son of mine is nine years and one day old," "This daughter of mine is nine years and one day old," [if] he is liable to bring an offering for them. But for flagellation, and for punishments, lo, this one is not believed.

T. 6:16 [If] his asses and his workers were bearing clean things and passing [some distance] before him, even if they were more than a mile away, lo, these are clean, because it is in the presumption of being guarded. If he said to them, "Go out, and I shall come after you," once they have left his eyesight, lo, these are unclean.

T. 6:17 Two say, "He was made unclean," and two say, "He was not made unclean" — [if the matter of doubt concerns] private domain, he is unclean. [If the matter of doubt concerns] public domain, he is clean.

M. 6:1 A place which was private domain and became public domain and once again was made private domain — when it is private domain, a matter of doubt concerning it is deemed unclean. When it is public domain, a matter of doubt concerning it is clean. He who was on the point of death in private domain — and they brought him out to the public domain, and brought him back to private domain — when he is in the private domain, a matter of doubt concerning him is deemed unclean. When he is in the public domain, a matter of doubt concerning him is clean.

T. 7:1 The dying man who is placed in a shop and entered the stoa — it is clean. [If] they brought him out of the stoa and brought him back to the shop a second time — it is unclean.

M. 6:2 Four matters of doubt do sages declare clean. How so? (1) the unclean person stands and the clean person passes by — (2) the clean person stands and the unclean person passes by — (3) the unclean thing is in the private domain and the clean thing is in the public domain — (4) the clean thing is in the private domain and the unclean thing is in the public domain — it is a matter of doubt whether he touched or whether he did not touch — it is a matter of doubt whether he overshadowed or whether he did not overshadow — it is a matter of doubt whether he moved or whether he did not move — sages declare clean.

M. 6:3 A tree which is standing in public domain, and the uncleanness is in it — one climbed to its top — there is doubt whether he touched or whether he did not touch — his matter of doubt is deemed unclean. He put his hand into the hole in which the uncleanness is located — it is a matter of doubt whether he touched or whether he did not touch — his matter of doubt is deemed unclean. A shop which is unclean and open to the public

domain — it is a matter of doubt whether he went in or whether he did not go in — his matter of doubt is deemed clean. h is a matter of doubt whether he touched or whether he did not touch — his matter of doubt is deemed clean. Two shops, one unclean and one clean — one entered one of them — it is a matter of doubt whether he entered the unclean one, or whether he entered the clean one — his matter of doubt is deemed unclean.

T. 7:2 There are things in the public domain which they have treated as private domain. A basket in the public domain which is ten handbreadths high, and the uncleanness is in it — it is a matter of doubt whether he touched or whether he did not touch — his matter of doubt is deemed clean. [If] he put his hand into it — it is a matter of doubt whether he touched or whether he did not touch — his matter of doubt is deemed unclean.

T. 7:3 If there was a basket [on his shoulder], and a loaf of heave-offering was wrapped in bast or in paper and placed in it — it is a matter of doubt whether another [person] touched or did not touch — its doubt is deemed clean. [If] he put his hand into it — it is a matter of doubt whether he touched or whether he did not touch — its matter of doubt is deemed unclean.

T. 7:4 An ass in the public domain, ten handbreadths high — and uncleanness is placed on top of it — it is a matter of doubt whether he touched or whether he did not touch — its matter of doubt is deemed clean. [If] he stretches out his hand on top of it — it is a matter of doubt whether he touched or whether he did not touch — its matter of doubt is deemed unclean. A rock in public domain, ten handbreadths high — and uncleanness is placed on top of it — it is a matter of doubt whether he touched or whether he did not touch — his matter of doubt is deemed clean. [If] someone climbed up to its top — it is a matter of doubt whether he touched or whether he did not touch — his matter of doubt is deemed unclean.

M. 6:4 As much as you can multiply doubts and doubts about doubts — in connection with private domain, it is unclean; in connection with public domain, it is clean. How so? One entered an alley, and (1) the uncleanness is in the courtyard — it is a matter of doubt whether he entered [the courtyard] or whether he did not enter — (2) uncleanness is in the house — it is a matter of doubt whether he entered or whether he did not enter — (3) and even if he did enter — it is a matter of doubt whether it was there or whether it was not there — (4) and even if it was there — it is a matter of doubt whether it contains sufficient bulk or whether it does not contain sufficient bulk — (5) and even if it does contain a sufficient bulk to convey uncleanness — it is a matter of doubt whether it is uncleanness or whether it is cleanness — (6) and even

if it is uncleanness — it is a matter of doubt whether he touched it or whether he did not touch his matter of doubt is deemed unclean.

M. 6:5 One entered the valley during the rainy season — and the uncleanness is in a certain field, and he said, "I walked in that place, but I do not know whether I entered that particular field, or whether I did not enter [it]" — sages declare unclean.

T. 7:8 And what is the dry season? Once the crop is gathered from it. And what is the rainy season? Once the second rain falls. [If] there were there clear fields — if one could stand on one side and see those that enter and those that leave on the other side — it is private property with respect to the Sabbath and public domain with respect to uncleanness. And if not, it is private property with respect to both.

M. 6:6 A doubt concerning private domain is deemed unclean — until one will say, "I did not touch it." A matter of doubt in the public domain is deemed clean — until one will say, "I did touch it." What is public domain? The paths of Bet Gilgul, and the like of them — [they are] private domain in regard to the Sabbath and public domain with regard to uncleanness. Paths which lead down to cisterns, pits, caverns, and winepresses are classified as private domain in regard to the Sabbath and as public domain in regard to uncleanness.

M. 6:7 The canyon — in the dry season — is private domain in respect to the Sabbath, and public domain in respect to uncleanness. And in the rainy season — it is private domain for both.

M. 6:8 A basilica — is private domain in respect to the Sabbath and public domain in respect to uncleanness.

T. 7:13 A basilica, the two doors of which are directly opposite one another — all the same is the rule applying to the middle and to the sides: it is private domain for the Sabbath and public domain for uncleanness

T. 7:12 A basilica which they open by day and lock by night — so long as it is open, it is public domain. [When] it is locked, it is private domain. You come out to rule, By day [a doubt concerning] it is clean, and by night [a doubt concerning] it is unclean.

M. 6:9 The forum — is private domain for the Sabbath, and public domain for uncleanness. And so too the sides. The colonnades are private domain for the Sabbath, and public domain for uncleanness. A courtyard which the public enters through one entry and leaves through another is private domain for the Sabbath and public domain for uncleanness.

T. 7:9 The paths which lead down to the wells, caves, and cisterns, and winepresses, and threshing floors, are private domain for the Sabbath and public domain for uncleanness.

T. 7:10 Alleys which go down to the sea or to the river, even though they are fenced off on either side, and the public climb over the fences and walk therein are private domain for the Sabbath and public domain for uncleanness.

T. 7:11 The roofs of the village on which a public path passes are private domain for the Sabbath and public domain for uncleanness. A garden, when it is guarded, is private domain. If it is not guarded, it is public domain.

We now move from the particular to the generic hermeneutics. Here too, the category-formation, Tohorot, lays claim to preeminence among the Halakhic compositions. It is compendious, comprehensive, articulate, and lucid: a mass of cases so constructed as to yield governing rules, exquisitely exemplified. A number of principles for the resolution of cases of doubt in matters of uncleanness are set forth, all together comprising a theory of probability readily defined. Although the hermeneutics is generic, nonetheless, the particular theory of the category-formation enters in wherever there is an opening, e.g., probability rests on the capacity of actors to form a lucid intentionality, excluding, then, a deaf-mute, imbecile, and minor; if we can interrogate an actor, a matter of doubt is resolved as unclean, if we cannot interrogate him, a matter of doubt is dismissed as clean. All unclean things [are adjudged] in accord with [their condition] at the moment that they are found; whoever lacks understanding to be interrogated — a matter of doubt concerning him is resolved in favor of cleanness; confirm the status quo; confirm the prevailing assumption; matters of doubt involving private domain are resolved as unclean, those involving public domain are resolved as clean. M. 4:7 then provides a further composite of types of cases where cases of doubt are resolved in favor of cleanness, e.g., concerning rulings of sages as against rules of the Torah, concerning sacrifices and the like. When it comes to liquids' contracting uncleanness, doubt are resolved as unclean, but when it comes to conveying uncleanness, the doubt is deemed clean; doubt about liquids as regards food is resolved as unclean, utensils, clean. M. 4:11 logs in yet another set of general rules. M. 5:2ff. take up the matter of probable outcomes, well-illustrated at M. 5:5. I cannot point to a more successful response to the generic hermeneutics of the Halakhah than this vast composite of cases illustrative of governing principles. At every point we can account for the case at hand by appeal to one or another of the commonsensical principles, chief of which is, confirm the (assumed) status quo.

IV. THE HABER AND THE 'AM HA'ARES

M. 7:1 The potter who left his pots and went down to drink — the innermost ones are clean. And the outermost ones are unclean. He who gives over his key to an *'am ha'ares* — the house is clean, for he gave him only [the charge of] guarding the key.

T. 8:1 He [the context requires: the *haber*] who gave a key to an *'am ha'ares* — the house is unclean. [If] he gave him the [key to the] outer [room] and did not give him [the key to] the inner [room], the outer one is unclean. And as to the inner, unclean is only [the space] up to the place to which he can stretch out his hand and touch. [If] there were there shelves ten handbreadths high and niches ten handbreadths high, unclean is only [the space] up to the place to which he can stretch out his hand and touch. [If] the outer room belongs to one [person] and the inner room to another [person], even though the clean things are placed on the side of the door of the inner [room], lo, they are clean. He who enters without permission, even though he stands at the side of clean things — they are clean. And so in the case of a gentile: one does not take into consideration [the possibility of his touching things] in connection with wine used for purposes of idolatry.

M. 7:2 He who leaves an *'am ha'ares* inside his house awake and found him awake — asleep and found him asleep — awake and found him asleep — the house is clean. [If he left him] sleeping and found him awake — unclean is only [the space] up to the place to which he stretch out his hand and touch.

T. 8:2 A *haber* who was sleeping in the house of an *'am ha'ares,* with his clothing folded up and lying under his head, and his sandals and his jug before him — lo, these are clean because they are in the presumption of being guarded.

M. 7:3 He who leaves workers in his house — unclean is only [the space] up to the place to which they can reach out their hands and touch.

T. 8:3 A *haber* who said to an *'am ha'ares,* "Go and sleep in the house" the whole house is in his domain. "Go and sleep on such-and-such a bed" — unclean is only that very bed, and the space up to which he can reach out his hand and touch from the bed. [If] he said to him, "Keep this cow for me, that it not enter the house" — "Keep this heifer for me, that it not break the utensils" — lo, these are clean, for he gave him only the task of guarding the cow alone. But if he said to him, "Guard this house for me that the cow should not enter it" — "Guard these utensils for me that the cow should not break them" — lo, they are unclean.]

M. 7:4 The wife of a *haber* who left the wife of an *'am ha'ares* grinding [grain] in her house — [if the sound of] the mill-stones ceased — the house is unclean. The millstones did not cease — unclean is only [the space] up to the place to which she can reach out her hand and touch. [If] they were two, one way or the other [whether or not the grinding ceased], unclean is only [the space] up to the place to which they can reach out their hands and touch.

T. 8:4 The wife of an 'am *ha'ares* grinds [grain] with the wife of a *haber* when she is unclean, but when she is clean, she should not grind [wheat with her].

M. 7:5 He who leaves an *'am ha'ares* in his house to guard it — when he sees those that enter and those that leave, the foods, liquids, and open clay utensils are unclean. But the couches and seats and clay utensils which are sealed with a tight seal are clean. And if he does not see either those that enter or those that leave, even if he was immobilized, even if he was tied up, everything is unclean.

T. 8:7 He who leaves an 'am *ha'ares* in his house to guard it and this one is immobile or tied up — when he can see those that enter and those that leave unclean is only [the space] up to the place which they can make unclean.

M. 7:6 The tax collectors who entered the house — the house is unclean. If there is a gentile with them, they are believed to state, "We did not enter." But they are not believed to state, "We entered, but we did not touch [anything]." The thieves who entered the house — unclean is only the place [trodden by] the feet of the thieves. And what do they render unclean? The foods, and the liquids, and clay utensils which are open. But the couches and the seats and clay utensils which are sealed with a tight seal are clean. If there is a gentile with them, or a woman, everything is unclean.

T. 8:5 The tax-collectors who went into the house — if they said, "We entered the house, but we did not touch anything," lo, these are believed, for the testimony which prohibited is the testimony which permitted. If there were others giving testimony concerning them that they entered the house, and they said, "We did not touch anything," they are not believed. When the pledge is in their hand, even though others do not give testimony about them, they are not believed, because the pledge gives testimony about them. If there was a gentile with them, even though the pledge is in their hand, even though the gentile gives testimony concerning them that they entered, and they said, "We did not touch anything," lo, these are believed, because the fear of the gentile is upon them.

T. 8:6 The thieves who entered the house — unclean is only [the space] up to the place to which they can stretch out their hands and touch from the place of the robbery.

M. 7:7 He who leaves his clothing in the wall niche of the bathhouse — [they are not clean] unless one give him [the attendant] the key, or a seal, or unless he will make a mark. He who leaves his utensils from one vintage to the next vintage — his utensils are clean. And in the case of an Israelite, [they are not clean] unless he will testify, "In my heart was [the intention] to guard them."

T. 8:8 He who leaves his utensils in the wall niches of a bath house — he locked and sealed — even though he came and found the lock open, and the seal spoiled — it is clean. The seal of which they spoke [suffices] even if [it is] of mud, even if [it is] a spindle. He who stuffs his utensils in the wall niches of a bath house — they are unclean, because the gentile may be interrogated concerning them.

M. 7:8 He who was clean, and changed his mind about eating [heave offering] — they [the foodstuffs] are unclean. [If] his hands were clean, and he changed his mind about eating, even though he said, "I know that my hands have not been made unclean," his hands are unclean, for the hands are busy.

M. 7:9 The woman who entered in to take out a piece of bread for a beggar, and she came out and found him standing by the side of loaves [of bread] of heave offering — and so, the woman who went out and found her girl friend stirring up coals under a pot of heave offering — it is clean.

T. 8:9 He who purchases utensils from gentile craftsmen, and he who gives over utensils to gentile craftsmen — they are unclean with midras-uncleanness and clean of corpse-uncleanness. And he who purchases utensils from craftsmen who are *'ammé ha'ares* and he who gives over utensils to craftsmen who are *'ammé ha'ares* they are unclean with midras-uncleanness and unclean with corpse-uncleanness. [If] one left his utensils before an *'am ha'ares* and said to him, "Guard these for me" — they are unclean with midras-uncleanness and clean of corpse-uncleanness. [If] he put them on his shoulder, they are unclean with midras-uncleanness [and unclean with] corpse-uncleanness.

T. 8:11 [If] one left his utensils in the bath and came and found them as they were [originally left] — lo, these are clean. But they instruct him not to do so with clean things. [If] one left his winepress and his cistern and entered the town, even though he came and found an *'am ha'ares* beside them, they are clean. And so in the case of a gentile: One does not take into consideration the matter of wine used for the purposes of idolatry.

T. 8:12 An *'am ha'ares* who came to be sprinkled — they sprinkle on him and on his utensils only after three days. But a *haber* who came to be sprinkled — they sprinkle on him and on his utensils forthwith.

T. 8:13 [If] one was dressed in a shirt and wrapped in a cloak, and he said, "My concern was for the shirt, and my concern was not for the cloak" the shirt is clean, and the cloak is unclean. [If] a basket was on his shoulder, and a shovel was in it, [if] he said, "My concern was for the basket, and my concern was not for the shovel," the basket is clean, and the shovel is unclean.

T. 8:14 [If] one was making use of the jar in the assumption that it was of unconsecrated food and afterward it was found to contain heave-offering, lo, this is clean, and it is prohibited to be eaten, because it is a matter of doubt concerning one who has immersed on the selfsame day and awaits sunset for the completion of purification. [If] they said to him concerning that which was clean, "It is suspended" — lo, this is unclean. And if he said, "Lo, I shall leave it until I shall inquire concerning it" — lo, this is clean.

T. 8:15 Unclean and clean liquids [are] in the house — they follow [the status of] the larger part. WM'SH A woman filtered unclean and clean liquids into a jar of heave-offering, and the case came before sages. And they did not declare it unclean, because she did not cease to be concerned for it.

M. 8:1 He who lives with an *'am ha'ares* in a courtyard, and forgot utensils in the courtyard — even jars tightly sealed with a stopper, or an oven tightly sealed with a stopper — lo, these are unclean.

T. 9:1 A *haber* and an *'am ha'ares* who were dwelling in a courtyard and who forgot utensils in the courtyard — that which is suitable to become unclean with midras-uncleanness is [deemed to have been] made unclean with midras-uncleanness, and that which is suitable to become unclean with corpse-uncleanness is [deemed to have been] made unclean with corpse-uncleanness. This one has a *Sukkah* before his door, and that one has a *Sukkah* before his door — this one has a partition before his door, and that one has a partition before his door — this one leaves his utensils in his *Sukkah,* and that one leaves his utensils in his *Sukkah,* this one leaves his utensils by his partition, and that one leaves his utensils by his partition — all [the objects] are clean.

T. 9:2 This one has a *Sukkah* or partition before the door of his fellow, and that one has *a Sukkah* or partition before the door of his fellow — this one leaves his utensils in his *Sukkah* or partition before the door of his fellow, and that one leaves his utensil by the *Sukkah* or partition before his fellow's door — lo, these are unclean, for this one has the right to enter, and that one has the right to enter.

T. 9:3 A *haber* who left food and liquid on a well and went down to drink they are clean, for others do not handle them. But a *haber* who was selling food and liquid at the door of his shop and went inside [the shop] — lo, these are unclean, because others do handle them.

T. 9:4 An *'am ha'ares is* believed concerning the immersion of something unclean with corpse-uncleanness, but he is not believed concerning the immersion of something unclean with *maddaf*-uncleanness.

T. 9:5 A *haber* who died and left produce — they follow the status of the greater part of that which is brought in [to storage]. If the greater part of that which is brought in [to storage] is unconsecrated food, [the whole is regarded as] unconsecrated food, and if the greater part of that which is brought in [to storage] is heave-offering, [then the whole is deemed] heave-offering.

T. 9:6 [If] he [a *haber*] left clean [foods], lo, they are [regarded as] clean [foods]. [If] he left utensils, lo, they are regarded as unclean, for I say, "They were sprinkled, but not repeated[ly sprinkled], or repeated, but not immersed, "or possibly he did not sprinkle them at all."" A *haber* who died and left produce, even if on that very day he gathered them in, lo, they are in the presumption of having been properly prepared [tithed]. An *'am ha'ares* who took on himself [the obligations of the *haber],* and who had clean foods, and who said, "It is perfectly clear to me that they have not been made unclean" — When others had been engaged therewith, they are prohibited to him and prohibited to everyone else. [If] only he himself [was engaged therewith], they are permitted to him and prohibited to everyone else.

T. 9:7 A gentile who converted and who had wine and who said, "It is perfectly clear to me that it has not been made unclean" — when others were engaged therewith, it is prohibited to him and prohibited to everyone else. [If the man] himself [was engaged therewith], it is permitted to him and prohibited to everyone else.

M. 8:2 He who deposits utensils with an *'am ha'ares* — they are unclean with corpse uncleanness and unclean with midras uncleanness. If he [the *'am ha'ares*] knows him [the depositor], that he eats heave offering, they are clean of corpse uncleanness but unclean with midras uncleanness [the non-observant Israelite will refrain from touching things, but he cannot be expected to refrain from sitting down on chairs.]

M. 8:3 He who loses something on one day and found it on the same day — it is clean. [If he lost it) by day and found it [the next] night, [lost it] by night and found it [the next] day [lost

it] by day and found it on the next day — it is unclean. This is the general principle: Any object over which has passed the night or part of it [the night] — it is unclean. He who spreads out utensils [to dry] — in the public domain — they are clean. And [if he did so] in private domain — they are unclean. And if he was guarding them [in private domain], they are clean. [If] they fell, and, [having lost sight of them], he went to bring them in, they are unclean. [If] his dipper fell into the well of an *'am ha'ares* and he went to get some — thing with which to get it up — it is unclean, because it rested in the domain of an *'am ha'ares* for one moment.

T. 9:8 He who loses [something] and finds [it] in private property — and a night passed over it — it is unclean with midras-uncleanness and unclean with corpse-uncleanness. [If he lost them] in public domain — and a night passed over them — they are unclean with midras-uncleanness, and clean in regard to corpse-uncleanness.

M. 8:4 He who leaves his house open and found it open, locked and found it locked, open and found it locked — it is clean. [If he left it] locked, and found it open — it is clean, for there were thieves, but they changed their minds and went away.

M. 8:5 The wife of an *'am ha'ares* who went into the house of a *haber* to get his [the *haber*'s] son, or his daughter, or his beast — the house is clean, because she entered without permission.

T. 9:11 The roof of a *haber* is beside the roof of the *'am ha'ares* — the *haber* lays out utensils there and leaves clean things there, and on condition that the *'am ha'ares* cannot reach out his hand and touch. The roof of the *haber is* above the roof of the *'am ha'ares* — even though the *'am ha'ares* can reach out his hand and touch — the *haber* lays out utensils there and leaves clean things there. And so with a gentile: one does not take into consideration the possibility of wine used for idolatrous practice.

T. 9:12 [If] his dipper fell into the well of an *'am ha'ares* — *lo,* this is unclean. But it is clean when it comes up

We turn to a subset of problems of doubt, those that concern, in particular, what an Israelite who does not observe the laws of cultic cleanness outside of the Temple is likely to do with the things belonging to one who does. We have to establish guidelines to deal with a variety of particular cases, and, as is the Halakhic way, these guidelines emerge from illustrative cases, only occasionally being formulated as generalizations. The basic principle once more is, confirm the status quo, as at M. 8:4. But what that means in the case at hand requires amplification. The governing premise is, the *'am ha'ares* who is subject to supervision will not deliberately impart uncleanness to the food or property of the *haber,* and he will keep his word and carry out the *haber's* instructions. But if the *'am ha'ares* is in charge, then the probabilities shift. The *'am ha'ares* does not observe the purity laws, so the status quo is confirmed: here too, all things being equal, he will not keep laws he ordinarily ignores. The *'am ha'ares* is assumed to handle whatever is subject to his dominion. The outer limits of plausibility are outlined at M. 7:6, the governing premise at T. 9:1: where the non-observant Israelite has every right to enter, everything is deemed at his disposal and hence unclean to its maximum extent.

V. CONCLUDING MISCELLANIES AND REPRISE. UNCLEANNESS OF FOODS, LIQUIDS, CONNECTION

M. 8:6 A general rule did they state in connection with clean [foods]: Whatever is set aside for human consumption — it is susceptible to uncleanness until it is unfit for food for a dog. And whatever is not set aside for human consumption — it is insusceptible to uncleanness until it is designated for man. How so? A young pigeon which fell into the winepress, and one gave thought to it to bring it up for a gentile — it is susceptible to uncleanness. [And if one gave thought to bring it up] for a dog — it is insusceptible to uncleanness. [If] a deaf-mute, an imbecile, or a minor gave thought to it, it is insusceptible to uncleanness. If they brought it up, it is susceptible to uncleanness, for they have the power of deed, but they do not have the power of [effective] intention.

T. 9:13 Wheat which comes out with the turds of the oxen and barley which comes out with the turds of the cattle — even though one gave thought to them to make use of them for food are not susceptible to uncleanness [with the uncleanness affecting] food. [If] one gathered them for food, they are susceptible to uncleanness [with the uncleanness affecting] food. Urine — even though one gathered it for drink — his intention is null.

M. 8:7 The outer sides of utensils which were made unclean with liquids — liquids which were made unclean on the outer sides of the utensils — render what they touch unclean at one remove and render unfit at one [further] remove. Lo, this one [heave offering] says, "The things that made you [liquids] unclean did not make me unclean, but you made me unclean."

M. 8:8 (1) a kneading trough which lay on an incline, (2) and the [unclean] dough is above, (3) and running liquid is below — three pieces of dough [together making up] an egg's bulk — they are not joined together. And two — they are joined together. And if it was standing liquid, even if [the pieces of dough that made up the egg's bulk] were small as a mustard seed — it is

joined together.

T. 9:15 A kneading-trough which is unclean with corpse-uncleanness — they do not knead in it grain of unconsecrated food, and they do not lay out in it dough of heave-offering. But if one wants, he may bring grain of unconsecrated food and put it in it, and lay on it dough of heave-offering, and on condition that the dough should not touch the trough.

M. 8:9 A stick which is wholly covered by unclean liquids — it is unclean until one will immerse the whole thing. A jet [of liquid], [water on] an incline, and flowing liquid — are not a connector either for uncleanness or for cleanness. The rut [of water] is a connector for uncleanness and for cleanness.

M. 9:1 Olives — from what time do they receive uncleanness? After the work of preparing them is completed.

M. 9:2 [If] one has finished gathering but is going to buy [morel — finished buying [more] but is going to borrow [still more] — [if] a time of mourning or a wedding feast befell him, or an accident — even [if] Zabim and Zabot [= Lev. 15] walk on them, they are clean. [If] unclean liquids fell on them, unclean is only the place which they touched. And the sap which comes forth from them is clean.

T. 10:1 When its preparation will be completed.

T. 10:3 And why did they say that sap which exudes from the bale [of olives made up] for the olive-press is susceptible to uncleanness? Because it is not possible for the serial fluid of olives not to contain particles of oil. Sap which exudes from oil is susceptible to uncleanness. That which exudes from the vat is insusceptible. [If] one gathered it and made it into a bale [of olives for the press], it is susceptible to uncleanness.

M. 9:3 [When] the work of preparing them is completed, lo, these are susceptible to uncleanness. [If] unclean liquids fell on them — the sap which exudes from them — it is unclean.

T. 10:4 He who packs his olives in two groups — once one of them is completed, they [the olives in that group] are susceptible to receive uncleanness. He who cuts his olives in the Upper Galilee and is going to bring them down to Lower Galilee — they do not receive uncleanness until he brings them down to Lower Galilee. If before he cut them he gave thought to them, they are insusceptible to uncleanness. [If he did so] after he cut them, they have been rendered susceptible to receive uncleanness. He who completes work on his olives and is going to sell them — they are insusceptible to uncleanness. [He who completes work on his olives and is going] to adorn them with leaves, they are susceptible to receive uncleanness.

T. 10:5 He who purchases a vat of olives from the gentile, if he is gathering them on the ground, [or: if there are olives to be gathered, lying on the ground,] let him prepare it in cleanness. [And he who purchases] from an Israelite, [the Israelite] is believed to say, "I did not complete work on it." [If] he had a clump of olives and wants to prepare them in cleanness, even though he is going to add [only] a *qab* or two *qabs* of olives to the clump, lo, these are insusceptible to uncleanness; and on condition that he not practice deception; but if he practiced deception, lo, these are susceptible to uncleanness.

T. 10:6 He who stacks his olives in the domain of an *'am ha'ares* and locked and placed a seal — he does not scruple lest there is there another key or another seal. And even though he came and found the lock open, or the seal disarranged, it is insusceptible to receive uncleanness. The seal of which they spoke may be even a bit of mud, and even a spindle of wood.

M. 9:5 He who leaves olives in the press so that they will grow soft — so that they will be easy to press — lo, these are susceptible to uncleanness. [If he does so] so that they will grow soft so that he may salt them — they are not susceptible to uncleanness. He who crushes olives [of heave offering] with unclean hands — he has rendered them unclean.

T. 10:7 [If] there were there holes and cracks, he does not scruple lest one have thrust in a reed and moved the [olives] about. [If] there were there windows of four handbreadths, they are treated as doors.

T. 10:8 He who stacks [his olives] in his house — he prepares a partition for them from the ground to the beams. And on condition that they should [not] be shaken up on account of the partition. He who stacks [his olives] in the press is like him who stacks in his house.

T. 10:9 He who completes work on his olives and left one basket — let him give it before the priest, and bring him the key.

T. 10:11 The olive which one crushed with unclean hands — it has not been rendered susceptible to uncleanness. [If he did so in order] to dry them with salt — (and) it has (not) been rendered susceptible to uncleanness. [If he did so] in order to know whether there is water in it, it has not been rendered susceptible to uncleanness. [If] he had a mass of olives and is going to turn it over, once he has driven a stake into it, even if there are many clumps in it, lo, these are not connected to one another.

M. 9:6 He who leaves his olives on the roof to dry them, even if they are [piled] a cubit in height — they are not made susceptible to uncleanness. [If] he put them in the house so that they might putrefy and is going to bring them up to the roof — [if] he

put them on the roof to putrefy or to open — lo, these are susceptible to uncleanness. [If] he put them in the house until he could keep watch over his roof, or so until he might bring them to some other place — they are not susceptible to uncleanness.

M. 9:7 [If] one wanted to take from them [enough for] a single pressing, or [enough for] two pressings — let him set apart in a state of uncleanness and cover up in a state of uncleanness.

T. 10:12 And on condition that he not uproot the whole clump. But in a place in which they are accustomed to leave a sufficient amount for a pressing, one leaves enough for a single pressing. In a place in which they are accustomed to leave a sufficient amount for a small olive press, one leaves sufficient for a small olive press. [If they are accustomed to leave enough for] a small olive press with a cylindrical beam, one leaves enough for a small olive press with a cylindrical beam. And on condition that one not uproot the whole clump. And if one has uprooted the whole clump, lo, these are susceptible to uncleanness. And on condition that one not practice deception. And if one has practiced deception, lo, these are susceptible to uncleanness. And he who stacks in the press is like him who stacks in his house.

M. 9:8 The [dead] creeping thing which is found in the millstones — unclean is only the place which it touches. [If] it was running liquid — the whole is unclean. [If] it is found on the leaves [which cover up the mass of olives], let them ask the olive press workers to state, "We did not touch." [If] it was touching the mass, even if it is the size of a barley grain — it is unclean.

M. 9:9 [If the insect] was found on top of broken-off blocks, and it touches as much as an egg's bulk — it is unclean. [If it touched] broken-off blocks on top of other broken-off blocks, even though it touches as much as an egg's bulk — unclean is only the place which it touches. [If an insect is found] between the wall and the olives, it [the mass of olives] is clean. [If] it is found on the roof, [those still in] the vat are clean. [If] it is found in the vat, those on the roof are unclean. [If] it is found burned [and clean] on the olives — and so a scorched rag — it is clean. For all [conditions of] uncleanness are [decided in accord with] the time that they are found.

T. 11:1 [If] a dead creeping thing is found on the roof, unclean is only the roof. [If it is found] in the vat, unclean is only the vat. [If] it is found in a clump [of olives] and on the roof — [if found in the next] three days, the vat is unclean. [If it is found] after three days, the vat is clean.

T. 11:2 He who cuts pieces from the dough, and a dead creeping thing is found in the piece, the dough is clean. [If] it is found in the dough, unclean is only the dough. [If it is found] in the piece which is cut off, unclean is only the piece. [If] it is found inside the piece which is cut off, the whole is unclean.

T. 11:3 [If] a dead creeping thing is found in the upper one, unclean is only the upper one. [If] it is found in the lower one, unclean is only the lower one. [If] it is found on clods and touched as much as an egg's bulk [of crumbs], it is unclean. Clods which are on clods — even though it touched as much as an egg's bulk — unclean is only the place which it touched.

M. 10:2 The olive workers who were entering and leaving, and unclean liquids were in the olive press — if there is [sufficient space] between the liquids and the olives so that they can dry their feet on the ground — lo, these [olives] are clean. The olive workers and the grape gatherers before whom uncleanness was found — they are believed to say, "We did not touch it." And so the children among them. They go outside the door of the olive press and defecate behind the wall, and they are clean. How far are they to go and be clean? So far that one may [still] see them.

M. 10:4 He who places [grapes into the winepress] from [what was stored in] baskets or from what was spread out on the ground — he places with unclean hands. And he separates his heave offering in cleanness. [He who puts grapes into the winepress] from the grape basket or from what is spread out on leaves — all agree that he puts them in with clean hands. And if he puts them in with unclean hands, he has rendered them unclean.

M. 10:5 He [who is unclean] who eats [grapes] from the baskets and from what is spread out on the ground — even though they burst open and were dripping into the winepress — lo, the press is clean. [If one ate from grapes which were] in the grape basket and from what is spread out on leaves, and there fell from it [into the vat] a single berry — if it had a seal, [what is in the vat] is clean. If it had no seal, [what is in the vat] is unclean. If [a cluster of] grapes [with stalks] fell from it [into the vat] and one trampled them in an empty part, if there was there an egg's bulk exactly, it [the vat] is clean. [If there is there] more than an egg's bulk, it [the vat] is unclean, since as soon as the first drop exuded, it was made unclean, by [the remainder which is] an egg's bulk in volume.

T. 11:4 Grapes — until when do they receive uncleanness as food? Until the time that they will trample them, warp and woof. And [if] there remain of them whole dried berries, they receive uncleanness as food. Olives — until when do they receive uncleanness as food? Until one will press them. [If] one has crushed them but there remain of them whole dried berries, they receive uncleanness as food.

T. 11:5 And what are uncrushed olives and grapes? Those that exude from under the beam or from under the peat and from the grape-skins. [If] one gathered them for food, they receive uncleanness as food. And the grape pits and the skins, even though one has gathered them for food — his intention is null.

T. 11:6 He who weighs grapes in the balance, even though wine flows on his hands — and even though he gave thought to it — it is insusceptible. He who presses grapes in a jug, even though [the juice] flows on his hands — it is insusceptible. And so with respect to the gentile: One does scruple on account of wine used for idolatrous purposes.

T. 11:7 He who cuts grapes of his vineyard for the market — if he did not find a market for them, he returns them to the vat. [He who cuts] olives for the market — [if] he did not find a market for them, he returns them to the press. Even though he brings them to the market in unclean baskets and in unclean containers, they are clean. [When] they have entered the domain of the vat and the domain of the press, they are made susceptible to receive uncleanness.

T. 11:8 He who purchases from that which is lying on the ground — [if he purchases] from an Israelite, let him do the work in uncleanness. [If he purchases them] from a gentile, let him do the work in cleanness. [He who purchases] from what is lying on the ground on leaves — whether from an Israelite or from a gentile, let him prepare them in uncleanness.

T. 11:9 He who purchases [olives] from what is lying on the ground from an Israelite — [intending] to make them into dried olives — lo, this one prepares his olives in cleanness. He who eats [grapes] from the baskets and from what is lying on the ground — [if] he ate and left over as much as a *se'ah* or two *se'ahs*. Even though he spread them out for the vat, and threw them into the vat, [even though he spread them out for the vat] and the wine spurts on the grapes, it is clean. And so in the case of the gentile: one does not scruple on account of wine used for idolatrous purposes.

T. 11:10 [If] a single berry fell from it — if it has a seal, it is clean. [If] it does not have a seal, it is unclean. Under what circumstances? When one [who is unclean] has touched the place on which the liquid is located. [If] one did not touch the place on which the liquid is located, it is clean.

M. 10:6 He who was standing and talking at the edge of the cistern, and spit spurted from his mouth — it is a matter of doubt whether it reached the pit or whether it did not reach the pit — the matter of doubt is deemed clean.

M. 10:7 He who emptied out the cistern, and a dead creeping thing was found in the first [jarful] — they all are un-

clean. [If it was found] in the last [jarful] — it is unclean, but all the rest are clean. Under what circumstances? When he drew out [the wine] with each one [of the jars]. But if he was drawing out with a ladling jar, [if] a dead creeping thing was found in one of them, it alone is unclean. Under what circumstances? When he examined but did not cover up, or he covered but did not inspect. [If he] was both inspecting and covering — and a dead creeping thing is found — in [one] jar — the whole [cistern] is unclean; in the cistern — the whole [cistern] is unclean; in the ladling jar — the whole [cistern] is unclean.

T. 11:13 He who empties the cistern one by one [filling one jar at a time] and the dead creeping thing is found in the first jar — they all are unclean. [If it is found] in the last jar, the last jar is unclean, but the rest of them are clean. [If it is found] in the middle jar, from it and following, the jars are unclean; from it and the foregoing, the jars are clean. Under what circumstances? When one examined but did not cover, or covered but did not examine. [If] he was examining and covering, and a dead creeping thing is found in one of them, it alone is unclean.

M. 10:8 [The space] between the rollers and the grape skins is public domain. [The part of] the vineyard which is in front of the grape gatherers is private domain. [That which is] behind the grape gatherers is public domain. Under what circumstances? When the public goes in by one end and goes out by the other. An implement of the olive press and of the winepress and the olive truss, when they are of wood, one dries them off and they are clean. When they are of reed grass, one leaves them unused for twelve months, or one scalds them in hot water.

T. 11:15 The upper cistern is public domain, and the lower is private domain — under what circumstances? When the public enters through one way and leave through another. [If] there is there only a single door, or only a single breach, this and that are private domain.

T. 11:16 He whose wine-vats and olive-presses were unclean and who wants to clean them: [as to] the boards and the two posts supporting the beams of the press and the troughs — he dries them, and they are clean. The cylinders of twigs and of hemp — he has to dry out. The cylinders of bast and of reeds — he has to leave unused. And how long does he leave them unused? Twelve months. And just as he dries for cleanness, so he dries for wine used for idolatrous purposes.

The miscellanies respond to a variety of principles of the generic hermeneutics. The first is, we confirm the prevailing situation. If something is assumed to be intended for human consumption, it remains susceptible to uncleanness as food until even a dog will not eat it. Whatever is not designated for human consumption remains insusceptible until it is designated for man's food. But the power of intentionality is limited to those of sound senses, so M. 8:6, a fundamental exercise. How liquids flow and the consequences for the transmission of uncleanness are dealt with at M. 8:7-9. Then we turn to particular liquids, olives and their oil, M. 9:1ff. A reprise of the resolution of cases of doubt is set forth at M. 9:8ff. It is difficult to explain the cogency or the rationale for this composite, in light of the remarkable cogency of the prior ones.

IV. THE HERMENEUTICS OF TOHOROT

A. WHAT FUSES THE HALAKHIC DATA INTO A CATEGORY-FORMATION?

When sages wished to organize a basic category called "purities" — Tohorot in Hebrew — as was their way, they identified data that cohered and yielded a cogent account of matters. We seek to identify their reasons for that judgment. I see two that are particular to the topic, two that are generic but adapted for the requirements of the topic. We should have no category-formation without the particular hermeneutics, but we also should not have the category-formation that we do have without the generic hermeneutics. Let me set forth as a sequence the topics at hand, indicating where the particular and the generic hermeneutics, respectively, come to bear:

1. the particular hermeneutics of intentionality, realized in the analysis of the relationship between sources of uncleanness and removes or successive levels of sanctification;
2. the particular hermeneutics of intentionality, realized in the analysis of the relationship between Fathers and Offspring of uncleanness;
3. the generic hermeneutics covering probabilities, realized in sorting out matters of doubt in accord with sages' assessment of likely outcomes;
4. the generic hermeneutics covering probabilities, realized in the analysis of the relationship of the *haber* and the *'am ha'ares* — what the later is likely to do in relationship to susceptible but clean food or drink belonging to the former.

We have already established that the system finds its dynamics — and therefore its problematics — in intentionality, which permeates the entire structure and renders it coherent. But we need not invoke so general a fact as the pervasive presence of considerations of attitude or will. The matter of intentionality time and again is expressed in so many words, not only implicitly, for example in the following:

> He who leaves his clothing in the wall niche of the bathhouse — they are not clean unless one give him the attendant the key, or a seal, or unless he will make a mark. He who leaves his utensils from one vintage to the next vintage — his utensils are clean. And in the case of an Israelite, they are not clean unless he will testify, "In my heart was the intention to guard them"
>
> M. 7:7

On the other hand, if someone had the intentionality of eating food in the status of priestly rations and so was in a state of cultic purity, as soon as he changes his mind about doing so, we classify the man as unclean; once the intention changes, the consequent attitude and activity no longer suffice to preserve, by happenstance, the cleanness of the person. Either he intends to keep the purity rules and so is assumed to succeed, or he does not intend to keep them, and, sources of contamination being abundant and, considering removes from the original source, enduring and ubiquitous, we simply assign the now-thoughtless person to the status of uncleanness. That represents a sizable corpus of cases that work out the particular hermeneutics of the category-formation.

But stated in sequence, the four main foci of Tohorot hold together because to the sages they make a single statement, from logical beginning to necessary end,[2] and the order is critical to the message that is set forth. That statement fuses in response to the requirements of the generic hermeneutics, though critical components realize the particular hermeneutics introduced at section i. How does the generic hermeneutics fuse the data into a coherent category-formation?

Before us we contemplate an intangible world of confusion, actual and potential:

[1] among classes of things and persons that are both alike and not alike:

[2] among things that may contract uncleanness but also attain sanctification;

[3] among sources of uncleanness; among things that may

---

[2] With the qualification that I cannot explain what I call "the concluding miscellany." It uncommon for category-formations of the Halakhah to trail off in a miscellaneous composite.

be unclean or clean;

[4] among persons who are Israelites all together, but who may or may not keep certain laws of the Torah.

What the Halakhah accomplishes is the same thing throughout: to identify things that are to begin with alike — that stand along a single continuum, that bear traits in common — but that also exhibit differentiating qualities. Extrapolating from cases, the Halakhah then offers the governing rules that sort out these mixtures of things that are both alike and unlike. The Halakhah tells us how to differentiate the unlike among the like, so to sort out confusion and clarify the categories that pertain.

Take the categories one by one. Sources of uncleanness form a single classification; but we differentiate between the primary source and removes therefrom, that is, successive contacts: the source, what has touched the source, what has touched what has touched the source, and so on into the outer reaches of imagination. Thus, in philosophical terms, we distinguish what is primary from what is secondary and derivative, that is, between efficient and proximate causes. And again, sources of uncleanness form one category, but some sources are more virulent than others, that is to say, some sources of uncleanness produce powerful and long-lasting effects, others limited and transient ones; some affect many things, others only a few; some transmit uncleanness only if touched, others when overshadowed, or when carried even though not touched, and so on. The two points of engagement — removes, Fathers/offspring — clearly correspond, as we move from the source of uncleanness through the successive removes, and from the Father of uncleanness through the diminishing effects of the Offspring thereof. So much for differentiating between sources of uncleanness and among their effects: a labor of identifying the lines of order and structure that separate uncleanness from uncleanness and differentiate their affects upon food and drink and clothing at various levels of sanctification: this affects that, but not the other thing; this is affected by that, but not the other thing.

What about what is affected by sources of uncleanness? That question carries us from corpses, spit, and blood of certain origin, to food, drink, and human beings. The third subdivision of the Halakhah as set forth by the Mishnah and the Tosefta involves food and drink, the fourth, persons. In both cases we confront the same problem: how to deal with doubt as to the status, in respect to uncleanness, of food and drink, on the one side, and persons, on the other. What persons, food, and utensils have in common is that all may be made unclean, but, from the perspective of the Halakhah, they also may attain cultic cleanness, and, in the setting of the household as much as the Temple, ought to. That with which we have to reckon, then, is whether in an unguarded moment they have contracted uncleanness.

We resolve doubt as to the classification of food and drink by appeal to probabilities of a variety of orders. It is more probable that the status quo has prevailed than that it has not; it is more probable that what is dragged, and so can touch something, has touched the unclean thing than that what is tossed, and so cannot touch, has made contact. Common sense about the more or the less probable, however, is joined to certain principles that appear to be arbitrary but that in fact appeal to their own inner logic. Because we want the householder to maintain a high state of alertness concerning sources of uncleanness, we declare that cases of doubt in private property are treated as unclean. Because the public domain contains many imponderables and cannot be closed off to the faithful, we declare cases of doubt in public property to be treated as clean. Now that position is counter-intuitive, since in the public domain circulate gentiles, whose persons and secretions are by definition unclean, as well as Israelites who do not keep this aspect of the Halakhah. And, given the distractions of crowds, one is more likely there than in private domain to step on unclean spit or urine deriving from gentiles. And who is to know the "history" of an object — what the one who touched it has touched, and what that has touched, backward for however many removes from the initial source of uncleanness? Reason therefore suggests that a case of doubt in public domain should be resolved in favor of uncleanness, and in private, cleanness. So here the system concerns itself with its larger goal — sanctifying the household and its table — and mitigates its more extreme possibilities. Where people can and should take care, they are held to a high standard. Where circumstances make difficult a constant state of alertness amid a barrage of occasions for contamination, they are not. That is where the logic of public policy takes priority over the logic of probabilities of contamination, an outer limit to the obsessive mentality that is potential in the system.

So much for food, drink, and utensils, what about persons? Here we classify the category of Israelites, differentiating the *haber* from the *'am ha'ares,* that is, those who prepare their ordinary food as though it were heave-offering or Holy Things from those who do not. The former take care not to contract uncleanness or to remove its effects through immersion. The latter do not. Then how do the two classes of Israelites interact, and, more to the point, how do the ones who keep the purity-laws determine the status of their persons and property that has been subject to the disposition of those who do not keep those laws? Here again, as we have seen, a few comprehensive principles accommodate the cases and problems at hand; these have already been specified.

B. THE ACTIVITY OF THE CATEGORY-FORMATION

INTENTIONALITY: The taxonomic power of intentionality comes to expression, among many definitive statements, in the following, which is one of the clearest, at T. 2:5: Honey which oozes from the hive of bees receives uncleanness as liquid. If one gave thought to it as food, it receives uncleanness as food. Oil is neither food nor liquid. If one gave thought to it to make use of it as food and not as liquid his intention is of no effect. Blood which congealed is neither food nor liquid. If one gave thought to it to make use of it as food, it receives uncleanness as food. And if one gave thought to use it as liquid his intention is null. It would be difficult to find a more explicit statement that matters of uncleanness are entirely relative to the attitude of the Israelite than the following:

> He who was clean, and changed his mind about eating [heave offering] — they [the foodstuffs] are unclean. [If] his hands were clean, and he changed his mind about eating, even though he said, "I know that my hands have not been made unclean," his hands are unclean, for the hands are busy.
>
> M. 7:8

The condition of the man has not changed, but his attitude has, and that suffices to render him unclean for eating heave-offering. Once the hands are no longer supervised, they are assumed to contract uncleanness — a good measure of the alertness that the intent to preserve cultic cleanness is assumed to bring about. But how intentionality reigns supreme remains to be seen.

That same matter of intentionality and preparation of a substance to serve as food comes to expression in a striking way. At what point does something enter into the system of cultic uncleanness as food? It is when people regard it as food. At what point does something leave the system and become insusceptible to uncleanness as food? When people will not eat it. So at both entry and departure into and out of the system, the attitude of man toward the substance governs the status of the substance, and intrinsic traits register only at man's wish, e.g., the rotting of the meat. How this works out in ordinary terms is simple. Whatever people identify as suitable for human consumption is susceptible until proven otherwise, that is, "until it is unfit for food for a dog." And whatever is not ordinarily eaten by man remains insusceptible until it is explicitly designated for human consumption. So the thinking exhibited in the Halakhah of Uqsin about intentionality to use a substance for food comes to the surface once more, in a statement of remarkable elegance (M. 8:6).

The program goes over other principles pertinent to food in general. A recurrent consideration is, how large a volume of the substance is required to be taken into account? That is, the requisite volume to enter the system. Since the system is set into motion by man's intentionality and attitude, we need to know what sort of standard measure dictates the volume of a substance that man takes into account to begin with — much as was the case for Kelim. A further issue concerns the status as to uncleanness of the one who consumes such substance, matters of joining together to receive uncleanness along with the main body of the matter and to impart uncleanness thereto and form part of the volume to attain the requisite amount.

INTENTIONALITY AND REMOVES OF UNCLEANNESS: That brings us back to the topic of "removes," meaning, the chain of contacts between the source of uncleanness and extensions thereof. We might regard the matter as a formulation in odd terms of the matter of causality, with its various degrees: primary, secondary, and so on. Here the Halakhah takes up a matter to which we have made only casual reference, the conception that uncleanness is transmitted not only through direct but through indirect effect. The details are not hard to grasp, though some of the governing rules prove arbitrary. The basic principle is this: If someone or something contracts uncleanness from a primary source of uncleanness ("Father of Uncleanness") such as a corpse, he is in the status of uncleanness in the first remove from that source. What touches him or it then is in the status of uncleanness in the second remove, what touches what is unclean in the second remove enters the third remove, and so beyond. So assessing the "remove" from the original source of uncleanness enters the picture.

With what consequence? The matter of "removes" makes a difference in the affect upon things or persons touched in a succession of removes, and the condition as to uncleanness of those thing or persons. That, in turn, depends upon the sensitivity to uncleanness of what is touched. We already know the criterion: the higher in the hierarchy of sanctification, the more susceptible, or sensitive, to uncleanness. Therefore what is in the status of Holy Things will be affected by uncleanness transmitted through a higher number of removes than what is in the status of heave-offering (priestly rations), what is in the status of heave-offering will be affected by uncleanness transmitted through a diminished number of removes, and so downward. At the end, at a given remove from the original source, something may be unfit, that is, treated as unclean, but it will not transmit uncleanness at all. Then the Halakhah differentiates what is unclean from what is unfit. Food may be unfit for consumption by those who eat ordinary food as though it were holy, but it is not necessarily unclean within the system of cultic contamination, having reached a remove so far from the initial source as to have lost that capacity to convey contamination even while retaining its classification of unfitness. That category corresponds to the ruling in jurisprudence that an action is forbidden but if done not subject to penalty.

The correspondence of the hierarchy of sanctification with the hierarchy of contamination is fully exposed in both the Mishnah's and the Tosefta's statements of the topic that we examined at the opening of the Halakhah of Kelim, and it is recapitulated here. As is often the case, the Tosefta will prove still more systematic than the Mishnah. The opening statement establishes the pattern for the rest. The uncleanness emitted by a dead creeping thing imparts uncleanness at three removes from the original dead frog; at the fourth remove, what is affected is unfit, but not unclean so far as affecting a fifth remove is concerned. And that pertains to matters of Holy Things, deriving from, or designated for, the altar. For food in the status of heave-offering, the chain is reduced by one remove. As to unconsecrated food, it is reduced by yet another remove. Since, when it becomes unclean, liquid is deemed unclean in the first remove, no matter the source of the uncleanness or the number of removes involved, the picture shifts, so T. 1:5.

> T. 1:5 The creeping thing renders unclean at three removes and unfit at one further remove in connection with Holy Things; and renders unclean at two removes and unfit at one further remove in connection with heave-offering. It renders unclean at one remove and unfit at one remove in connection with unconsecrated food.
>
> Liquid renders unclean at two removes and unfit at one remove in connection with Holy Things. It renders unclean at one remove and unfit at one remove in connection with Heave-offering. And it spoils unconsecrated food.

Now a further set of cases of the working of removes in relationship to the source of uncleanness is laid out; here I indent expository material:

> T. 1:6 The hands convey uncleanness at one remove and render unfit at one remove in connection with Holy Things, and render heave-offering unfit, and the rule governing the uncleanness of hands has no bearing upon unconsecrated food.
>
> In respect to what sort of Holy Things did they speak? Concerning Holy Things of the sanctuary which are sanctified, for example, loaves of thanksgiving and the wafers of the Nazir over which the sacrifice has been slaughtered and meal-offerings which were mixed in a utensil.

> But loaves of thanksgiving and wafers of a Nazir over which the sacrifice was not slaughtered and meal-offerings which were not mixed in a utensil are like neither Holy Things nor unconsecrated food, but they are like heave-offering. And the dead creeping thing renders unclean at two removes and spoils at one remove in their case.
>
> T. 1:7 Loaves of Holy Things — in their holes is liquid — and the aforementioned liquid of Holy Things is made unclean in the case of one of them by a dead creeping thing — they all are in the first remove of uncleanness. In the case of heave-offering, it imparts uncleanness at two removes and spoils heave-offering at one further remove. In the case of unconsecrated food, it imparts uncleanness at one remove and spoils heave-offering at one further remove.
>
> You have no liquid (of Holy Things) which touches something unclean in the third remove and is unclean except for Holy Things alone. But food which is unclean in the second remove which touched the liquid of the olive-press — it the liquid is unclean.

The correlation of sanctification and susceptibility to uncleanness thus is exquisitely spelled out.

Like M. Hag. 2:5ff., M. Toh. 2:3-5 correlate susceptibility to uncleanness with a position in the hierarchy of sanctification. The rules make this matter explicit for [1] unconsecrated food, [2] heave offering, and [3] Holy Things. The first-named is unclean and imparts uncleanness at the first remove from the Father of Uncleanness; food that touches food in the first remove, that is, at the second, is unfit but does not convey uncleanness. And at the third remove, unconsecrated food is entirely unaffected. Heave-offering adds a remove, and Holy Things yet another. At this point we recall the primacy of intentionality in the entire system and ask, where, in the present rather complex matter, do we identify a place for human attitude? In fact, it is omnipresent for a simple reason: it is man who has originally assigned to each body of food the status that it enjoys. He is the one who designates grain as unconsecrated and available for his household's meals; as priestly rations and therefore sanctified to the priesthood; or as Holy Things for presentation in the Temple. Grain that has had exactly the same "history" of contacts with a Father of Uncleanness, or what has contacted a Father (first remove) or what has contacted that (second remove) by reason of the householder's intentionality will then be classified differently as to uncleanness.

Here again, — to continue our reading of M. 2:3ff. as a statement of generative principles — we deal with a system of complex relationships, a set of grids that are interposed and interleaved. The key language at M. 2:6 then raises the question of how food is prepared, which is to say, the degree of punctiliousness that the householder has observed in preparing a given volume of food. And here, once more, the attitude of the householder provides the key to all relationships. Has he prepared heave offering in conditions of cleanness pertaining to Holy Things? Has he prepared ordinary food in conditions of cleanness demanded for — in accord with the discipline that applies to — Holy Things? Then he has indicated a higher state of alertness to the possibility of cultic contamination than he would have sustained to attain conditions of cleanness demanded for ordinary food or for lower steps in the hierarchy of sanctification. Then the system of removes will dictate the classification of said food, depending upon the status imputed to the food by the householder and upon the actions he has taken by reason of the status he has assigned to the food.

But do matters change in substance, in actuality? Or do we deal with a gossamer web formed of intangibles such as emotion, attitude, and intention or aspiration? M. 2:8 makes its implacable judgment upon the whole: And unconsecrated food which is prepared in accord with the rules pertaining to Holy Things — lo, this is like unconsecrated food. Everything is relative, but then there is no way that intrinsic uncleanness or sanctification comes into view. The rules apply, but the substance of matters is unchanged by the householder's attitude — and yet, we see, the substance of matters makes slight impact upon the transactions portrayed here.

Physical traits nonetheless do make a difference in some aspects of the system — but only to underscore how all things end up relative to attitude. Now we further distinguish between solids and liquids, and here Scripture is held to make a contribution. Lev. 11:34 states, "Any food in it a clay utensil into which a dead creeping thing has fallen which may be eaten, upon which water may come, shall be unclean; and all drink which may be drunk from every such utensil shall be unclean." Solid food, then, imparts uncleanness to food and drink but not utensils, meaning, solid food is in the first remove of uncleanness, but utensils contract uncleanness only from a Father of Uncleanness; liquid that contracts uncleanness affects utensils. Not only so, but liquid contracts uncleanness from an offspring of uncleanness (what is in the first remove or beyond), as well as from a Father of uncleanness, and what touches liquid is classified in the first remove of uncleanness, exactly as the liquid itself. (The Halakhah of Parah goes over this matter as well.) Not only so, but liquid in any volume imparts uncleanness, while food does so only in the requisite volume (Albeck, p. 297).

That is the case, however, only of liquid that is subject to man's intentionality, which is to say, that man wants to use to moisten produce. Liquid that wets produce not with the owner's approval has no affect upon the produce. While systematically expounded in tractate Makhshirin, that principle, deriving from Lev. 11:34, 37 as sages read the verse, comes to the surface here: He who leaves his olives on the roof to dry them, even if they are piled a cubit in height — they are not made susceptible to uncleanness. If he put them in the house so that they might putrefy and is going to bring them up to the roof — if he put them on the roof to putrefy or to open — lo, these are susceptible to uncleanness. If he put them in the house until he could keep watch over his roof, or so until he might bring them to some other place — they are not susceptible to uncleanness. The difference is that when the man put the olives into the house to putrefy, he desires the liquid that will ooze and so wets down the olives by intention. But if he put them into the house not to hasten putrefaction but only to protect the olives from uncleanness until he can keep watch on the olives when spread out on the roof, then his intention defines the classification of the olives.

THE GENERIC HERMENEUTICS: THE EXEGETICAL OUTCOME: [1] Mixtures. The Halakhah of Tohorot frames matters, as we have come to expect, in terms of interstitial problems: what do we do when food unclean by a Father of Uncleanness, hence in the first remove, mixes with food unclean by an Offspring of Uncleanness, e.g., so that only when combined is the requisite volume of unclean food reached to impart uncleanness; then at what remove of uncleanness is food that is so contaminated? Here we see the intangibility of uncleanness itself. A bulk of food that is joined together and then divided turns out to move upward and downward in the scale of removes. Thus: an egg's bulk of food unclean in the first remove of uncleanness and an egg's bulk of food unclean in the second remove of uncleanness which one mixed together with one another — it is unclean in the first remove of uncleanness. If one divided them up — this is unclean in the second remove of uncleanness, and this is unclean in the second remove of uncleanness. The matter is stated still more clearly: A piece of dough, which was unclean in the first remove, and one stuck others to it, they all are unclean in the first remove. If they separated, it is unclean in the first remove, but all the rest are unclean in the second remove. So much for the matter of removes from uncleanness, the hierarchy of sanctification ascending upward, and uncleanness ascending downward.

THE GENERIC HERMENEUTICS: THE EXEGETICAL OUTCOME: [2] RESOLVING MATTERS OF DOUBT. Principles that permeate the Halakhah come to bear in concrete ways here. For example, the basic tendency to confirm the status quo explains the principle that what is dragged is assumed to have been contaminated, but what is thrown, not. But other considerations enter in. The first of these is the distinction between public domain and private domain. A matter of doubt concerning what is in public domain is resolved as clean, in private domain, unclean. That is to say, within the household itself, people are expected to pay extra care to avoid sources of uncleanness. In the public domain, where matters are more difficult — but the stakes much lower — matters of doubt are resolved as unclean. That decisions are guided by circumstance and relationship, not by intrinsic considerations, is made explicit time and again, e.g., among many cases: A place which was private domain and became public domain and once again was made private domain — when it is private domain, a matter of doubt concerning it is deemed unclean. When it is public domain, a matter of doubt concerning it is clean. So again we find no trace of a fixed and physical foundation to the matter of uncleanness; all things are relative, each in its context.

THE GENERIC HERMENEUTICS: THE EXEGETICAL OUTCOME: [3] MIXTURES OF CLASSES OF ISRAELITES AND DOUBTS AS TO THE PROBABLE RESULTS. When we come to the mixture of Israelites — the haber and the 'am ha'ares — at stake is not the person but the conduct of the two components of the social order contemplated by the Halakhah, those that keep the Halakhah of cleanness and those that do not. The Halakhah at hand sorts out the complexities of relationships between those who keep the purity-laws even outside of the holy city and the Temple and those who do not. These too involve the resolution of cases of doubt. But we should not miss what is subject to doubt. It is not only whether or not a pot has contracted uncleanness when it was not watched. It is how persons are likely to behave in situations when they are not supervised. And the problematics of the law finds definition in the question: to what extent do those at the upper side of the hierarchy of sanctification impute good faith to people at the lower end of the same hierarchy, that is, who in the household observe purity-laws only at specified times and occasions? So what is at issue is the status of the Israelite household that does not evince alert routine concern to avoid the sources and chains of uncleanness that Scripture designates.

The basic notion is, people will not touch and so contaminate what is not theirs, especially if they are warned not to do so: The woman who entered in to take out a piece of bread for a beggar, and she came out and found him standing by the side of loaves of bread of heave offering — it is clean. That is so in certain transactions. But if someone takes the view that he has every right to utilize an area, then he is assumed to handle whatever is lying about. Hence in a courtyard shared with an ordinary person, all utensils that are left forgotten there are assumed to be handled by that person and so to be contaminated. If, by contrast, the ordinary person is warned of the concerns of the observant one, he is assumed to take ordinary precautions. He will not expose to corpse-uncleanness what belongs to the observant person, but he may well sit down on his garments or other utensils or step on them, with the result that they contract pressure (midras) uncleanness: He who deposits utensils with an *'am ha'ares* — they are unclean with corpse uncleanness and unclean with midras uncleanness. If the *'am ha'ares* knows him the depositor, that he eats heave offering, they are clean of corpse uncleanness but unclean with midras-uncleanness. The key here, revealing the Halakhah's basic premise about the good faith and good will of the outsider, is the knowledge and the assumed response to that knowledge exhibited by the *'am ha'ares*.

The governing principles in determining matters of probability prove few, but sufficient for a broad variety of cases.

First, we confirm the status quo whenever possible. He who leaves his house open and found it open, locked and found it locked, open and found it locked — it is clean. If we leave a person in the house and find him as is, we assume nothing has changed; the house remains uncontaminated. But if the person was asleep and found awake, then we assume he will have touched whatever he can reach. Having been left asleep, the person who wakes up will not have been instructed as to what not to touch, so we assume that he touches whatever is near at hand. So too, we rely upon evidence interpreted in a commonsense way. A fine example of how that works is in the following: The wife of a *haber* who left the wife of an *'am ha'ares* grinding grain in her house — if the sound of the millstones ceased — the house is unclean. The millstones did not cease — unclean is only the space up to the place to which she can reach out her hand and touch. If the wife of the ordinary person stops grinding, we assume she touches whatever is at hand anywhere in the house. If she keeps grinding, we assume she touches only what she can reach from her place at the grindstone.

Second, where the ordinary person — the one who most of the time, except for the menstrual taboo, does not observe the purity laws in his household as these extend to the cultic status of food and drink — has no instructions, he will not take heed of those concerns important to the one who observes cultic cleanness even in connection with everyday food. But where there are instructions, the ordinary person will follow instructions faithfully and may be relied upon. That distinction, between the ordinary person who is under no charge and the one who has been given a responsibility, is expressed in simple and in complex rulings. Here is a simple one: He who gives over his key to an *'am ha'ares* — the house is clean, for he gave him only the charge of guarding the key. Now what the Halakhah expresses is confidence in the good faith of the *'am ha'ares*. But where no one is in charge, then we take for granted what can contract cultic uncleanness ordinarily will do so. Thus if the potter leaves the pots, the ones that people can handle, at the outside, are assumed to be unclean, the ones that people cannot reach retain their prior status. Through the Halakhah the sages set forth their confidence that people exhibit good will for the concerns of their neighbors, and if informed, they will avoid imparting uncleanness to their neighbors' property.

C. THE CONSISTENCY OF THE CATEGORY-FORMATION

The present category-formation exhibits uniform results, its principles of interpreting data repeatedly producing a coherent and cogent outcome. Indeed, it competes among the most coherent of them all — and most lay a compelling claim to cogency, start to finish. As usual, the particular hermeneutics takes first place, the generic, second.

D. THE GENERATIVITY OF THE CATEGORY-FORMATION

The category-formation, Tohorot, in its hermeneutics embodies the principles that generate much of the division of the Halakhah that bears the same title. The generativity of the category-formation at hand matches that of the entire division. In both the division and the category-formation before us, we deal with the role of the Israelite will in the working out of the story of corporate Israel. Let us begin with some simple data, which encompass all pertinent category-formations, not only the one at hand or merely those that belong to its division.

Sanctification is the established condition for family and property (caste status and marriage, on the one side, food, drink, clothing, utensils, on the other). What removes the family, its food, drink, clothing and utensils, from the status of sanctification interferes with what ought to be natural. Sources of uncleanness also come about by nature; sages adhere rigidly to the definition of those sources that Scripture establishes and do not add a single new source or extend an existing source in any consequential way (a judgment that will be modified only slightly when we come to the category-formation of Niddah-Zabim.).

Holy Israel, then, confronts round about, embodied in the nations and their corpse-uncleanness, all the intangible detritus of the sources of contamination analogous to death. Consequently Israel's task is constantly to remain alert and watchful, lest those contamination affect Israel. That attests to Israel's perpetual will to live in God's kingdom: "You shall be holy, for I the Lord your God am holy" (Lev. 19:3): separate for God's sake, obedient, as Adam was not, to God's complex command.

And, we now see, that means, Israel must watch not only whom it marries, what it eats and drinks and wears and where it stands and sits and lies. Israel also must pay attention to the genealogy of whom it marries and the history of what it eats and drinks: what the food it eats may have touched, who may have stood or sat upon the clothing that it wears and the beds on which it takes a rest. To preserve the condition it ought always to enjoy, which is, the state of sanctification, Israel has then to maintain a constant surveillance of the present and past of the world in which it lives and the people among whom it makes its life. Marrying without carefully investigating the genealogy of the Israelite family into which one marries can produce *mamzerim*, and sitting on a bench without finding out who has sat there before can produce uncleanness that can contaminate much else, and eating a piece of bread without knowing where it has been and who has touched it can diminish one's standing in the hierarchy of sanctification. Why all this? An attitude of alertness embodies the will to obey, there being no better evidence of the right intentionality than constant concern to respond to God's will with acts of affirmation. What Adam did not do in Eden, what Israel promised and failed to carry out at Sinai ("We shall do and we shall obey"), Israel educated in the Torah will realize in these acts of caring and concern.

The family, the space occupied by it for the sacred occasions (each man in "his place"), and the household's property in the full sense of the word — real estate, personalty, and movables — are treated as analogous to the sacred space, the Temple, occupied by the consecrated caste, the priesthood and their staff, and what is kept therein. What establishes the analogy, however, if not the very core of Tohorot? That is to say, the sources of change and disruption that threaten the cleanness, hence the sanctification of the Temple are the very same sources that threaten the norm of cleanness of the household. If the same uncleanness affects the Temple and the table, then the only difference is one of degree, not of kind, as the Halakhah states explicitly. All form a single continuum, some higher, some lower — just as this category-formation maintains. And the rest follows.

Now we see the sources for the generativity of the Halakhic category-formations represented best by the one before us, Tohorot. Those sources locate themselves in the context in which the texts that invoke intentionality find their place, the reason that the entire system treats cleanness and sanctification, or uncleanness and desacralization, as relative to the Israelite's attitude and will. What the Israelite values as food is therefore subject to his will. That, then, is what receives or conveys uncleanness as food, in accord with God's will for the same matter. What he does not value does not contract or transmit uncleanness; only that to which an Israelite to begin with pays attention counts for anything in the system of watchfulness with which we deal. What the Israelite values as a useful utensil may contract uncleanness. What the Israelite deems an essential part of a piece of fruit or vegetable is integral to the fruit or vegetable, adds to its volume, contracts from, or transmits to, the fruit or vegetable such uncleanness as takes effect. What the Israelite holds inedible or disgusting even for dog-food does not contract uncleanness as food. When the Israelite subjects to the cleanness-regulations of consecrated food what is merely everyday edibles, the rules of consecrated food pertain — even though the substance of the food is unchanged. In these and numerous other details the relativity of all things to intentionality comes to full and rich instantiation. So the Halakhah manages to say the same thing about many things, and the category-formation expands itself along lines the stretch out from the very core: *Of that for which Israel cares, there God's will governs.* For the dynamics derives from that test of wills that commences with a single tree's produce.

But the category-formation not only exhibits generative power, it also contains within itself the necessary limits of its own generativity. These emerge at the restrictions of the analogy, household to the Temple, that the Halakhah before us has laid down: the household is not the Temple, the table is not the altar. Something resembles, as treated as like, something else; something is not the same thing as that something else. The household may be compared to the Temple, the table may be treated as analogous, in the ways amply spelled out here, to the altar, upon the same continuum. But that is not the same thing as saying the table here is the altar there. That the Halakhah does not maintain; it forms an exercise in analogical thinking, not scientific inquiry. Sages think about the power of similitudes when they consider humanity: man is like God, so Scripture announces — but to be like God is not to be God! What differentiates that which is compared to the thing upon which the comparison is based is what separates the imitation from the real thing. And sages knew and valued that difference, and that is why the Halakhah in every line realizes that difference. And that makes all the more remarkable sages' extensive legislation to embody the imitation and realize it. If the table is like the altar in the way in which man is like God, then let us elaborate the meaning of the similitude, the uses of the analogy, the moral authority of the metaphor by reason of what generates the metaphor: the altar, God, respectively.

2.
TRACTATE MIQVAOT

I. THE DEFINITION OF THE CATEGORY-FORMATION

As usual, the category-formation — in this case, immersion-pools — announces its own hermeneutics, both the particular and the generic. As always, the category-formation takes up the former at the outset, the latter afterward. An outline of the category-formation leaves no doubt about the regnant theory of the selection and interpretation of data concerning the immersion-pool, a species of the genus, water that removes uncleanness:

I. THE PARTICULAR HERMENEUTICS OF ANALOGY AND CONTRAST: THE SIX GRADES OF GATHERINGS OF WATER
II. THE GENERIC HERMENEUTICS: DOUBTS. RESOLVING DOUBTS ABOUT IMMERSION AND IMMERSION-POOLS
III. THE GENERIC HERMENEUTICS. MIXTURES. DIVERSE VOLUME AND MIXTURES OF WATER OF IMMERSION-POOLS
IV. THE GENERIC HERMENEUTICS. MIXTURES. THE UNION OF POOLS TO FORM THE REQUISITE VOLUME OF WATER
V. THE GENERIC HERMENEUTICS. MIXTURES. WATER AND WINE, WATER AND MUD, WATER IN VARIOUS LOCALES
VI. THE GENERIC HERMENEUTICS: CONNECTION. USING THE IMMERSION POOL. THE MATTER OF INTERPOSITION

Units ii-vi, self-evidently, go over the familiar program of the generic hermeneutics, doubts, mixtures, connections, so the entire hermeneutics particular to Miqvaot is engaged in the opening unit. And there, a theory that Rabbinic Judaism forms its Halakhic hermeneutics in a process of analogical-contrastive analysis finds explicit validation. There, as my theory of matters leads us to expect, we deal with an exercise of hierarchical classification, making possible analogical-contrastive analysis, as the outline indicates. The opening unit sets explicitly forth the genus, water that serves to remove uncleanness, and six species thereof. Then it systematically conducts the work of comparison and contrast that, in other category-formations, I have hypothetically recapitulated on my own. Here the Halakhah not only identifies its particular hermeneutics but also makes explicit the process of analogical-contrastive analysis that has generated that hermeneutics.

The key-contrast, as we shall see, of the two like classifications of water — water that removes uncleanness — is between the third and the sixth of the six classifications, still water against running water. Here is where the generative hermeneutics enters. The former — the immersion-pool of forty seahs of still water — defines the problematic of the Halakhah, in these aspects:

[1] it must not be subjected to human intervention or intentionality,
[2] it must not be collected in utensils;
[3] but it must flow naturally (with the flow permissibly directed by man) to its collection-point in the pool.

And, conversely, drawn water imparts uncleanness and if poured into a collection of rain-water of a volume insufficient to constitute a valid immersion pool spoils the water into which it is poured. We recall, Parah requires exactly the opposite traits for the water that will mix with the ash of the red cow and remove corpse-uncleanness:

[1] it must be subjected to human intervention or intentionality at the most acute level,
[2] it must be collected in utensils;
[3] and it must not flow naturally but only as directed by human decision to its collection-point in the utensil.

By itself still water that has accumulated through rainfall bears one message, and in comparison with living water, the category-formation yields a still more eloquent one. The lesson of the classification, still water, seen on its own is that still water does not purify, only sunset does. That lesson is important at Tebul Yom but immaterial here. The latter — the contrast between still and living water — governs the Halakhic exposition before us, which can be understood only in the context of analogical-contrastive analysis. The companion species of the shared genus, Parah, then supplies the key to Miqvaot, living water for the one, still water for the other. Of the six kinds of water that the Halakhah differentiates for purposes of removing uncleanness, these two take priority, still water that in the requisite volume has collected from rain-drippings, which is to say, water that accumulates naturally from heaven, and living or spring or flowing water, from deep in the earth, which removes corpse-uncleanness and that of the Zab and of *nega'*-uncleanness.

What is it that turns still water from a source of uncleanness (if drawn) or a facilitator for the transmission of uncleanness (if poured upon seed through an act of will, in line with Lev. 11:34, 37=the category-formation, Makhshirin) to the medium for removing uncleanness of a certain classification? The matter may be expressed positively and negatively. It is the negative fact that the water has not served human purposes or been subjected to human activity. Water left in its natural condition, in sufficient volume, pouring down from heaven in the form of rain and collecting on its own upon the earth — that is Heaven's medium for removing uncleanness imparted by dead creeping things and certain other kinds of uncleanness. Living water, subjected to human intentionality and activity, drawn by man in a utensil, removes corpse-uncleanness and comparable types of uncleanness. The contrast between Parah's insistence on use of a valid utensil and Miqvaot's exclusion of the same is expressed in the following, among many cases:

> A potsherd which is sunk down into the ground of a cistern of a press — and rain fell, and it was filled up — lo, it [the water] is unfit, because it has been guided by means of a utensil.
>
> T. 3:1

Required to preserve passivity, man may only dig a hole into which rain-water will naturally flow. But that is how uncleanness takes place, by nature, rarely by an act of human intentionality.

And that match underscores the positive message in response to the particular hermeneutics. Just as uncleanness comes about by nature — nature's failing to realize its teleology, and not by human activity or intentionality, so nature serves to remove uncleanness and naturally to restore the normal condition of persons and objects, which is cleanness. Nature restores what nature has disrupted, the celestial removing the chthonic, so to speak. That is in two stages, still water marks the cessation of uncleanness, sunset the beginning of the new cycle of Israel in conformity with the purposive character of nature, as we shall note in connection with the status of Tebul Yom. Just as human intentionality cannot create sources of uncleanness, so, in the context of the immersion-pool and the kinds of uncleanness it removes, human intentionality cannot directly bring about the sources of purification. But the opposite rule pertains to purification water, which can be brought into being only through unremitting and intense intentionality on the part of all participants in the rite.

Now when we come to interpret the opposed rules of water for immersion pools and water for mixing with ash to form purification-water for removal of corpse-uncleanness, the question is simply stated. It is, why does still water unaffected by human agency restore the natural condition disrupted by uncleanness other than that of the corpse and its analogues, while by contrast purification-water systematically subjected to human intervention — constant attention, deliberate action, start to finish — alone removes corpse-uncleanness? We have then to account for the exclusion of man from the one process, the radical insistence upon his inclusion, in full deliberation, within the other. The contrastive process then produces the reason. We deal with two essentially distinct types of uncleanness, one ordinary and natural, the other extraordinary and in violation of nature. And in this matter we find the explanation for how the category-formation fuses its facts into a coherent statement. The dead creeping and counterpart sources of uncleanness are part of nature; death and media of uncleanness that are analogous thereto violate the natural course that God intended at creation.

The facts must carry their own message. Uncleanness that comes about by reason of any cause but death and its analogues is removed by the Heaven's own dispensation, not by man's intervention: rain-fall and the sunset marking the new creation suffice. To explain: ordinary purification is done by nature, resulting from natural processes. Water that falls from heaven and, unimpeded by man, collects in sufficient volume restores the natural condition of persons and objects that have contracted uncleanness at second hand or by reason of minor sources of contamination. Still water serves for the moment, until sunset marks the new now-clean spell in the story of the person or the object. But as to persons and objects that have contracted uncleanness from death, nature on its own cannot produce the kind of water that bears the power to remove that uncleanness and restore the condition of nature. Only man can. And man can do this, as Parah has shown us, only by the highest level of concentration, the most deliberate and focussed action. The water is not still, but flowing water: living water overcoming death. And the water is kept alive, in constant motion until it is stirred with the ash. Any extrinsic action spoils the water; stopping to rest on a bench, doing any deed other than required for the rite itself — these disrupt the circle of sanctification within the world of uncleanness that the burning of the cow has required.

So the facts lead us to the critical question at the heart of matters: why does the state of human intentionality govern in the confrontation with corpse-uncleanness? To that matter we turn at the end, for it is a question generated by the category-formation, but not limited to the framework thereof: a mark of the generativity of the hermeneutics that has governed the category-formation but that transcends it.

II. THE SCRIPTURAL FOUNDATIONS OF THE HALAKHIC CATEGORY-FORMATION

Of all this Scripture knows nothing, though to such a taxonomy of types of water, Scripture makes its contribution. When Scripture speaks of "putting into water" — immersing — an unclean person or garment, it further specifies, "and it shall be unclean until evening, then it will be clean." So immersion does not purify, but in a measure removes uncleanness. Scripture proves remarkably reticent to deal with questions involving how the "putting into water" is carried out, not defining the sort of water that works, as the pertinent verses show:

> Lev. 11:31-2: "Any anything upon which any of them [dead creeping things] falls when they are dead shall be unclean...it must be put into water and it shall be unclean until evening, then it shall be clean."
>
> Lev. 15:13: "And when he who has a discharge is cleansed of his discharge, then he shall count for himself seven clean days for his cleansing and wash his clothes and he shall bathe his body in running water and shall be clean."
>
> Lev. 11:32: "What is touched by a dead creeping thing must be put in water and it shall be unclean until evening; then it shall be clean."
>
> Lev. 11:40: "He also who carries the carcass shall wash his clothes and be unclean until evening."
>
> Lev. 14:8: "And he who is to be cleansed shall wash his clothes and shave off all his hair and bathe himself in water and he shall be clean."
>
> Lev. 15:5: "And any one who touches the Zab's bed shall wash his clothes and bathe himself in water, and he shall be unclean until evening."
>
> Lev. 15:16: "And if a man has a discharge of semen, he shall bathe his whole body in water and be unclean until evening."
>
> Lev. 15:21: "And whoever touches her bed shall wash his clothes and bathe himself in water and be unclean until evening.:"
>
> Lev. 15:27: "And whoever touches these things shall be unclean and shall wash his clothes and bathe himself in water and be unclean until evening."
>
> Lev. 16:28: "And he who burns them shall wash his clothes and bathe his body and afterward he may come into the camp."
>
> Lev.17:15: "And every person that eats what dies of itself...shall wash his clothes in water and be unclean until evening. Then he shall be clean."

Lev. 22:6-7: "The person who touches any such shall be unclean until evening and shall not eat of the holy things unless he has bathed his body in water. When the sun is down, he shall be clean."

Num. 10:7: "Then the priest shall wash his clothes and bathe his body in water and afterwards he shall come into the camp. And the priest shall be unclean until evening."

Num. 17:17: "And the clean person shall sprinkle upon the unclean...and he shall wash his clothes and bathe himself in water and at evening he shall be clean."

Dt. 23:11:12: "If there is among you any man who is not clean, but when evening comes, he shall bathe himself in water, and when the sun is down, he may come into the camp."

Scripture supplies no information about the character of the water into which the unclean object is to be put, how such water is collected, how much is required, and the like. Here is a case in which Scripture supplies facts, but the Halakhah, the context in which those facts are formed into a category-formation particular to the Halakhah.

III. THE EXPOSITION OF THE COMPONENTS OF THE GIVEN CATEGORY-FORMATION BY THE MISHNAH-TOSEFTA

I. SIX GRADES OF GATHERINGS OF WATER

M. 1:1 Six grades in gatherings [of water], this above that, and this above that: Water in ponds — (1) An unclean person drank, and a clean person drank — he is unclean. (2) An unclean person drank and drew water with a clean utensil — it is unclean. (3) An unclean person drank, and a loaf of heave offering fell — if he rinsed, it is unclean. And if he did not rinse, it is clean.

T. 1:1 Said R. Nehemiah, "Why have they said, 'If he did not rinse, it is clean?' For the water which is in the pond is not going to receive uncleanness until it is detached. [Even when] one has lifted it up, the clean predominates over the unclean."

T. 1:2 "And why have they said, 'If he rinsed, [it is unclean]?' The water which is on his hands is rendered susceptible to uncleanness and made unclean, and it makes the loaf unclean."

M. 1:2 (4) [If] one drew with an unclean utensil, and a clean person drank — he is unclean. (5) [If] one drew [water] with an unclean utensil and drew [water] with a clean utensil — it is unclean. (6) [If] one drew with an unclean utensil, and a loaf of heave offering fell [into the water], if he rinsed [it off], it is unclean, and if he did not rinse it, it is clean.

M. 1:3 (7) Unclean water fell, and a clean person drank — he is unclean. (8) [If] unclean water fell into it, and one drew with a clean utensil — it is unclean. (9) [If] unclean water fell, and a loaf of heave offering fell [into it], if he rinsed, it is unclean, and if he did not rinse, it is clean.

M. 1:4 [If] a corpse fell into it, or the unclean person walked in it, and a clean person drank — he is clean. All the same are (1) water of ponds, (2) water of cisterns, (3) water of ditches, (4) water of caverns, (5) water of rain drippings which have stopped, and (6) immersion pools which do not contain forty seahs: during the rainy season, all are clean. [When] the rain ends, those that are near the village and the road are unclean. And those that are far are clean, until the larger numbers of people have passed by.

T. 1:3 A pond into which wine, honey, or milk has fallen — they follow the majority. [If] olive-oil fell into it, even though it congealed, lo, this [pool] is unclean, because it is not possible for it to be freed from the particles of oil.

T. 1:4 Wine of heave-offering which fell on fruit — one should rinse them off, and they are permitted. And so olive-oil of heave-offering which fell into pieces of fruit — one should rinse them off, and they are permitted. Olive-oil of heave-offering which fell on wine — one should skim it off, and the wine is permitted. That which fell on brine — one should skim it off so that he annuls the taste of the olive-oil which is in it.

M. 1:5 When is the [the water's] purification? [If] they formed the greater part, even though they did not overflow. [When purified], they are suitable for dough-offering and for the washing of hands therefrom.

T. 1:5 The assumption concerning mud and puddles which are by the doors of shops in the public domain during the rainy-season — all are clean. [When] the rain ceased, lo, they are like dirty water which is in the market-places — they follow the majority.

T. 1:6 Dirty water and rain-water which got mixed together — whether in utensils or on the ground — it is unclean. [When] the rain ceased, those which are near the village and the road are unclean. Those which pools of water that are distant are clean until the larger number of people will walk there. Under what circumstances? In the case of a pool from which it is not possible to drink without one's footprints being discerned. But a pool from which it is possible to drink without one's footprints being discerned — [if] one found there the footprints of man [or] footprints of large cattle, it is unclean. [If one found there] footprints of small cattle, it is clean.

T. 1:7 A pool which does not contain forty *seahs* of water, and into which less than three *logs* of drawn water fell — it is suitable for unconsecrated food, for dough offering, and for heave offering, and for washing the hands therewith. And it is fit to be added to. [If] rain fell — [if] they formed the greater part and overflowed, — [if] they formed the greater part, even though they did not overflow — they are suitable for *dough offering* and for heave-offering and for washing the hands therewith. And it is fit to be added to. And how [is a case in which] they formed the greater part, even though they did not overflow?

T. 1:8 An immersion-pool which holds forty *se'ahs* and in it are nineteen *se'ahs,* and less than three *logs* of drawn water fell therein — once twenty-one *se'ahs* of rain-water have fallen in it is clean because they [rain-water] have formed the greater part.

T. 1:9 An immersion-pool which holds twenty *se'ahs,* and in it are nineteen *se'ahs,* and less than three *logs* of drawn water fell therein — it is unclean. Once one *se'ah* of rain-water has fallen therein, it is clean, because [now] it has overflowed. And how much must it overflow. Any amount at all. [If] there fell into three *logs* of unclean drawn water — it is unfit for *dough offering* and for heave-offering and for washing the hands therewith. And it is unfit to be added to. [If] the rain fell — until there will go forth from it its fullness and a bit more.

T. 1:10 [If] rain fell — [if] it formed the greater part, even though it did not overflow — it is suitable for *dough offering* and for heave-offering and for washing the hands therewith. And it is unfit to be added to, until there will go forth from it its fullness and a bit more.

T. 1:11 And how much is *and more?* Its fullness and more. An immersion-pool which holds twenty *se'ahs,* and in it are nineteen *se'ahs* — three *logs* of unclean water fell into it — and rain fell, and it was filled up — it [the water] always remains in [its] unfitness, until there will go forth from it its fullness and a bit more — some small amount more to remove the three *logs*.

T. 1:12 An immersion-pool which contains forty *se'ahs* less a *qartob* and three *logs* of unclean drawn water fell therein — they are unfit for dough offering and for heave-offering and for washing the hands therewith. And unfit to be added to. [If] less than three *logs* [fell in], even if they are all unfit [or: unclean], once a single *qartob* of rain-water fell therein — they are clean.

M. 1:6 Above them: Water of rain drippings which have not ceased. (1) [If] an unclean person drank [from it], and [afterward] a clean person drank — he is clean. (2) [If] an unclean person drank and drew [water] with a clean utensil — it is clean. (3)

[If] an unclean person drank, and a loaf of heave offering fell, even though he rinsed — it is clean. (4) [If] one drew with an unclean utensil, and a clean person drank — he is clean. (5) [If] one drew with an unclean utensil and drew with a clean utensil — it is clean. (6) [If] one drew with an unclean utensil, and a loaf of heave offering fell, even though he rinsed — it is clean. (7) [If] unclean water fell, and a clean person drank — he is clean, (8) [If] unclean water fell, and one drew with a clean utensil — it is clean. (9) [If] unclean water fell, and a loaf of heave offering fell, even though he rinsed — it is clean. They are suitable for heave offering and for rinsing the hands therefrom.

T. 1:13 And just as they are clean for immersion, so they are clean for everything. Above them: Rain-drippings which have not ceased — For they immerse [unclean] water in them. And they do not immerse in them man and hands and utensils. This is the general rule: Any place in which man immerses, hands and utensils immerse. [If] a man does not immerse, hands and utensils do not immerse. And what are rain-drippings? So long as the rains fall, and the mountains trickle [with water] lo, they are like the water of a spring. [If] they ceased to trickle, *lo,* they are like the water of pools.

M. 1:7 Above them: A pool of water which has forty seahs, in which they immerse and dunk. Above them: A spring, whose waters are sparse, and in which drawn water forms the greater part: it is equivalent (1) to the pool, to render clean by standing water; and (2) to a fountain, to dunk in it in any amount [of water] at all.

M. 1:8 Above them: Smitten [spring] water — which render clean when they are flowing.

M. 1:9 Above them: Living water — in which [take place] immersion for Zabim, and sprinkling for lepers; and which is suitable to mix the purification water.

T. 1:14 He who digs at the side of the ocean and at the side of the river, in a swampy place — lo, it [the water] counts as water in rain ponds. He who digs at the side of the spring — for so long as it [water] comes on account of the spring — even though it stops and starts seeping again, lo, it is like spring-water. [If] it again ceases to flow, lo, it is like the water of pools.

T. 1:15 A spring, the waters of which are sparse, and it [drawn water] formed the greater part and expanded — it cleanses when it is standing water. And it does not cleanse when it is flowing, except to the place to which it can reach in the first place.

The one point of interest at M. 1:1ff., on the water that when raised out of the pond (T. 1:1) is susceptible to uncleanness, comes third: if the loaf fell in and the person rinsed it, that means the loaf was wet down intentionally, and it is made susceptible and contracts uncleanness forthwith. If he did not rinse it, it means he did not want the loaf to be wet down, so, whatever the actual condition of the loaf, it is as if it were dry and insusceptible. The contrast between the classification of water at M. 1:1-5 and that at M. 1:6 is neatly drawn, and the continuation, which omits the generic hermeneutics operative at M. 1:1-6, is self-explanatory in its contrasts.

II. RESOLVING DOUBTS ABOUT IMMERSION AND IMMERSION-POOLS

M. 2:1 The unclean person who went down to immerse — it is a doubt whether he immersed or whether he did not immerse — [and] even if he did immerse — it is a doubt whether there are forty seahs in it, or whether there are not — two immersion pools, in one of which there are forty seahs, and in one of which there are not forty seahs — he immersed in one of them and does not know in which one of them he immersed — his matter of doubt is deemed unclean.

M. 2:2 An immersion pool which was measured and found lacking [forty seahs] — all things requiring cleanness which were made depending on it — retroactively — whether in private domain or whether in public domain. are unclean. Under what circumstances? With reference to a major uncleanness. But with reference to a minor uncleanness: for example, (1) [if] one ate [a half-loaf of] unclean foods, (2) drank [a quarter-qab of] unclean liquids, (3) one's head and the greater part of one's body came into drawn water, (4) or three logs of drawn water fell on one's head and the greater part of one's body and he went down to immerse — it is a matter of doubt whether he immersed or did not immerse — and even if he immersed, it is a matter of doubt whether there are forty seahs [of rainwater] in it or there are not [forty seahs] in it — two immersion pools, in one of which there are forty seahs, and in one of which there are not — one immersed in one of them and does not know in which one of them he immersed — his matter of doubt is deemed clean.

T. 1:16 An immersion-pool which was measured and found lacking — all the acts requiring cleanness which were carried out depending upon it whether this immersion-pool is in the private domain, or whether this immersion-pool is in the public domain — are unclean.

M. 2:3 A doubt about drawn water that sages have declared clean — it is a matter of doubt whether they [three logs of drawn water] fell or did not fall. [And] even if they did fall, it is a matter of doubt whether there are forty seahs in it or whether there are not — two immersion pools, in one of which there are forty seahs and in one of which there are not — it fell into one of them, and one does not know into which one of them it fell — its [the pool's] matter of doubt is deemed clean, because it has something upon which to depend. [If] both of them were less than forty seahs, and if [drawn water] fell into one of them and one does not know into which of them it fell — its matter of doubt is deemed unclean, for it has nothing upon which to depend. Whether in the first place or at the end, its measure is three logs of drawn water [to invalidate the immersion pool].

T. 2:1 An immersion-pool which one left empty and came and found full fit, because it involves a matter of doubt concerning drawn waters in an immersion-pool, and the assumption concerning immersion-pools is that they are fit.

T. 2:2 A water-duct which is pouring water into an immersion-pool, and a mortar is set at its [the duct's] side — and it is a matter of doubt whether it [water] is [pouring] from the water-duct to the immersion-pool, or whether it is [pouring] from the mortar into the immersion-pool — it is unfit, because the matter of unfitness is demonstrable. And if the greater part [of water] in the immersion-pool is fit, [Supply: it is fit] because this is a matter of doubt concerning drawn water in connection with an immersion-pool.

T. 2:3 Two immersion-pools which do not contain forty *se'ahs* [of rainwater], and three *logs* of drawn water fell [into one of them], and it is known into which of them it has fallen, and afterward, a second [volume, three further *logs* of drawn water] fell, but it is not known into which of them they have fallen — lo, I am able to attribute [the matter], saying, "To the place into which the first [three *logs* of drawn water] have fallen, there have the second ones fallen [as well]."

T. 2:4 Three *logs* [of drawn water] fell into one of them, and it is not known into which of them they fell, and afterward a second [volume of *logs* of drawn water] fell, and it is known into which of them they fell — one cannot attribute [the matter], saying, "Into the place into which the second ones have fallen, there did the first ones fall [as well]." In one [of the immersion-pools] there are forty *se'ahs* [of rain-water], and in one of them there are not [forty *se'ahs* of rain-water] — lo, I declare, "Into the one containing forty *se'ahs* of rain-water have they fallen." [If] one is drawn water and one is fit water — lo, I declare, "They have fallen into the drawn water."

T. 2:5 Two immersion-pools which do not contain forty *se'ahs* [of rainwater], and three *logs* [of drawn water] have fallen into one of them, and it is not known into which of them they have fallen — and afterward rain came, and they [the two pools] were filled up [with suitable water] — R. Yosé says, "They say to him that he should not immerse in [either] one of them. But if he did immerse in one of them and prepared things requiring cleanness, because this is a matter of doubt concerning drawn water in respect to an immersion-pool [supply: they are deemed clean]. To what is the matter likened? To a person, one of whose hands has been made unclean, and it is not known which of them [is unclean]. They say to him that he should not prepare things requiring cleanness with either one of them. But if he did prepare things requiring cleanness with one of them, they are clean, because it is a matter of doubt involving the hands."

T. 2:6 Two immersion-pools — one containing forty *se'ahs* [of rain-water] and one not containing [forty *se'ahs* of rain-water] — one immersed in one of them on account of a condition of uncleanness deriving from a major source of uncleanness and prepared clean things, [he immersed] in the first and prepared [things requiring cleanness], [he immersed] in the second and prepared [things requiring cleanness], [if] these and those are lying [before him] — the first are held in a state of suspense, and the second are clean. Under what circumstances? When [we deal with] a condition of uncleanness deriving from a major source of uncleanness. But [if we deal with] a condition of uncleanness deriving from a minor source of uncleanness, these and those are clean.

T. 2:7 [If] he immersed in one of them on account of a condition of uncleanness deriving from a minor source of uncleanness and prepared things requiring cleanness — they are clean. [If] between times he was made unclean by a major source of uncleanness, and he immersed in the second [pool] and prepared [things requiring conditions of cleanness] — these and those are lying [before him] — lo, these prove [the condition of one another and both are kept in a state of suspense]. [If] the first were eaten, and [or] made [definitely] unclean, or perished before the second were prepared — the second are deemed clean. [If this took place] after the second were prepared, the second are held in a state of suspense.

T. 2:8 [If] he immersed in one of them on account of a condition of uncleanness deriving from a major source of uncleanness and prepared things requiring cleanness, they are suspended. [If] he was made unclean in the meantime by a minor source of uncleanness, and he immersed in the second [pool] and prepared things requiring cleanness — they are deemed clean. [And if] these touched the others, the first are held in a state of suspense, and the second are burned.

[If] he immersed in one of them on account of a condition of uncleanness deriving from a minor source of uncleanness, and prepared clean things, they are deemed clean. [If] he was made unclean in the meantime by a major source of uncleanness and immersed and prepared things requiring cleanness, they are held in a state of suspense, [And if] these touched those, the second are held in a state of suspense and the first are burned.

T. 2:9 Two immersion-pools of forty *se'ahs* each, one containing drawn [water], and one containing suitable [water] — and one immersed in one of them on account of a condition of uncleanness deriving from a major source of uncleanness and prepared things requiring cleanness — they are held in a state of suspense. [If he immersed] in the second and prepared things requiring cleanness — they are clean. [If he immersed] in the first and did not prepare things requiring cleanness, then immersed in the second and prepared things requiring cleanness — they are clean. [If he immersed] in the first and prepared [things requiring cleanness], [then immersed] in the second and prepared [things requiring cleanness] — [if] these and those are lying [before him] — the first are suspended, and the second are clean. Under what circumstances? In the case of a condition of uncleanness deriving from a major source of uncleanness. But in the case of a condition of uncleanness deriving from a minor source of uncleanness, these and those are held in a state of suspense.

T. 2:10 [If] two people went down and immersed in the two of them, one unclean with a condition of uncleanness deriving from a major source of uncleanness, and one unclean on account of a minor source of uncleanness — he who immerses on account of a major source of uncleanness is unclean. And the one who immerses on account of uncleanness deriving from a minor source of uncleanness is clean. One who is unclean with uncleanness deriving from a major source of uncleanness and one who immerses to cool himself — he who immerses on account of uncleanness deriving from a major source of uncleanness is unclean, and the one who immerses to cool himself is clean. One is unclean with uncleanness deriving from a minor source of uncleanness, and one immerses to cool himself — both of them are kept in a state of suspense. To what is the matter likened? To two paths, one unclean and one clean, and there were two who went in the two of them and prepared things requiring cleanness. In the case of one there is sufficient intelligence for interrogation, and in the case of the other there is not sufficient intelligence for interrogation — in the case of the private domain, both of them are kept in a state of suspense. In the case of public domain, the one who has intelligence for interrogation in a matter of doubt is deemed to be unclean. And the one who does not have intelligence for interrogation in a matter of doubt is deemed clean.

T. 2:11 Two immersion-pools, each containing twenty *se'ahs*. one with drawn water, and one with suitable water — one immersed to cool himself in one of them and prepared things requiring cleanness — they are clean. [If he then immersed] in the second, and prepared things requiring cleanness — they are burned. [If one immersed] in the first and did not prepare [things requiring cleanness], [and then immersed] in the second and prepared [things requiring cleanness] — they are burned. [If one immersed] in the first and prepared things requiring cleanness, and [then immersed] in the second [and prepared things requiring cleanness] — if these and those are lying before him — the first are deemed clean, and the second are to be burned.

T. 2:12 Two women who engaged in preparing a bird which is suitable to produce [only] one] *sela'* of blood, after a while, on this one a *sela'* of blood is found, and a *sela'* of blood is found on the other — both of them are in disarray.

Because we confirm the status quo, M. 2:1's rule follows, and that is made explicit in the case of M. 2:2. If, however, we can find reason to declare clean, M. 2:3, we take that into account.

III. DIVERSE VOLUME AND MIXTURES OF WATER OF IMMERSION-POOLS

M. 2:5 An [empty] ritual pool which has in it three holes of drawn water, each one [containing] a log [of drawn water] — if it is known that forty seahs of suitable water have fallen into it, before the water spread to the third hole, it is fit. And if not, it is unfit.

M. 2:6 He who scrapes up mud [from the pool containing less than forty seahs, and heaps it] by the sides, and three logs [of water] drained from it — it is fit. [If] he was removing [the mud away from the pool] and three logs [of water] drained [down] into the pool, it is unfit.

T. 3:1 A potsherd which is sunk down into the ground of a cistern of a press — and rain fell, and it was filled up — lo, it [the water] is unfit, because it has been guided by means of a utensil.

T. 3:2 [If] there were [poured] on one's head three *logs* of drawn water, and one went down and immersed in an immersion-pool which contains [exactly] forty *se'ahs* — it is fit. [If] one squeezed it out into it, it is unfit. [If] one dunked a thick [wet] blanket into it, and three *logs* [of drawn water] exuded from it into the immersion-pool, it is fit. [If] one squeezed it [water] from it [the blanket], it is unfit.

T. 3:3 A legion which is passing from place to place, and so a caravan [or: a cow] which is passing from place to place and they splashed with their hands or their feet (and) three *logs* into the immersion-pool — it is fit. And not only so, but even if they made an immersion-pool in the first place, it is fit.

T. 3:4 And what is mud which is measured with the water? R. Yohanan b. Beroqah says, "That which is measured in a *log.*" R. Yosé says, "That which goes forth in a funnel." And what is the measuring rod? This is the shuttle containing the spool. The mud which is on the sides counts in the measure of forty *se'ahs.* but they do not immerse in it. Three holes [containing water] in a gulch — the lowest and the uppermost are of twenty *se'ahs* each, and the middle one is of forty *se'ahs* — the rivulet of rain-water enters into them and goes out of them — One way or the other, they immerse only in the middle one, in which forty *se'ahs* have come to a standstill.

M. 2:7 He who leaves [empty] wine jars on the top of the roof to dry them, and they filled with water — he breaks them, or turns them upside down. But he does not empty them out [into a cistern].

M. 2:8 The plasterer who forgot a lime pot in the cistern, and it filled with water if there was any amount of water flowing on top of it [the pot], one way or the other, he does break it.

M. 2:9 He who arranges [empty] wine jars inside the cistern, and they filled with water, even though the cistern soaked up [all] its water, lo, this one breaks [them].

M. 2:10 A ritual pool which contains forty seahs of water and mud — they dunk [objects] in the water, and [them] in the mud. In what sort of mud do they immerse [objects]? In mud on the surface of which the water flows. [If] there was water on one side [only], they immerse in water, and they do not immerse in mud. Of what sort of mud did they speak? In mud in which a reed will sink on its own.

M. 3:1 Two immersion pools which [respectively] do not contain forty seahs — and into this one fell a log and a half [of drawn water], and into that one [fell] a log and a half and [then] they were mingled together are fit, since the category of unfitness never applied to them. But: an immersion pool which does not contain forty seahs [of fit water] — and three logs of drawn water fell into it — and it was divided into two [parts] — is unfit, since the category of unfitness applied to it. It always remains in its unfitness, until there will go forth from it its fullness and more.

M. 3:2 How so? The cistern which is in the courtyard — and three logs [of drawn water] fell into it — it always remains in its state of unfitness, until there will go forth from it its fullness

and more. Or: until one will set up in the courtyard [another pool containing] forty seahs, and the upper [water] will be cleaned by the lower one.

M. 3:3 A cistern which is full of drawn water, and the water channel enters it and leaves from it — always is in its state of unfitness, until it will be reckoned that there do not remain of the first [unfit water] three logs. Two who were pouring [drawn water] into the immersion pool, this one [pours in] a log and a half — and this one pours in a log and a half — he who wrings out his garment and puts in [drawn water] from many places — and he who empties out the water cooler and puts in [water] from many places — sages declare unfit.

T. 3:5 Two pools of [exactly] forty *se'ahs* [of fit water] in each — this one on top of that one — and three *logs* fell into the upper one, and they were diverted and came into the lower one — it is suitable, for I say, "The forty *se'ahs* were complete before three *logs* came down."

T. 3:6 Two immersion-pools, each containing twenty *se'ahs* — and this is beside that one — and three *logs* of drawn water fell into one of them, and they were diverted and came into its fellow — it is suitable.

M. 3:4 [If three logs of drawn water fell or are poured into a pool] from one utensil, from two, and from three, they join together. [If three logs of drawn water fell into a pool] from four utensils, they do not join together. A person who had an emission of semen who was sick, upon whom nine qabs of water fell — and a clean person on whose head and the greater part of whose body three logs of drawn water fell — from one utensil, from two, and from three — they join together. From four — they do not join together. Under what circumstances? When the second began before the first ceased. And under what circumstances? When he did not intend to add more [drawn water]. But if he intended to add more, even one qartob in the entire year they join together to form three logs [of drawn water].

T. 3:8 Three *logs* [which fell] into an immersion-pool — and one who had an emission of semen who was ill, upon whom nine *qabs* of water have fallen — a clean person on whose head and the greater part of whose body three *logs* of drawn water have fallen — if it is from one utensil, two or three, they join together; if from four, they do not join together.

T. 3:9 He who enters drawn water except for his finger-tips — even if only his head and the greater part of his body entered into drawn water, he is unclean. [If] there entered drawn water on his head but not the greater part of his body, or the greater part of his body but not his head, or his head and the greater part of his body, whether from the top or from the side came [into drawn water] — he is clean, until his head [and greater part of his body] will enter into drawn water in accord with the normal way [of doing so].

T. 3:10 [If] part of it [the water] is drawn water and part of it is not drawn water — [or if it is drawn water] into which wine, honey, or milk has fallen — he is clean — until it will be wholly drawn water. Even if he is clean, and it [the drawn water] is clean, he is made unclean and renders it unclean. Lo, this one says, "He made me unclean, and I made him unclean."

T. 3:11 A clean person on whose head and the greater part of whose body three *logs* of drawn water have fallen is unclean. [If] they fell on his head but not on the greater part of his body, on the greater part of his body but not on his head [if] they fell on his head and on the greater part of his body whether from above or whether from the side — he is clean — until they fall on his head and the greater part of his body in the usual way.

T. 3:12 [If] part of it was drawn water and part of it was not drawn water [if] there fell into it wine, honey, or milk — he is clean, until it will be entirely drawn water. And even if he is clean, and it is clean, he is made unclean, and renders it unclean. Lo, this one says, "He made me unclean, and I made him unclean."

T. 3:13 R. Ishmael says, "[If] they [the three *logs* of drawn water] are clean, he remains clean, on account of the following argument a *fortiori*. And if when the rule concerning other liquids mixed with water is that they render the body unfit if one drinks a quarter-qab, the rule is not that the clean is like the unclean, in a situation in which liquids mixed with water do not render the body unfit, when three *logs* fall, is it not logical that we should not regard the clean as equivalent to the unclean?"

T. 3:14 An immersion-pool will prove the matter: For it is not the rule that other liquids which fall into it are treated as water. And [here the law] treats the clean as equivalent to the unclean.

M. 4:1 He who leaves utensils under the waterspout — all the same are large utensils and small utensils — and even utensils made of dung, of stone, and of dirt — it [the water] renders the immersion pool unfit in the case of the one who leaves or forgets.

M. 4:2 He who leaves a tray under the waterspout if it has a rim, it [water gathered in it] renders the immersion pool unfit. And if not, it does not render the immersion pool unfit. [If] he set it upright to rinse [it], one way or the other, it does not render the immersion pool unfit.

T. 4:1 A tray which one put beneath the water-spout to rinse [it]. and so too: utensils which one placed under the water-spout to rinse them — the first drops of water [as they fall onto the tray or utensil] are susceptible to receive uncleanness. [If] the requisite volume of forty *se'ahs* of rain water is completed, lo, these are fit. A water-spout which one hewed out and afterward affixed spoils the immersion-pool.

M. 4:3 He who makes a cavity in the waterspout to catch the pebbles [in the rainwater] — [if it is] of wood, [it renders the immersion pool invalid as a receptacle to catch rainwater if it holds] any amount at all. [And if it is] of earthenware, [it renders the immersion pool invalid if it holds] a quarter-log. [If] pebbles were rolling about inside it [the hole], they render the immersion pool unfit. [If] dirt fell into it and it was pressed tight, it is fit. A water pipe which is narrow on one side and the other and wide in the middle does not spoil [the immersion pool], since it is not made as a receptacle.

M. 4:4 Drawn water and rainwater which mingled in the courtyard, or in a hollow, or on the steps of a cave — if the greater part is formed by fit [water], it is fit, and if the greater part is [formed by] unfit [water], it is unfit. Half and half — it is unfit. When? At the time that they mingled together before they reached the immersion pool. [If] they [each] were flowing in an unbroken stream into the water — if it is known that forty seahs of fit water fell into it before three logs of drawn water fell into it, it is fit. And if not, it is unfit.

T. 4:2 Water which is drawn on its own in buckets from the ocean and from the river, and that which goes up on the water-pump spoil the immersion-pool.

T. 4 :3 A roof on top of which there are twenty-one *se'ahs* of rain-water — one draws water and carries it on the shoulder and puts in it nineteen *se'ahs,* opens [a sluice], and mingles them in the courtyard.

T. 4:4 [If] there were forty *se'ahs* [on the roof], and it [the roof] was broken through, and they [the forty *se'ahs* of rain-water] came [flowed] into the house it [the water] is ft. But [as they are flowing into the house] they do not dunk [utensils] in them, for they do not dunk in air. [If] one of its ends [the water-stream from the roof] reaches the ground, they do immerse in it. But they do not immerse in air.

M. 4:5 The trough which is [hewn] in the rock — (1) they do not draw water from it, (2) they do not mix [ashes of the red cow and water] in it, (3) they do not sprinkle from it, (4) it does not require a tightly stopped-up cover, and (5) it does not spoil the immersion pool. [If] it was a [movable] utensil, and one [then] attached it [to the rock] with plaster — (1) they do draw in it, (2)

they do mix in it, (3) they do sprinkle from it, (4) it does require a tightly stopped-up cover, and (5) it does spoil the immersion pool. [If] it was perforated below or on the side, and it cannot hold any amount of water — it is suitable. And how large a hole must there be [so it is no longer a utensil with a receptacle]? As large as the spout of a water-skin.

T. 4:6 A reservoir which distributes water [in pipes] among the villages, if it was perforated by a hole the size of the stopper of a water-skin, does not spoil the immersion-pool, and if not, it spoils the immersion-pool. This law did the people of Assya bring up three festival seasons to Yabneh, and at the third season, they declared it fit — even if it was perforated by a hole the size of a needle.

T. 4:7 Under what circumstances? When [it is perforated] from the side. But [if it is perforated] from the bottom, it does not spoil the immersion-pool [even at less than the requisite hole of a stopper]. And if it was able to serve as a receptacle from the perforation and downward, [holding] any amount at all [of water], it spoils the immersion-pool. [If] one stopped it up with plaster or with building materials, it does not spoil the immersion-pool. [If one stopped it up] with plaster and with gypsum, it does spoil the immersion-pool. [If one put it] on the ground [thereby stuffing up the hole] or on plaster and gypsum, or [if] one plastered it with mud on the sides, it does not spoil the immersion-pool.

M. 5:1 [The water of] a spring which one passed over [into] the trough is unfit. [If] one passed it over the edge in any amount — valid is what is outside [of the trough], for the [water of] a spring renders clean in any quantity at all. [If] one passed it over [into] a pond, and one [then] stopped it up, lo, it [the pond] is like an immersion pool. [If one then] went and made it continue to flow, it is [still] unfit for Zabs and for lepers and for mixing purification water therewith, until one knows that the first [water] has flowed away.

T. 4:8 A spring which flows to the bidet, and from the bidet to the pool — the first drops, as they flow — lo, they are unfit, because they are drawn water. What should one do? One should perforate it at the "eye of the beard" in any amount at all. And it will come out that the small part of the water cleans the larger part. One stops up the flow by a corpse. Water which flows over the furrows and the indentation — one dunks [utensils] in them [if the waters are] at a height of the thickness of a garlic peel and the breadth of the stopper of the water-skin.

M. 5:3 A spring which is drawn like a centipede — [if] one added to it [drawn water] and it was made to flow further — lo, it is as it was. [If] it [the spring] was standing [still] and one added to it [drawn water], and made it flow further — it is equivalent to an immersion pool, to purify in standing water, and to a spring, to immerse therein in any amount. [It is subject to polythetic classification, being an interstitial case.]

T. 4:9 A spring which is drawn out like a centipede — and it [drawn water] formed the greater part over it [spring-water] — and made it [the channel] wider — it renders clean in a hollow [like an immersion-pool]. And it does not purify when it is flowing, except up to the place to which it was able to reach in the first place.

M. 5:5 Flowing water is like a spring. And that which drips is like an immersion pool. Testified R. Sadoq concerning flowing water which was more than dripping water [with which it was mixed] that it is fit. And dripping water which one made into flowing water, one sticks in even a staff, even a reed, even a Zab and a Zabah, one goes down and dips.

Mixtures of valid and invalid water form the focus of this sizable composite, e.g., M. 4:4's standard case, where we resolve a case of mixture by assigning the status of the whole to that of the predominant part. The contrast between M. 4:5's treatment of water in a trough for use in an immersion pool and the same for use in purification-water realizes the particular hermeneutics. Once an immersion-pool lacks the requisite volume, it falls into the category of a pool that is susceptible to uncleanness. But if it is lacking and valid water is mingled with the water in the pool, it recovers its status as an effective immersion pool. M. 3:1-3 go over this ground.

IV. THE UNION OF POOLS TO FORM THE REQUISITE VOLUME OF WATER

M. 5:6 A wave which broke off, and in it are forty seahs — and it fell on man and on utensils — they are clean. Any place in which are forty seahs. they dip and dunk: They dunk (1) in trenches, (2) in ditches, and (3) in the tracks of an ass which are mixed in the valley. They do not dunk in the rain-stream. One dams it with utensils and dips in it. And utensils with which one dammed — they are not deemed to have been dunked thereby.

T. 4:5 A wave [of water] which was detached from the sea or from the river — they do not immerse in it, for they do not immerse in air. If the two ends [of the wave] touched the ground, they do immerse in it, but they do not immerse in the crest [of the wave].

T. 4:10 What is the rain-stream? Rain-water which comes down an incline. they do not dunk in it unless there will be before it a circle containing forty *se'ahs*.

M. 6:1 Any [pool of water] which is mingled with [water of] an immersion pool is [deemed to be as valid] as the immersion pool. Holes of the cave and clefts of the cave — one dunks in them as they are. A pit of the cavern — they do not dunk in it unless it [the hole between the pit and the immersion pool] is as large as the spout of a water-skin. Said R. Judah, "When is that the case? At the time that it stands by itself. But if it does not stand by itself, they dunk in it just as it is."

T. 5:1 Holes on the rim of the immersion-pool, and so tracks of the hooves of cattle — if [the water in these] is joined together [with water in an immersion-pool] by a hole the size of the stopper of the water-skin — they dunk therein. And if not, they do not dunk therein. The projections which are in the immersion-pool — they dunk therein, and on condition that they are mingled together through a hole the size of the stopper of the water-skin.

T. 5:2 A trough which is full of utensils — and one brought it[s water] into touch with an immersion-pool — it requires [mingling of water through] a hole the size of the spout of the water-skin. But a spring [suffices] with [an intermingling] of any amount at all. In regard to a large utensil [we require a hole the size of] four handbreadths. [And in the case of a small one], its greater part.

M. 6:2 A bucket which is full of utensils, which one dunked — lo, they [the utensils] are clean. And if it did not immerse, the water is not mingled [with that of the immersion pool], until it [the water in the bucket] is mingled [with the water of the pool] by [a stream) the size of the spout of a water-skin.

T. 5:3 A kettle which is full of utensils, and one brought it into touch with [the water of] an immersion-pool even though its mouth is narrow, in any amount at all, the utensils which are in it are clean. [If] one tipped it on its side, [the water in the kettle and that in the immersion-pool are not intermingled] until there will be a hole in its mouth the size of the spout of a water-skin.

M. 6:3 Three immersion pools — in this one are twenty seahs [of fit water], and in this one are twenty seahs [of fit water], and in this one are twenty seahs of drawn water — and [the one containing] drawn [water] is at the side — and three people went down and dipped in them, and it [the water in the three pools] was mingled together — the immersion pools are clean. And the people who immersed are clean. [If] the one containing drawn [water] was in the middle, and three people went down and immersed in them, and they were mingled together — the immersion pools are as they were. And those who immersed are as they were.

T. 3:7 Two immersion-pools, each containing twenty *se'ahs,* one with drawn water, and one with fit water — two went down and brought the two into contact and immersed in them — even if it [water] was red and turned white, or white and turned red — the immersion-pools remain as they were, and the ones who immersed remain as they were.

M. 6:4 The sponge and the bucket which contained three logs of water, and they fell into the immersion pool — they have not rendered it unfit. For they said only, "Three logs which fell."

M. 6:5 The box and the chest which are in the sea — they do not dunk in them, unless they were pierced to the size of the stopper of the water-skin. R. Judah says, "In the case of a large utensil, four handbreadths. And in the case of a small one, its greater part [must be broken down]." If it was a sack or a basket — they dunk in them as they are, since the water is mixed together. [If] they were set under the water pipe, they do not spoil the immersion pool. But they dunk them and bring [them] out in the ordinary way.

M. 6:6 A defective earthenware vessel which is in the immersion pool, and one dunked the utensils in it — they are clean from their uncleanness. But they are unclean because of the clay utensil. If the water flowed over the top of it in any amount at all, they are clean. A spring which comes up out of an oven, and one went down and immersed in it — he is clean. And his hands are unclean. And if it was higher than it by the height of his hands, even his hands are clean.

T. 5:4 A spring which emerges through the oven, and one immersed in it a radish and a gourd [in order to rinse them off] — if the water overflowed on top of it to their full [bulk], lo, they are clean. The two fingers of which they have spoken — [they are in accord with the] average man. And not [in accord with] the four which are in the handbreadth. An olive's bulk of carrion, a lentil's bulk of the insect — [if] there is a doubt whether they form the requisite bulk or do not form the requisite bulk — it is unclean. For any matter the principle [of contamination] of which derives from the Torah, but the requisite measure of which derives from the words of Scribes — its matter of doubt is deemed unclean.

M. 6:7 The intermingling of immersion pools is through a hole the size of the spout of a water-skin, in the thickness and capacity — two fingers turned around in full. [If there is] doubt whether it is the size of the spout of a water-skin or not the size of the spout of a water-skin, it is unfit, because it derives from the Torah. And so: the olive's bulk of a corpse, and the olive's bulk of carrion, and the lentil's bulk of a [dead] creeping thing. Whatever stops up the spout of the water-skin diminishes it.

M. 6:8 They clean immersion pools: a higher pool by the lower pool, and a distant by a nearby [pool]. How so? One brings a pipe of earthenware or lead, and puts his hand under it until it is filled with water, and draws it along and makes it touch. Even by as much as a hair's breadth suffices. [If] the upper one contains forty seahs [of fit water], and in the lower pool there is nothing — one draws [water and carries it] on the shoulder and puts it into the upper one, until there will descend into the lower one forty seahs.

T. 5:5 They clean the immersion-pools, the upper by the lower, and the distant by that which is near — how so? One brings a pipe of wood or of bone or of glass and places his hand(s) [under] the lower [end of the pipe] until it will be filled with water, and conveys it, and touches it [the water of the pool to the water of the pipe]. Even if it is [touching] by as little as a hair's breadth, it suffices. And if the pipe is bent in any measure at all, it is unfit. Under what circumstances? When they were on top of the other. But if they were side by side, he brings a knee-shaped pipe on one side, and a knee-shaped pipe on the other side, and a pipe in the middle — and he touches [the water of the one to that of the other] and descends and immerses.

M. 6:9 A wall which is between two immersion pools which was cracked perpendicularly — it joins together. [If the crack is] horizontal, it does not join together, until there will be in one place a hole the size of the spout of a water-skin. [If] they flow together into one another through a hole [in the top of the dividing wall, they can be included together] if the height [of the connecting stream] is [only] the thickness of a garlic peel and the breadth, the size of the spout of a water-skin.

T. 5:6 A wall is between two immersion-pools which was cracked horizontally — it joins together. And [if it was cracked] perpendicularly, it does not join together. [If] they flow together into one another, a full handbreadth over the whole breadth of the split is required for intermingling of water.

M. 6:10 The outlet of a bath — if the bath holds a quarter-log before the water reaches the outlet, it is valid, and if not, it is invalid.

T. 5:7 [If] the corpse is in the bath house, the furnace-room is unclean. [If] the corpse is in the furnace-room, the bath house is unclean, because of the outlet. He who touches the outlet is unclean, but he is clean when he ascends [from the water].

M. 6:11 The filter of the bath — the lower [pipe] is full of drawn water, and the upper [pipe] is full of fit water — if [the space] in front of the hole [holds] three logs [of drawn water] — it is unfit [as an immersion pool].

T. 5:8 The filter which is in the bath — the lower one is full of drawn water — and the upper one is full of fit water — and on condition that it be opposite the hole — and it contributes to the measure of forty seahs.

Once one mingles the valid water of an immersion pool with another body of water, the whole is deemed completely mixed, with the result that the entire volume is valid. How this is done is spelled out in the present composite.

V. WATER AND WINE, WATER AND MUD, WATER IN VARIOUS LOCALES

M. 7:1 There are things which raise the immersion pool and do not invalidate [it], invalidate and do not raise, do not raise and do not invalidate. These raise and do not invalidate: (1) the snow, (2) hail, (3) hoarfrost, (4) ice, (5) salt, and (6) thin mud. How do they raise and not invalidate? An immersion pool which has forty seahs, but one — a seah of one of them fell into it and raised it — they thus turn out raising and not invalidating [the immersion pool].

M. 7:2 These invalidate and do not raise: (1) [Drawn] water, whether unclean or clean,(2) and water in which food has been pressed or (3) seethed, (4) and grape skin wine before it has fermented. How do they spoil and not raise [the immersion pool]? An immersion pool which has forty seahs [of fit water], less a qartob and a qartob of one of them fell into it — they have not raised it[s volume]. It spoils it at three logs. But (1) other liquids, and (2) fruit juice, and (3) brine, and (4) fish brine, and (5) grape skin wine which has fermented — sometimes they raise, and sometimes they do not raise. How so? An immersion pool which contains forty seahs, lacking one — a seah of one of them fell into it — it does not raise it. [If] it contained forty seahs, and one put in a seah and took out a seah — lo, this is fit.

T. 5:8 Snowballs which are sunk down into an immersion-pool — lo, they raise the level of the water.

T. 5:9 Water in which food has been pressed or seethed, and olive-water they immerse in it, and on condition that it does not contain sediment of oil. And the grape-skin wine before it has fermented — they do not immerse in it.

M. 7:3 [If] one rinsed in it [an immersion pool] baskets of olives and baskets of grapes, and they changed its color, it is valid. [If] wine and olive sap fell into it and changed its color, it is unfit. What should one do? He should wait on it until rain falls

and its color returns to the color of water. [If] there were forty seahs [of fit water] in it, one may draw [water in buckets and carry it] on his shoulder and pour it into it, until its [the pool's] color returns to the color of water.

M. 7:4 [If] wine or olive sap fell into it and changed the color of part of it [the water], and forty seahs of [fit] water are not in it — lo, this one should not immerse in it.

T. 5:10 An immersion-pool which does not have forty *se'ahs* [of fit water], and one puts into it wine, and its color changes — it is not made unfit in the measure of three *logs*. And not only so, but even if its color returned to what it had been, [the pool] is fit [to be added to]. [If] there were in it forty *se'ahs* [of fit water], and wine fell in and its color changed in part, he who immerses, whether in the place of the water or in the place of the wine, is as if he did not immerse. [If] three *logs* of wine fell in, it is as if they did not fall in. [If] it was drawn water and one made it touch — [if] he made it touch at the place of the wine, this and this have not become clean. [If] one touched [them together] at the place where the water is located, it is clean. [If he touched it] at the place [at which] the wine [is located], it is not clean.

T. 5:11 A jar which broke in the Great Sea and the color of that place is like the color of that wine — he who immerses in that place is as if he did not immerse. And not only so, but even if a loaf of heave-offering fell there, it is unclean.

M. 7:5 Three logs of [drawn] water — and into them fell a qartob of wine — and lo, their color is the color of wine — and they fell into the immersion pool — they have not rendered it unfit. Three logs of water, lacking a qartob — and a qartob of milk fell into them, and lo, their color is the color of the water — and they fell into the immersion pool — they have not rendered it unfit.

M. 7:6 An immersion pool which contains exactly forty seahs — two people went down and immersed in it, one after the other — the first is clean, and the second is unclean. [If] one immersed the thick mantle in it and brought it up, and part of it is touching the water, it [the pool still] is clean. The cushion or mattress of leather once one has lifted their lips out of the water, the water in them is deemed drawn water. What should he do? He should immerse them and raise them by their bottoms.

T. 5:12 An immersion-pool which contains exactly forty *se'ahs,* and two people went down and immersed one after the other — the first is clean, and the second is unclean. What should one do? While the first still is in the water, one should draw [water in utensils and carry it] on the shoulder and put it into it, and it is clean.

T. 5:13 [If] one immersed in it a large kettle. lo, this is unclean, because the water gushes forth. What should one do? He puts it in with its mouth downward and turns it over and immerses it, and raises it up by its bottom.

M. 7:7 [If] one immersed the bed therein, even though its legs sink down into thick mud — it is clean, because the water touched them before [the mud did]. An immersion pool, the water of which is [tool shallow [to cover the body] — one presses down, even with bundles of wood, even with bundles of reeds, so that the [level of the] water may rise,. and he goes down and immerses. An [unclean] needle which is located on the steps of the cavern — [if] one stirred the water to and fro — after a wave has broken over it, it is clean.

T. 5:14 He who jumps into an immersion-pool, lo, such a one is blameworthy. He who immerses twice in an immersion-pool, lo, this one is blameworthy. This one says to his fellow, "Press your hand down on me in the immersion-pool" — lo, this one is blameworthy.

M. 8:1 The Land of Israel is clean, and its immersion pools are clean. The immersion pools of the peoples which are [located] outside of the Land are fit for those who have had a seminal issue, even though they have been filled with water from a swape well. Those which are in the Land of Israel which are outside the town gate are fit even for menstruating women. Those which are inside the town gate are fit for those who have had a seminal issue. And they are unfit for all [other] unclean people.

T. 6:1 Samaritan territory [in the Land of Israel] is clean, [and] its immersion-pools and its dwellings and its paths are clean. The land of the gentiles [in the Land of Israel] is unclean, [and] its immersion-pools and its dwellings and its paths are unclean. The immersion-pools of the gentiles which are outside of the Land are fit for those who have suffered a pollution, and unfit for all [other] unclean Israelites. Those in the Land of Israel which are outside the town gate are fit for all unclean people, and it does not need saying, for an Israelite who has had a seminal emission. And those which are inside the gate are unfit for those who have had a seminal issue, and, it does not require saying, for all unclean people.

T. 6:4 A bath whose bath-attendants are gentiles, when its filters are open to the private domain, is unclean. [When they are open] to the public domain, it is clean [fit]. A bath whose bath-attendants are gentiles, and which an Israelite entered in the morning and touched [the waters of which to a fit immersion- pool] — even though this [gentile] goes in and the other comes out, is clean. [If] it was locked or if it was designated as private property, it is unclean.]

M. 8:2 These are those who have had a seminal emission who require immersion: [if] one noticed urine [issuing] in drops or turbid — at the outset, he is clean. [If these occur] in the middle or at the end [of urinating], he is unclean. [If he notices them] from beginning to end of urination, he is clean. [If they are] white and viscous, he is unclean. He who dreams erotic dreams by night and arose and found his flesh [penis] heated is [assumed to be] unclean.

M. 8:4 A gentile woman who discharged semen from an Israelite is unclean, An Israelite woman who discharged semen from a gentile is clean. The woman who had sexual relations and went down and immersed but did not clean the house is as if she did not immerse. A person who has had an emission who immersed and did not first urinate when he does urinate is unclean.

T. 6:5 He who dreams erotic dreams by night and arose and found his flesh hot is unclean. [If] he dreamt erotic dreams but was not heated, or [if] he was heated but did not dream erotic dreams, he is clean.

T. 6:7 The semen of an Israelite under all circumstances, lo, this is unclean. And that of a gentile, under all circumstances, is clean, except for the urine in which it is located. All those concerning which they have said that they are clean [are clean] for unconsecrated food and unclean for heave-offering, except for the woman who discharges semen, who is unclean for unconsecrated food.

The opening exposition, M. 7:1ff. classifies various liquids in solid form or in mixtures in relationship to the immersion pool. The criteria for classifying the mixtures are standard, not particular to the category-formation at hand, e.g., which component of the mixture imparts its traits to the entire mixture?

VI. USING THE IMMERSION POOL. THE MATTER OF INTERPOSITION

M. 8:5 A menstruating woman who placed coins in her mouth and went down and immersed is clean on account of her uncleanness [as a menstruant], but she is unclean because of her spit. If she put her hair in her mouth, closed her hand, pressed her lips together — it is as if she did not immerse. He who kept hold on a man or on utensils and immersed them — they are unclean. And if he rinsed his hand in the water, they are clean. The private parts, [and] the wrinkles — it is not necessary that water should come into them.

M. 9:1 These interpose on man: 1. threads of wool, 2. and threads of flax, 3. and the ribbons which are on the heads of girls. R. Judah says, "Those of wool and those of hair do not interpose, because the water enters into them."

M. 9:2 4. the matted hair over the heart, 5. and [on] the beard, 6. and the woman's privy parts, 7. the pus outside the eye, 8. and the hardened pus outside the wound, 9. and the bandage which is on it, 10. and dried juice, 11. and dried clots of excrement which are on his flesh, 12. and dough which is under the fingernail, 13. and sweat crumbs, 14. and miry clay, 15. and potter's clay, 16. and road clay. What is miry clay? This is clay of pits, as it is written, And he brought me up out of a horrible pit, out of the miry clay (Ps. 40:3). Potter's clay is in accord with its literal sense. And road clay? The pegs by the roadsides in which they do not dip and in which they do not dunk. And all other mud — they dunk in it when it is wet. And one should not dip with the dust which is [still] on his feet. And one should not dunk the kettle with soot, unless one scrapes.

M. 9:3 These are [things] which do not interpose: 1. matted hair of the head, 2. and of the armpits, 3. and of the privy parts of a man. Whatever one takes note of interposes, and whatever one does not take note of does not interpose.

M. 9:4 4. Pus in the eye, 5. and hardened pus in the wound, 6. and moist fruit juice, 7. and moist excrement which is on his flesh, 8. and excrement which is under the fingernail, 9. and a fingernail which is dangling: 10. downy hair of the child is not unclean and does not convey uncleanness. The membrane that grows over a sore is susceptible to uncleanness and conveys uncleanness.

T. 6:8 And as [to the things about which] they have said, "They interpose," and as [to the things about which] they have said, "They do not interpose" they do not convey uncleanness and do not receive cleanness, except for the membrane on the sore. And the bandage which is on the sore, and the splints which are on the fracture, and the chains, and the ear-rings, and the beads, and the rings, when they are tightly-bound, interpose, and when they are loosely bound, they do not interpose.

T. 6:9 A dry poultice which is on the sore, and the eye-paint which is in the eye — lo, these do not interpose. The blood, and the ink, and the honey, and the milk, and mulberry juice, and fig juice, and sycamore juice, and carob juice — when they are dry, interpose, and when they are moist, they do not interpose. And all other juices, whether wet or dry — lo, these interpose for they are gummy. Stains of fruit juice, and the eye-paint which is outside the eye — lo, these interpose.

T. 6:10 And excrement under the fingernail which is not opposite the flesh, the mud, and the dough under the fingernail even opposite the flesh do [not] interpose. The downy hair of an adult, about which he is not fastidious, and the limb and flesh which are dangling in the case of a man, lo, these do interpose.

T. 6:14 And what are the pegs by the road-sides? Those on which people walk in the rainy season, and they are rubbed against [and stick to the garments].Ss As to clothing: [mud] on one side does not interpose. On both sides, it interposes.

T. 7:1 [If] one tied his hands and feet together and sat down in a stream of water — if the water covered his whole [body], he is clean. And if not, he is unclean. [If] his hands and feet were covered with dust, and he went down and immersed in an immersion-pool which contains forty *se'ahs,* he is clean. [If] he rubbed [his hands or feet], or [if] he immersed in hot water, he is unclean. A kettle which is full of soot and which one immersed is unclean. [If] one polished it or immersed it in hot water, it is clean.

T. 7:10 [If] there was a single hair outside of the sore, and its head cleaves to the sore, or [if] there were on him two hairs, and their tops cleaved to the knots surrounding the anus or excrement, lo, these interpose. [If] there were on him two hairs on his eyelids below, and they pierce a way through to the eyelids above — this was a case, and five sages in Lud took a vote concerning it and declared it unclean.

M. 9:5 These interpose in utensils: (1) pitch, (2) and the gum of myrrh. On glass utensils — whether inside or outside. On the table, and on the tray, and on the couch — on the clean ones, they interpose, and on the dirty ones, they do not interpose. On the beds belonging to the householder it interposes, and on those be — longing to the poor man, it does not interpose. On the saddle of the householder it interposes, and on that of the water-skin carriers, it does not interpose. On a packsaddle it interposes.

M. 9:6 On garments: On one side, it does not interpose. On both sides, it interposes.

M. 9:7 [As to] the aprons of pitch workers or potters or tree trimmers — they do not interpose. This is the general rule: Whatever one takes note of interposes, and whatever one does not take note of does not interpose.

T. 6:11 Whatever [substances] interpose in utensils, interpose in the case of the menstruating woman and in the case of the convert at the time of immersion. And in connection with [immersion for eating] unconsecrated food, they do not interpose.

T. 6:12 A ring which one put into a brick of wet mud, and which one immersed, is clean. If it was miry clay and [mud] like it, it is as if one did not immerse it.

T. 6:13 A flagon which is full of unclean water, and moist mud is placed on its mouth — if the water reaches down into the mud, and one dunked it, it is clean. If it was miry clay and its equivalents, it is as if one did not immerse it.

T. 6:15 Pitch which is on the cup and which is on the flask — [if] it is on its inside, it interposes; and [if] it is on the outside, it does not interpose. Under what circumstances? At the factory. But [if it belongs to] the householder, whether it is inside it or on its outer parts, lo, this interposes. In the case of a tray and dish, whether it is on the inside or whether it is on the outside, whether at the factory or at home, lo, this interposes.

T. 6:16 Gum of myrrh and resin, whether in the case of a cup or in the case of a flask, or whether in the case of the tray or whether in the case of the dish, whether on the inside, or on the outside whether at the factory or at home — lo, these interpose. [Mud] on the sandal: — [if it is] on its inside and above, it interposes and [if it is] on the lower part [of the inside], it does not interpose. And [mud] on the bench: [if it is] on top [or] on the sides, it interposes, and if it is below, it does not interpose.

T. 6:17 [As to] pieces of excrement which are on the toilet and on the chairs [or: pots] — those which are pressed down — whether on the inside or on the outside, whether below or on the sides, lo, these interpose. Those which are on the bed of the householder — if it is on the outer frame it interposes, and if it is on the inner, it does not interpose.

T. 6:18 Moist wine lees which are in the cup and the flask, and the fluff on a chain or a bell, and the mud and the dough which are on the handle of the ax and on the handle of a shovel — lo, these do not interpose. [If] they turned solid, lo, they interpose.

M. 10:1 All handles of utensils (1) which one affixed not in their usual fashion, or (2) which one affixed in their usual fashion but did not fix firmly, or (3) which one did fix firmly but which broke — lo, these interpose. A utensil which one immersed downward — it is as if it did not immerse. [If] one immersed it in its usual way, without [immersing] the handle, [it is not deemed immersed] until he will turn it on its side. A utensil which is narrow on both ends and broad in the middle is not clean until one will turn it on its side. A flask the mouth of which is turned downward is not clean until one will make a hole on its side. The ink-pot of an ordinary person is not clean until one will make a hole in its side. The ink-pot of Joseph the Priest was perforated on

its side.

T. 6:19 All handles of utensils which are affixed in the ordinary way, lo, these do not interpose. [If] one put pitch or wax, whether in the place of the hollow [of the handle] or whether in the place of the spout, lo, these do not interpose. [If] one put them in not in the normal way, lo, these interpose. [If] one put pitch or wax, whether in the place of the hole or in the place of the spout, lo, these interpose.

T. 6:20 All handles of utensils which broke, for example, the handle of the sickle, and the handle of the knife, if they serve their original function, interpose, and if not, they do not interpose.

T. 6:21 The sickle, the handle of which was broken within that part of the handle which is indispensable in using the tool, does not interpose, because it is equivalent to the private parts. [If it is broken] beyond the indispensable part of the handle, if it serves its original function, it does not interpose; and if not, lo, this interposes. [If] one joined it with reed grass or with rope, lo, this interposes. [If] one affixed it with resin, lo, this does not interpose.

T. 6:22 A utensil which is narrow on both ends and broad in the middle, for example a quarter-measure and a half-quarter measure — can never have purification, until one will turn it on its side. A flask, the rim of which is flattened downwards into its midst, and the shoulders of which are high, and so a flagon, the rim of which is flattened downwards into its midst and the shoulders of which are high — can never have purification until one will turn it [on its side].

T. 6:23 A flask the lip of which is turned outward — one immerses it and raises it by its bottom.

M. 10:2 (1) The mattress and (2) the pillow of leather — lo, these require that the water come into them. (1) The round pillow, and (2) the ball, and (3) the shoemaker's last, and (4) the amulet, and (5) the phylactery do not require that the water come into them. This is the general principle: Whatever it is not the way to put in and take out — they immerse sealed up.

M. 10:3 These [are objects] which do not require that the water enter into them: 1. the knots of the poor man, 2. and the tassels, 3. and the knotted thong of the sandal, 4. and the phylactery of the head when it is fastened tightly, 5. and that of the arm when it does not move up and down, 6. and the hand-grip of a water-skin, 7. and the hand-grip of a shepherd's wallet.

M. 10:4 These are [objects] which require that the water enter into them: 1. the knot of undergarments which [is tied to] the shoulder, 2. and the hem of sheets (-it is necessary to unstitch-) 3. and the phylactery of the head when it is not fastened tightly, 4. and that of the arm when it moves up and down, 5. and the

straps of a sandal. And clothing which one immersed washed — [they must remain in the water merely] until they bulge. If one immersed them dry, [they must remain in the water] until they will bulge and cease from bulging.

T. 7:2 Baskets of the wine-press and of the olive-press — [when] they [the holes therein] are tightly packed [by grapes or olives] — one needs [to clean them by] picking. And [when] they are loose, one needs to shake [them loose, so water will permeate the basket]. The knots of the money-bag and of the bands, and the knots of the shoe and sandal, and the knots of the hole of a shirt [of a woman] — these interpose. The knots of the fringes of a money-bag, and bands, and the knots of the thongs of the shoe, and the sandal, and the knot of the undergarment which is on the shoulder, and the sheet the fringes of which one tied up, lo, these interpose. [If] they were knotted on their own, lo, these do not interpose.

T. 7:3 The knots of the poor person about which he is fastidious and [those] of the householder — lo, these interpose. And the knots of the householder about which he is not fastidious and those of the poor man — lo, these do not interpose.

M. 10:5 All handles of utensils which are too long and which one is going to cut off — one immerses them up to the place of [their proper] measure. The chain of a large bucket [is immersed to a length of] four handbreadths [from the bucket], and that of a small [bucket] is [immersed to a length of] ten [handbreadths from the bucket]. They immerse them up to the place of [their proper] measure. The rope which is tied to the basket is not connected, unless one has sewed [it on to the bucket].

T. 7:3B And R. Judah says, "One has to immerse the whole thing on account of [the place where the handle is intended to be] lopped off." And so did R. Judah say in the name of R. Tarfon, "One has to immerse the entire ring."

M. 10:6 They do immerse [unclean] hot water in cold [immersion pool water], and not cold in hot, and not fresh water in foul, and not foul water in fresh. An [unclean] utensil which is full of liquid and which one immersed is as if it did not immerse. [If it is] full of urine, they regard it as if it were water. [If it is] full of purification water, [it is not clean] until the water [of the immersion pool that enters the utensil] exceeds the purification water.

T. 7:4 A utensil which is full of wine and which one immersed, if its [the wine's] color is [so diluted as to be] annulled, it is clean, and if not, it is unclean. [If] it was filled with white wine or milk, if it [the water of the immersion-pool that enters the utensil] exceeds it [the wine or milk], it is clean. If not it is unclean.

M. 10:7 All [unclean] foods join together to render the body unfit [for eating heave offering] at the measure of a half a loaf. All [unclean] liquids join together to render the body unfit at the measure of a quarter-log. This [rule] is more strict in the case of one who drinks unclean liquids than in the case of an immersion pool, for [in the present case] they treat other liquids as equivalent to water.

T. 7:5 All foods join together to render the body invalid in the measure of a half a loaf — in the time that it takes to eat a loaf. [If] one ate and went back and ate again and went back and ate again, if from the beginning of the first act of eating to the end of the last act of eating, [the time has elapsed which is] sufficient for eating a loaf, they join together, and if not, they do not join together. And they do not require him who eats less than the required measure to go down and immerse. But one who eats in accord with the established measure goes down and immerses. [If] one ate less than the established measure and goes down and immerses in the middle, he is unclean.

T. 7:6 They permitted a woman who is pregnant to taste a small quantity [of unclean food], because of the danger to life.

T. 7:7 All liquids join together to render the body invalid for eating heave-offering — in [the case of one who] drinks a quarter-log in the time it takes to eat a loaf [or: to drink a quarter-log]. [If] one drank and went and drank again and went and drank again, if [the time elapsed] from the beginning of the first act of drinking to the end of the last act of drinking is sufficient for the drinking of a quarter-log [or: to eat a loaf], they join together, and if not, they do not join together. They do not make him liable who drinks less than the established measure to go down and immerse. But he drinks in the established measure and goes down and immerses. [If] one drank less than the established measure and went down and immersed in the middle, he is clean. They permitted a woman who touches something which has touched an object unclean with corpse-uncleanness to suckle her child, and he is clean.

M. 10:8 [If] one ate unclean food or drank unclean liquids, immersed, then vomited them up — they are unclean, because they are not cleaned with the body. [If] he drank unclean water, immersed, and vomited it up — it is clean, because it is cleaned with the body. If one swallowed a clean ring, entered the Tent of the corpse, was sprinkled and repeated the sprinkling and immersed and then vomited it up — lo, it is as it was [clean]. If one swallowed an unclean ring, he immerses, eats heave offering, then vomited it up — it is unclean and renders him unclean. An arrow which is stuck in a man — when it is apparent to the eye, it interposes, and if it is not apparent to the eye, he immerses and

eats his heave offering.

T. 7:8 [If] one swallowed an olive's bulk of corpse-matter and entered a house, it is clean, for whatever is swallowed by man or cattle or beast or fowl is clean. [If] it decomposed or emerged from below [the rectum], it is clean. [If] one drank unclean water and vomited it up, it is unclean, because it was made unclean when it went out. [If] one immersed, or [if] it decomposed or it came out below, it is clean. [If] one drank other [unclean] liquids even though he immersed and vomited them out, they are unclean, because they are not made clean in the body. [If] they decomposed or went forth, they are clean.

T. 7:9 A cow which drank unclean water and vomited it up — it is unclean, because it is not made clean in the body. [If] it decomposed or went out below, it is clean. He into whose knee an arrow penetrated — lo, this interposes. Under what circumstances? In the case of one made of metal. But in the case of one made of wood, lo, this interposes. And if the flesh formed a membrane over it, all agree that it does not interpose, for whatever is swallowed up in man, cattle, beast, and fowl is clean [If] pieces of gravel or splinters went into the cracks beneath his feet, it does not interpose, because it is like the privy parts.

What interposes between man and the water of the immersion pool and so impedes the process of purification through contact with the water is what man takes into account, and what does not interpose is that of which he does not take cognizance. So attitude governs: Whatever one takes note of interposes, and whatever one does not take note of does not interpose. The rule for handles carries us to the matter of connection and is familiar in its principle from Kelim.

IV. THE HERMENEUTICS OF MIQVAOT

A. WHAT FUSES THE HALAKHIC DATA INTO A CATEGORY-FORMATION?

While dealing with the hierarchization of six classifications of water, at its center the Halakhah contrasts the immersion pool of forty seahs of still water with the flowing water of the spring, which, in any volume at all, purifies. Here is where the analogical-contrastive analysis takes place, and so far as the Halakhic data fuse into a coherent category-formation, here is where the particular hermeneutics is realized. All the rest of the category-formation in detail responds to the program of the generic kind, which depends upon the particular hermeneutics for everything but its problematics. The two classifications of water that purifies are alike in that both accomplish purification through water (excluding fire, breakage, and other media Scripture identifies); they are different solely in the obvious fact that spring-water flows, and the immersion-pool is a gathering of still water. Spring water, deriving from the earth, and immersion-pool-water, deriving from heaven, are equivalent in their purificatory power, so long as they are preserved in their natural form. Then living water removes corpse-uncleanness, and still water, uncleanness of other classifications, in general, of much less virulence.

The principal interest of the Halakhah is in the definition of that water that serves for removing uncleanness through immersion in a valid immersion-pool, and nearly the entire repertoire of detailed, analytical exercises concerns the collection and utilization of that pool's water. That is what fuses the halakhic data into the category-formation, Miqvaot, and to that matter, all else is subordinate. Essentially, the Halakhah makes two points, one concerning the character of the water, which carries the entire particular hermeneutics of the category-formation, the other, its required volume, which precipitates many of the problems raised by the generic hermeneutics. In this context, we note, it is the generic hermeneutics that predominates, so to claim that the particular hermeneutics fuses the halakhic data into the present category-formation is to overstate matters. The Halakhic tractate does not fuse so much as it holds together nicely by reason of its topic, not because of the cogency of the twin-hermeneutics, particular and generic, that yields the exegetical program for the topical exposition. In this respect, the paramount position of the particular hermeneutics in Kelim and Ohalot forms a striking contrast. Take away the generic hermeneutics and we still have formidable category-formations in both cases. Remove the generic hermeneutics from Miqvaot and we scarcely have a category-formation worthy of the name, substantive and encompassing.

The particular hermeneutics nonetheless is exquisitely realized, and, situated at the outset, the beautifully articulated composite makes the statement that is unique to the category-formation. The opening unit could not state matters more lucidly or expose its generative method more clearly than it does in its taxonomy of types of water and their hierarchization.[3] Water that has flowed and collected naturally or that flows on its own removes uncleanness; drawn water will not. Stagnant pool water serves for cleanness for dough-offering and

---

[3] For the microbiological bases for these same distinctions among types of water, see Aloys Hüttermann, "Water and Purity: Microbiology and the Precepts of the Torah, Mishnah, and Talmud," in *Annual of Rabbinic Judaism, Ancient, Medieval, and Modern* (Leiden, 1999: E. J. Brill), ed. by Alan J. Avery-Peck, Volume I. Hütterman explains why flowing water or water in cisterns differs from the other types of water listed here.

for washing hands; rain water that still flows is suitable for washing for heave-offering and hand-washing; immersion pool water in the correct volume is suitable for removing uncleanness from men and utensils; and living or flowing spring water serves for removing corpse-uncleanness and that which is analogous to it.

Let me spell out this hierarchical classification-scheme, fully exposed in the Halakhah.

[1] Water in insufficient volume or of inappropriate character both receives and transmits uncleanness. Such water is called "water in ponds." But it encompasses a variety of types of water; what all have in common is that they are of insufficient volume: All the same are (1) water of ponds, (2) water of cisterns, (3) water of ditches, (4) water of caverns, (5) water of rain drippings which have stopped, and (6) immersion pools which do not contain forty seahs. During the rainy season, all such collections of water are clean. When the rain ends, those that are near the village and the road are unclean. And those that are far are clean, until the larger numbers of people have passed by. That is the kind of water that fully participates in the system of uncleanness.

[2] Then we come to water that serves for immersion-pools, meaning, water that, in requisite volume, removes uncleanness. At this next level we deal with bodies of water that are still receiving the run-off of rain. Such bodies of water do not contract uncleanness but remove uncleanness. These serve for immersion. The suitable type of water — rain-drippings — is defined as follows: "And what are rain-drippings? So long as the rains fall, and the mountains trickle with water lo, they are like the water of a spring. If they ceased to trickle, *lo,* they are like the water of pools."

[3] The third level of water is constituted by a pool of water, collected rain-drippings, that has the requisite volume, forty seahs, to cover the body of a person who immerses therein. Such a pool of water is suitable for immersion for removal of uncleanness or for dunking utensils for the same purpose.

[4] The fourth level is flowing, or spring-water, mixed with drawn water that forms the larger part of the volume. That is interstitial, bearing traits of the immersion-pool and of the spring. It removes uncleanness, like standing water, and it may serve in any small volume at all to clean utensils. The full measure of forty seahs required for still water is not required for spring water.

[5] The fifth sort is spring water that is "smitten," or turbid at times; when that water flows, it serves.

[6] Sixth, at the apex is flowing, or living water, which serves for the purification rites for removing corpse-uncleanness and its counterparts, the uncleanness of the Zab and of the *nega'*.

That, some and substance, sets forth the category-formation in all of its particularity: cogent and orderly and proportionate and compelling. All the rest of the category-formation serves to ask the conventional exegetical questions of clarification that the generic hermeneutics precipitates.

B. THE ACTIVITY OF THE CATEGORY-FORMATION

WATER FOR THE IMMERSION-POOL, ITS CHARACTER AND VOLUME. The water of type three, collected rain-drippings, for the immersion-pool must accumulate naturally, deriving from the run-off of rain and equivalent natural sources, e.g., sea-water. It may not be drawn by human action. But by the indirect action of man it may be led into the pool on its own, e.g., in a duct. So the main point is that it must not be drawn water or in any way collected through human intentionality and intervention. In volume, the immersion pool must be comprised of sufficient water to cover the entire body of a human being. Insufficient pools may be intermingled through a whole of a given size. One may further pipe valid water, e.g., a higher pool may be emptied into a lower pool to form the requisite volume. But one may not carry or draw the water. As we noted, what validates water for the purification-rite invalidates it for the immersion-pool. Drawn water may be used to augment the volume of a valid pool, meaning, a small quantity of drawn water is neutralized by, and fully integrated with, valid water. If water collects in jugs, one may break the jugs or turn them outside down, with the water flowing naturally into the cistern. But he may not pick up the jugs and empty them into the cistern. Mud of an appropriate character may serve.

If an immersion pool is of insufficient volume, the addition of water in solid form, e.g., snow, hail, ice, and the like, may raise the volume to the required level. Drawn water, by contrast, invalidates the insufficient volume of rain-water and does not raise it to the requisite volume. If wine or olive sap change the color of the pool, the pool is unfit until the color of water is restored. If two people descend into an immersion pool that contains exactly forty seahs of water, the first is clean by the immersion, but the second is not, because the first party has removed enough water to reduce the volume to less than is required.

DRAWN WATER, HUMAN INTERVENTION. CASES. Any sort of man-made utensil serving as a catchment for gathering rain-water is ruled out. He who makes a cavity in the waterspout to catch the pebbles in the rainwater — if it is of wood, it renders the immersion pool invalid as a receptacle to catch rainwater if it holds any amount at all. And if it is of earthenware, it renders the immersion pool invalid if it holds a quarter-log. While a man-made utensil may not be used, a trough hewn in rock is permitted, but one that was free-standing and then attached to the rock is forbidden. And, conversely, a trough hewn in the rock may not be used for drawing water for use with the ashes of the red cow or mixing the ashes or sprinkling said water. Spring water that one passed into a trough is unfit, but what flows over the edge remains in its status as free-flowing water. Spring water may be drawn forward, and it also may be augmented by drawn water. If spring water was standing still and augmented with drawn water and made to flow further, it is deemed an immersion pool, that is, it purifies in still water, but also is equivalent to spring for immersion in even less than forty seahs.

Drawn water absolutely may not be used for the immersion pool; a person on the greater part of whose body drawn water is poured in the volume of three logs is unclean. The Tosefta's formulation is clear: A clean person on whose head and the greater part of whose body three *logs* of drawn water have fallen is unclean. If they fell on his head but not on the greater part of his body, on the greater part of his body but not on his head if they fell on his head and on the greater part of his body whether from above or whether from the side — he is clean — until they fall on his head and the greater part of his body in the usual way. Accordingly, water that is subject to human action and intent not only does not purify but contaminates.

THE USE OF THE IMMERSION POOL: The person must immerse fully, even to the fingertips, and the pool must contain forty seahs of water to make that immersion possible. Cases of doubt in instances of major uncleanness are generally resolved in favor of the status quo; the unclean person is assumed to remain unclean who has not definitively immersed in a valid pool. In instances of minor uncleanness, they are resolved in favor of cleanness.

Issues of interposition carry us to the generic hermeneutics of connection and mixture. The water must be able to reach all parts of the body-surface; what interposes between the water and the person invalidates the immersion. The same is so for utensils; pitch and the like interpose. This is expressed very simply: A menstruating woman who placed coins in her mouth and went down and immersed is clean on account of her uncleanness as a menstruant, but she is unclean because of her spit. If she put her hair in her mouth, closed her hand, pressed her lips together — it is as if she did not immerse. He who kept hold on a man or on utensils and immersed them — they are unclean. And if he rinsed his hand in the water, they are clean. As to handles, if they are tightly affixed in the ordinary way, they are integral to the utensil and do not interpose.

Here is a point at which intentionality enters in. Whatever one takes note of interposes, and whatever one does not take note of does not interpose. If one is going to cut off part of a handle, the part that he is not going to cut off is part of the utensil and affected by its immersion. All of these rulings express in context the principles of the Halakhah of Kelim and Uqsin.

C. THE CONSISTENCY OF THE CATEGORY-FORMATION

The particular hermeneutics cannot be said to pervade the category-formation. The topical exposition responds to the generic hermeneutics.

D. THE GENERATIVITY OF THE CATEGORY-FORMATION

The paradox of water is that it both contracts and also removes uncleanness. It imparts susceptibility to uncleanness, when deliberately put onto seed for example, and among other liquids water also receives uncleanness when touched by a source of uncleanness. But under some conditions, in correct volume, deriving from the appropriate source, water also has the power to diminish or even remove uncleanness, still water the former, flowing water the latter. So, it is clear, the Halakhic structure deals with diverse classifications of water, on the one side, and with rules governing those classifications of water that bear the power to remove uncleanness but then do not themselves receive uncleanness, on the other. But within the present category-formation, only one component of the entire structure is represented, the particular type of water that Heaven provides and man must not affect. Once that point is made, nothing follows, so far as I can see. That component does not lead to conceptions that, by reason of the principle that is contained in a given case, transcend the topic under discussion. By that criterion, we cannot point to how generative power of the particular hermeneutics vastly extends the limits of present category-formative.

But when we take a step back and see Miqvaot and Parah as they should be seen — species of a common genus — then matters change considerably.[4] Parah insists that man intervene in the preparation of the water for the purification-mixture that will remove corpse uncleanness, Miqvaot forbids man from intervening in the preparation of the water for the purification of uncleanness of other sorts. Why is the uncleanness of the soul treated differently?

The contrast points to a judgment that leads us beyond the limits of the category-formation, Miqvaot, the point of its generativity. Man's supreme act of will, embodying intentionality in highly-purposive activity, can overcome

[4] The contrast is further adumbrated to be sure in our results for Negaim and Zabim as well, as we shall see presently.

even the effects of death. If the Halakhah wished to say, man can overcome death through the correct and deliberate attitude, it could not have embodied that message in more powerful language than the activities required for the formulation of purification-water. *Man's act of will overcomes the uncleanness of death, just as man's willful act of deliberate rebellion brought about death to begin with.* Man restores what man has disrupted. As to the rest, man refrains from deliberate action, and nature, providing purifying water from heaven, accomplishes the restoration. That is because the other forms of uncleanness come about by nature's own failure to realize itself, so nature provides the medium of the removal of the consequence: water that Heaven supplies naturally matches nature's condition. But since death comes about by reason of Adam's and Eve's original act of will, their heirs' supreme act of concentration and deliberation upon doing things as God wants them done is required to bring about the preparation of the medium of purification. That view of matters is made explicit in the Aggadic account, part of which we have already noted, of how Adam acknowledged that he bore full responsibility for his own fate, and built into the human condition, therefore, is that same recognition:

A. It is written, "Thus said the Lord, What wrong did your fathers find in me that they went far from me and went after worthlessness and became worthless?" (Jer. 2:5)

B. Said R. Isaac, "This refers to one who leaves the scroll of the Torah and departs. Concerning him, Scripture says, 'What wrong did your fathers find in me that they went far from me.'"

C. "Said the Holy One, blessed be He, to the Israelites, 'My children, your fathers found no wrong with me, but you have found wrong with me.'"

Now a case — the archetypal one, man himself — will illustrate the generalization contained within the statement of Isaac. People who violate the Torah do so on their own volition, not by reason of a tradition of rebellion. They therefore bear responsibility for their own sins. Man is the archetype; he brings upon himself his own death:

J. "So too all the generations came to the first Man, saying to him, 'Is it possible that the Holy One, blessed be He, is imposing the attribute of justice on you?'

K. He said to them, "God forbid. I am the one who has brought about my own death. Thus did he command me, saying to me, 'Of all the trees of the garden you may eat, but of the tree of the knowledge of good and evil you may not eat' (Gen. 2:17).

> When I violated his instructions, I brought about my own death,
>
> for it is written, 'On the day on which you eat it, you will surely die' (Gen. 2:17)."
>
> Pesiqta deRab Kahana XIV:V.1

God is not at fault for Adam's fall; Adam brought about his own death. It was through an act of deliberation and will. So let an act of deliberation and will remove the consequence corpse-uncleanness. Had the Halakhah wished in its terms and categories to accomplish a reprise of the story of man's fall, it could not have made a more eloquent statement than it does in the contrast between the Halakhah of Miqvaot and that of Parah. To what man has caused man must pay full mind, and nature restoring itself to its own purposive condition takes care of the rest.

3.
TRACTATES ZABIM AND NIDDAH

I. THE DEFINITION OF THE CATEGORY-FORMATION

When it comes to the tractates Zabim and Niddah, Scripture defines the two as a single category-formation, and part of a still larger coherent complex. This it does by setting forth both sources of uncleanness, flux (zob) and menstrual blood, in the same pattern and context at Leviticus 15. They are not readily differentiated as to character or consequence.[5] From the perspective of analysis of the traits of Halakhic category-formations, too, the two topics themselves form part of a single species, set forth in Lev. 12-15, human bodily flux that contaminates in a severe way, with the same variables and consequences. That cogent species therefore is to be contrasted with the species, bodily flux that does not contaminate in a severe way or at all. The way in which the entire species, human beings that produce contaminating fluids, is joined together suggests that we are going to deal with a coherent set:

> M. 10:4 (1) The Zab, (2) the Zabah, [Lev.15] (3) the menstruating woman [Lev. 15], (4) the woman who has given birth [Lev. 12], and (5) the person afflicted with the skin ailment [Lev. 13-14], who died impart uncleanness through being carried [even without contact] until the flesh has decayed. A gentile who dies is clean in respect to imparting uncleanness through being carried. A menstruating woman is only one who dies during her menstrual period.

In fact, while here and there organizing the sub-species of the set for hierarchical classification, the Halakhah presents no category-formation for Lev. 12, equivalent to Negaim for Lev. 13-14 and Zabim and Niddah for Lev. 15, nor

---

[5] Full disclosure requires the further admission that I cannot discern a hermeneutics particular to Niddah; the entire category-formation, as we shall see, consists of exegetical problems precipitated by the generic hermeneutics of the Halakhah as that hermeneutics intersects with the topical data. The outline, given later, leaves no doubt on that score. Zabim, by contrast, proves remarkably rich in exegetical expressions of the particular hermeneutics that is in play. That explains, also, why I treat the two tractates in the order, Zabim, then Niddah. In any event I register the claim that the Halakhah's category-formation responds to the character and imperatives of Scripture's.

does anything remotely comparable to a category-formation attend to the uncleanness of the gentile. Not only so, but while Negaim and Ohalot can be shown to form a speciated genus, the interplay of Negaim and Ohalot with Zabim-Niddah does not compare. So while details of the law of the one intersect with those of the other, the large-scale construction of the category-formations, the hermeneutical theory of the selection and interpretation of data for them, and the exegetical program consequent upon said theory — all of these critical issues of order and construction focus our attention not on the huge, complex super-genus that encompasses all unclean bodily excretions but only on the component of that genus formed by the inseparable Halakhic category-formations, Zabim and Niddah.

What I shall show is, Zabim-Niddah emerge out of a hermeneutics based on a governing theory of the teleology of human sexuality and its physical expression. When the physical conditions of sexuality conform to the natural purpose that defines them, they yield no uncleanness or a minor, ephemeral uncleanness. When those conditions do not conform, the signifying excretion produces a principal form of uncleanness, one that, in important ways, compares and contrasts with that of the corpse. But explaining how that proposition is reached and setting forth the evidence and argument that sustain it require a measure of patience for the necessary, systematic, step-by-step exposition. So we begin from the genus and proceed to the speciation and subspeciation, all the time attempting to recapitulate the thought-processes of analogical-contrastive analysis that, within the theory of this project, produced the particular hermeneutics of the Halakhic category-formation.

THE GENUS: HUMAN SOURCES OF UNCLEANNESS, LIVING AND DEAD. The genus, sources of uncleanness deriving from human beings, encompasses the corpse and the uncleanness exuded from a living person. All have in common the exclusion of considerations of intentionality, attitude, or deliberation. . A single criterion governs every species of this genus, one that we have already met: man or woman cannot generate by an act of deliberation an unclean body fluid whether genital semen or genital blood, just as they cannot form by an act of will a source of uncleanness represented by the corpse or the dead creeping thing. Were we to simplify matters and say, as to what contracts uncleanness, man's will disposes, but as to what imparts uncleanness, nature's work imposes, we should not be far off the mark. The initial speciation and hierarchical classification present no surprise. The corpse is wholly a source of uncleanness, whether solid or liquid, or, as explained at Ohalot, gaseous. The animate sources of uncleanness from living persons all are in liquid form.[6] We

[6] The dry form of the excretion possesses contaminating force too, and the differentiation between liquid and dry form is undertaken, but this is random, e.g., M.

need not dwell on the hierarchization of the classifications of data; as to the unclean excretions of the corpse as against those of the living person; the former are at the highest level of uncleanness. In the taxonomic process, the corpse defines the generative analogy for all else.

The sources of uncleanness deriving from human beings bear each its own distinctive traits as well. While the former, the corpse, constitutes a Father of fathers of uncleanness, turning what touches it into a Father of uncleanness, and what touches that into an Offspring, the latter is a mere Father of uncleanness, and what touches it falls merely into the first remove of uncleanness. So virulence is the first variable. But the process of disseminating contamination forms a more important one. Once the mere pressure — without direct physical contact, but mere weight — of the Zab or Zabah has been applied to something used for lying or sitting, that suffices to impart uncleanness. Not only so, but then the chair or bed imparts uncleanness to one who touches it. It renders such a one unclean in the first remove, and then the clothing of such a person — in contact with the one who is wearing it — is unclean in the second remove. How further does an animate source of uncleanness affect others in a way in which a corpse or a dead creeping thing does not? The spit of such a person conveys uncleanness, as much as does his touch (contact), as much as does his pressure or weight to the object or person bearing that weight.

But there is an important point of commonalty with the corpse. The purification process for the person afflicted with flux-uncleanness takes seven days, just as does the purification process of a person who is afflicted with Nega'-uncleanness or a father of uncleanness by reason of contact with a corpse. Immersion now is required, and the uncleanness thereafter passes at sunset, the beginning of a new day. The matter of offerings varies with the character of the source of uncleanness, as Scripture makes explicit, and forms a point of speciation and hierarchization; when offerings are required, that is a sign of a more virulent uncleanness. So much for the broad speciation of the indicated genus. Now to the particular category-formation and its hermeneutics: what data, how constituted into statements upon what generative issues?

THE SPECIES: SOURCES OF UNCLEANNESS THAT EXUDE FROM A LIVING PERSON: It is among the sources of uncleanness produced by living persons that the present work of sub-speciation and hierarchization takes place. Here, therefore, we seek to identify the results of analogical-contrastive reasoning that produce a particular hermeneutics to guide selection and interpretation of data for Zabim-Niddah. The point is now simply stated: what, exactly, signifies the uncleanness, with what effect? The answers to those questions comprise the hermeneutics that guides the selection and interpretation of the data of Zabim-

Niddah.[7]

These sources of uncleanness that flows from a living person are specified at Leviticus 12-15: vaginal flow of the woman after child birth (Lev. 12), who for a week for a male, two weeks for a female, offspring produces vaginal blood that is a source of uncleanness (and then, thirty-three days for a male, sixty-six for a female, the vaginal flux is deemed clean), the person afflicted with the skin-ailment (Lev. 13-14), the woman, called a Zabah who produces vaginal blood (classified as flux, by which I translate *zob*) *not* during her regular menstrual period (Lev. 15), and the man, called a Zab, who produces semen not via an erection (Lev. 15). The Halakhah treats them as a single coherent taxon, joined as they are by common indicative traits of origin and also common effects:

> He who touches the Zab and the Zabah and the menstruating woman (Lev. 15) and the woman after childbirth (Lev. 12) and the person afflicted with the skin ailment (Lev. 13-14) a bed or a chair

---

[7] Now the impasse announced at Note 2 is circumvented. The items there that violate the lines of structure and order of the Halakhic category-formation, that constitute law, halakhah, but not, on their own, species of the category-formation(s) of the Halakhah, play no definitive role in the process of category-formation and the definition of the hermeneutics of the result. Had the category-formation found definition in the distinction of liquid and solid forms of uncleanness, with systematic work on that distinction, then the sub-species would have emerged along the lines spelled out there. But that is a distinction that makes a practical difference while making no impact upon the hermeneutics that governs. That rather jarring result underscores the specificity and purposive character of the hermeneutical process that I claim hypothetically to reconstruct. I allege that, in this project, I can identify the hermeneutics that has generated the category-formations as we know them: their choices of data and their reading of their data. In pointing to data that can have contributed to the hermeneutical work but, by reason of the character of the category-formations that we do have, do not make that contribution, I underscore the probative value of our results. That is to say, I can explain what I can explain, and I can also identify anomalies and so construct a null hypothesis. That is simple enough. If I am wrong in my basic reading of matters, then I should find it impossible, by reason of a plethora of exceptions, to establish any rules at all — to explain anything in a consistent and systematic way. That is manifestly not the case. But if I am right in that basic reading, then I should be able to identify, in so complex a corpus of laws, compositions and even composites that are not inert and not mere formalities ("miscellaneous composites") that point to theories of category-formation and consequent hermeneutics other than the one I have found serviceable for the vast part of the whole of the halakhah, the law viewed as a mass. Here I can show such anomalies: the unkept promises of laws formed into adumbrations of absent category-formations, and, more to the point, hints of an absent hermeneutics.

> [that any of these have lain or sat upon] imparts uncleanness at two removes and renders [heave offering] unfit at one further remove
>
> M. Zab. 5:6

So we see a common source and common effects, all made explicit. We may take one step further. The persons afflicted with these bodily excretions bear in common with those affected by Nega'-uncleanness the status of interstitiality. Just as the latter is suspended between death and life, like a corpse but not like a corpse, so the former falls between two defined conditions. But the conditions are not the same as the distinction between life and death, and herein we find our first point of sub-speciation.

TELEOLOGICAL HERMENEUTICS. AN INITIAL OBSERVATION: That point concerns teleology — the theory of the purpose and goal that things are meant to effect, the reason they are made — whether realized whether unrealized. The variable then is teleological. In bodily excretions that produce uncleanness we deal with semen or vaginal blood outside of the menstrual period that cannot carry out the purpose that by nature the one or the other realizes, which is participation in the process of procreating life. Such non-productive semen, such vaginal flow outside of the normal cycle of procreation violate their own innate teleology. "Zob" or flux in the case of male semen falls in the middle, between semen of an erection and semen that is not emitted at all. The former carries out its purpose; it is unclean, to be sure, but at a reduced level of uncleanness; the latter of course is clean. When we come to the three types of blood that a woman produces, the same considerations apply. Some blood signifies cleanness; it is the blood that exudes beyond the specified time after birth of a child, marking the realization of the purpose of the female sexual organs. Some blood signifies uncleanness within the reproductive cycle, menstrual blood, with a routine purification process. But some blood, Zob, signifies uncleanness not within the menstrual cycle, and that blood, when it ceases, imposes an elaborate process of purification. That is the blood in the woman, like the semen of a flaccid penis, that signifies the failure of the reproductive organs to fulfill their teleology. The purification process for the Zab or Zabah is comparable to that for corpse-uncleanness, involving seven days and an offering.

On that basis, the Halakhah differentiates between blood that marks a phase in the reproductive cycle and blood that is not unclean by reason of constituting menstrual blood at all (a matter of intense interest to the sages in the Halakhah of Niddah, as we shall see). Semen should either serve for reproduction or not be emitted; if the former, it is a source of a mild form of uncleanness, as Scripture specifies; if the latter, it goes without saying, it produces no uncleanness. Blood should either form part of the reproductive cycle, signifying uncleanness on its own count,[8] or it should not be classified as menstrual blood at all, therefore, once more, not a source of uncleanness.

The same general consideration, distinguishing between body-fluids of the same physical properties that realize the teleology of an object from those that do not, encompasses the things that are affected by the person suffering flux-uncleanness. The man or woman afflicted with flux-uncleanness, the Zab or Zabah, transmits uncleanness to that on which they sit or lie, even though they do not touch the chair or bed. That classification of uncleanness, called Midras- or pressure-uncleanness, entails a realized teleology too, since it pertains only to objects that bear ordinarily are used to bear weight or pressure, that is, beds and chairs and things analogous to them. When those objects are used for the purpose for which they are made by a person afflicted with flux, they receive Midras-uncleanness. If such a person sits on a pot, not used for sitting, it is unaffected by Midras-uncleanness. The Halakhah of Kelim has already shown us that objects not used for sitting or lying, e.g., pots and pans, are not susceptible to the Midras- or pressure-uncleanness transmitted by a Zab or a Zabah.

MENSTRUAL BLOOD AS AGAINST FLUX, COMPARED AND CONTRASTED: The clear distinction among [1] clean genital blood, [2] genital blood unclean as menstrual blood, and [3] genital blood unclean as flux, requires that we focus on the latter two and ask, how do the two sub-species of female bodily excretions, vaginal blood that is menstrual as against vaginal blood that is Zob compare and contrast? Here Scripture itself does the work of analogical-contrastive analysis. At issue in Scripture is the character of a woman's vaginal secretions or blood: when does it appear, how is it classified? The distinction between menstrual or Niddah-blood and Zibah-blood, the former part of the seven days of the procreative cycle, the latter not, but rather part of the eleven days that separate one menstrual period from another, yields very little difference in actuality, except at the point of purification. The one is vaginal blood that flows during the woman's established menstrual cycle. The other is vaginal blood that flows during the eleven clean days between one cycle and another; these are called Zibah-days, in that blood that flows during the eleven days between menstrual cycles is deemed *Zob,* as we have already established in the Halakhah of Zabim-Niddah. In some ways — those that have to do with actualities — the two types of vaginal flow are comparable, in others, they contrast. But it is a distinction that makes a huge difference: the Zob bears

---

[8] The Halakhah rigidly differentiates the uncleanness of menstrual blood from the uncleanness of Zob-blood in a woman, just as Scripture does. The distinct rites of purification validate that distinction, which distinction forms the starting point of the Halakhic system of Zabim-Niddah.

with it the stench of death and its uncleanness is removed in a Temple rite, therefore one that is comparable to, though of less elaborate character than, the rite to remove corpse-uncleanness.

If we compare Scripture's presentation of the two forms of animate female-sources of uncleanness, we see how they relate, starting with the menstruating woman.

The first thing we notice is that while the menstrual period is limited, the uncleanness attaching to the Zabah is indeterminate. The woman who menstruates may before and afterward engage in sexual relations and become pregnant. The Zabah, perpetually unclean, may not engage in sexual relations and so may not become pregnant. She is removed from the entire procreative process so long as her excretions continue.

The second thing we see is that while the Niddah accomplishes purification through immersion and sunset, the Zabah undergoes an elaborate cultic rite, comparable to the rite of purification after contracting corpse-uncleanness. So while the signification of the uncleanness — vaginal flux — is the same, the circumstances as to timing and longevity vastly distinguish the one from the other, and, as I shall suggest presently, the distinction makes a massive difference in our reading of what is at stake. Here is the Torah's presentation of the pertinent Halakhah:

> MENSTRUAL UNCLEANNESS: When a woman has a discharge, her discharge being blood from her body, she shall remain in her impurity seven days;
>
> 1. Whoever touches her shall be unclean until evening.
> 2. Anything that she lies on during her impurity shall be unclean; and anything that she sits on shall be unclean.
> 3. Anyone who touches her bedding shall wash his clothes, bathe in water, and remain unclean until evening; and anyone who touches any object on which she has sat shall wash his clothes, bathe in water, and remain unclean until evening. Be it the bedding or be it the object on which she has sat, on touching it he shall be unclean until evening.
> 4. And if a man lies with her, her impurity is communicated to him; he shall be unclean seven days, and any bedding on which he lies shall become unclean.

The Zabah is presented as follows:

> 1. THE ZABAH: "When a woman has had a discharge of blood for many days, not at the time of her impurity, or when she has a discharge beyond her period of impurity, she shall be

unclean as though at the time of her impurity, as long as her discharge lasts."

2. Any bedding on which she lies while her discharge lasts shall be for her like bedding during her impurity; and any object on which she sits shall become unclean as it does during her impurity;

3. whoever touches them shall be unclean; he shall wash his clothes, bathe in water, and remain unclean until evening.

4. When she becomes clean of her discharge, she shall count off seven days, and after that she shall be clean. On the eighth day she shall take two turtledoves or two pigeons and bring them to the priest at the entrance of the tent of meeting. The priest shall offer the one as a sin-offering and the other as a burnt-offering; and the priest shall make expiation on her behalf, for her unclean discharge, before the Lord.

The menstruating woman and the Zabah (or Zab, for the male) convey uncleanness through touch, and both serve as Fathers of uncleanness, setting into the first remove of uncleanness whatever they touch. One who touches what they have lain upon or sat upon immerses, awaits sunset, and is then clean. As to sexual relations, the menstruating woman imparts her own status to the one with whom she has sexual relations, and he imparts pressure-uncleanness by sitting and lying as well. As to the Zabah, touching produces the same result; no provision is made for sexual relations. A cultic purification-rite is provided for her, but not for the menstruating woman, who, at the end of her period, simply immerses and waits for sunset. She is then in the first remove, her period having concluded.

So while the concrete effects of the respective sources of vaginal uncleanness coincide, the purification-rite contrasts sharply. The Zabah purifies herself in a blood-rite at the Temple. The purification-rite, not required for the menstruating woman, marks the woman as suitable to reenter the procreative cycle; the flux has removed her from that cycle, the cessation signifies her suitability once more.

And this brings us to the principal result of the analogical-contrastive process that encompasses Niddah and Zabim and yields a hermeneutics for them both. The facts at hand suffice to show that *Zibah-blood signifies an aberration in the procreative cycle, Niddah-blood proves integral to that cycle.* The one is irregular and disrupts normal sexual relations, marking the woman as one who, at that point, may not reproduce life (any more than, from sages' view, the semen emitted by a flaccid penis can reproduce life). The other is regular, integral to the normal sexual cycle, and marks the woman as one wholly integrated to the cycle of reproduction. Then the entire sequence —

eleven Zibah-days, seven Niddah-days — forms an account of the woman's relationship to the procreative cycle, which involves three possibilities:

[1] she wholly participates, having sexual relations, receiving semen and not emitting unclean blood;
[2] she is wholly excluded, not having sexual relations at all,
[3] and she is temporarily excluded but remains sexually accessible, which is why the Torah makes provision for the status of one who, in her period, does have sexual relations with her.

Viewed together, the Halakhah of Zabim and of Niddah make a single coherent statement, one that emerges in the process of analogy and contrast, classification and hierarchization of the result. The contrast between blood in the Niddah-days and blood in the Zibah-days frames the issue at hand. That is why I claim, we cannot understand the Halakhah of Niddah outside of the framework of the Halakhah of Zabim, and, in the nature of things, the contrary is also the case. The points of intersection, that is, the consequences of uncleanness imparted by vaginal blood, and the points of differentiation, that is, sexuality and the purification rite, respectively, leave no choice. We must consider Niddah and Zabim as a single statement within the Halakhah, of which Zabim forms the main lines of thought, Niddah the subordinated and secondary results thereof.[9]

THE TELEOLOGICAL HERMENEUTICS OF THE CATEGORY-FORMATION, ZABIM-NIDDAH: The analogical-contrastive analysis has directed our attention to the heart of matters, which is the character of Zob and of its flow. Zob or flux is genital discharge that by its nature cannot accomplish that for which it is created, its purpose or teleology. In a word, the physical world portrayed here finds its definitive traits in the teleology of things, which yields the meetings and the matchings that produce the Halakhah of Zabim-Niddah. The uncleanness generated by sexual fluids that do not realize their teleology passes via pressure, analogous to that of the sexual relation, to objects that serve for sexuality. When the teleological physics of sexual fluids accomplish its goal, it brings about life. Then, consequently, a minor uncleanness is brought about by semen properly ejaculated, and so too with vaginal blood of an episodic character outside the regular period.

When the teleology — the procreation of life — of the sexual parts, en-

[9] And that explains why the particular hermeneutics of the whole finds its place in Zabim's Halakhah, the generic hermeneutics defining the exegetical program of Niddah.

compassing further the objects used for sexual intercourse, and extending even to the activities and exertions characteristic thereof — when that teleology is not realized, then severe uncleanness results. That uncleanness then overspreads each of the components of procreation that has not realized its purpose:

[1] SOURCE OF UNCLEANNESS: the fluid itself, now source of uncleanness analogous to corpse-uncleanness;

[2] MEDIUM FOR THE TRANSMISSION OF UNCLEANNESS (MIDRAS-UNCLEANNESS): the activity, exerting pressure, now medium for disseminating not life but uncleanness; and spatial location in relationship to the Zab/Zabah: above or beneath, analogous to the uncleanness transmitted via spatial relation to the corpse and to the person afflicted with Nega'-uncleanness; and

[3] DISTINCTIVE RECIPIENT (OBJECT) OF UNCLEANNESS: the bed and analogous objects, now the focus of not procreative activity but contamination.

That is to say, the fluid itself should bring about procreation (for a man) or form part of the procreative process (for a woman). It does not. Pressure upon a bed, e.g., in sexual relations, should be part of the normal procreative process. In this context, it is not. The bed and analogous objects, which are flat, do not form receptacles to receive corpse-uncleanness. Here, in flat form, unlike other wooden or leather utensils, they do receive uncleanness, Midras-uncleanness.[10] At each point, the analogical-contrastive analysis has yielded the results of contrast: what under one set of conditions is either not a source of uncleanness or a source of minor uncleanness under another set is a source of major uncleanness, *comparable in medium of dissemination of uncleanness to that of the corpse, and comparable in the purification-process of seven days to that of the corpse*. An activity that under normal circumstances does not serve to disseminate uncleanness now does. Objects that when flat do not receive uncleanness now do. When the procreative organs function in a way contrary to their teleology, they produce the opposite of life, the consequence of death, which is uncleanness, a conclusion required, as I said, by the character of the purification-rite. Analogy serves as much as contrast to allow us to reconstruct the reasoning-process that has yielded the result before us.

Let us make that result very concrete. Not realizing their tasks within

---

[10] To be sure, once they have received Midras-uncleanness, if they then are dismantled, they retain the status of uncleanness, as Kelim has shown us time and again. The status, once imparted, remains, though, we recall, some Tannaite opinion deems that fact anomalous.

the teleological physics at hand:

[1] the fluid is unclean,
[2] the bed and analogous objects become the unique foci of the uncleanness of said fluid, and
[3] the activity — pressure — serves as the medium not of life but of anti-life, such as, we now realize, cultic uncleanness disseminated through Midras-uncleanness in particular represents.

FLUX-UNCLEANNESS AND CORPSE-UNCLEANNESS: In the continuum established by comparison, then contrast, how are we to compare and contrast the uncleanness of the soul, the seven-day uncleanness of the corpse and corpse-matter, with the uncleanness of *Zob*? When we examine, the uncleanness exuding from the Zab or Zabah, encompassing not only the flux itself, whether semen or blood, but the body-fluids, e.g., the spit, the urine, of a person so afflicted, we find an interesting fact. Zob or flux does not constitute a Father of Fathers of Uncleanness as the corpse does. The Zabah or Zab is a Father of uncleanness, contaminating the garments and utensils of someone who touches her or him, also those things that bear her or his weight. These are made unclean in the first remove. So the virulence of the escaping soul — itself capable of creating objects that are Fathers of uncleanness — vastly exceeds that of the genital excretions that do not realize their purpose.

Different in degree, however, they form a common genus. The character of *Zob*-fluid and the uncleanness of the soul that we examined in the context of corpse-uncleanness share the common quality that, when touched, both sorts of fluid impart uncleanness. If there is an object suitable to serve as a bed or chair or saddle that lies underneath a stone, and a Zab or Zabah bears down on the stone, e.g., stands, sits, lies or leans on it or hangs from it, because he is supported by the stone, the bed or chair that bears the weight of the intervening stone is itself contaminated. But corpse-uncleanness — e.g., a receptacle containing a bone — not touched but nonetheless the *weight* of which is carried produces no effect, e.g., through an intervening layer of disconnected material, while *Zob*-uncleanness that is not contacted but the weight of which is carried does produce its uncleanness. So corpse-uncleanness possesses a tangibility, a tactility, that *Zob*-uncleanness lacks, and *Zob*-uncleanness responds to forces that affect corpse-uncleanness little or not at all. What is the difference?

Using our imagination of the workings of the physics of liquids in this odd context, we may on that basis differentiate the uncleanness of the corpse from the uncleanness of flux. The one, while thick, diffuses into the air of a contained space. It is therefore comparable to a gaseous substance; but, as we noted, it flows like a heavy gas, analogous to a viscous fluid, along fairly firm lines, within a sizable space, a squared handbreadth. So while comparable to a gaseous substance, it remains, if invisible, thick and tactile. *Zob*, by contrast, does not diffuse in the air. It is a heavy, squishy, still-intangible liquid. It permeates the objects that are congruent to its effects ("susceptible to *Zob*-uncleanness," which is to say, objects used for lying and sitting, encompassing also carpets and benches and the like). Then, if a clean person bears down, the *Zob* under pressure is excreted upward onto the clean person, even through intervening, disconnected layers of material; the transmission takes place by reason of pressure, not contact.

That conception comes to expression in many cases, not only in Zabim but also in Niddah, e.g. the following: the Zab and the clean person who sat in a ship or on a raft, or who rode together on a beast, even though their clothes do not touch, lo, these are unclean with Midras uncleanness. If they sat on a plank, or on a bench, or on a bed frame, and on the beam, when they are infirm — if they climbed up on a tree which was shaky, on a branch which was shaky on a firm tree — if they climbed up on an Egyptian ladder when it is not fastened with a nail, on the bridge, and on the beam, and on the door, when they are not fastened with clay, they are unclean.

Now how are we to differentiate the gaseous corpse-uncleanness, which does not respond to pressure, from comparable *Zob*-uncleanness, which does? A difference in (imagined) viscosity ought to explain matters. Corpse-uncleanness flows within a guiding framework (under pressure, spurts upward and downward, we recall). But it does not permeate and pass through intervening fabric, however flimsy ("tent") or other materials. *Zob*-uncleanness under pressure is not guided along the lines of that which conveys the pressure — the tent for example — but flows right into, and through, the fabric or other material that contains it. Hence seen in physical terms, the Zob is dense, glutinous and a squishy semifluid, the uncleanness of the soul is attenuated, spare and light.

But those physical traits on their own do not suffice to explain the difference as to the modes of movement between the uncleanness exuding from the corpse and that emitted by the sexual organs, male or female. Specifically, why should the latter classification of uncleanness flow so as to pass through the stone on which the Zab exerts pressure through direct contact, as well as weight, to the bed beneath, on which the Zab exerts pressure not through contact but only through weight? Why should a receptacle contain corpse-uncleanness but not the uncleanness of *Zob*, that is, why should a receptacle be unaffected by Midras- or pressure uncleanness of a Zab or Zabah? Asked in that way, the question bears its own answer. We deal in *Zob* with a kind of uncleanness that matches, that responds to, its own origin, assignment, and character. To make these specific, let me say: its origin in sexual organs, its assignment, procreation, and its character defined by a dysfunction in those organs. Sexually-generated fluid that, by (sages') definition cannot accomplish the purpose that, by nature, sexually-generated fluid is supposed to achieve — procreation of life — affects, as we noted in another context, those sorts of objects that serve sexually, ones used for lying and the like, but not those sorts of objects that under normal circumstances do not serve sexually, receptacles, for example.

THE WORKING OF THE PARTICULAR HERMENEUTICS OF ZABIM-NIDDAH: CORPSE-UNCLEANNESS AND DISSEMINATION OF UNCLEANNESS THROUGH SPATIAL RELATIONSHIPS WITH THE SOURCE OF UNCLEANNESS, AS WITH THE CORPSE: Let us now address the matter to which I briefly made reference a moment ago, namely, the particular rule of spatial relationship in the transmission of uncleanness of a Zab or Zabah, because there we shall see the inexorable operation of the principle of realized or unrealized teleology as the key to all else, affecting both the source and the subject of contamination. The corpse conveys uncleanness to what it overshadows, or to what overshadows it. So too the person suffering from Nega'-uncleanness produces a comparable effect, so we have seen in Ohalot and Negaim, respectively. As with the corpse and the person afflicted with the skin ailment described at Lev. 13, the uncleanness is transmitted through spatial relationships not involving direct, physical contact, whether through pressure or actual touching. There are three parallel results of comparable spatial relationships:

[1] overshadowing the corpse or being overshadowed by it,

[2] the person afflicted with the skin ailment within a contained space,

[3] so too the Zab or Zabah in relationship to a bed or chair.

In all three instances, location within a demarcated spatial relationship with the source of uncleanness, not only actual contact, direct or through pressure (as the case requires), serves as cause of dissemination of uncleanness from the source to the focus thereof.

The comparison having been worked out, the contrast now brings us to the paradoxical fact of the Halakhah. It is that overshadowing serves corpse-uncleanness and *Zob*-uncleanness, but that is only with powerful distinctions, and that involves each in its own way. What overshadows a corpse contracts corpse-uncleanness, and what a corpse overshadows is contaminated by corpse-uncleanness. That is without regard to the character of the objects. We do not, furthermore, differentiate between the two locations of the corpse relative to the object in relationship thereto. So locative relationship and substantive character play no role in the transmission of corpse-uncleanness through overshadowing. The corpse that overshadows or is overshadowed produces its effects without regard to what is affected. But that is not how matters are with *Zob*-uncleanness. Here we do differentiate, in the situation of overshadowing, between the character of two classes of objects. And, concomitantly, we also differentiate locatively, between the two locations that said classes of objects take up: above, below the Zab. So we have two variables as to the character of objects, and two variables as to their location, and, further, these variables produce opposite results, the locative for the substantive, as the case requires.

Here are some of the exemplary facts, which make the whole explicit.

[1] If a Zab overshadows food and drink, unlike the corpse he has no affect upon them.

[2] But if food or drink are located above the Zab, they are made unclean.

Why the mirror-relationships? What is located where the Zab lies or sits but cannot serve for lying or sitting is unaffected by him; what is located where the Zab cannot lie or sit and cannot serve for lying or sitting — thus what in relationship to the Zab is in its natural location, not in its unnatural location — is affected by him. So he functions as does a corpse in conveying uncleanness, the medium is the same; but he does not impart uncleanness as does a corpse. What does not conform in relationship to the Zab to its natural location is affected by him; what conforms is not. So considerations of teleology enter in once more.

THE TELEOLOGICAL HERMENEUTICS OF ZABIM-NIDDAH FULLY EXPOSED: Here again, a teleological logic comes into play through analogical-contrastive dialectics, then, with the things that enjoy their natural relationship to the Zab subject to his effect, those not, not; and then the opposite comes into force: what the Zab cannot use for lying that is located where the Zab cannot lie down is affected by the Zab! So considerations of fulfilling the physical purpose for which the thing is shaped take over, even here. To state matters simply: teleological physics dictates the course of contamination by *Zob* and the results, for things affected by that contamination, as well. And it is a simple teleology, which we identified at the very outset: what serves for procreation is distinguished, in respect to *Zob*-uncleanness, from what does not. And the rest follows.

What we confront, therefore, is a physics permeated by teleology: the flow of fluids in response to the condition or purpose of that to which, or from which, they flow, and not in response only to their own character, e.g., to the density of the atoms that comprise the fluid and define its viscosity. That which matches the character of an object or its purpose flows to that object or its purpose, and the invisible flow itself conforms to the character of the activity conducted with said object. The bed, used for lying or sitting, then is affected by pressure, carried on in acts of lying or sitting; the particular uncleanness at hand, sexual excretions in a non-procreative framework, affects those objects that by their nature serve, through those actions that by their nature produce, procreation.

When sexual activity bearing the potential of procreation takes place, a transient uncleanness results — that of healthy semen, which passes upon immersion and sunset, as Scripture says. When sexual excretions lacking that potential take place, a virulent uncleanness takes over, life replaced by anti-life, by a form of death nearly as virulent as the death that takes over the life of a man and causes the excretion of the soul. The soul of the fully-realized man or woman is thick, the unrealized, proto-soul of *Zob*, thin. But the former can be contained in physical limits, as it was in the body, while the latter flows teleologically, its character and therefore its purpose overriding the substantive, physical traits, or physical traits responding to teleological matches (whichever formulation better serves).

In this same context, moreover, the difference in the rite of purification of the Niddah and the Zabah emerges as entirely rational within the system. The Niddah's purification-rite is analogous to the purification-rite of the man who has emitted semen in the normal course of procreation, and for the same reason: the Niddah has passed through a natural stage in the procreative cycle. When menstrual uncleanness ends and she reverts to the condition of cleanness required for propagation of life in conditions of sanctification, she immerses and awaits sunset. She need not undergo a cultic rite of purification because she has never been removed from the cycle of life. Niddah-blood then bears no analogy to the blood of a corpse, but Zabah-blood does. That is because, within the teleological physiology as much as the teleological physics of the system, Niddah-blood fulfils its teleology, Zabah-blood does not. That is why it is comparable to corpse-matter in its purification-rite.

FROM HERMENEUTICS TO HALAKHAH: The particular hermeneutics of the Halakhah of Zabim-Niddah tends to surface in details. But the generic hermeneutics of the Halakhah defines the exegetical program of bits and pieces of Zabim but nearly all of Niddah, as we shall see in detail. Here is the outline of Zabim:

I. BECOMING UNCLEAN AS A ZAB

II. TRANSFERRING THE UNCLEANNESS OF THE ZAB. PRESSURE

III. Transferring the Uncleanness of the Zab. Generalizations

The ways in which the particular hermeneutics frame the exegetical task will become clear in section iii. The outline of Niddah shows that issues of doubt ("retroactivity") and interstitiality predominate; without Zabim, we should find practically inaccessible the particular hermeneutics of Niddah:

I. Retroactive Contamination

II. Unclean Excretions

A. Unclean Blood
B. The Status of Abortions as to Uncleanness
C. Samaritan, Sadducee, and Gentile Women
D. Status of Blood Produced in Labor
E. Status of Blood Produced in the Zibah-Period
F. Status of Blood Produced in a Caesarian Section
G. Point at which Unclean Fluid Imparts Uncleanness

III. Rules Applicable at Various Ages

IV. Doubts in Connection with Unclean Excretions

A. Bloodstains and Other Matters Subject to Doubt
B. Blood of Menstruating Woman, Flesh of a Corpse
C. Doubts about Creeping Things, Bloodstains
D. Bloodstains Doubtfully-Unclean blood] of Israelites, Gentiles, and Samaritans
E. Doubts about Bloodstains and Drops of Blood
F. The Fixed Period

V. Concluding Miscellanies

A. Girl Married before Puberty: status of Blood
B. Doubts about Cleanness re Failure to Examine
C. Uncleanness of the Zab, the Menstruating Woman
D. Status of a Woman in the Period of Purifying after Childbirth

The program of Niddah begins with the interstitial question of doubt: how do we deal with cases of unclarity as to the exact point at which the period has begun, with special reference to the status of the man who is engaged in sexual relations with the woman at that moment? That illustrates, at the outset, that, so far as the particular hermeneutics is concerned, Niddah on its own finds remarkably little to say that bears fundamental importance.

II. SCRIPTURE'S DEFINITION OF THE HALAKHIC CATEGORY-FORMATION

The Halakhic givens of the matter derive mainly from Scripture. The relevant verses of Scripture are first, Lev. 12:1-8, for the woman after childbirth, then Lev. 15:1-33, encompassing in a single statement both the flux (*zob*) of the Zab and the Zabah, and semen and menstrual blood, that is, excretions of the sexual organs that do not, and that do, pertain to the cycle of procreation, the former breaking, the latter establishing, that cycle. Lev. 12:1-8 follow:

> "The Lord spoke to Moses, saying, Speak to the Israelite people thus: When a woman at childbirth bears a male, she shall be unclean seven days; she shall be unclean as at the time of her menstrual infirmity. On the eighth day the flesh of his foreskin shall be circumcised. She shall remain in a state of blood purification for thirty-three days. She shall not touch any consecrated thing, nor enter the sanctuary until her period of purification is completed. If she shall bear a female, she shall be unclean two weeks as during her menstruation, and she shall remain in a state of blood purification for sixty-six days. On the completion of her period of purification, for either son or daughter, she shall bring to the priest, at the entrance of the tent of meeting, a lamb in its first year for a burnt-offering, and a pigeon or a turtledove for a sin-offering. He shall offer it before the Lord and make expiation on her behalf; she shall then be clean from her flow of blood. Such are the rituals concerning her who bears a child, male or female. If however her means do not suffice for a sheep, she shall take two turtledoves or two pigeons, one for a burnt-offering and the other for a sin-offering. The priest shall make expiation on her behalf and she shall be clean."

Here we have vaginal blood that for seven or fourteen days is deemed unclean in the classification of menstrual blood and then for thirty-three or sixty-six days is deemed altogether clean. The important point to note is that vaginal blood is not always deemed a mark of uncleanness, but, in the case at hand, is deemed clean. But, we also notice, a rite of purification is required for the vaginal flow that is classified as unclean. So in that regard — the cultic purification-rite — the woman after childbirth is comparable to the Zabah, and not to the woman who has menstruated, as we shall now observe in Lev. 15:1-33, which follow:

THE ZAB AND THE ZABAH

"The Lord spoke to Moses and Aaron, saying, Speak to the Israelite people and say to them: When any man has a discharge issuing from his member, [that is, the Zab], he is unclean. The uncleanness from his discharge shall mean the following - whether his member runs with the discharge or is stopped up so that there is no discharge, his uncleanness means this: Any bedding on which the one with the discharge lies shall be unclean, and every object on which he sits shall be unclean. Anyone who touches his bedding shall wash his clothes, bathe in water, and remain unclean until evening. Whoever sits on an object on which the one with the discharge has sat shall wash his clothes, bathe in water, and remain unclean until evening. Whoever touches the body of the one with the discharge shall wash his clothes, bathe in water, and remain unclean until evening. If one with a discharge spits on one who is clean, the latter shall wash his clothes, bathe in water, and remain unclean until evening. Any means for riding that one with a discharge has mounted shall be unclean. Whoever touches anything that was under him shall be unclean until evening; and whoever carries such things shall wash his clothes, bathe in water, and remain unclean until evening. If one with a discharge, without having rinsed his hands in water, touches another person, that person shall wash his clothes, bathe in water, and remain unclean until evening. An earthen vessel that one with a discharge touches shall be broken; and any wooden implement shall be rinsed with water. When one with a discharge becomes clean of his discharge, he shall count off seven days for his cleansing, wash his clothes and bathe his body in fresh water; then he shall be clean. On the eighth day he shall take two turtledoves or two pigeons and come before the Lord at the entrance of the tent of meeting and give them to the priest. The priest shall offer them, the one as a sin-offering and the other as a burnt-offering. Thus the priest shall make expiation on his behalf, for his discharge, before the Lord.

THE UNCLEANNESS OF SEMEN

When a man has an emission of semen, he shall bathe his whole body in water and remain unclean until evening. All cloth or leather on which semen falls shall be washed in water and remain unclean until evening. And if a man has carnal relations with a woman, they shall

> bathe in water and remain unclean until evening.
>
> MENSTRUAL UNCLEANNESS
>
> When a woman has a discharge, her discharge being blood from her body, she shall remain in her impurity seven days; whoever touches her shall be unclean until evening. Anything that she lies on during her impurity shall be unclean; and anything that she sits on shall be unclean. Anyone who touches her bedding shall wash his clothes, bathe in water, and remain unclean until evening; and anyone who touches any object on which she has sat shall wash his clothes, bathe in water, and remain unclean until evening. Be it the bedding or be it the object on which she has sat, on touching it he shall be unclean until evening. And if a man lies with her, her impurity is communicated to him; he shall be unclean seven days, and any bedding on which he lies shall become unclean.
>
> THE ZABAH
>
> When a woman has had a discharge of blood for many days, not at the time of her impurity, or when she has a discharge beyond her period of impurity, she shall be unclean as though at the time of her impurity, as long as her discharge lasts. Any bedding on which she lies while her discharge lasts shall be for her like bedding during her impurity; and any object on which she sits shall become unclean as it does during her impurity; whoever touches them shall be unclean; he shall wash his clothes, bathe in water, and remain unclean until evening. When she becomes clean of her discharge, she shall count off seven days, and after that she shall be clean. On the eighth day she shall take two turtledoves or two pigeons and bring them to the priest at the entrance of the tent of meeting. The priest shall offer the one as a sin-offering and the other as a burnt-offering; and the priest shall make expiation on her behalf, for her unclean discharge, before the Lord. You shall put the Israelites on guard against their uncleanness, lest they die through their uncleanness by defiling my tabernacle which is among them.
>
> Such is the ritual concerning him who has a discharge: concerning him who has an emission or semen and becomes unclean thereby, and concerning her who is in menstrual infirmity, and concerning anyone male or female who has a discharge and concerning a man who lies with an unclean woman" (Lev. 15:1-33).

Scripture's point of emphasis throughout is on four matters,

[1] the character of the discharge that signifies flux-uncleanness,

[2] the effects of the status of uncleanness: objects that are subject to uncleanness,

[3] how the uncleanness is transmitted; and

[4] the mode of purification and attendant cultic rite signifying the regaining of the normal status of cleanness.

The variable that guides us is obvious: is a woman excluded from, or included within, the procreative cycle. If her vaginal flow does not remove her from acts of procreation (in fact or at least in theory), then no purification-rite is called for; if she is utterly excluded from the process, then it is. The Zabah, it is assumed, simply cannot become pregnant and will not engage in sexual relations; the Torah makes no provision for that possibility. The menstruating woman may find herself in a situation in which, inadvertently, she has sexual relations during her period, with the specified consequences for her mate: he enters her status as to uncleanness.

III. THE EXPOSITION OF THE COMPONENTS OF THE GIVEN CATEGORY-FORMATION BY THE MISHNAH-TOSEFTA: ZABIM

I. BECOMING UNCLEAN AS A ZAB

M. 1:1 He who sees one appearance of flux is like one who has had a seminal emission. [If] he saw one [appearance of flux], and on the second day it ceased, and on the third day he saw two, or one as profuse as two — he imparts uncleanness to bed and chair, and is required to immerse in running water, but is free of the obligation to bring an offering.

T. 1:1 He who sees one appearance of flux — he is like one who has had a nocturnal emission .

T. 1:2 He who moves the appearance [of flux] — he is clean. His bed and his chair — it is clean.

T. 1:3 [If] one saw two appearances [of flux] — he who moves the first is clean, and [he who moves] the second is unclean. Beds and chairs [on] which [he sat] between the first and the second [appearance of flux] are clean. [If] he saw one as profuse as two — unclean is only the one who moves the last drop alone.

M. 1:2 He who sees semen on the third day of the counting of his flux has lost only that day. [This is the case] in which he sees semen. But if he saw flux, even on the seventh day, he has lost [all the days] which are before it.

M. 1:3 [If] he saw one on one day and two on the next day, two on one day and one on the following day, three on three [successive] days, or three nights — lo, this one is entirely a Zab.

M. 1:4 [If] he saw one, and it ceased for sufficient time for him to immerse and dry himself, and afterward he saw two, or one profuse as two, or [if] he saw two, or one profuse as two, and it ceased for sufficient time for him to immerse and dry himself, and afterward he saw one, lo, this one is entirely a Zab.

M. 1:5 [If] he saw one [flux] as profuse as three, which is sufficient for one to go from Gad Yon to Shiloah, which is time enough for two immersions and two dryings,. lo, this one is entirely a Zab. [If] he saw one which is profuse as two, he imparts uncleanness to bed and chair, and requires immersion in running water, and is free of the obligation to bring a sacrifice.

T. 1:9 Any semen which imparts uncleanness in the case of priests causes the loss [of a day] in the case of the Zab. The Zab is permitted to have sexual relations on the day of the completion of his counting, and [if he does so], loses only that day alone. How so? [If] he saw [semen] [even] at the eve of the eighth day, he counts as at the first and brings another sacrifice. [If] he saw on the eighth day, he counts as at the first and brings two offerings. How much is sufficient time for immersion and drying off. Sufficient time for one to descend and to immerse and to ascend and to dry off.

T. 1:10 And how much is the measure of a profuse appearance [of flux]? As [much time as it takes to go] from Gad Yon to Shiloah, which is the same [as the amount of time required for] two immersions and two acts of drying off.

T. 1:11 They made a parable. To what is the matter comparable? [It is comparable] to a rope of a hundred cubits in length. How so? [If] one saw at the beginning a hundred, and at the end fifty, and at the end a hundred cubit. Lo, this is entirely a Zab. [If] one saw at the beginning a hundred, in the middle fifty, and at the end, a hundred, or at the beginning a hundred and afterward fifty and at the end a hundred, lo, this is not entirely a Zab. [If] it ceased and one saw between one appearance and another sixty cubits or seventy cubits and afterward he sees [flux], all the more so is it his uncleanness. This is the principle: So long as it is profuse, all the more so is it his uncleanness.

T. 1:12 How so? [If] he saw three appearances [of flux], if there is not sufficient time between the first and the third for immersion and an act of drying off, he has at hand only one [flux]. [If] he saw one profuse as two — [if] there is sufficient time from the beginning of its [flow] to its end for immersion and an act of drying off, he has in hand two appearances. If not, he has in hand only one.

M. 1:6 [If] he saw one by day and one at twilight, one at twilight and one on the following day — if it is known that part of the appearance was on one day and part of it on the next, he is

certain as to the sacrifice and as to uncleanness. If it is a matter of doubt whether part of the appearance [of flux] appeared on one day and part on the next, he is certain as to uncleanness but in doubt as to the requirement to bring a sacrifice. [If] he saw [flux] on two days at twilight [on each day], he is in doubt as to imparting uncleanness and in doubt as to bring a sacrifice. [If he saw] one [appearance of flux] at twilight, he is in doubt [even as to] uncleanness.

M. 2:1 All are susceptible to uncleanness through flux, even converts, even slaves, (1) whether freed or not freed, a deaf-mute, imbecile, or minor, a eunuch by castration and a eunuch by nature. As to a tumtom [a person without distinct sexual characteristics] and androgyne [a person with the sexual traits of both sexes] — they place upon them the stringencies that apply to man and the stringencies that apply to woman: (1) they are susceptible to uncleanness through blood, like a woman, (2) and through white [flow], like a man. (3) And their status as to uncleanness remains in doubt.

T. 2:1 The gentiles and the convert and the resident alien are not susceptible to uncleanness through flux. But even though they are not susceptible to uncleanness through flux they [in fact] are unclean like Zabs in every respect. And on their account they burn heave-offering. But they are not liable on their account for contamination of the sanctuary and its holy things.

T. 2:2 A tumtom and an androgyne who saw either white or red flow — on their account they do not burn heave-offering. And they are not liable on their account for contamination of the sanctuary and its holy things. [If] they saw white and red flow simultaneously, they do burn heave- offering on their account. But they are not liable on their account for contamination of the sanctuary and its holy things.

T. 2:3 He who touches semen and red flow and enters the sanctuary is free [of obligation]. He who touched his own white flow and red flow and entered the sanctuary is liable. [If] he was counting [clean days] on account of white flow and saw red flow, [or if he was counting clean days] on account of red flow and saw white flow, lo this one does not lose [the day on which the one or the other appeared].

M. 2:2 In seven ways do they examine the Zab before he is confirmed as to flux: (1) as to what he had eaten, (2) as to what he had drunk, (3) and as to what he had carried; (4) as to whether he had jumped, (5) as to whether he was ill; (6) as to what he had seen, and (7) as to what he had fantasized — [if] he fantasized before he [actually] saw, or saw before fantasizing. Once one is con-

firmed as to flux, they do not examine him [further]. [Any flux which happens] inadvertently, and any that is subject to doubt, and his semen [all] are unclean, for there is now a basis for the matter [of deeming them unclean]. [If] he saw the first [flow of flux], they do examine him, [In the case of] the second, they do examine him. In [the case of the] third, they do not examine him.

T. 2:5 As to a Zab, they attribute it to food — and to any kind of food.

T. 2:6 As to a child, they attribute [his flux] to five things: to food, to drink, to a carrying something, and to jumping during his and his mother's illness.

M. 2:3 He who sees semen does not become susceptible to uncleanness by flux for twenty-four hours. A gentile who saw semen and converted [thereafter] — forthwith is he susceptible to uncleanness by reason of flux. She who sees blood and the one who is in hard labor — [the time during which she is not susceptible to uncleanness by reason of flux is] twenty-four hours. He who smites his slave — the day or two [Ex. 21:21] is twenty-four hours. A dog who ate the flesh of a corpse — for three days of twenty-four hours, lo, it [continues] in its natural state.

T. 2:4 And what is the difference between flux and semen? Flux comes from a limp penis, and semen from an erection. Flux is like the white of a crushed egg, and semen is congealed like the white of an egg which is not crushed. Red semen is clean, and the woman attributes [red flow] to it.

T. 2:7 A gentile who saw semen and converted — forthwith is he susceptible to uncleanness by reason of flux. Under what circumstances? When he converted when already circumcised. But if he was circumcised and afterward saw [semen], they attribute it to it so long as he is distressed [recovering from the circumcision], whether he is gentile or Israelite.

T. 2:8 He who finds a corpse lying across the breadth of the path — a Nazir and one who is going to eat his Passover is clean. And as to heave-offering, he is unclean. Under what circumstances? [If] there is no place to pass [except across the corpse itself]. But [if] there is a place to pass, even for heave-offering is he clean. Under what circumstances? When he goes by foot. But [if] he carries or rides on a beast, he is unclean. For the one who goes on his own two feet may possibly not touch and not overshadow and not move [the corpse]. But it is not possible for him [who carries or rides] not to touch and not to overshadow and not to move [the corpse]. [If] it is not possible for him not to touch, overshadow, and move, he is unclean. And in the case of a corpse which is spread about in bits and pieces, he is clean. Under what circumstances? In the case of the uncleanness of the nethermost depths. But if it is a case of certain uncleanness, he is unclean.

T. 2:9 What is the uncleanness of the nethermost depths? That [is a case in which] no one else anywhere in the world knew about the presence of the corpse-matter. But [if] anyone else in the world knew about the presence of corpse-matter, this is not deemed uncleanness of the nethermost depth. [If] one found it buried in straw or in dirt or in pebbles, lo, this constitutes uncleanness in the nethermost depths. But a corpse which is buried in water and in darkness and in the crevices of rocks — this is not deemed a grave in the nethermost depths. A grave in the nethermost depths applies only to the corpse alone.

We start with a problem of interstitiality. Producing flux on three successive days marks the uncleanness of the Zab (or Zabah). What if the flux comes sporadically or in uneven volume? The solution is as interstitial as the circumstance it addresses: uncleanness that is removed by immersion, without the obligation of an offering. A second problem of the same classification is the appearance of flux and of semen on alternate days, M. 1:2. M. 1:3-5, 6 then go over other possibilities and resolve them. The Tosefta at T. 1:9 introduces the analogical-contrastive analysis, now of semen produced by priests, which marks them unclean, and semen produced by a Zab. The interstitialities having been disposed of, M. 2:1 then lays out one primary component of the particular hermeneutics: the susceptibility to differentiated uncleanness for Israelites only, M. 2:1/T. 2:1. Here, it is the Tosefta, not the Mishnah, that makes the primary statement. M. 2:2 makes a statement of equally fundamental importance: the flux must come naturally and not through human stimulus. The next unit carries forward the exegesis precipitated by the particular hermeneutics.

II. TRANSFERRING THE UNCLEANNESS OF THE ZAB. PRESSURE

M. 2:4 The Zab imparts uncleanness to the bed in five ways so that it imparts uncleanness to man and imparts uncleanness to garments: (1) standing, (2) sitting, (3) lying, (4) suspended, and (5) leaning. And the bed imparts uncleanness to man in seven ways so that he imparts uncleanness to clothing: (1) standing, (2) sitting, (3) lying, (4) suspended, (5) leaning, (6) through [direct] , and (7) through carrying.

M. 3:1 The Zab and the clean person who sat in a ship or on a raft, or who rode [together] on a beast, even though their clothes do not touch, lo, these are unclean with Midras uncleanness. [If] they sat on a plank, or on a bench, or on a bed frame,

and on the beam, when they are infirm — [if] they climbed up on a tree which was shaky, on a branch which was shaky on a firm tree — [if they climbed up] on an Egyptian ladder when it is not fastened with a nail, on the bridge, and on the beam, and on the door, when they are not fastened with clay, they are unclean.

M. 3:2 [If] they [both] close or open [door] — [there is no transfer of uncleanness] unless this one closes and this one opens. [If] the one lifts the other out of the pit — [If] they twist ropes together — [there is no transfer of uncleanness] unless this one is pulling one way, and that one is pulling the other way. [If] they weave [together], whether standing or sitting, or grind wheat together — [If] they unload the ass or load it up, when their burden is heavy, they are unclean. When their burden is light, they are clean. And all of them are clean for members of the congregation and unclean [for those who eat] heave offering.

T. 4:1 [If] a clean person hits the unclean, the clothes of the clean person are clean. [If] an unclean person hits the clean since if the clean person draws back, lo, the unclean person falls down, the clothes of the clean person are unclean.

M. 3:3 The Zab and the clean person who sat in a large ship [if] they sat on the plank, on the bench, on the bed frame, and on the beam, when they are not infirm — [if] they climbed up into a tree which is firm, onto a branch which is firm, and onto a Tyrian or Egyptian ladder when it is affixed firmly with a nail, on the bridge, on the beam, and on the door, when they are fastened with clay, even on one side — they are clean. [If] the clean person hits the unclean person — he is clean. [If] the unclean person hits the clean person, he is unclean, for if the clean person should draw back, lo, the unclean person would fall down.

M. 4:2 [If a Zab] knocked against the king beam, against the rafter frame, against the waterspout, and against the fixed shelf, even though it is made with ropes, against the oven, and against the flour mill's container or lower millstone or the jack of a hand mill or an olive grinder's seah — measure [if a loaf of bread made of heave offering fell from any of these], it is clean.

M. 4:3 [If] he knocked against the door, against the door-pin, against the lock, against the rudder, and against the mill frame — and against a tree which is infirm, and against a branch which is infirm but on a solid tree — against an Egyptian ladder when it is not fastened with a nail — against the bridge, against the beam, and against the door when they are not held firm with clay — they are unclean. Against the chest, box, or cupboard — they are unclean.

T. 4:6 [If a Zab] knocked against an oven — [if] from it fell a loaf of heave-offering, it is clean. And if there was shard cleaving onto it, it is unclean. [If a Zab] knocked against the door-pin, the lock, and the door, they are unclean. [If a Zab knocked against] the chest, box, or cupboard, even though they hold [the requisite] volume — [they are unclean]. And if they were shifted, they are unclean. This is the principle: Whatever is through the force of trembling is clean; through the force of shaking is unclean.

M. 4:4 A Zab who was lying on five benches, or on five bags — lengthwise, they are unclean, breadth-wise, they are clean. [If] he slept — [if] there is a doubt whether he rolled over on them, they are unclean. [If] he was lying on six seats, with his two hands on two, his two feet on two, his head on one, and his body on one — unclean is only this one which is under the body. [If] he is standing on two chairs — [if] they are far from one another, they are clean.

M. 4:5 Ten cloaks, one on top of the other — [if] he slept on the topmost one, they are all unclean. [If] the Zab is on one side of a balance, and a bed or chair is opposite him [on the other balance], [if] the Zab went down, they are clean. [If] they went down [outweighing the Zab and thus lifting him up], they are unclean.

M. 4:6 [If] the Zab is on one side of the scale and food and drink are on the second, they are unclean. [But] in the case of a corpse, all is clean, except for the man. This is more strict in the case of the Zab than in the case of the corpse. And more strict is the rule in the case of the corpse than in the case of the Zab, for the Zab makes [unclean] the bed and chair which are under him so that they impart uncleanness to man and impart uncleanness to clothing, and [imparts] to what is above him maddaf uncleanness so that it imparts uncleanness to food and drink, which the corpse does not effect. More strict is the rule in the case of the corpse, for the corpse imparts uncleanness in the Tent and imparts uncleanness for seven days, which uncleanness the Zab does not effect.

T. 4:8 [If] the Zab is on one side of the scale and a bed or a chair is opposite him, if the Zab goes down, it imparts uncleanness at one remove and renders [heave-offering] unfit at one. And if it outweighed the Zab, it imparts uncleanness at two removes and renders [heave-offering] unfit at one remove. In the case of a man, whether he outweighs the Zab or whether the Zab outweighs him, he imparts uncleanness at one remove and renders [heave-offering] unfit at one remove.

T. 4:9 [If] a Zab is on one side of the scale and food and drink are on the second side, even if it is only slightly distant from the ground, they impose upon it the stringent rulings applying to that which [who] carries and the stringent rulings applying to that which [who] is carried. [If] he [a Zab] sat on top of a small press with a cylindrical beam utensils which are in the roller are unclean. [If he sat] on the fuller's press when it is loaded with stones, utensils which are under it are clean. When it goes back over the utensils [clothes], utensils which are under it become unclean.

T. 3:1 A more strict rule applies to the Zab than to the Zabah, and [a more strict rule applies] to the Zabah than to the Zab. For the Zab must [for purification] enter into running water. But the Zabah need not enter into running water. The Zab is susceptible to uncleanness through flux on the very day that he is born. But the Zabah [is not susceptible until] ten days [after birth]. If the Zab saw three occurrences of flux in three days, he is made unclean by them. But the Zabah sometimes sees three appearances on three successive days and is not made unclean by them. As to the Zab, his days do not stand before him, which is not the case for the Zabah. The Zab's sort [of fluid] does not cause him to lose a day, which is not the case for the Zabah. The Zab is made unclean by white [flow], which is not the case with the Zabah.

T. 3:2 More strict is the rule applying to the Zabah than to the Zab: For the Zabah imparts uncleanness to bed and chair on account of an appearance of unclean flow of any amount at all. She imparts uncleanness to the one who has intercourse with her. And she imparts uncleanness during the antecedent twenty-four hour period. And she imparts uncleanness internally as externally, And she imparts uncleanness in cases of inadvertence. And she imparts uncleanness through red flow — none of which is the case for the Zab.

T. 3:3 More strict is the rule applying to the Zab than to one unclean by corpse-uncleanness, and [more strict is the rule applying to] the one unclean by corpse-uncleanness than to the Zab: For the Zab makes a bed and chair under him render man unclean and render garments unclean and [imparts] to what is above him maddaf-uncleanness and makes food and drink unclean — [forms of uncleanness] which the corpse does not impart. His flux and his spit and his urine impart stringent uncleanness. And he imparts uncleanness by means of contact to a utensil which is subject to purification by rinsing, and by means of shifting to a clay utensil. And he is liable for a sacrifice and is required to enter running water for his purification, which is not the case for the one who is unclean by reason of corpse-uncleanness. More strict is the rule applying to one unclean by corpse-uncleanness: For the one suffering corpse-uncleanness requires sprinkling [with purification-water] on the third and seventh day, which is not the case for the Zab.

T. 3:4 More strict is the rule applying to the Zab than that applying to the person afflicted with the skin-ailment, and [more strict is the rule applying] to the person afflicted with the skin-ailment than applies to the Zab: For the Zab requires purification through entry into running water, which is not the case for the person afflicted with the skin-ailment . More strict is the rule applying to the person afflicted with the skin-ailment . For the person afflicted with the skin-ailment imparts uncleanness through entry, which is not the case for the Zab.

T. 3:5 More strict is the rule applying to the Zabah than to the person afflicted with the skin-ailment at. and [more strict is the rule applying] to the person afflicted with the skin-ailment at than to the Zabah: For the Zabah imparts uncleanness to one who has intercourse with her, which is not the case for the person afflicted with the skin-ailment at. More strict is the rule applying to the person afflicted with the skin-ailment For the person afflicted with the skin-ailment at imparts uncleanness through coming into a house. And she requires sprinkling with running water, which is not the case for the Zabah.

M. 4:7 [If] he was sitting on the bed, and four cloaks were under the four legs of the bed, they are unclean, because it [the bed] cannot stand on three [legs]. [If] he was riding on a beast, and four cloaks were under the four hooves of the beast, they are clean, because it can stand on three [hooves]. [If] there was a single cloak under its two forelegs, under its two hind-legs, under a foreleg and a hind-leg, it is unclean. [If] he sat on the beam of the olive press, utensils which are in the roller are unclean. [If he sat] on the fuller's press, the garments under it are clean.

The workings of Midras-uncleanness — pressure exerted without necessary contact between the source of the uncleanness and that which is affected by it — are beautifully spelled out, with a range of illustrative cases to make the necessary points. Any independent exertion of pressure on the part of the Zab that produces affects for susceptible persons or objects suffices. Here is Halakhah at its finest: exegetical cases generated by a common hermeneutical issue, which is not articulated but systematically instantiated. M. 4:6 then concludes with the comparison of midras- and corpse-uncleanness, yielding the triumph of Maddaf-uncleanness with its reversal of possibilities. And the Tosefta's counterpart, T. 3:1-5, is not only better articulated but more systematic.

III. TRANSFERRING THE UNCLEANNESS OF THE ZAB. GENERALIZATIONS

M. 5:1 He who touches the Zab, or whom the Zab touches, he who moves the Zab, or whom the Zab moves imparts uncleanness to food and drink and utensils which may be cleaned through rinsing when [he is in] contact but not when he carries [such objects]. A general rule did R. Joshua state: "Whoever imparts uncleanness to clothes, when he is in contact imparts uncleanness to food and drink, putting [them] into the first remove, and to the hands, putting [them] into the second remove. But he does not impart uncleanness either to man or to clay utensils. After he separates from the things which make him unclean, he imparts uncleanness to liquid, putting [it] into the first remove, and to food and the hands, putting [them] into the second remove, And he does not impart uncleanness to clothes."

M. 5:2 **And further: Another general rule did they state: Whatever is carried above the Zab is unclean. And whatever the Zab is carried upon is clean, except for something which is suitable for sitting and lying, and [except for] man. How so? [If] the finger of the Zab is under the course of stones, and the clean person is above them, he imparts uncleanness at two removes and renders [heave offering] unfit at one [still further remove]. [When] he separates, he imparts uncleanness at one remove and renders unfit at one [still further remove]. [If] the unclean person is above them and the clean person is below them, he imparts uncleanness at two removes and renders unfit at one [still further remove]. [When] he separates, he imparts uncleanness at one remove and renders unfit at one [still further remove]. [If] food and drink, bed and chair, and maddaf [articles not used for sitting and lying] are above [the course of stones, and the Zab's finger was below], they impart uncleanness at two removes [or: one remove] and render unfit at one. [When] they separate, they impart uncleanness at one remove and render unfit at one remove. [And if] the bed and chair are below them [and the Zab's finger was above, they impart uncleanness at two removes and render unfit at one.[When] they separate, they impart uncleanness at two removes and render unfit at one. [If] food and drink and maddaf are below them [and the Zab's finger was above the course of stones], they remain clean.**

T. 5:1 The Torah has imposed a more stringent rule upon food and drink and maddaf [an object not used for sitting and lying] which are above the Zab, than upon food and drink and maddaf which are under the Zab; upon bed and chair which are under the Zab, than upon bed and chair which are above the Zab and upon maddaf [an object not used for lying and sitting] which is above the Zab, than upon bed and chair which are above the Zab; upon man, whether above the Zab or below the Zab, than upon bed and chair which are above the Zab. [If] something connected to the unclean person is on a clean person, on part of him, [if] something connected to a clean person is on the unclean person on part of him — in the case of the Zab, he is unclean, in the case of the bed, he is clean. [If] the greater part of the unclean person is on the clean person, on part of him, [if] the greater part of a clean person is on the unclean person, on part of him — whether on the Zab or on the bed — he is unclean. [If] part of the unclean person is on a clean person, on part of him, [if] part of the clean person is on the unclean, on part of him — in the case of the Zab, it is unclean. In the case of the bed [of the Zab], it is clean.

M. 5:3 Whatever carries and is carried on top of a bed is clean, except for man. Whatever carries or is carried on top of carrion is clean, except for him who shifts [it]. Whatever carries or is carried on top of the corpse is clean, except for that which overshadows, and except for man when he shifts [it].

M. 5:4 [If] part of one who is unclean is on top of him who is clean, or [if] part of one who is clean is on top of one who is unclean, or [if] that which is connected to someone who is unclean is on top of someone who is clean, or [if] that which is connected to one who is clean is on top of the one who is unclean — he is unclean.

M. 5:5 [If] the unclean person is on part of the bed, and the clean person is on part of the bed, he is unclean. [If] part of the unclean person is on the bed, and part of the clean person is on the bed, he is clean. It turns out that uncleanness enters it and leaves it through its lesser part. And so: A loaf of bread made of heave offering flour which is placed on top of a bed, and paper is between, whether it is above or below, is clean. And so with a stone afflicted with a plague-mark, it [the loaf] is clean.

T. 5:2 What are the connectors? They are the teeth, the fingernails, the hair, and the backbone. What are the parts? They are the fingertips of the hands and the toes.36 His phlegm, and his mucous, and his saliva, and his snot, lo, they are like his spit. His tear and the blood of his wound and the milk of a woman and blood which exudes from his mouth and from his penis impart uncleanness as liquid. His flux, his spit, and his urine impart stringent uncleanness. His semen imparts uncleanness when it is carried, because it is not possible for semen to be emitted without a trace of urine to be contained therein.

M. 5:6 He who touches the Zab and the Zabah and the menstruating woman and the woman after childbirth and the per-

son afflicted with the skin ailment, a bed or a chair [that any of these have lain or sat upon] imparts uncleanness at two removes and renders [heave offering] unfit at one further remove. [If] he separated, he imparts uncleanness at one remove and renders unfit at one further remove. All the same are the one who touches and the one who shifts, and all the same are the one who carries and the one who is carried.

M. 5:7 **He who touches the flux of the Zab, and his spit, his semen, his urine, and the blood of the menstruating woman imparts uncleanness at two removes and renders unfit at one. [If] he separated, he imparts uncleanness at one remove and renders unfit at one. All the same are the one who touches and the one who shifts.**

M. 5:8 **He who carries the saddle, and he who is carried on it, and he who moves it imparts uncleanness at two removes and renders unfit at one. [If] he separated, he imparts uncleanness at one remove and renders unfit at one remove. He who carries the carrion and purification water sufficient in volume for sprinkling imparts uncleanness at two removes and renders unfit at one. [If] he separated, he imparts uncleanness at one remove and renders unfit at one.**

M. 5:9 **He who eats the carrion of a clean bird, when it is in his gullet, imparts uncleanness at two removes and renders unfit at one. [If] he put his head into the contained airspace of the oven, the oven is clean. [If] he vomited it up or swallowed it, he imparts uncleanness at one remove and renders unfit at one. And when it is in his mouth before he swallows it [so that it enters his gullet], he is clean.**

M. 5:10 **He who touches a dead creeping thing, and semen, and one who is made unclean by reason of a corpse, and the person afflicted with the skin ailment during the period of his counting [clean days, preparatory to the purification rite], and purification water insufficient in volume for sprinkling, and carrion, and a saddle imparts uncleanness at one remove and renders unfit at one remove. This is the general rule: Whatever touches any one of all the Fathers of Uncleanness which are listed in the Torah imparts uncleanness at one remove and renders unfit at one remove, except for man. [If] one separated, he imparts uncleanness at one remove and renders unfit at one remove.**

T. 5:3 Utensils which touch the Zab and the Zabah and the menstruating woman and the woman after childbirth and the person afflicted with the skin-ailment and the bed and the chair impart uncleanness at two removes and spoil [heave-offering] at one [further remove]. [If] they separated, they impart uncleanness at one remove and render unfit at one remove. He who touches, and he who carries, and he who shifts on account of carrying — none of these applies to them.

T. 5:4 He who touches the flux of the Zab and his spit and his semen, his urine and the blood of the menstruating woman imparts uncleanness at two removes and renders unfit at one. [If] he separated, he imparts uncleanness at one remove and renders unfit at one remove. All the same is the one who touches and the one who carries. He who carries and he who shifts — [these] do not apply to them. For you have nothing not animate which imparts uncleanness through shifting. And you have nothing which imparts uncleanness through shifting except for something which is animate.

T. 5:9 He who eats of the carrion of a clean bird, bones, sinews, the cluster of eggs, blood and flesh — [if] it is alive, he is clean. [If] he eats of the ovaries, crop, intestines, or [if] he melted the fat and swallowed it, he is unclean. [If] he wrapped it in bast and swallowed it, he is clean. [if] he wrapped it in lettuce and swallowed it, he is unclean. [If] he vomited it up and swallowed it, he imparts uncleanness at two removes and renders unfit at one [further remove]. [If] he swallowed it and went and vomited it up and it is located in his gullet, he imparts uncleanness at one remove and renders unfit at one remove. [If] he swallowed it, and it is not of the volume of an olive, he is clean in every respect. [If] he took a claw and ate it, if it is of the volume of an olive, he is unclean, and if not, he is clean.

T. 5:10 [If] the carrion of a beast is inside [him] and in his mouth, he is unclean. [If it is] in his gullet, he is clean. [If] the carrion of the fowl is inside [him] and in his mouth, he is clean. [If] it is in his gullet, he is unclean. You come out to say that in a situation in which this imparts uncleanness, the other imparts cleanness, and in a case in which the other imparts cleanness, this imparts uncleanness.

T. 5:11 The carrion of clean fowl is in the measure of an olive in respect to the gullet. And this is one of the thirteen things which have been stated in connection with the carrion of the clean fowl. The carrion of the unclean fowl is in the measure of half of a loaf to render the body unfit.

T. 5:12 He who eats a limb from a living animal, whether from beast or wild animal or clean fowl — in any measure at all, [he is liable]. [If] they are unclean, [he is clean] until they are of the volume of an olive. He who eats of the carrion of the unclean fowl, lo, this one incurs only forty stripes.

M. 5:11 One who has had a seminal emission is like one who has touched a dead creeping thing. He who has sexual relations with a menstruating woman is like one who is unclean by reason of corpse uncleanness. But more strict is the rule concern-

ing the one who has sexual relations with a menstruating woman: for he imparts uncleanness to bed and chair with a minor sort of uncleanness, [rendering the bed and chair capable of] imparting uncleanness to food and drink.

T. 5:5 He who touches the fringes of the saddle and the wool of carrion [and] purification-water which contains sufficient volume for sprinkling imparts uncleanness at two removes and renders unfit at one. [If] he separated, he imparts uncleanness at one remove and renders unfit at one. In the case of the horn of carrion and the wood of the saddle and purification-water which lacks sufficient volume for sprinkling, he imparts uncleanness at one remove and renders unfit at one remove. [If] he separated, he imparts uncleanness at one remove and renders unfit at one remove. He who touches one who has had intercourse with a menstruating woman and [who touches] an idol imparts uncleanness at one remove and renders [heave-offering] unfit at one remove, whether man or utensils.

T. 5:6 An idol is [unclean] in the status of a dead creeping thing, and its appurtenances likewise are unclean in the status of a dead creeping thing, as it is said, "You shall utterly detest it" [Deut. 7:26].

T. 5:7 He who pokes his head and the greater part of his body into a temple of idolatry is unclean. Utensils which he stuck into the contained airspace of a temple of idolatry are unclean. The stools and chairs, the greater part of which he put into a temple of idolatry, are unclean.

T. 5:8 Wine which one saw a gentile offer up as a libation, if it is of the volume of an olive's bulk, imparts stringent uncleanness. And if not, it imparts only the uncleanness of liquid. And the remainder of the gentile's wine, even though it is prohibited on account of wine used for idolatrous libations, imparts only the uncleanness of unclean liquid alone.

M. 5:12 These render heave offering unfit: he who eats food unclean in the first remove; and he who eats food unclean in the second remove; and he who drinks unclean liquid; he whose head and the greater part of whose body enters drawn water; and one who was clean on whose head and the greater part of whose body three logs of drawn water fall; and the book, and the hands, and the tebul-yom; and food and utensils which have been made unclean by [unclean] liquids.

As though the exposition of the working of Midras-uncleanness and Maddaf-uncleanness were insufficient, we now are given a systematic reprise, in general terms. M. 5:1's generalization adds its own point, having to do with the difference between the Zab's moving and touching objects not susceptible to

Midras-uncleanness. If an object is not used for lying or sitting, it is rendered unclean by the Zab's direct contact, but not by his movement or pressure. Joshua's general rule then introduces considerations of removes: he is a Father of uncleanness, a stage lower than the corpse. Along these same lines of systematic hierarchical classification, M. 5:2 gives us the required comparison of the Zab's and the corpse's affect upon objects that are located above or beneath the source of uncleanness. The Zab overshadowed by objects of any character imparts uncleanness to them; but he imparts uncleanness only to objects used for sitting and lying upon which he is carried. The particular hermeneutics then comes to full realization in the exposition that follows. As though that did not suffice, T. 5:1 provides a still more systematic statement. M. 5:3 completes the picture of the affects of spatial relationships, with special reference to being carried on top of a bed, carrion, and a corpse, and that sets the stage for the interstitial problems that follow, M. 5:4-5. M. 5:6 then turns from the exegesis of Midras-uncleanness and its extension in Maddaf-uncleanness to the uncleanness of animate sources of bodily uncleanness listed in Lev. 12-15, treated as a single category-formation, just as we have done in this account of matters. All produce the same effects as to contact, that is, they are all in the same status as to uncleanness, Fathers of uncleanness, yielding Offspring in the form of those persons or things that have direct contact with them. M. 5:7 proceeds to a secondary refinement. M. 5:8-10+11, 12, take up secondary issues: Merkab (saddle) uncleanness, the uncleanness of the carrion of a clean bird, and a dead creeping thing and the like — all of the sources now classified and hierarchized. I cannot imagine a more lucid exhibition of the hermeneutics of comparison and contrast than this wonderful composition. And if that did not suffice, the Tosefta builds on the foundation of the Mishnah a still more effective elaboration of the same hermeneutics. We have here nothing short of a handbook for the presentation of the methods of analogical-contrastive analysis, not only the issues, of sources of uncleanness. To claim that we reconstruct the thought-processes that yielded the hermeneutics that guided the exegesis of the Halakhic data in their category-formations, their organization and rationalization, is a vast overstatement. All we do in these exercises is follow the Mishnah as a Handbook of the Halakhah, and the Tosefta as a complementary recapitulation of that Handbook and an improvement on it: the whole a user's guide to a system remarkably complex in its articulation, amazingly coherent and simple in its operation.

IV. THE EXPOSITION OF THE COMPONENTS OF THE GIVEN CATEGORY-FORMATION BY THE MISHNAH-TOSEFTA: NIDDAH

I. RETROACTIVE CONTAMINATION

M. 1:1 [The woman is held to have been unclean only] during [the preceding] twenty-four hours [when] this lessens the period from the examination to the [last] examination, [and she is held to have been unclean only] during the period from examination to examination [when] this lessens the period of twenty-four hours. Every woman who has a fixed period — sufficient for her is her time. She who makes use of test rags, lo, this is equivalent to an examination, which lessens either the period of the twenty-four hours or the period from examination to examination.

T. 1:1 How does a period of twenty-four hours diminish the period from one examination to the next examination? [If] she examined herself after the Sabbath and found herself clean and spent Monday and Tuesday and did not examine herself, and on Wednesday she examined herself and found herself unclean — lo, this one imparts uncleanness in the preceding twenty-four hour period and not from one examination to the next.

T. 1:2 How does the period from one examination to the next examination diminish the period of twenty-four hours? [If] she examined herself in the morning and found herself clean and spent the second hour and the third hour, not examining herself, and then at the fourth hour examined herself and found herself unclean — lo, this renders unclean from examination to examination and not in a given twenty-four hour period. And this is that to which they referred, saying, The period of twenty four hours is diminished by the period from one examination to the next examination, and the period from one examination to the next examination is diminished by the period of twenty-four hours.

M. 1:2 How [is the case in which] her time suffices for her? [If] she was sitting on the bed and engaged in things requiring cleanness and arose and saw [a drop of blood], she is unclean, but all of those [things requiring cleanness] are clean. Even though they have said, "She renders unclean [whatever she touched during the preceding] twenty-four-hour period," she takes count [of the days prescribed in the Torah] only from the time that she saw a drop of blood.

M. 1:3 Four women [fall into the category of those for whom the] time [of first seeing blood] suffices: (1) the virgin, (2) the pregnant woman, (3) the nursing mother, and (4) the old lady.

Y. 1:3 l:1 Thus is the teaching of the Mishnah: Any girl who has not seen menstrual blood in her life, and even though she is married. They [thus spoke of a virgin as to blood[, that is, a girl who had never menstruated], not a virgin as to the hymen. There are cases in which a girl is a virgin as to blood and not virgin as to the hymen. There are cases in which she is a virgin as to the hymen but is not a virgin as to blood. [A girl is] a virgin as to the hymen when she produced a drop of blood and afterward was married. [She is a] virgin as to blood when she was married and afterward produced a drop of blood.

M. 1:4 Who is (1) the virgin? Any girl who never in her life saw a drop of blood, even though she is married. (2) A pregnant woman? Once it is known that the foetus is present. (3) A nursing mother? Until she will wean her son. [If] she gave her son to a wet nurse, weaned him, or he died — sufficient for her is her time.

M. 1:5 (4) Who is an old woman? Any woman for whom three periods have gone by without a flow near to the time of her old age.

T. 1:6 Who is a virgin? Any girl who has never seen a drop of blood in her life and even if she is married and had children, I call her a virgin until she will see the first drop of menstrual blood. It comes out that they did not refer to virgin in respect to the tokens of virginity but a virgin in respect to menstrual blood.

T. 1:7 Who is a pregnant woman? Once the presence of the foetus is recognized — Three months, as it is said, "And it came to pass at the end of three months" [Gen. 38:24]. [If] she was in the presumption of being pregnant and saw a drop of blood and afterward she miscarried something which is not a human foetus — sufficient for her is her time. And even though there is no Scriptural proof of the matter, there is a Scriptural allusion to the matter: "We were With child, we writhed, we have as it were brought forth wind" [Is. 26:18].

T. 1:8 A girl who did not reach her time for seeing blood and who saw a drop of blood — at the first and at the second appearance of the blood, sufficient for her is her time. [But when she sees] the third [drop of blood], she imparts uncleanness [to what she touched] during the preceding twenty-four hour period. [If] she missed her flow for three periods and then saw a drop of blood, sufficient for her is her time. And once [a girl] has reached her time for seeing blood, and she saw a first drop, sufficient for her is her time, and [after she saw] a second, she imparts uncleanness during the preceding twenty-four hour period. And at the third [period] — sufficient for her is her time. [If] she missed three periods and then she saw a drop of blood, she imparts uncleanness during the preceding twenty-four hour period.

T. 1:9 And from what time is a girl likely to see a drop of blood? From the time that she will produce two pubic hairs.

T. 1:11 [If] an old lady missed three periods and then saw a drop of blood — sufficient for her is her time. [If] she [again] missed three periods and saw a drop of blood, [still] sufficient for her is her time. [If] she [again] missed three periods and saw a drop of blood, lo, she is equivalent to all other women. She imparts uncleanness for the preceding twenty-four hours or from one examination to the next. Not [only] that she has settled on a fixed period, but even if she has diminished, [or] she has added to it. [If] she missed three of them and saw a drop of blood, sufficient for her is her time. [If] she [again] missed the three of them and saw a drop of blood, sufficient for her is her time. [If] she [again] missed the three of them and saw a drop of blood, lo she is like all other women and conveys uncleanness for the preceding twenty-four hour period or from one examination to the next. But that she has established a period. for herself.

T. 1:12 The four women concerning whom they have said, Sufficient for them is their time — how so? [If] she saw a blood stain and afterward saw a drop of blood — sufficient for her is her time. [If] she missed three periods between one appearance and another appearance of blood and did not see a drop of blood and afterward saw a drop of blood — sufficient for her is her time. [If] she missed three periods during the days of her purifying and did not see a drop of blood, and afterward saw a drop of blood, sufficient for her is her time.

T. 2:4 A woman is obligated to care for her child for twenty-four months. The same rule applies both to her child and to one that is given her as a son to suckle. The woman to whom a son is given to suckle should not do [additional] work [while caring] for him and should not suckle another child with him.

T. 2:5 An infant who recognizes his mother — they do not give him to a wet-nurse because of the danger to life. An infant sucks from the gentile woman and from the unclean cow, and from any of them does he suck, and even on the Sabbath. [If] he was weaned, it is prohibited.

T. 2:6 Three kinds of women have intercourse with a contraceptive device: a girl under age, a pregnant woman, and a nursing mother. A girl under age — lest she become pregnant and die. What is a girl under age? From eleven years and one day until twelve years and one day. One younger than that or older than that — one has intercourse in the normal way. Therefore one has intercourse in the normal way and does not scruple. A pregnant woman — lest she make the fetus into a sandal. A nursing mother — lest she kill her infant.

T. 2:7 A man should not marry a woman made pregnant by his fellow or one who is nursing the child of his fellow, as it is said, "Do not remove an ancient landmark or enter the fields of the fatherless" [Prov. 23:10].

M. 1:6 And of what case did they speak when they said, "Sufficient for her is her time"? Of the case of the first appearance of a drop of blood. But in the case of the second appearance of such a drop of blood, she conveys uncleanness to whatever she touched during the preceding twenty-four hours. But if she saw the first flow by reason of constraint [through abnormal causes], even in the case of the second drop of blood, sufficient for her is her time.

T. 1:3 A tumtom [one whose sex is unknown] and an androgyne who saw [a drop of blood] — sufficient for them is their time. A female proselyte who saw a drop of blood for the first time, sufficient for her is the time [at which she saw the drop of blood]. And she who sees a drop of blood [caused] abnormally — sufficient for her is her time.

T. 1:4 What is a case of seeing a drop of blood caused abnormally? 1. [If] she was sick and saw a drop of blood — 2. [If] she jumped and saw a drop of blood — 3. [If] her husband hit her and she saw a drop of blood — 4. [If] she was bearing a heavy burden and saw a drop of blood — — this is a matter of an abnormal cause. And what is the sort of case for which her time is sufficient? [If] she sat down on a bed and on a chair and on a bench and was engaged in preparing things requiring cleanness and had intercourse and then got up and saw a drop of blood — he [the husband] is clean, and the things requiring cleanness are clean.

M. 1:7 Even though they have said, "Sufficient for her is her time," (1) she must nonetheless examine herself, except for (a) the menstruating woman, and (b) the woman who is sitting in the blood of her purifying [after having given birth]. And (2) she makes use of test rags, except for (a) the one who is sitting in the blood of her purifying, and (b) a virgin, whose drops of blood are clean. And (3) twice must she [who has a fixed period] examine herself: (a) in the morning and (b) at twilight, and (c) when she prepares for sexual relations. Beyond these examinations, women of the priestly caste [must examine themselves] when they eat heave offering.

M. 2:1 Any hand which makes many examinations — in the case of women is to be praised and in the case of men is to be cut off. The [woman who is] a deaf-mute, and imbecile, or blind, or a woman who is deranged — if there are women of sound

senses, they care for them, and they eat heave offering. It is the way of Israelite women to make use of two test rags, one for him and one for her. The pious prepare yet a third, to take care of the house.

T. 2:8 Any hand which makes many examinations — in the case of women is to be praised; in the case of men is to be cut off. Under what circumstances? With reference to seminal emission But if it is with reference to flux — Any hand which makes many examinations, lo, it is to be praised.

T. 2:9 An imbecile [male] — they dunk him and feed him with heave offering [food] in the evening. And they watch him as to sleeping, and if he went to sleep and got up, he is forthwith unclean. put it on him and inspect its contents. If inside it semen is found, he is unclean, and if not, he is clean.

M. 2:2 If it [a drop of blood] is found on his, they are unclean and liable for a sacrifice. If it is found on hers at the time itself, they are unclean [for seven days] and liable for a sacrifice. If it is found on hers after a while, their uncleanness remains in doubt, and they are exempt from an offering.

M. 2:3 What is meant by "after a while"? Sufficient time that the woman may descend from the bed and wash her face [sexual organs]. And afterward [if a drop of blood appears], she imparts uncleanness [to objects she touched] during the preceding twenty-four-hour period but does not impart uncleanness [as a menstruant for seven days] to him who has had sexual relations with her. She imparts uncleanness to him who has sexual relations with her in the case of one who sees a bloodstain, that she imparts uncleanness to him who has sexual relations with her.

T. 3:1 All the women concerning whom sages have said, 'Sufficient for them is their time' — their blood stain is like their appearance [of blood], and a minor who is apt to see blood is subject to the rule of blood stains.

T. 3:2 Every woman who has a fixed period — her blood stain imparts uncleanness retroactively. For if she sees [blood] not at the time of her fixed period, it imparts uncleanness to objects she touched during the preceding twenty-four hours.

T. 3:5 Sometimes blood stains do put a woman into the category of one afflicted with flux, How so? [If] she puts on herself five shirts which had been examined by her, if she saw on them three drops [of blood] on three days, or [if] she saw a blood stain and afterward she saw two unclean days lo, this one takes account of the possibility of flux.' [As to the meaning of] "forthwith" they drew an analogy. To what is the matter compared? To the attendant and the witness who stood behind the lintel. Once the attendant went out, the witness forthwith entered. This is "forthwith."

T. 3:6 After a time of which they spoke — after the time sufficient for drying, and not after the time sufficient for examination. And what is the meaning of after a time? After sufficient time for the woman to get off the bed and wash her face.

T. 3:7 During this period, they are unclean as a matter of doubt and free of the obligation of a sacrifice [sin-offering] but liable for the suspensive guilt-offering.

T. 3:8 A pregnant woman and a nursing mother — the one who has intercourse with them is clean, and [so in the case of] any woman who has a fixed period. And all other women are unclean in respect to contact, and clean in respect to intercourse. Under what circumstances? When he left her clean. But if he left her unclean, lo, she remains in the presumption of being unclean, until she shall tell him, "I am clean for you."

M. 2:4 "All women are assumed to be clean for their husbands. Those that come home from a trip — their wives are assumed to be clean for them. It suffices for her [to make use of] two test rags for the entire night."

To Zabim, Niddah joins a systematic particularization of the established results of the stated hermeneutics of comparison and contrast. Just as, in addition to its power of generalization, Zabim has take up the particulars having to do with the Zab and Zabah, so in the same context, Niddah does the same for the menstrual uncleanness. Having no occasion to invoke the particular hermeneutics, the framers of the category-formation (or, as I should prefer, the other principal component of the category-formation) relied upon generic hermeneutics for their exegetical program. The best comes first: the problem of doubt as to when a woman's period has begun, therefore the status of objects she has touched in the period beginning with the last point at which she knew she was clean and ending with the first point at which she knew she was unclean. Essentially, we aim to confirm the status quo; the comparison of the present classification of doubt with the counterpart, the status of the woman accused of adultery, is undertaken in the Bavli's analysis of the matter, a most imaginative exercise. While the exegetical problems are elaborately worked out, the basic principles present no complexities whatsoever, a mark of the workings of the generic hermeneutics.

II. UNCLEAN EXCRETIONS

A. *UNCLEAN BLOOD*

M. 2:5 The sages made a parable in connection with the woman: (1) the room, (2) the front hall, and (3) the room upstairs. Blood in the room is unclean. If it is found in the front hall, a matter of doubt concerning it is deemed unclean, since it is assumed to come from the fountain [uterus].

T. 3:9 Blood which is found in the front-hall — they burn heave-offering on its account and are liable on its account for contamination of the sanctuary and its holy things. That which exudes from the room — if it is known that it is blood caused by a blow, it is clean, and if not, it is unclean. [If] it is in doubt whether it is blood of the room or blood caused by a blow, it is unclean.

T. 3:10 It comes out that one rules, there are three matters of doubt concerning a woman. As to [a blood stain on] her flesh, if it is in doubt whether it is clean or unclean, it is unclean. And as to [a blood stain on] her clothing, if it is a matter of doubt whether it is unclean or clean, it is clean. And as to matters of contact and shifting, they follow the majority.

M. 2:6 Five [colors of] blood are unclean in a woman: (1) red, and (2) black, and (3) bright crocus color, and (4) [blood] which is like water mixed with earth, and (5) [blood which is] like water mixed with wine. [Blood which is] yellow — sages declare clean.

M. 2:7 What is the red [color]? Like the blood of a wound. Black? Like ink sediment. If it is deeper than this, it is unclean, but if it is lighter than this, it is clean. And bright crocus color? Like the brightest shade in it. Like earthy water? [A color like that produced when] over dirt from the valley of Bet Kerem water is made to float. [A color] like water mixed with wine? Two parts of water, and one part of wine — [making use of] wine of Sharon.

T. 3:11 Black as ink sediment — [if] it is deeper than this, it is unclean [if] it is lighter than this, even like stibium, it is clean. Not that from the beginning of its formation it [black blood] was black, but when it was discharged, it turned black. To what is the matter comparable? To the blood caused by a blow. [For] once it begins to flow, it turns black. Bright crocus color — Like the bright color which is on top, and not on the bottom, on a wet one, and not on a dry one; as one examines it in the shade, and not as one examines it in sunlight. [As to dirt] which is like them: They examine them when they are turbid, and they do not examine them when they are clear. [If] they became clear, they do not go and make them turbid a second time, for there is no limit to water and dirt. Like water mixed with wine: Two parts water, and one part wine, from the wine of the Sharon — Similar to that of the Carmel, new and not old.

Since the Halakhah differentiates among types of vaginal excretions, unclean as menstrual blood forming only one type, the taxonomic process has to do the work of classification and hierarchization.

B. *THE STATUS OF ABORTIONS AS TO UNCLEANNESS*

M. 3:1 She who produces a piece [a shapeless object] — if there is blood with it, she is unclean, and if not, she is clean.

T. 4:1 She who produces a piece [a shapeless object] — they cut it open. If there is blood in side it, lo, this one is a menstruate. If not, she is not a menstruate.

M. 3:2 She who produces [an abortion] like a rind, like a hair, like dust, like red flies — let her put them into water. If they dissolve [into blood], she is unclean [as a menstruant], and if not she is clean. She who produces [an abortion] like fish, locusts, insects, and creeping things — if there is blood with them, she is unclean. And if not, she is clean. She who produces [an abortion] like a beast, wild animal, or bird, whether unclean or clean — anything which does not bear [some aspect] of the human form is not deemed a foetus.

T. 4:2 She who produces [an abortion] like a rind, like a hair, like dust, like red flies — they crush it, together with spit, on the fingernail. If it dissolves, lo, this one is a menstruant, and if not, she is not deemed a menstruant.

M. 3:3 She who aborts a sac filled with water, filled with blood, filled with dry matter [matter of various colors], does not take into consideration the possibility that this is a valid birth. But if [a limb] had formed, let her sit [out the days of uncleanness and cleanness] for both male and female.

T. 4:10 The umbilical cord is a connector in man, up to handbreadth, to receive uncleanness and to impart uncleanness. But in a beast, it is not a connector. A caul which goes forth over the skin of the flesh of man, whether alive or dead, lo, this is clean and permitted for enjoyment. And what is a sac, the limbs of which are formed?

T. 4:11 They do not estimate it [the fetus] with water, because the water is hard and disturbs its shape. And they estimate it only in oil, because the oil is soft and makes it clear. And they examine it only in sunlight.

T. 4:12 She who produces an abortion which was not formed — it is not a valid birth.

M. 3:4 She who aborts [an abortion shaped like] a sandal or a placenta — let her sit [out the days of uncleanness and cleanness] for both male and female. [If] there is a placenta in a house, the house is unclean. Not that the placenta is the child, but because there is no placenta which does not contain part of the child.

T. 4:7 The facial features of which they spoke may be any one of the features of the face except for the ears. The sandal of which they spoke is similar to the sandal, a fish in the sea.

T. 4:8 And why did they say, A sandal? Is it not so that there is no sandal with which there also is not a bit of embryo? [But they have so ruled because of the] possibility that she will produce with it a male and so be in disarray in respect to a female. Or [because of the] possibility that she will produce two, one [a female child] before sunset and one [the sandal] after sunset, and it will turn out that she counts the beginning of her period of menstruation in accordance with the first and the beginning of her period of menstruation in accordance with the second.

T. 4:9 The placenta of which they spoke — in its first stage it is like the thread of the warp, and its head is like a lupine, and it is hollow like a trumpet. And there is no placenta less in size than a handbreadth. And why did they refer to a placenta? And is it not so that there is no placenta without a bit of the child with it.

M. 3:5 She who produces a *tumtom* [an offspring without discernible sexual characteristics] or an androgyne [an offspring with the traits of both sexes] — let her sit [out the days of uncleanness and cleanness] for both male and female. [If she bore twins,] a *tumtom* and a male child, an androgyne and a male child — let her sit [out the days of uncleanness] for both male and female. [If she bore] a *tumtom* and a female, an androgyne and a female — let her sit [out the days of uncleanness] for a female only. [If] it emerged in pieces or feet foremost — once the greater part of it has gone forth, lo, it is as if it were fully born. [If] it came forth in the normal way, [it is not deemed born] until the greater part of its head has come forth. And what is the greater part of its head? Once its forehead has come forth.

T. 4:14 [If] it came out in pieces or feet foremost, it is not deemed a foetus, until the greater part of it will emerge. If it emerged in the normal way before its greater part emerged. And what is the greater part of its head. This is its forehead.

T. 4:15 She who aborts a creature with a body which is not shaped or a creature with a head which is not shaped — it is not a viable birth. [If it has] a hand which is shaped or a foot which is shaped, lo, this is a viable birth. [If it has] a hand which is unshaped or a foot which is unshaped, it is not a viable birth. [If it has] a body which is unshaped, it is not a viable birth. What is a body which is unshaped? [One lacking a part] that one may take from the living person and he would survive — lo this is a viable birth. [One lacking a part that one may take] from the living person and he would die — lo, this is not a viable birth.

B. 3:5 I.3/28B A *TUMTOM* OR AN ANDROGYNE THAT PRODUCED A DROP OF WHITE EXCRETION OR A DROP OF RED EXCRETION — NEITHER IS LIABLE ON ACCOUNT OF ENTERING THE TEMPLE [SINCE THEY ARE NOT DEEMED UNCLEAN, E.G., BY REASON OF THE ZIBAH-UNCLEANNESS DESCRIBED AT LEV. 15 OR BY REASON OF MENSTRUATION], NOR ON THEIR ACCOUNT DO THEY BURN PRIESTLY RATIONS [THAT THEY MAY HAVE TOUCHED AFTER PRODUCING THE EXCRETION]. IF, HOWEVER, THEY SHOULD PRODUCE A DROP OF WHITE EXCRETION AND OF RED SIMULTANEOUSLY, WHILE THEY STILL ARE NOT LIABLE FOR ENTERING THE TEMPLE, THEY DO ON THEIR ACCOUNT BURN PRIESTLY RATIONS THAT THEY HAVE TOUCHED.

M. 3:6 She who aborts and what it is not known [masculine or feminine] — let her sit [out the days of uncleanness and cleanness] for both male and female. [If] it is not known whether or not it was a human foetus, let her sit [out the days of uncleanness and cleanness] for a male and for female and also for menstruation.

T. 4:16 She who aborts and it is not known what it is [male or female] — let her sit out [the days of uncleanness and cleanness] for a male and for a female and for menstruation. And why have they said [that she should be unclean] as a menstruating woman? That if she should see blood on the thirty-fourth day, [and if] she should go back and see it on the forty-first day, she should turn out to count the beginning of her menstrual period from the first and the beginning of her menstrual cycle from the last [such appearance]. And why did they say a [she should sit out the days of uncleanness and cleanness of a] female? That if she should see blood on the seventy-fourth day and she should see blood on the eighty-first day, she should turn out to count the beginning of her menstrual period from the first and the beginning of her menstrual period from the last [such appearance].

M. 3:7 She who miscarries on the fortieth day does not take account of the possibility that it is a human foetus. [If this takes place] on the forty-first day [after intercourse], however, [she does take account of that possibility, and so] let her sit [out the days of uncleanness] for a male, for a female, and for menstruation. All the same is the process of the formation of the male and female — both are completed on the forty-first day.

Having defined the norm, we now address the interstitial classification: abortions in various conditions. Has the woman produced a valid offspring, in which case the rules of Lev. 12 take over? And then we have to determine whether the offspring is male or female. Or is it menstrual blood, in which case she is unclean? Or is it blood of a clean order, e.g., internal bleeding, in which case she is clean? The cases sort out the issues of interstitiality consequent upon the definitions given earlier.

C. *SAMARITAN, SADDUCEE, AND GENTILE WOMEN*

M. 4:1 Samaritan women are deemed menstruants from their cradle. And Samaritans convey uncleanness to a couch beneath as to a cover above, because [by the Israelite method of reckoning the period of menstrual uncleanness] they have intercourse with menstruating women, and continue unclean for any sort of blood [not differentiating unclean from clean]. But those [who have contact] with them are not liable for entering the sanctuary and do not burn heave offering on their account, because the uncleanness affecting them is a matter of doubt.

T. 5:1 Samaritan women from their cradle are deemed menstruants. And Samaritans convey uncleanness to a [couch] beneath as to [a cover] above, because they have intercourse with menstruating women, for they [Samaritan women] continue unclean [for seven days] for any sort of blood — a day on which she is clean, she counts among the seven.

M. 4:2 When Sadducean women are accustomed to follow in the way of their fathers, lo, they are like Samaritan women. [If] they left [those ways] to walk in the ways of Israel, lo, they are like Israel.

T. 5:2 Sadducean women, when they are accustomed to follow in the ways of their fathers, lo, they are like Samaritans. [If] they left [those ways to walk] in the ways of Israel, lo, they are like Israel[ites].

T. 5:4 Israelite girls, when they are minors, before they have reached the age of puberty, lo, they are assumed to be clean, and the women do not examine them. When they have reached the age of puberty, lo, they are assumed to be clean, but the women do examine them.

M. 4:3 The blood of a gentile woman, and the blood of purifying of a woman with *sara'at* [the skin ailment of Lev. 13] — it is in the classification of her spit and urine [which convey uncleanness when wet but not when dried up]. The blood of a woman who has not immersed after childbirth — it imparts uncleanness wet and dry. A woman who has given birth while in the status of one who has a flux, — it [her spit and her urine] conveys

uncleanness whether wet or dry.

Samaritans and Sadducees constitute interstitial classes of another order. The former keep the laws of the Torah in writing, but this they do not correctly interpret; only "Israel" does, meaning, the Israel guided by sages' traditions in the interpretation of the Torah. The particular point at issue is whether some vaginal excretions are clean, as sages maintain, hence the place of the composition. Sadducean women are treated as analogous.

D. *STATUS OF BLOOD PRODUCED IN LABOR*

M. 4:4 A woman in labor is deemed to be a menstruant. [If] a woman was in hard travail for three days during the eleven days, and [if] she enjoyed a respite for twenty-four hours and [then] gave birth lo, this one is one who has given birth as a Zabah [while in the status of one who has a flux]. For she has had relief from the pain and not from the blood.

T. 5:7 A woman in protracted labor — for how long should she have respite [so that blood appearing thereafter indicates that] she is a Zabah? Twenty-four hours.

T. 5:8 She who is in labor before giving birth, lo, she is deemed a menstruant. [If] during the eleven days [of Zibah] she was in hard labor and had respite for one day, labor for one day and respite for two days, respite for one day and hard labor for one day and respite for one day — she gives birth in the status of a Zabah. [If] she had respite for two days and was in labor for one day, respite for one day and labor for two days, labor for one day and respite for one day, and labor for one day — she has not given birth as a Zabah. This is the general rule: [When] the respite comes immediately before the childbirth, she gives birth as a Zabah. [If] the labor is immediately before the childbirth, she does not give birth as a Zabah. [If] she had labor for two days and had respite for one, even though she went and had hard labor afterward, she gives birth as a Zabah.

T. 5:10 There can be a case in which a woman is in hard labor for twenty five days and not be a Zabah. How so? Two not at her time, and seven of menstruation, and two after her [menstrual] period, fourteen days which giving birth to a female child [causes to be clean] . But it is not possible for her to be in labor twenty-six days. Where there is no child, she gives birth as a Zabah.

T. 5:11 There can be a case of a woman who sees blood on a hundred days and is not deemed a Zabah on their account: Two not at her time, and seven during her menstrual period, and two after her menstrual period, and eighty after having given birth to a female, and seven during her menstrual cycle and two after her menstrual period.

T. 5:12 [If] she was in labor for three days, one after another, she is prohibited to her house [to have intercourse] and forbidden to eat heave offering. [If] one was in the assumption of being pregnant and went into labor and afterward aborted something which is not a viable birth, she has given birth as a Zabah. She who went into hard labor, and it [the baby] went forth by way of her side, has given birth in the status of a Zabah. The blood which goes forth from there is unclean.

M. 4:6 She who is in protracted labor during the eighty days [of cleanness] after the birth of a female — any blood which she sees is clean, until the child emerges.

The exposition of interstitial issues moves on to the status of the blood produced by a woman in labor, as distinct from that that is produced after the birth of the child. It is menstrual, but then it may be Zob, and each produces its own consequences.

E. *STATUS OF BLOOD PRODUCED IN THE ZIBAH-PERIOD*

M. 4:7 All the eleven days that follow the seven days of menstruation] a woman is in the assumption of being clean. [If] she sat down and did not examine herself accidentally, under constraint, [or if] willfully she did not examine herself, she is clean. [Once] the time of her period has come and she has not examined herself, lo, this one is deemed unclean. But during the [seven clean] days [that must be counted by the] man or woman that has a flux, or [the one day of cleanness to be counted] by her that awaits day against day — [during that time,] lo, these are in the assumption of being unclean.

The division of vaginal blood between the seven days in which the blood is menstrual and the eleven following in which the blood is Zob is defined.

F. *STATUS OF BLOOD PRODUCED IN A CAESAREAN SECTION*

M. 5:1 As to that which goes forth from the side [delivered by Caesarian section] — they do not sit out the days of uncleanness and the days of cleanness on its account. And they are not liable for an offering [of childbirth].

M. 5:1-2 "All women impart uncleanness [by reason of blood] in the outer house, as it is said, "And her issue [even while still] in her flesh will be unclean [blood]" (Lev. 15:19)." But the Zab and the one who has had an emission do not impart unclean-

ness until their uncleanness will [actually] come forth [through ejaculation]. [If] one was eating heave offering and felt his limbs tremble, he holds on to the penis and swallows the heave offering. And they are made unclean by any amount [of discharge] at all, even though it is like a grain of mustard, and less than that.

T. 5:13 She who ejects semen — [if it is] on the inside — it [the semen] is unclean .

B. 5:1-2 III.1/42A A MENSTRUANT [AFTER SHE HAS PRODUCED BLOOD ONE TIME DURING HER MENSTRUAL DAYS], A WOMAN AFFLICTED BY FLUX-UNCLEANNESS, A WOMAN WHO HAS HAD A SINGLE FLUX AND COUNTS DAY AGAINST DAY [SO THAT IF SHE COUNTS A CLEAN DAY FOR THE UNCLEAN ONE, SHE IS THEN CLEAN] AND A WOMAN AFTER CHILDBIRTH ALL IMPART UNCLEANNESS INTERNALLY [AS SOON AS THE DISCHARGE HAS MADE ITS WAY INTO THE VAGINA] AS WELL AS EXTERNALLY.

Interstitiality meets its outer limit: blood that is not vaginal, but that is produced in a circumstance analogous to that which is, is null, M. 5:1.

III. RULES APPLICABLE AT VARIOUS AGES

M. 5:3 A girl one day old [who sees a drop of blood] (1) is made unclean as a menstruant. A girl ten days old [who passed the first seven days as a menstruant and then had a flow on the next three consecutive days] (2) becomes unclean through Zibah. A boy one day old (3) becomes unclean through Zibah, (4) becomes unclean through plagues, (5) becomes unclean through corpse uncleanness. And he imposes the requirement of levirate marriage, frees [a sister-in-law] from the requirement of levirate marriage, makes it permissible for one to eat heave offering, makes it impermissible for one to eat heave offering, inherits, and causes to inherit. And he who kills him is liable. And lo, he is like his father and his mother and all his relatives as a full bridegroom.

M. 5:4 A girl three years and one day old is betrothed by intercourse. And if a levir has had intercourse with her, he has acquired her. And they are liable on her account because of the law [prohibiting intercourse with] a married woman. And she imparts uncleanness to him who has intercourse with her [when she is menstruating] to convey uncleanness to the lower as to the upper layer. [If] she was married to a priest, she eats heave offering. [If] one of those who are unfit [for marriage] has intercourse with her, he has rendered her unfit to marry into the priesthood. [If] one of all those who are forbidden in the Torah to have inter-

course with her did so, they are put to death on her account. But she is free of responsibility. [If] she is younger than that [age], [intercourse with her] is like putting a finger in the eye.

M. 5:5 A boy nine years and one day old who had intercourse with his deceased childless brother's widow has acquired her. But he does not give her a writ of divorce until he comes of age. And he is made unclean by a menstruating woman, to convey uncleanness to the lower as to the upper layer. And he disqualifies a priest's daughter from eating priestly rations, but [if he was a priest, by his act of sexual relations, he] does not render [a woman] qualified to eat heave offering. And [by an act of bestiality] he spoils a beast for use on the altar. And it is stoned on his account. And if he had intercourse with any of all the prohibited relationships stated in the Torah, they are put to death on his account. But he is free of responsibility.

T. 5:14 A girl one day old may be a menstruant.

T. 6:1 An Ammonite, Moabite, Egyptian, Edomite, Samaritan, Netin, or Mamzer, [all] at the age of nine years and one day, who had intercourse with the daughter of a priest, Levite, and Israelite has rendered her unfit for marriage to the priesthood.

T. 6:2 A boy nine years and one day old who produced two hairs — it is a mole. A boy nine years and one day old and up to twelve years and one day old who produced two pubic hairs — it is a mole. [A boy] from twelve years and one day old and up to thirteen years and one day old who produced two pubic hairs, lo, he is equivalent to a man in. every respect. A boy fourteen years and fifteen years old who has not produced two pubic hairs, lo, he is like a boy nine years and one day old in every respect. A boy twenty years old who has not produced two pubic hairs, even though he produces them thereafter, lo, he is like a eunuch in every respect. A girl twenty years old who has not produced two pubic hairs, even though she produced them thereafter, lo, she is treated as sterile in all respects.

B. 5:5 1:1/45A THE LAW HAS TREATED AS EQUIVALENT THE ACT OF SEXUAL RELATIONS OF A BOY NINE YEARS OLD AND AN ACT OF BESPEAKING [IN WHICH A DECEASED CHILDLESS WIDOW'S BROTHER DECLARES HIS INTENT OF CONSUMMATING THE LEVIRATE MARRIAGE WITH THE WIDOW] IN THE CASE OF AN ADULT. JUST AS AN ACT OF BESPEAKING IN THE CASE OF AN ADULT NECESSITATES A WRITE OF DIVORCE IN RESPECT TO HIS ACT OF BESPEAKING AND THE RITE OF REMOVING THE SHOE IN REGARD TO THE MARITAL BOND THAT IS PRESENT BY REASON OF THE LEVIRATE CONNECTION, SO IN THE CASE OF A BOY NINE YEARS OLD WHO HAS HAD SEXUAL RELATIONS, AN ACT OF BESPEAKING NECESSITATES A WRIT OF DIVORCE IN RESPECT TO HIS ACT OF BESPEAKING AND THE RITE OF REMOVING THE SHOE IN REGARD

TO THE MARITAL BOND THAT IS PRESENT BY REASON OF THE LEVIRATE CONNECTION.

M. 5:6 A girl eleven years and one day old — her vows are examined. A girl twelve years and one day old — her vows are confirmed. And they examine throughout the twelfth year. A boy eleven years and one day old — his vows are examined. A boy thirteen years and one day old — his vows are confirmed. And they examine through the thirteenth year. Before this time, even though they have said, "We know before Whom we have vowed," "for Whose [sanctity] we have sanctified" — their vows are not vows, and that which they have sanctified is deemed not sanctified. After this time, even though they said, "We do not know before Whom we have vowed," "for Whose [sanctity] we have sanctified" — their vow is a vow, and that which they have sanctified is deemed sanctified.

T. 5:15 During the period in which the son and daughter are interrogated, even though [better: if] they said, "[We know] to Whom we have taken a vow, and to Whom we have sanctified an object," their vows are vows, and [things subject to] their acts of sanctification are deemed sanctified.

M. 5:7 Sages have made a parable in regard to the woman: (1) an unripe fig, (2) a ripening fig, and (3) a fully ripe fig. An unripe fig — she is still a little girl. And a ripening fig — these are the days of her girlhood. In both periods her father is entitled to keep as his own whatever she finds and to retain her wages and to annul her vows. A fully ripe fig — once she has grown up, her father has no further right over her.

M. 5:9 A girl twenty years old who has not produced two pubic hairs — let her bring evidence that she is twenty years old and she is then declared sterile: she does not perform the act of *halisah* [removing the shoe to sever a levirate connection] and does not enter into levirate marriage. A boy twenty years old who has not produced two pubic hairs — let him bring evidence that he is twenty years old, and he is declared a eunuch.

M. 6:1 [If] the token [of puberty] below appeared before that above, [the girl] either carries out the rite of removing the shoe to abrogate a levirate connection [*halisah*] or she actually enters levirate marriage. [If] the upper token appeared before the lower one, even though it is not possible [for the upper to appear before the lower] — she either carries out the rite of *halisah* or enters into levirate marriage. Because they have said, "It is possible for the lower token to appear before the upper one appears, but it is not possible for the upper one to appear before the lower one appears."

T. 6:10 Whatever imparts uncleanness in the Tent imparts uncleanness lasting seven days, but there is that which imparts uncleanness which lasts for seven days but does not impart uncleanness in the Tent. Whatever has horns has hooves, and there is that which has hooves and does not have horns. Whoever has the right to take charity has the right to take the tithe of the poor, and there is that one who takes the tithe of the poor and does not take charity.

M. 6:11 A girl who has produced two pubic hairs [after twelve years and one day] either performs the rite of *halisah* or enters into levirate marriage, and she is liable for all the commandments which are stated in the Torah. And so a boy who has produced two pubic hairs is liable for all the commandments which are stated in the Torah. And he is appropriate to be subjected to the law of the rebellious son from the time that he produces two hairs until he has grown an encircling beard — (the lower and not the upper [is meant], but the sages spoke in chaste language). A girl who has produced two pubic hairs no longer is able to exercise the right of refusal.

T. 6:7 The two pubic hairs of which they spoke [establish puberty] even [if] one is on the hand and one on the foot, one in the armpit and one in the loin, even two between two joints of his fingers — lo, these join together.

T. 6:8 All those who are inspected are inspected only by women. A woman is permitted to testify in such wise as to impose a stringent ruling but not to impose a lenient ruling. A woman is permitted to testify, "She is a minor," so that she should not carry out the rite of halisah. And "she is an adult," so that she should not exercise the right of refusal. But she is not permitted to testify, saying, "She is a minor," so that the girl may exercise the right of refusal, or, "She is an adult," so that she may carry out the rite of halisah.

The definition of unclean excretions continues with a large exposition of definitive facts. I see no point at which the particular hermeneutics enters in. As children grow up, the pass from one unambiguous status to another, but en route, through an interstitial condition: neither fully minor nor completely mature. That is what is spelled out here. This is another text-book case of the workings of the generic hermeneutics, many of its archetypal problems finding exemplification here.

IV. DOUBTS IN CONNECTION WITH UNCLEAN EXCRETIONS

A. *BLOODSTAINS AND OTHER MATTERS SUBJECT TO DOUBT*

M. 6:13 She who sees a bloodstain [on her garment] — lo, she is in disarray. Bloodstains are not subject [to the law of uncleanness] because of Zibah-flux.

M. 6:14 She who sees [blood] — [1] on the eleventh day at twilight, [2] at the beginning of her menstrual period, [3] or at the end of her menstrual period, [4] at the beginning of her period of [those days on which the appearance of blood is classified as the blood of flux, or Zibah, and not as menstrual blood], [5] or at the end of the period of [those days on which the appearance of blood is classified as the blood of flux, or Zibah, and not as menstrual blood], [6] on the fortieth day [of cleanness] for the male child, [7] or on the eightieth day of cleanness of the female child — at twilight in [the case of] all of them — lo, these err.

B. 6:14 II.1/54A IF A WOMAN IS UNCLEAN ON ONE DAY AND CLEAN ON THE NEXT [WITH NO DISCHARGE AT NIGHT], SHE MAY HAVE SEXUAL RELATIONS ON THE EIGHTH DAY, [COUNTING FROM THE ONE ON WHICH HER FIRST DISCHARGE TOOK PLACE; ON THE EIGHTH DAY HER CLEANNESS IS ESTABLISHED BEYOND DOUBT, SINCE HER UNCLEAN PERIOD OF MENSTRUATION ENDED WITH THE SEVENTH, AND THE EIGHTH DAY IS ONE OF HER ALTERNATE, CLEAN DAYS], AND WITH ITS NIGHT WITH IT [SINCE SHE PRODUCES NO BLOOD BY NIGHT]. AND ALSO ON FOUR NIGHTS OUT OF EVERY EIGHTEEN DAYS [AGAIN COUNTING FROM THE DAY OF THE FIRST DISCHARGE. AS SHE NEVER DISCHARGES ON THREE CONSECUTIVE DAYS, SHE CAN NEVER BECOME UNCLEAN AS CONFIRMED WITH FLUX-UNCLEANNESS, WHICH WOULD REQUIRE SEVEN CLEAN DAYS TO PASS. WHEN SHE DISCHARGES ON THE NINTH DAY, ONE OF THE ALTERNATIVE UNCLEAN DAYS, AS A PERSON AFFLICTED WITH MINOR FLUX UNCLEANNESS, HAVING HAD A DISCHARGE ON ONE OF THE ELEVEN DAYS IN WHICH THE APPEARANCE OF BLOOD IS CLASSIFIED AS FLUX, SHE HAS TO ALLOW A CLEAN DAY TO PASS, WHICH IS THE TENTH, AND SHE MAY HAVE SEXUAL RELATIONS ON THE NIGHT FOLLOWING. THEN IF THERE IS A DISCHARGE ON THE ELEVENTH DAY, ONE OF THE ALTERNATE UNCLEAN DAYS, SHE ALLOWS THE TWELFTH DAY TO PASS, AND HAS SEXUAL RELATIONS ON THE FOLLOWING NIGHT, AND SO TOO WITH THE FOURTEENTH AND THE SIXTEENTH. SO WHEN EIGHTEEN DAYS HAVE PASSED, WITH THE SUNSET OF THE EIGHTEENTH DAY, SHE HAS IN ADDITION TO THE EIGHTH DAY AND NIGHT FOLLOWING IT THE FOUR NIGHTS THAT FOLLOW THE TENTH, TWELFTH, FOURTEENTH, AND SIXTEENTH DAYS, RESPECTIVELY. THE NIGHT FOLLOWING THE EIGHTEENTH DAY IS

AGAIN ONE IN WHICH PERFORMANCE OF SEXUAL RELATIONS IS ALLOWED, BUT IT BELONGS TO THE NEXT CYCLE.] IF, HOWEVER, SHE PRODUCED BLOOD BY NIGHT, SHE MAY HAVE SEXUAL RELATIONS ONLY ON THE EIGHTH DAY ALONE. [SHE HAS SEXUAL RELATIONS ON THE EIGHTH DAY AFTER HER FIRST DISCHARGE. ON THE DAY SHE IS DEFINITELY CLEAN, SINCE HER DISCHARGE DOES NOT APPEAR UNTIL EVENING. THE PREVIOUS NIGHT SHE IS CLEAN, SINCE WITH THE DAY PRECEDING IT, THE SEVENTH, HER UNCLEAN, MENSTRUAL PERIOD HAD ENDED. DURING THE FIRST SEVEN DAYS THEN SHE IS UNCLEAN AS A MENSTRUANT, AND IN THE NIGHT FOLLOWING THE EIGHTH, ONE OF THE ALTERNATIVE, UNCLEAN NIGHTS, SHE IS UNCLEAN WITH A MINOR FLUX-UNCLEANNESS, AND MUST ALLOW ONE DAY, THE NINTH, TO PASS. ON THE NIGHT FOLLOWING THE NINTH, ANOTHER OF THE ALTERNATE UNCLEAN NIGHTS, SHE IS AGAIN UNCLEAN WITH A MINOR FLUX-UNCLEANNESS, SO SHE HAS TO ALLOW A DAY TO PASS, THE TENTH, AND SO TO THE END OF EIGHTEEN DAYS, WHEN A NEW CYCLE OF THE SAME NUMBER OF DAYS BEGINS, IN WHICH SHE IS ALLOWED MARITAL RELATIONS ON THE EIGHTH DAY AND THE NIGHT PRECEDING IT ONLY.] IF THE PATTERN INVOLVES TWO DAYS AS UNCLEAN FOLLOWED BY TWO DAYS AS CLEAN, SHE HAS SEXUAL RELATIONS ON THE EIGHTH DAY, THE TWELFTH, THE SIXTEENTH, AND THE TWENTIETH. IF THE WOMAN IS UNCLEAN FOR THREE DAYS AND CLEAN FOR THREE DAYS, SHE HAS SEXUAL RELATIONS FOR TWO DAYS, AND THEN SHE DOES NOT HAVE SEXUAL RELATIONS ANY MORE DURING A GIVEN CYCLE]. [AFTER THE TWELFTH DAY SHE WILL NOT ATTAIN CLEANNESS. THE THIRTEENTH, FOURTEENTH, AND FIFTEENTH, THREE OF THE ALTERNATIVE THREE UNCLEAN DAYS, WILL BE UNCLEAN DAYS WITHIN HER ZIBAH-PERIOD THAT SUBJECT HER TO THE RESTRICTIONS OF MAJOR FLUX-UNCLEANNESS, SO SHE MUST HAVE SEVEN CLEAN DAYS, BUT WITH THE ALTERNATIVE UNCLEAN DAYS, SHE WILL NOT HAVE A FULL PERIOD OF SEVEN CLEAN DAYS]. IF SHE HAS FOUR UNCLEAN DAYS AND FOUR CLEAN DAYS IN ALTERNATION, SHE MAY HAVE SEXUAL RELATIONS ON ONE DAY, AND THEN SHE DOES NOT HAVE SEXUAL RELATIONS ANY MORE DURING A GIVEN CYCLE]. IF SHE HAS FIVE UNCLEAN DAYS AND FIVE CLEAN DAYS, SHE HAS SEXUAL RELATIONS FOR THREE DAYS, AND THEN SHE DOES NOT HAVE SEXUAL RELATIONS ANY MORE DURING A GIVEN CYCLE]. IF SHE HAS SIX UNCLEAN DAYS AND SIX CLEAN DAYS, SHE MAY HAVE SEXUAL RELATIONS FOR FIVE DAYS, AND THEN SHE DOES NOT HAVE SEXUAL RELATIONS ANY MORE DURING A GIVEN CYCLE]. IF SHE HAS SEVEN UNCLEAN DAYS AND SEVEN CLEAN DAYS, SHE MAY HAVE SEXUAL RELATIONS A QUARTER OUT OF EVERY TWENTY-EIGHT DAYS [SEVEN OUT OF TWENTY-EIGHT] [MADE UP AS FOLLOWS: SEVEN UNCLEAN DAYS OF MENSTRUATION, SEVEN DAYS OF CLEANNESS IN WHICH

SEXUAL RELATIONS ARE PERMITTED, SEVEN DAYS OF UNCLEANNESS AS CONFIRMED WITH FLUX-UNCLEANNESS, SEVEN CLEAN DAYS THAT MUST BE NOTED, AND SO WITH EACH CYCLE OF TWENTY-EIGHT DAYS]. IF SHE HAS EIGHT UNCLEAN DAYS AND EIGHT CLEAN DAYS, SHE HAS SEXUAL RELATIONS FOR FIFTEEN DAYS OUR OF EVERY FORTY-EIGHT.

Bloodstains may or may not represent menstrual blood; they do not stand for flux. The time at which a drop of blood appears may produce doubt, e.g., the time may not belong definitively either to the menstrual or to the Zibah-day, and the like.

B. *BLOOD OF MENSTRUATING WOMAN, FLESH OF A CORPSE*

M. 7:1 The blood of the menstruating woman and the flesh of a corpse impart uncleanness when they are wet, and (2) impart uncleanness when they are dry. But the [Zab's] flux, phlegm, spit, and the dead creeping thing, carrion, and semen (3) impart uncleanness when they are wet, and (4) do not impart uncleanness when they are dry. And if they can be soaked and return to their former condition, they (5) impart uncleanness when they are wet, and they (6) impart uncleanness when they are dry. And how long are they to be soaked? In lukewarm water, for twenty-four hours.

T. 6:11 The blood of a menstruating woman and the flesh of the corpse all these which became moldy — lo, they are clean.

The analogical-contrastive analysis of bodily sources of uncleanness, encompassing the lot of them, corpse-matter and menstrual blood and Zob and the dead creeping thing, carrion, and semen, yields a single category-formation, so far as the distinction between what is wet and what is dry.

C. *DOUBTS ABOUT CREEPING THINGS, BLOODSTAINS*

M. 7:2 The creeping thing which is found in the alleyway imparts uncleanness retroactively, until one will state "I inspected this alleyway and there was no creeping thing in it," or until the time that it [last] was cleaned. And so: a bloodstain which is found on a garment imparts uncleanness retroactively, until one will state, "I inspected this garment, and there was no bloodstain on it," or until such time as it was [last] washed. And it imparts uncleanness whether wet or dry.

T. 6:14 A spade which was stolen from the house — it [the house] is unclean retroactively, until one will state, "I inspected this place, and it was here."

We confirm the status quo, a familiar principle.

D. *BLOODSTAINS DOUBTFULLY-UNCLEAN BLOOD] OF ISRAELITES, GENTILES, AND SAMARITANS*

M. 7:3 All the bloodstains which come from Reqem are clean. Those which come from among the gentiles are clean. Those which come from among Israelites and from among Samaritans — sages declare clean, because they are not suspect in regard to their bloodstains.

M. 7:4 All bloodstains that are found anywhere are clean, except for those which are found in the rooms or around places of uncleanness. The place of uncleanness of Samaritans imparts uncleanness by overshadowing, because they are assumed to bury their miscarriages there.

M. 7:5 They are believed to say, "We buried the abortions there," or, "We did not bury [abortions there]." They are believed to say concerning a beast whether it had born a firstling or had not born a firstling. They are believed concerning the marking out of graves. But they are not believed either about interlaced foliage or protruding stones or about a *bet haperas* [a grave area, that is, an area possibly contaminated by corpse matter]. This is the principle: [Concerning] something about which they are suspect they are not believed.

T. 6:16 The Samaritan is believed to say, "A grave which was ploughed up by me is not a grave," for he testifies solely about the grave itself. And [he is believed if he says of] a tree which overshadows [the grave], "There is not a grave [beneath it]," for he testifies only about the grave itself.

Now the disposition of bloodstains is subjected to the standard rule: confirm the presumed status quo.

E. *DOUBTS ABOUT BLOODSTAINS AND DROPS OF BLOOD*

M. 8:1 She who sees a bloodstain on her body — [if] it was near the pudenda, she is unclean. And [if] it was not near the pudenda, she is clean. [If it was] on her heel or on the end of her big toe, she is unclean. [If it was] on her thigh or on her feet on the inside, she is unclean. [And if it was] on the outside, she is clean. [If it was] on both sides, she is clean. [If] she saw it on her garment, [if it is] from the belt and downward, she is unclean; from the belt and upward, she is clean. [If] she saw it on the sleeve of her garment, if it reaches to opposite the pudenda, she is unclean, and if not, she is clean. [If] she had stripped it off or put it on during the night, wherever a bloodstain is located, she is un-

clean, since it can have been turned about. And so in the case of a pallium.

T. 6:19 [If] it is found on her ribbons, lo, this one is unclean, because when she lets it loose, it touches the pudenda. And if there was a wound on her neck, and it is found on her shoulder, lo, this one blames it [on the neck-wound]. [If] it [the wound] is found on her thigh, lo, this one blames it [on the blood on the thigh]. And they do not take account of the possibility that her hand brought it down there. [If] it is found on her hand, she is unclean, because the hands are always busy.

T. 6:20 [If] there were on her two blood stains, one above and one below, even if the one below is large and the one above is small, she blames the lower one [on the upper one], up to the size of a split bean, for I say, "From the place from which the upper one came, the lower one came also." [If] there were two blood stains on her breast, one above and one below, even though the lower one is large and the upper one is small, she blames the lower one [on the upper one], up to the size of a split bean, for I say, "From the place from which the upper one came, the lower one came."

T. 7:1 [If] it was found on the sleeve of her tunic, if it reaches to opposite the pudenda, she is unclean, and if not she is clean.

T. 7:3 A short girl who put on the garment of a tall girl, and a tall girl who put on the garment of a short girl — [if] it is found near the pudenda of the tall girl, they are both unclean. [If] it is found near the pudenda of the short girl, she is unclean, but the tall girl is clean. Two of them [who] were grinding with a handmill, and it [blood] was found on the foot of the inner one — they are both unclean. [If] it is found on the foot of the outer one, she is unclean and her girl-friend is clean. [If] it is found between them [both are unclean] — this was a case: It was found on the edge of a bath, and on an olive leaf with which she was lighting the oven — And the case came before sages, and they declared them unclean.

B. 8:1 IV.3 IF A WOMAN PUT ON THREE GARMENTS THAT HAD BEEN EXAMINED FOR HER, IF SHE CAN ATTRIBUTE BLOOD, SHE DOES SO, AND EVEN TO THE UNDERGARMENT. IF SHE CANNOT ATTRIBUTE THE BLOOD TO ANY EXTERNAL SOURCE, SHE DOES NOT DO SO, AND EVEN IF THE BLOOD IS ON THE OUTERMOST GARMENT [T. NID. 7:2A-D]. HOW IS THIS SO? IF SHE HAD GONE THROUGH THE MARKETPLACE OF BUTCHERS, SHE ASSIGNS THE BLOOD TO THAT CAUSE, AND EVEN IF IT IS FOUND ON THE UNDERGARMENT. IF SHE HAD NOT PASSED THROUGH THE MARKETPLACE OF THE BUTCHERS, EVEN IF BLOOD IS FOUND ON THE OUTERMOST GARMENT, SHE DOES NOT ASSIGN THE BLOOD TO SOME EXTERNAL CAUSE.

M. 8:2 And she blames it on any thing on which she can blame it: [if] she slaughtered a beast, a wild animal, or a bird, or if she was busy with [anything which causes] bloodstains, or if she sat down beside people who were engaged in them [anything that produces bloodstains]. [If] she killed a louse, lo, this one blames [blood that may turn up] on it. How much may she blame on it? And [it may be attributed to a louse] even though she did not kill it. And she blames it on her son or her husband. If there is a wound [covered by a scab] on her and it can open again and bleed she may blame it on that.

T. 6:17 She blames [the bloodstain] on anything on which she can blame it. [If] there is a matter of doubt whether or not she has passed through the market of the butchers, lo, this one does not blame [it on the blood of slaughtered animals]. [If] she passed through, [but] it is a matter of doubt whether [blood] spurted on her or did not spurt on her, lo, this one blames [it on blood's spurting on her]. [If] she was handling things which are red, she does not blame [on these things] a stain which is black. [If] she was handling a small quantity [of blood], she does not blame on it a large quantity.

T. 6:18 If a woman had a wound on her neck in a position in which the blood stain might be attributed to blood from the wound, she may so assign it; but if it was on her shoulder, in which case she cannot assign bloodstains to such a wound, she may not do so, and we do not suggest that it is possible that she had taken the blood with her hand and transferred it to some other place.

T. 7:2 [If] she put on five garments which were examined for her, and [if] it was found on the innermost one, lo, this one blames it on an external source. And if she cannot blame it she does not blame it.

M. 9:1 The woman who was doing her needs [urinating] and who saw blood [with the urine] — one way or the other she is clean.

M. 9:2 A man and a woman who did their needs [urinated] into a pot, and blood was found on the water — it is unclean, for it is not the way of the man to produce blood, but the assumption concerning blood [is that it derives] from the woman.

T. 7:9 Blood which comes out with the excrement is clean. Blood which drips out, whether before the water or after the water, is unclean . A bloodstain which is attributed [to a clean source] is clean. And that which concerns contacts and shiftings — they follow the majority.

M. 9:3 [If a woman] lent her garment to a gentile woman, or to a menstruating woman [and blood was found on the garment after it was returned and worn by the owner] — lo, this one

blames it on her. Three women who wore a single garment, or who sat on a single [wooden] bench, and blood was found on it — they are all unclean. [If] they sat on a stone bench, or on the bench in a bathhouse [and blood was found on it] —it is clean. Anything which is not susceptible to receive uncleanness does not receive [uncleanness through] bloodstains.

M. 9:4 Three women who were sleeping in one bed, and blood was found under one of them — they all are unclean. [If] one of them examined herself and was found unclean —she is unclean. And the [other] two of them are clean. And they attribute it [the blood] to one another. And if they were not apt to see a flow of blood, they regard them as if they were apt to see a flow of blood.

M. 9:5 Three women who were sleeping in one bed, and blood was found under the middle one — they all are unclean. [If it was found] under the one on the inside, the two on the inside are unclean. But the outer one is clean. [If it was found] under the one on the outside, the two on the outside are unclean, and the one on the inside is clean.

T. 8:5 All pregnant women are one and nursing mothers one, and they do not attribute it to one another. A pregnant woman, a nursing mother, and an old woman — they do not attribute the blood to one another.

M. 9:6-7 Seven substances do they pass over the bloodstain [to see whether it is blood or dye]: (1) tasteless spit, and (2) water from boiled grits, and (3) urine, and (4) niter, and (5) lye-soap, (6) Cimolian earth, and (7) lion's leaf. [If] one immersed it and prepared things requiring cleanness depending upon it, [if] one rubbed on it these seven substances and it did not disappear, (1) lo, this is dye. (2) The things requiring cleanness are deemed clean, and (3) one does not have to immerse. [If] it passed away or became faded, (1) lo, this is a bloodstain, and (2) the things requiring cleanness are deemed unclean, and (3) one has to immerse. What is tasteless spit? That of one who has eaten nothing. What is water from boiled grits? Paste made from grits of peeled beans. Urine? That which has fermented. And one must scour [the stain] with each of the seven substances three times. [If] one rubbed them on not in order, or [if] one rubbed in all seven substances at once, he has done nothing whatsoever.

T. 8:8 What is tasteless spit? [Spit of] anyone who has tasted nothing since the preceding evening, even the entire day. [If] one slept for the entire day, he does not produce tasteless spit. [If] he was awake all night, he does produce tasteless spit.

T. 8:9 Water from boiled grits? — a paste made of grits of peeled beans. Urine? — urine which has fermented. And how much must they have fermented? For three days.

T. 8:10 Niter — this is Alexandrian niter. Soap, Cimolian earth, and lion's leaf — from any place. One rinses and does not have to dry. [If] one passed them over not in their [given] order, the former are not counted, but the latter are counted.

T. 8:11 [If] one passed the seven substances on it, and it did not pass away, and one did it a second time and [then] it did pass away [and if he prepared] things requiring cleanness, they are deemed c lean . [If he passed over it] the six substances, and it did not go away, and one cleaned it with soap, and it went away, things requiring cleanness are suspended, for if he had passed soap over it in the first place, it would have gone away.

T. 8:12 As to blood which certainly is menstrual blood, one does not pass over it the seven substances. A dyed garment is not made unclean through blood stains.

T. 8:13 A garment in which a blood stain has been lost — one passes over it the seven substances.

The origin of the bloodstain is subject to doubt. We resolve the doubt by appealing to the obvious probabilities. Here the Halakhah aims at accepting any plausible evidence of cleanness: "she blames it on anything on which she can."

F. *THE FIXED PERIOD*

M. 9:8 Any woman who has a fixed period — [it is] sufficient for her [to reckon her period of uncleanness, thus of having imparted uncleanness to objects she touched from] her [set] time. And these are [the tokens] of fixed periods [premenstrual syndrome]: [if before discharging menstrual blood] she (1) yawns, or (2) sneezed, or (3) felt pain in the top of her stomach or the bottom of her bowels or (4) discharges, or (5) a kind of shuddering takes hold of her. And so with similar phenomena. And any woman who has established [that the presence of one of these tokens signals the onset of her period] three times, lo, this is a fixed period.

M. 9:9 [If] she habitually saw blood at the beginning of [symptoms of] periods, all things requiring cleanness which she prepared while the [symptoms of] periods are in progress are unclean. [If she usually saw blood] at the end of [symptoms of] periods, all the things requiring cleanness which she prepared while [the symptoms of] the periods lasted are deemed clean.

M. 9:10 [If] she habitually saw blood on the fifteenth day of the month and changed her pattern and saw blood on the twentieth day, [sexual relations on] this day and that day are prohibited. [If] she twice changed to the twentieth day, this day and that day are prohibited. [If] she three times changed to the twentieth day, the fifteenth day is now permitted, and she has established for herself a fixed period on the twentieth day. For a woman does not establish for herself a fixed period until she has established it three times. And she is not cleaned from [uncleanness imposed by] a fixed period until it will have been uprooted from her three times.

T. 9:1 [If] she habitually saw blood at the beginning of the period, all the things requiring cleanness which she prepared at the beginning of the period and at the middle of the period and at the end of the period are unclean. [If she usually saw blood] at the middle of the period, all the things requiring cleanness which she prepared at the beginning of the period are clean. All the things requiring cleanness at the middle of the period are unclean . At the end of the period — all the things requiring cleanness which she prepared at the beginning of the period and at the middle of the period are clean. And all things requiring cleanness at the end of the period are unclean .

The fixed period, which resolves all questions of doubt, comes at the end and is defined.

V. CONCLUDING MISCELLANIES

A. *GIRL MARRIED BEFORE PUBERTY: STATUS OF BLOOD*

M. 9:11 Woman as regards [the blood of] virginity are like vines. (1) There is a vine whose wine is red, and (2) there is a vine whose wine is black, and (3) there is a vine whose wine is abundant, and (4) there is a vine whose wine is sparse.

M. 10:1 A girl whose time for seeing [blood] [age of menstruation] had not yet come and who was married — they give her until the wound will heal. [If] her time for seeing [blood] came and she was married — they give her the first night until the end of the Sabbath day, [which is to say,] four nights. [If] she saw blood [before marriage] and still was in her father's house [when married] — all the night is hers.

T. 9:3 [If] she habitually saw blood on the fifteenth day, and she changed her pattern to the seventeenth day, this and that are prohibited. [If] she changed to the sixteenth day, the fifteenth day and the seventeenth day are unclean. The sixteenth day is clean.

T. 9:4 [If] she changed to the eighteenth day, the three of them are clean, and unclean is only the eighteenth day alone. [If] she usually saw blood on the twentieth day and changed to the thirtieth day, this one and that one are prohibited, but she is permitted to have intercourse from the twentieth day to the thirtieth day. And if she saw blood on the twentieth day, she is permitted to have intercourse on the thirtieth day, because her period comes in good order. [If] she did not see on the twentieth day, she is prohibited to have intercourse on the thirtieth day.

T. 9:5 She who sees blood imparts uncleanness [to objects which she touched] during the preceding twenty-four hours. And to what does she impart uncleanness? Food and drink and objects used for lying and sitting and clay utensils which are tightly sealed. And she is in disarray [as to her fixed period]. And she does not impart uncleanness to the one who has intercourse with her. And she does not count seven days from its appearance but from the time that she saw blood.

T. 9:6 She who sees a blood stain imparts uncleanness retroactively. And to what does she impart uncleanness? Food and drink and objects used for lying and sitting and open clay utensils. And she is in disarray [as to her fixed period]. And she imparts uncleanness to the one who has intercourse with her. But she does not count seven days from its appearance but from the time that she saw [blood]. And in any case [the uncleanness] is held in suspense and [consecrated food] is not burned.

B. 10:1 IV.4/65B-66A SHE WHO PRODUCES BLOOD ON ACCOUNT OF HAVING SEXUAL RELATIONS MAY HAVE SEXUAL RELATIONS ONCE, TWICE, AND A THIRD TIME. FROM THAT POINT ONWARD, SHE MAY HAVE SEXUAL RELATIONS ONLY IF SHE IS DIVORCED AND MARRIED TO SOMEONE ELSE. IF SHE REMARRIED AND THEN PRODUCED BLOOD ON ACCOUNT OF HAVING SEXUAL RELATIONS, SHE MAY HAVE SEXUAL RELATIONS ONCE, TWICE, AND A THIRD TIME. FROM THAT POINT ONWARD, SHE MAY HAVE SEXUAL RELATIONS ONLY IF SHE IS DIVORCED AND MARRIED TO SOMEONE ELSE. IF SHE REMARRIED AND THEN PRODUCED BLOOD ON ACCOUNT OF HAVING SEXUAL RELATIONS, SHE MAY HAVE SEXUAL RELATIONS ONCE, TWICE, AND A THIRD TIME. FROM THAT POINT ONWARD, SHE MAY HAVE SEXUAL RELATIONS ONLY IF SHE EXAMINES HERSELF. HOW DOES SHE EXAMINE HERSELF? SHE BRINGS A TUBE, WITH A PAINT STICK WITHIN, AND AN ABSORBENT AT THE TOP. IF BLOOD IS FOUND ON THE TOP OF THE ABSORBENT, THEN IT IS KNOWN THAT THE BLOOD COMES FROM THE SOURCE [THE UTERUS]. IF BLOOD IS NOT FOUND ON THE TOP, THEN IT IS KNOWN THAT THE BLOOD COMES FROM THE SIDES OF THE WOMB.. AND IF SHE HAS A SORE ON THAT SPOT, THEN THE BLOOD IS

ATTRIBUTED TO HER SORE. AND IF SHE HAS A FIXED PERIOD, SHE ATTRIBUTES THE BLOOD TO HER FIXED PERIOD. AND IF THE BLOOD OF HER WOUND IS DIFFERENT FROM THE BLOOD THAT SHE PRODUCES IN HER MENSTRUAL PERIOD, SHE DOES NOT ATTRIBUTE THE BLOOD TO THE WOUND.

The concluding miscellanies commence with the blood produced by a pre-pubescent girl in the act of intercourse.

B. *DOUBTS ABOUT CLEANNESS RE FAILURE TO EXAMINE*

M. 10:2 A menstruating woman who examined herself on the seventh day at dawn and found herself to be clean — at twilight she did not mark her separation [by immersion] — and after some days examined herself and found herself unclean — lo, she is assumed to be clean. [If] she examined herself on the seventh day at dawn and found herself unclean, and at twilight she did not mark her separation, and after a time she examined herself and found herself clean, lo, this one is in the assumption of being unclean. And she imparts uncleanness [to articles that she had touched] during the preceding twenty-four hours and from one examination to the preceding examination. And if she has a fixed period, sufficient for her is her time. Even [if] she examined herself on the second day of her menstrual period and found herself clean, and at twilight [of the seventh day] she did not mark her separation, and after a time she examined herself and found herself unclean, lo, this one is in the assumption of being clean.

T. 8:1 Lo, [if a woman] was married and saw blood during intercourse she has intercourse one time, and a second and a third. Thereafter, she may not have intercourse, but she is to be divorced and married to someone else. [If] she was married [to another man] and saw blood during inter course, she has intercourse one time, and a second, and third. Thereafter she should not have sexual relations. But she should be divorced and married to some other.

T. 8:2 And how many times is she permitted to remarry? Up to three times. Thereafter she should not be married unless she examines herself with a reed. How do they examine her? One brings a reed and puts inside it a painting stick and brings an absorbent and puts it on the head of the painting stick. [If] it [blood] is found on its head, lo, this is unclean, because it is blood of uterus [menstrual blood]. And [if it is found] on the sides, lo, [there is no flow from the uterus and] this one is clean, because it is blood rubbed off [from a wound on the sides of the vagina]. If she has a fixed period, lo, this one takes account of her fixed period. If she has a wound, lo, she attributes it to it. But if blood of her menstrual period was different from blood of her wound, lo, this one does not attribute it to it.

T. 8:4 [If] she was examining herself with the right [hand] and it is unclean, with the left [hand] and it is clean, she should examine only with the left. [If she was examining herself] in the courtyard and it is clean, in the antechamber and it is unclean, she should examine only in the courtyard. [If she examined] herself, and she is unclean, [if she was examined] by her girl-friend and she was clean, she should be examined only by her girl friend.

T. 9:8 [And the girl] whose time for seeing blood has come [and she was married] — if she interrupted and saw blood not on account of sexual relations [and then produced blood], lo, this one is unclean as a menstruant. They give her the first night only. [If] the color of the blood changed and she saw [blood], lo, this one is unclean as a menstruant.

T. 9:9 And all of them who have seen [blood] — they examine them with a reed, except for the virgin, for her blood is clean, because it is hymeneal blood . And in regard to all other appearances of blood, all is in accord with the nature of the blood.

T. 9:10 The blood of menstruation is red. Hymeneal blood is dim. Blood of menstruation is turbid. Hymeneal blood is not turbid. Blood of menstruation is from the source. Hymeneal blood is from the sides

T. 9:12 [If] she examined herself and her garment and lent it to her girl friend and afterward blood is found on it, she is clean and her girl-friend at tributes it to her.

We confirm the established presumption in the case of doubt outlined here.

C. *UNCLEANNESS OF THE ZAB, THE MENSTRUATING WOMAN*

M. 10:4 (1) The Zab, (2) the Zabah, (3) the menstruating woman, (4) the woman who has given birth, and (5) the person afflicted with the skin ailment [Lev. 13-14], who died impart uncleanness through being carried [even without contact] until the flesh has decayed. A gentile who dies is clean in respect to imparting uncleanness through being carried. A menstruating woman is only one who dies during her menstrual period.

M. 10:5 The woman who died and from whom a quarter-*log* of blood exuded — it [a drop of blood] imparts uncleanness by reason of producing a bloodstain, and it [a quarter-*log*] imparts uncleanness by means of overshadowing.

T. 9:14 The Zab and the Zabah and the menstruating woman and the woman who has given birth and the person afflicted with the skin ailment who died impart uncleanness when they are carried — until the flesh will rot. And they impart uncleanness only [if one carries] their larger part. And they impart uncleanness only by decree of the scribes.

T. 9:16 At first they would immerse objects on account of [contact with] women who had died while in their menstrual period. They reverted to immerse because of every one of them [whether they died menstruating or not], because of the respect due to women. And first they would bring out incense before those who had [died of] intestinal illness. They reverted to bring out incense before everyone, because of the honor owing to the dead. At first they would bring out the rich on a bed and poor in a box. They reverted to bring them out, whether on a bed or in a box, because of the respect owing to the poor.

T. 9:17 At first they would bring [food] to the house of mourning of the poor in a colored glass utensil and to the rich in white glass. They reverted to carry either in colored or in white glass because of the honor owing to the poor. At first whoever had a corpse found that the deceased's expenses were more difficult to bear than the death of the person. Everyone began leaving their dead and running away. Rabban Gamaliel behaved toward himself...Everyone behaved as did Rabban Gamaliel.

T. 9:18 At first meat eaten for desire was regarded as insusceptible to uncleanness. They reverted to decree concerning it that it should be subject to uncleanness of the hands. They reverted and decreed concerning it that it should be subject to uncleanness through contact. They reverted and decreed concerning it that it should be like carrion itself and impart uncleanness through carrying. They reverted and said every olive-pressing made in connection with meat of desire is unclean for Holy Things but clean for heave-offering. They reverted and ruled that this applies to a beast and not to fowl.

Once more we cover all the animate sources of uncleanness of Lev. 12-15, now with attention to the post-mortem effects of their particular, shared classification of uncleanness. It remains a source of uncleanness, distinct from corpse-uncleanness, for the stated period. That means if someone bears the weight of the corpse of such a person, without contact, he becomes unclean under the rules of Lev. 12-15, now with special attention to those of Lev. 15.

D. *STATUS OF A WOMAN IN THE PERIOD OF PURIFYING AFTER CHILDBIRTH*

M. 10:6 At first did they say, "She who is sitting out the blood of purifying did pour water out for washing the Passover offering." They reverted to rule, "Lo, she is like one who has

touched one who is unclean by reason of corpse uncleanness, so far as Holy Things are concerned."

M. 10:7 She eats tithe and sets apart dough offering and brings near [to the other dough the vessel in which she has put the portion set apart as dough offering] to designate it as dough offering, and if some of her spit and blood of purifying fell on a loaf of heave offering, that it is clean. She does not require immersion at the end.

The penultimate rule clarifies a detail of Lev. 12.

E. *SHE WHO SEES BLOOD ON THE ELEVENTH DAY OF THE ZIBAH PERIOD*

M. 10:8 She who sees [blood] on the eleventh day [the last day of the eleven days of the Zibah-period, during which all flow of blood is classified as flux, and the next day is the first day of the menstrual period] and immersed in the evening and had intercourse — they are free of the obligation to bring the sacrifice. [If] she immersed on the day after it [the first day of her menstrual cycle of seven days] and had intercourse and afterward saw a drop of blood — lo, such a one is a glutton [but in no way culpable]. The woman who sees a drop of blood during the [first ten of the] eleven [Zibah-] days and immersed in the evening and had intercourse, [since as one who has experienced a discharge on a Zibah-day, she has to allow a clean day to pass before she can regard herself as clean] they impart uncleanness to objects which are used for sitting and lying and are liable for a sacrifice. If she immersed on the day afterward [so that part of the day had passed without flux] and had intercourse, lo, this is bad conduct, but [whether] things which they touch [are made unclean] or [whether] their sexual intercourse [is culpable] are matters which are left in suspense.

We conclude with another interstitial problem.

V. THE HERMENEUTICS OF ZABIM-NIDDAH

A. WHAT FUSES THE HALAKHIC DATA INTO A CATEGORY-FORMATION?

The several species, bodily flux that contaminates, all together comprise a species of the genus, sources of uncleanness — whether solid or liquid or gaseous — deriving from human beings. That genus encompasses the items at hand, along with the corpse and the person afflicted with Nega'-uncleanness.

For reasons amply spelled out in section i, the Halakhah fuses within the results of analogical-contrastive analysis of the genus, "bodily excretions that produce virulent uncleanness," as speciated into flux and corpse-uncleanness. To see how the fusion takes place in analogical-contrastive analysis, let us begin with the summary that Tosefta — true to its character as the source of generalizations of the Mishnah's exemplary cases — provides (at T. Zab. 3:3-5):

> More strict is the rule applying to the Zab than to one unclean by corpse-uncleanness, and more strict is the rule applying to the one unclean by corpse-uncleanness than to the Zab: For the Zab makes a bed and chair under him render man unclean and render garments unclean and imparts to what is above him *maddaf*-uncleanness the uncleanness affecting objects not used for sitting or lying that are located above a Zab in relationship to a Zab and makes food and drink unclean — forms of uncleanness which the corpse does not impart. His flux and his spit and his urine impart stringent uncleanness. And by means of contact he imparts uncleanness to a utensil that is subject to purification by rinsing, and by means of shifting to a clay utensil. And he is liable for a sacrifice and is required to enter running water for his purification, which is not the case for the one who is unclean by reason of corpse-uncleanness. More strict is the rule applying to one unclean by corpse-uncleanness: For the one suffering corpse-uncleanness requires sprinkling with purification-water on the third and seventh day, which is not the case for the Zab.
>
> T. 3:3

> More strict is the rule applying to the Zab than that applying to the person afflicted with the skin-ailment, and [more strict is the rule applying] to the person afflicted with the skin-ailment than applies to the Zab: For the Zab requires purification through entry into running water, which is not the case for the person afflicted with the skin-ailment . More strict is the rule applying to the person afflicted with the skin-ailment. For the person afflicted with the skin-ailment imparts uncleanness through entry, which is not the case for the Zab.
>
> T. 3:4

> More strict is the rule applying to the Zabah than to the person afflicted with the skin-ailment at. and [more strict is the rule applying] to the person afflicted with the skin-ailment at than to the Zabah: For the Zabah imparts uncleanness to one who has intercourse with her, which is not the case for the person afflicted with the skin-ailment at. More strict is the rule applying to the person afflicted with the skin-ailment For the person afflicted with the skin-ailment at imparts uncleanness through coming into a house. And she requires

sprinkling with running water, which is not the case for the Zabah.

T. 3:5

The work of hierarchical classification is never more beautifully accomplished than by a passage such as this elegant statement. While the Mishnah contains some compositions that compare, the Tosefta makes of them its métier.

What further fuses the Halakhic data of unclean excretions produced by man into a category-formation is a familiar set, a negative fact matched by a positive one. The negative is familiar. Intentionality plays no role in the capacity to transmit uncleanness imputed to the man; the corpse transmits uncleanness *ex opere operato,* from the moment of death, about which the deceased was not consulted, and so too the menstruating woman, man afflicted with flux or the Zab, and the woman or the Zabah afflicted with flux outside of her regular period, effect uncleanness willy-nilly. The woman's period does not depend upon her intentionality. And equally probatively, the Halakhah lays great stress that the flux of the Zab and the Zabah that bears the power to contaminate — semen from the one, blood from the other — make its appearance on its own. The blood or semen must come about without the connivance of the afflicted party. The teleological principle that permeates the whole underscores the exclusion of man's or woman's will.

And that leads us at the very heart of the Halakhah of Zabim-Niddah: the analogy to death, having been contrastively articulated. Why does the Halakhah defining sources of uncleanness exclude all consideration of the attitude or intentionality of the animate being, the man or woman, who becomes a source of uncleanness? Because of the indicative trait of the governing analogy, death. That, self-evidently, is, we die willy-nilly, neither by intention nor by plan, and to death our attitude is null. What by its nature compares with death also contaminates like death, which comes whether or not it is wanted. Then the details of the law flow from the natural teleology that governs: excretions of the sexual organs that by their nature cannot procreate life, affect objects used in that process, and that is accomplished by means of activities analogous to the sexual act or integral thereto: Zob or semen from a flaccid penis affect beds and like objects through pressure. The goal is for life to be created and maintained in accord with the teleology of matters. Man and woman were made to procreate, to participate in creation. When they do so, they enter fulfill their purpose, when not, they become sources of uncleanness in the specific ways set forth by Zabim-Niddah.

B. THE ACTIVITY OF THE CATEGORY-FORMATION: ZABIM

The particular hermeneutics of Zabim-Niddah, with its stress on the results of analogical-contrastive analysis of types of bodily excretions and its interest in issues of teleology, predominates in Zabim; the generic hermeneutics makes only a modest contribution to the Halakhic exposition.

ZOB AND SUSCEPTIBILITY TO UNCLEANNESS AS A ZAB: What classification of animate beings produces *zob,* that is, contaminating flux from the genitals? What is that *zob*? And how is such *zob* produced? These are the critical questions that the Halakhah undertakes to answer, and, as we shall see, the answers form the exegetical response to the particular hermeneutics of Zabim-Niddah.

The first question is answered through the intersection of the Mishnah's and the Tosefta's rule. The entire system of differentiated sources and effects of uncleanness that envelops the household and classifies its food, clothing, utensils and furniture as clean and cult-worthy or unclean and not pertains only to Israel and forms a vast system that realizes in the details of the here and now the sanctification of Israel. The Tosefta makes that statement in its own laconic language: "All are susceptible to uncleanness through flux, even converts, even slaves, whether freed or not freed, a deaf-mute, imbecile, or minor, a eunuch by castration and a eunuch by nature. Gentiles and the convert and the resident alien are not susceptible to uncleanness through flux." That is because the gentiles form a vast undifferentiated world, unclean with corpse-uncleanness by nature, a realm of death, gentiles' uncleanness is inherent. So when it comes to the Halakhah of the uncleanness of the Zabah and the Zabah, we deal only with Israelites. And, given the nature of *zob* — a genital excretion — we deal with Israelites in the household in particular, in their normal, licit marital relationships.

The answer to the second question, What is that *zob*? It is, in the case of a male, semen emitted by a flaccid penis, and in the case of a female, blood emitted by the genitals not during the established menstrual period. So as usual, the system of sanctification and uncleanness forms a vast exercise in classification: semen and blood, like food and drink and clothing and furniture, may fall into one or another taxon, as circumstances defined by nature dictate.

And what differentiates semen classified as unclean in a minor way from the semen deemed to fall into the category of *zob*? The answer is made explicit — again by the Tosefta — as follows: And what is the difference between flux and semen? Flux comes from a limp penis, and semen from an erection. Flux is like the white of a crushed egg, and semen is congealed like the white of an egg which is not crushed. Red semen is clean, and the woman attributes red flow to it. The uncleanness that results from a healthy ejaculation, meaning, one that at least potentially can accomplish its purpose, procreation, is routine and minor, as Scripture states explicitly, and as M. 5:11 recapitulates: One who has had a seminal emission is like one who has touched a dead creeping thing. Purification then requires mere immersion and sunset, nothing more. By contrast, one confirmed as a Zab or Zabah undergoes a purification rite comparable to that required after corpse-uncleanness, a seven-day period, immersion, then an offering on the eighth day — a considerable difference. The key is the imputation of a seven-day process of purification, guaranteeing that the victim has fully recovered from his affliction. When *zob* can realize or conform to its teleologically-dictated purpose, then it is unclean in a minor way. But when *zob* violates that teleology, it is unclean in the league of a corpse.

Who or what differentiates between the teleologically-valid semen (that capable of impregnating a woman) and semen deemed invalid *zob*? The third question is answered with equal clarity: *zob* of either male (semen) or female (blood) comes about solely by nature; it cannot derive from an extrinsic cause of the flow of semen, let alone from his own engagement. If a man ejaculated after eating or drinking or jumping or fantasizing, this is not unclean semen in the category of *zob*. Physical causes, e.g., food, activity, or psychological causes, e.g., fantasizing — these may produce a flow of semen, but that semen does not qualify as *zob*. So in Zabim we deal with Israelites who produce genital flux through no activity of their own. It is nature's own flawed semen, semen that violates its own teleology. Man cannot bring it about by an act of will, any more than by an act of will he turns himself into a source of corpse-uncleanness, releasing his soul to contaminate until contained.

The Halakhah contributes fundamental considerations to the definition of uncleanness deriving from the sexual parts. Scripture speaks of a man's discharge; the Halakhah wants such a discharge to take place on three successive days or in three ample, distinct flows even on one day. When it comes to flux of a woman, the Halakhah likewise concerns itself with three such appearances on three successive days; only then is the matter confirmed. The consequent, abundant possibilities of doubt preoccupy sages. Much of the law concerns itself with interstitial cases of one kind or another.

ZOB AND THE SUSCEPTIBILITY TO UNCLEANNESS OF THE ZABAH: A flow of vaginal blood may bear diverse significations; it may be menstrual blood, it may be zibah-blood, and it may be natural blood. Blood that flows during a regularly-established period is classified as menstrual. Blood that flows in the eleven days between periods — called zibah-days — is classified as *zob*, hence zibah-days' blood. Now if blood appears on one of the eleven zibah-days, what is the consequence? The woman immerses in the evening.

Then she has to wait out the next day to make sure that there is no further flow of blood. If there is none, she is clean and permitted to have regular sexual relations with her husband. If there are appearances of blood on the three successive days during the period of the zibah-days, the woman is classified as a Zabah. In both cases — differentiated menstrual- or zibah-blood —the consequence, uncleanness, is the same.

THE GENERIC HERMENEUTICS OF THE ZAB AND THE ZABAH: Driven by the generic hermeneutics, much of the Halakhah pursues the question of ambiguous data on the matter. What is at stake here in particular is the woman's status as to procreation. If she is established as unclean for her period, then after the period, for the next eleven days, she is permitted to have sexual relations, until the advent of the next regular period. If the blood flows during the zibah-days, however, then an irregular flow, from day to day, prevents her from participating in the procreative process, and that exclusion from normal sexual relations, by reason of the intermittent, irregular flow, may continue for a long time. So the distinction between menstrual- and *zob*-blood makes a great difference. By the latter the woman is marked as not a fit vehicle for procreation.

A flow of semen from the flaccid penis forms the counterpart to the vaginal flux of the woman. He who sees semen does not become susceptible to uncleanness by flux for twenty-four hours. One such flow does not establish uncleanness, three on successive days do. The issues must be separate and distinct from one another but need not appear on different days. Problems therefore arise when "clean days," that is, days on which no flux makes an appearance, intervene between days of flux. But the Torah also treats as unclean the flow of semen from the erect penis. But it is uncleanness in a different classification, as the Written Torah makes clear. The former uncleanness persists; it yields contamination through pressure, not only contact; only when the discharge stops for a week is the man clean, and then a rite of purification is required. But contrast, an emission of semen in the normal manner produces uncleanness removed through immersion and sunset. So we need to differentiate the relationship of semen to flux, as at M. 1:2. Then we face the sequence of interstitial cases — not clean, but not confirmed as unclean — that the details of the law address. Here again, a man who produces semen not in the normal framework of the reproductive life is excluded by nature from the procreative process. The Zab and the Zabah belong to holy Israel, but nature removes them from the natural processes by which the sanctity of Israel is propagated, namely, in bed.

THE MEDIA FOR TRANSMITTING UNCLEANNESS: The special medium, pressure, that transmits the uncleanness of the sexual organs matches the way by which those organs realize their teleology. As sexual activity takes place through not only making contact or touching but also exerting pressure, bringing about procreative ejaculation, so uncleanness is transmitted through not only contact but also pressure, specifically, to objects bearing the weight of a person afflicted with the uncleanness of flux. Since sexual activity commonly takes place where people lie, objects used for lying (and, concomitantly, for sitting) are susceptible to the pressure-uncleanness of the sexually-based sources of uncleanness. So a fully-realized teleological logic governs throughout.

But how to sort out the diverse media that take effect for the dissemination of diverse, differentiated sources of uncleanness? As usual, the Halakhah forms the ideal instrument for acute, systematic differentiation, through analogical-contrastive logic, between and among things that are both alike and not alike. And, as usual, the framers of the authoritative statement of the Halakhah, the Mishnah, provide a systematic statement of the matter. That brings us to the exquisite exposition of the Halakhah that is provided by Zabim Chapter Five. There we deal with the means for transferring uncleanness, direct contact, pressure, carrying, shifting, and overshadowing. Of these modes, it is the last item that is of special interest, because it is the point at which the comparison of *zob*- and corpse-uncleanness becomes necessary, and, with that comparison we reach the exegetical key for understanding the Halakhah of Zabim-Niddah.

How does the Mishnah frame matters? The Mishnah's key rule is at M. 5:2: Whatever is carried above the Zab is unclean. And whatever the Zab is carried upon is clean, except for something which is suitable for sitting and lying, and except for man. Here we find a striking paradox. If something is used for lying or sitting and the Zab is carried thereon, the object is unclean; but if it is food or drink that bears his weight, the food or drink is unaffected by him. And then, a mirror-image is taken: whatever is carried above the Zab, not bearing his weight, is unclean, inclusive of food and drink. So the Zab possesses no power of transmitting uncleanness by overshadowing, but he transmits uncleanness to what overshadows him (thus: maddaf-uncleanness). First comes the teleological definition of what is subject to his pressure, which is, what can be used for lying and the like, then comes the antithesis; first comes the location, what is beneath, then comes the antithesis, what is above. It is an amazingly logical system that is set forth, each point then generating its consequence within the same simple logical structure.

So *zob*-uncleanness is transmitted through direct contact, carrying (pressure), shifting, and overshadowing, while corpse-uncleanness is transmitted through direct contact and overshadowing. In both cases, we meet our old friend, the distinction of removes of uncleanness. We make a distinction between the situation that prevails when one is in actual contact with the source of uncleanness from that which prevails after one lets go. We further distinguish modes of transmission of uncleanness to the various sorts of objects that receive the uncleanness — a critical point for corpse-uncleanness, when it comes to receptacles, and for *zob* and other pressure-uncleanness when it comes to the matter at hand. We then identify the bed and the chair, things used for lying and sitting, other objects not used for sitting and lying (maddaf-objects) and food and drink. The Zab imparts uncleanness to objects that bear his weight and what are not shifted by him, which, absent contact or overshadowing, corpse-matter cannot do.

That is the point of T. 5:1: the Torah has imposed a more stringent rule upon food and drink and maddaf an object not used for sitting and lying which are above the Zab, than upon food and drink and maddaf which are under the Zab; upon bed and chair which are under the Zab, than upon bed and chair which are above the Zab and upon maddaf an object not used for lying and sitting which is above the Zab, than upon bed and chair which are above the Zab; upon man, whether above the Zab or below the Zab, than upon bed and chair which are above the Zab.

THE EFFECT OF *ZOB*-UNCLEANNESS SUCH AS IS TRANSMITTED BY PRESSURE (MIDRAS): What are the consequences of *zob*-uncleanness for the Israelite household? An object appropriate to receive uncleanness from the Zab or Zabah — the bed and analogous objects — becomes unclean when the Zab or Zabah has stood, sat, lain or leaned, upon, or been suspended from, said object. Then the object imparts uncleanness to another person who stands, sits, lies, upon, or is suspended from, the object itself; the bed or analogous object likewise imparts uncleanness to one who carries its weight or to one who touches it ("contact"). It does not convey uncleanness to one who overshadows it, or to one whom it overshadows; it does not function as does corpse-uncleanness. The uncleanness of Zabim-Niddah bears its own message, aligned alongside, but distinct from, the message of the uncleanness of Ohalot. This is stated at M. Nid. 6:3 as follows: Whatever is susceptible to Midras uncleanness is susceptible to corpse uncleanness, but there is that which is susceptible to corpse uncleanness and is not susceptible to Midras uncleanness. The Talmud to the same passage proceeds:

III.1A. Whatever is susceptible to Midras uncleanness is susceptible to corpse uncleanness, but there is that which is susceptible to corpse uncleanness and is not susceptible to Midras uncleanness:

B. Whatever is suitable to contract Midras-uncleanness contracts corpse-uncleanness, but there are things that are suitable to contract corpse-uncleanness but not Midras-uncleanness.

C. What is encompassed by that statement? What is encompassed is a seah-measure and a tarqab-measure, for it has been taught on Tannaite authority:

D. "And he who sits on any thing" (Lev. 15:6) — might one suppose that if one turned over a seah-measure and sat down on it, or a tarqab-measure and sat down upon it, it will be unclean?

E. Scripture states, "On which he who has an issue has sat" (Lev. 15:6), meaning, that which is designated as an object for sitting, which then excludes something concerning which people may say, "Get up and let us do our work with that object."

So while the two sources of uncleanness — the corpse, *Zob* — produce a single consequence, uncleanness, each functions in its own way, and that must be each for its own reasons. That is made explicit at T. 3:3, our starting point.

C. THE ACTIVITY OF THE CATEGORY-FORMATION: NIDDAH

If the particular hermeneutics of Zabim-Niddah predominates in Zabim, the generic hermeneutics of the Halakhah governs in Niddah. From the outset, when Tractate Niddah sets forth Halakhah on the uncleanness of certain vaginal flows, the category-formation commences with cases of doubt in connection with that same matter. These fluids are menstrual blood, the abortion, and the like; the women are classified as Israelite, Samaritan, Sadducean, and so on. The animate source of uncleanness — here, the woman — has to take precautions to ascertain her status, and the net effect of the Halakhah is to require the woman to pay close attention to the condition of her vagina. The woman who has a fixed period still has to examine herself in the morning, at twilight, and before having sexual relations. That imposes considerations of cultic cleanness on a variety of homely situations. A man concerned with seminal emission, by contrast, is discouraged from doing the same, but if his motive is to look out for flux, he is praised as well. While considerations of eating priestly rations in the state of cultic cleanness register, the premise of the Halakhah throughout places us in the home of an ordinary caste-Israelite. Then, if a drop of blood is found on the man's cloth, the man is assumed to have had sexual relations with a menstruating woman; so too, if it is found on hers at the time of intercourse. But if it is found on hers later on, the matter is not certain. The upshot is, sexual relations are subject to considerations of cultic cleanness, even when the prevailing assumption is that both parties are cultically clean for the act.

Cases of doubt give way to problems of classification and confusion or mixtures. Here again, considerations of uncleanness require that we sort out the sources of an uncleanness that is, physically, undifferentiated — what class of woman with an affiliation in Israel has produced the blood? But it goes without saying, it is in the setting of holy Israel that the entire matter is worked out. Gentile women are unclean by definition, and considerations of Niddah- or Zibah-blood do not pertain. Scripture speaks of Israel, not gentiles. But the spit and urine of the gentile are unclean, for the gentile is classified as a Zab, and the blood of the gentile woman is unclean just as are the urine and spit of the Zab (when wet, not when dry). But Samaritan and Sadducean women are Israelites and the pertinent distinctions among types of blood do apply. Because they continue unclean for any sort of blood not differentiating unclean from clean, Samaritan women miscalculate, not differentiating one type of blood from another, and hence impart uncleanness to everything on which they sit or lie. In their power to differentiate among types of blood, knowing the difference between menstrual and other classifications of vaginal excretions, sages thus distinguish (their) Israel from all others claiming to form part of Israel.

Interstitiality enters in as well. Specifically, since the menstruating woman takes her position in-between the two poles — wholly participating in the procreative process, wholly excluded from it — we must find entirely predictable that a principal problematic of the law concerns cases of doubt in yet another context. That is to say, since in the sequence from the menstrual period to the clean days and back to the menstrual period, a woman participates in the cycle of procreation, what we need to know is how to deal with uncertainty as to her particular status at a given moment. How do we deal with the status of objects that the woman has touched in the interval between the moment at which she knew for certain she was clean and the one at which he discovered she was menstruating? The Niddah's procreative interstitiality — she can procreate, as a Zabah cannot, and for that reason is deemed at some moments clean, at some, unclean, in a way in which a Zabah is never deemed clean — then accounts for what is at stake in the Halakhah . What is involved is retrospective, and thus retroactive contamination, that is to say, how do we classify persons or objects that have had contact with the woman at the time at which her status is uncertain?

The solution of the Halakhah is to mediate between two points of certainty. We confirm the prevailing supposition for which evidence is available. The woman is assumed to remain perpetually alert as to her status, inspecting her sexual organs for spots of blood. So if we look backward from the moment of discovery of blood, we come to a point at which the woman has last inspected herself and found herself clean. Then all objects she has touched from that last inspection to the point of discovery of the blood may be deemed unclean. Or we may impose an arbitrary standard of twenty-four hours, in the assumption that, inspection of no, the woman is unlikely to have missed a vaginal flow for longer than that span of time. The Halakhah takes the view that each span of time — the period from the last inspection, the arbitrary period of twenty-four hours — lessens the other, so that the longest interval of uncertainty is twenty-four hours. But if a woman has a fixed period, that establishes the presumptive fact and decides the issue. She then assumes that at no time prior to the advent of her regular period has she produced vaginal blood, inspection or no. Once the period is established, we have ample evidence on how to resolve situations subject to doubt. Thus if a woman habitually saw blood at the beginning of [symptoms of] periods, all things requiring cleanness which she prepared while the symptoms of periods are in progress are unclean. If she usually saw blood at the end of symptoms of periods, all the things requiring cleanness which she prepared while the symptoms of the periods lasted are deemed clean. Rules of this kind present no surprises, working out commonsense distinctions as they do.

Sages claim to accomplish the differentiation among types of vaginal blood: (1) the room, (2) the front hall, and (3) the room upstairs. Blood from "the room" is deemed unclean, so too from the "front hall," which is also uterine. What is from "the room upstairs" is clean. Blood may derive from the bladder, and blood mixed with urine therefore is clean. Red spots may be dye, not blood at all. So too if blood is found on a woman's garments, a matter of doubt is resolved as clean; if it is on her flesh, a matter of doubt is resolved as unclean. Sages moreover differentiate by the color of the blood, so Tosefta makes matters explicit: Black as ink sediment — [if] it is deeper than this, it is unclean [if] it is lighter than this, even like stibium, it is clean, and so throughout.

They further distinguish between blood produced by an abortion, determining whether or not the vaginal blood derives from childbirth or from the menstrual period. Thus, if the foetus bears human form, it is deemed to have been a birth and the rules of Lev. 12 apply; if not, the woman is clean, or, if the event takes place during her menstrual period, is regarded as nothing more than a menstruant. But then the sex of the foetus has to be determined, and sages supply rules for doing so. So too if a woman excretes blood during labor not in her menstrual period, then the blood is attributed to labor and the woman is not deemed a menstruant.

Because they fall into the classification of substances that impart uncleanness, the blood of the menstruating woman, the flux and blood of the Zab, the dead creeping thing, carrion, and semen all have to be compared and contrasted as well. The point of differentiation concerns the power to contaminate whether wet or dry. The blood of the menstruating woman and the flesh of a corpse impart uncleanness when they are wet, and impart uncleanness when they are dry. But the Zab's flux, phlegm, spit, and the dead creeping thing, carrion, and semen impart uncleanness when they are wet, and do not impart uncleanness when they are dry. If they can be soaked and return to their former condition, they impart uncleanness when they are wet, and they impart uncleanness when they are dry. So the difference is not absolute but relative. If the substances that do not impart uncleanness when dry can in fact be restored through soaking, they revert to their original virulence.

The real question then pertains to what menstrual blood and corpse-matter bear in common, and once we ask that question, we find ourselves with a possible, if only tentative answer, already supplied in the Halakhah of Ohalot: the interplay of soul and body must come into consideration. Menstrual blood now is treated as equivalent to corpse-matter, meaning, both contain remnants of the soul, the one having been permeated by the soul, which is now the principal source of uncleanness, the other (so it appears) deriving from the cache of potential souls; but that is only a guess as to what accounts for the position of the Halakhah at M. 7:1. In any event T. Zabim 5:1 has already prepared us for systematic comparisons and contrasts of this kind.

The generic hermeneutics identifies ambiguities as to classification or status, and so naturally, we raise the question: What happens when death overtakes one of the animate sources of uncleanness under consideration here? If a Zab or Zabah, a menstruating woman or a woman unclean after childbirth or a person suffering the skin ailment dies, how does the uncleanness emanating from them disseminate? It is through carriage, even without contact; the same is so for a gentile. That is so until the flesh rots. In this aspect, then, the named animate sources of uncleanness differ from the corpse. The upshot is, the particular kind of uncleanness affecting the named classes of persons continues to classify the persons at hand, and they are not now deemed mere corpses along with all other corpses. The uncleanness that has enveloped them defines the working of the uncleanness that exudes from them, even after death; only when the flesh rots do they enter the taxon of ordinary corpses.

Except at the specified times, cultic cleanness defines the natural condition of the Israelite. Thus all the eleven days that follow the seven days of menstruation a woman is in the assumption of being clean. If she sat down and did not examine herself accidentally, under constraint, or if willfully she did not examine herself, she is clean. Once the time of her period has come and she has not examined herself, lo, this one is deemed unclean. The upshot is, a woman is assumed to be cultically clean until evidence to the contrary presents itself. On that basis, if a virgin who has not yet menstruated is married, she is assumed to be cultically clean through the honeymoon, the blood deriving as it does from the hymen: A girl whose time for seeing [blood] [age of menstruation] had not yet come and who was married — they give her [that is, she is assumed to be clean and not producing menstrual blood] until the wound will heal. If her time for seeing blood came and she was married — they give her the first night until the end of the Sabbath day, [which is to say,] four nights. If she saw blood before marriage, having had a period, and still was in her father's house when married — all the night is hers. So too if a woman has completed her period and examined herself and found that she was clean, but did not immerse at twilight at the end of her seventh day, and later on found she was unclean, she is assumed to have been clean to that point. As to the corresponding situation of the Zabah and Zab, we have a dispute as follows:

MISHNAH-TRACTATE NIDDAH 10:3

A. The Zab and the Zabah who examined themselves on the first day and found themselves to be clean,

B. [and who examined themselves] on the seventh day and found themselves to be clean,

C. and on the remaining, intervening days did not examine themselves —

D. R. Eliezer says, "Lo, they are in the assumption of being clean."

E. R. Joshua says, "They have only the first day and the seventh day alone [as clean days]."

F. R. Aqiba says, "They have only the seventh day alone [as a clean day]."

BAVLI 10:3 I.1/68B

I.1 A. It has been taught on Tannaite authority:

B. Said R. Eliezer to R. Joshua, "How can you say that the first day and the seventh day are clean, but the intervening days are unclean? In your opinion, you are counting clean days even though they are interrupted by unclean days, but the Torah has said, 'After that she shall be clean' (Lev. 15:28), meaning, after all of them, meaning, uncleanness may not intervene among the clean days."

C. R. Joshua said to him, "Do you not also concur that one counts with interruptions [of intervening days] in the case of the Nazirite who sits underneath overhanging branches [under which corpse matter is also located], or in the case of a Zab who produces a flux during the days of his counting — these too count clean days even though the clean days are interrupted with unclean days, though the Torah has said, 'But the former days shall be void' (Num. 6:12)" [T. Nid. 9:13A-B].

E. A Tannaite statement: R. Yosé and R. Simeon say, "The

> opinion of R. Eliezer seems to us better than the opinion of R. Joshua, but the opinion of R. Aqiba is better than the opinions of both of them; but the law follows R. Eliezer" [T. Nid. 9:13C-D]

Eliezer treats cleanness as the prevailing assumption, the condition that reflects the natural situation, and Aqiba takes the opposite position: what is established as fact is all that we take into account. The Halakhah then explicitly deems the cleanness of Israel to define its natural condition, the norm violated by uncleanness.

D. THE GENERATIVITY OF THE CATEGORY-FORMATION

Here what the category-formation does not encompass signals the generative power that inheres. Let me explain. Life is to be created and sustained in conditions of cultic cleanness such as the Torah defines, so not only food but sex is subject to uncleanness-rules, and sexual activities, as much as ordinary meals, raise issues of cultic cleanness. This is the one area of cultic cleanness and uncleanness laid out at Leviticus Chapters Eleven through Fifteen that Scripture itself declares in so many words to pertain to the household, not only the cult. In concrete terms, Scripture is explicit that sexual relations may not take place during the menstrual period: "And if a man lies with her, her impurity is communicated to him; he shall be unclean seven days, and any bedding on which he lies shall become unclean." Whether or not the governing consideration pertains to entry into the tabernacle is not specified; the Halakhah takes for granted that sexual relations may not take place in the woman's menstrual period, and considerations of cleanness, made explicit in Scripture, then pertain to preserving cultic cleanness at home, not only in connection with entry into the Temple.

In that context, the Halakhic system makes its more encompassing statement. The goal of nature, its telos in procreation, pertains to Israel, the propagation of the holy people. Sages make that point explicitly. With a system so permeated by the conviction that things bear a natural purpose and accomplish a goal that is set for them by their very nature, we must identify the central and generative focus of the teleology realized in uncleanness or sanctification. So we ask ourselves, Who matters, who makes a difference? The answer, repeated in one sector of the Halakhah after another, is, only the Israelite. It is his or her life-force that comes under scrutiny. It is that life-force, that semen or that blood, that accomplishing its teleology procreates life and yields a minor form of uncleanness, but, not accomplishing its teleology, is deemed analogous to the departing soul. What does it take to constitute an animate source of uncleanness, affecting the Israelite household, when it comes to the sexual organs? The first and most important consideration is, only Israelites produce flux capable of effecting contamination under the laws of Zabim-Niddah. Gentiles, meaning, idolaters, do not. The Halakhah of Niddah makes that point explicit. Their body fluids contaminate under other rubrics of uncleanness, but in general they contaminate like corpses and not like animate beings. They, their persons, their body-fluids, their land — all represent a realm of undifferentiated death, contrasting with the highly differentiated life attaching to holy Israel. In the articulation of the Halakhah of sources of uncleanness deriving from human beings, therefore, we see the mark of the generativity of the category-formation, Zabim-Niddah in the exclusion of category-formations altogether, which, within the governing hermeneutics, we are able to explain.

4.
TRACTATE MAKHSHIRIN

I. THE DEFINITION OF THE CATEGORY-FORMATION

The category-formation, Makhshirin, dealing with the power of water, when deliberately applied to dry grain or produce, to impart susceptibility to uncleanness, forms a massive, rather abstract theoretical essay, realized through practical problems, on issues of intentionality. The basic fact that precipitates the Halakhic inquiry is expressed at Lev. 11:37: "And if any part of their carcass falls upon any seed for sowing that is to be sown, it is clean; but if water be put on the seed and any part of their carcass falls on it, it is unclean to you." This is understood by the sages responsible for the category-formation to mean, [1] dry produce is insusceptible to uncleanness, [2] produce that is that has been intentionally wet down, is susceptible, and [3] produce that has been unintentionally wet down remains insusceptible. So the hermeneutical focus of the category-formation finds definition in issues of intentionality. But their specific character can be discerned only when we reconstruct the process of analogical-contrastive analysis of species of a common genus, which we shall undertake in a moment.

How, first of all, may we account for this conception of the interaction of intentionality with the processes of nature? A case permits explaining what is at stake. A householder takes flour, which is dry and has not been deliberately wet down. The flour has been kept dry because once wet down, it moulders and gets maggoty. So before he needs to use the flour to bake bread, the householder keeps it dry. The dry flour then is inert. The householder further takes yeast. That too, on its own, is null. But, having put the two together, the householder adds water. Fermentation begins. That is the point at which the flour and yeast become susceptible to uncleanness. What adding water accomplishes is the beginning of life-processes: the water, yeast, and flour become living dough. At that moment, which the householder has precipitated by a purposive action, when the process of kneading dough to bake bread commences with the irrigation of the yeast and the dough, all is changed. The dough congeals, the yeast buds and ferments, producing its sugar, carbon dioxide, and ethanol. At that exact moment, the very instant of animation, at which the bread begins to live, the householder goes on the alert for contaminating dangers to the bread. So in a cuisine based on bread (not potatoes, not rice, sorghum, poppy, sesame, or pulse, for example) what is at stake in "wetting down seed," based on the analogy of adding water to dry flour and yeast, is the point at which produce begins the fermentation-process by which it becomes maximally edible and useful to the householder.

The moment of deliberately wetting grain down defines the hour of conflict between life-processes — embodied in fermentation and leavening — and death's agents, corpse-matter, dead creeping things and the like. This is in concrete ways. But the contest is one of wills, and only when Israel's will is engaged does the contest of life and death commence, embodied as it is in cleanness yielding sanctification and uncleanness embodying death. So that contest of wills is precipitated — *les jeux son fait,* one may say — only if Israel cares, carries out an act of will. If not, then neither sanctification nor uncleanness registers; the transaction is as null as if it took place outside of the Land of Israel or under the auspices of a gentile. Israel's act of will brings to the surface the potentiality of sanctification and the danger of uncleanness to match. The Israelite's will and intention and the act that realizes the life-processes that he wishes to nurture endow with consequence what by nature happens willy-nilly. Deliberation brings about the status of sanctification for Israel and therefore brings about the threat to sanctification that uncleanness poses.

Makhshirin then deals with willful application of water or other liquids that have the power to impart to grain and produce the status of susceptibility to uncleanness. Here the possibility of analogical-contrastive analysis becomes real. The hypothetical thought-process that has defined the particular hermeneutics of Makhshirin requires a companion-species to form a genus. If Makhshirin — liquids that impart susceptibility to uncleanness —forms a species of the genus, water (or other liquids of the same classification), what constitutes the counterpart and opposite, alike and unlike? It can only be the species, water or other liquids that do not have the capacity to impart to grain and produce the status of susceptibility to uncleanness. In the context already established, our genus is comprised by water (and comparable liquids) of two types: [1] that liquid (water and its companions) that responds to man's will, and [2] that which does not respond to man's will; [1] that liquid with the power to impart susceptibility to uncleanness, [2] that without. So to state the hermeneutical center, the theory of the selection and interpretation of the data of Makhshirin, here are the species that form components of the genus.

[1] There are liquids that are unclean and therefore impart uncleanness to whatever is susceptible to uncleanness without regard to man's attitude toward them. For example, sages understand corpse-uncleanness as a viscous liquid that flows in the dimensions of a square handbreadth. If corpse-uncleanness is the model of other uncleanness, then sages will deem quite routine the notion that uncleanness of other liquids, e.g., that which exudes from

the dead creeping thing, will correspond: they are unclean and impart uncleanness without regard to man's attitude.

[2] If one species of the common genus is will to which man's intentionality is irrelevant, then the counterpart, comparable, species, can only be, liquid that participates in the system of uncleanness but that enters the system only upon the invitation of man's intentionality.

The analogical-contrastive analysis then yields the particular hermeneutics of the category-formation of Makhshirin. Liquid possesses on its own no objective taxonomic traits; whether or not something is wet by itself forms no indicator, no variable. The category-foundation, by reason of its particular hermeneutics, differentiates water of two types:

[1] that which has deliberately been applied to the produce, and
[2] that which has come upon the produce not with the householder's approval.

The produce may be wet down, but if it is without the householder's plan and intention, that is null. The householder's desire to use the water to wet his seed marks the point at which water is classified as bearing the power to impart susceptibility to uncleanness. How the two classifications of water differ is made explicit in the outline of the category-formation:

I. INTENTION: DIVISIBLE OR INDIVISIBLE

II. WATER CAPABLE OF IMPARTING SUSCEPTIBILITY MIXED WITH WATER INCAPABLE OF IMPARTING SUSCEPTIBILITY

III. ABSORPTION OF WATER

IV. WATER USED FOR ONE PURPOSE: ITS STATUS AS TO A SECONDARY PURPOSE

V. THE STREAM AS A CONNECTOR

VI. THE INSUSCEPTIBILITY OF LIQUIDS THAT ARE NOT USED INTENTIONALLY

VII. THE LIQUIDS THAT HAVE THE POWER TO IMPART SUSCEPTIBILITY TO UNCLEANNESS

What is implicit in this outline is simple: water that is subject to human intentionality has the power to impart susceptibility; then water that man does not deliberately apply to produce does not exercise that power. As usual, the particular hermeneutics then make its appearance at the outset, in unit I, yielding a problem of a generic character at unit II, mixtures of water of one status with water of another status; the problem of mixtures and connections at unit III; interstitiality at unit IV; connection at unit V, and a miscellany of clarifying rules, defining the type of liquid that does, or that does not, enter the system at unit VI-VII.

The category-formation thus forms yet another highly coherent essay on the centrality of human intentionality in inaugurating the process by which the sources of contamination take effect upon the foci and loci of contamination: the persons, things, and locations that can be affected by uncleanness. The Halakhah of Kelim has registered the same conception. Only deliberate action by man renders a utensil or food susceptible to uncleanness. As to Kelim, susceptibility to uncleanness by human agency is imparted to what is whole, complete, and useful. When it comes to water or other pertinent liquids, the same considerations come into play. Nature alone can produce that which contaminates, and nature produces that which purifies. But man by his deliberate action renders susceptible to uncleanness that which he values, finds useful, deems worthwhile, whether utensils or food. Specifically, human agency inaugurates the processes of contamination, so the system is activated by the work of thinking man, which renders susceptible to uncleanness that which man values. Natural sources of uncleanness, natural media of purification — these await the pleasure of man to do their work. Of all this, Scripture knows little, if anything.

II. THE SCRIPTURAL FOUNDATIONS OF THE HALAKHIC CATEGORY-FORMATION

As is often so for the Halakhah of the Oral Torah, Scripture contributes the facts, sages the problematics. That is to say, sages understand Lev. 11:34, 37, to hold that produce that is dry is unaffected by uncleanness from any source and falls outside of the system. Only when produce is wet down is it susceptible. They further take as a fact that produce that is wet down by the intent of the owner is affected, but that wet down inadvertently, under duress, or by third parties is not. We look in vain for the Written Torah's recognition of that fact. The pertinent verses are these:

> Lev. 11:29-34, pass.: "And these are unclean to you among the swarming things that swarm upon the earth...These are unclean to

> you among all that swarm; whoever touches them when they are dead shall be unclean until the evening. And anything upon which any of them falls when they are dead shall be unclean...And if any of them falls into any earthen vessel, all that is in it shall be unclean, and you shall break it. Any food in it that may be eaten, upon which water may come, shall be unclean; and all drink that may be drunk from every such vessel shall be unclean."
>
> Lev. 11:37: "And if any part of their carcass falls upon any seed for sowing that is to be sown, it is clean; but if water be put on the seed and any part of their carcass falls on it, it is unclean to you."

The predicate that is yielded, for the formulation of the law, by the pertinent verses is, "If water be put...," meaning, if the farmer deliberately wets down seed or produce, then the produce is susceptible to uncleanness and is made unclean by any source of uncleanness (not just a dead creeping thing), a detail of the process of homogenization, as to effect, of the sources of uncleanness to which reference is made in the preceding chapter.

III. THE EXPOSITION OF THE COMPONENTS OF THE GIVEN CATEGORY-FORMATION BY THE MISHNAH-TOSEFTA

I. INTENTION: DIVISIBLE OR INDIVISIBLE

> **M. 1:1 Any liquid which in the beginning is acceptable, even though at the end it is not acceptable, or which at the end is acceptable, even though at the beginning it is not acceptable — lo, this is under the law, "If water be put" (Lev. 11:34). Unclean liquids impart uncleanness [whether they are] acceptable or not acceptable.**
>
> **M. 1:2 He who shakes the tree to bring down from it fruit, or [who shakes the tree to bring down from it] that which is unclean — it is not under the law, "If water be put." [If one shakes the tree] to bring down from it liquids — The House of Shammai say, "Those [drops] which fell and [those] which [remain] on it are under the law, 'If water be put' (Lev. 11:34)." The House of Hillel say, "Those which fall are under the law, 'If water be put.' And those which [remain] on it are not under the law, 'If water be put' (Lev. 11:34), because [the man] intends that they should fall from [the tree in] its entirety."**
>
> **M. 1:3 He who shakes the tree, and it fell on its fellow — or [if he shakes] a bush and it fell on another [bush], and under them are (1) seeds or (2) vegetables which are attached to the**

ground — the House of Shammai say, "[They are] under the law, 'If water be put' (Lev. 11:34)." The House of Hillel say, "They are not under the law, 'If water be put' (Lev. 11:34)." There is no liquid in the Torah which is unclean before a person actually intends [to make use of it] and puts it on, as it is said, "And if water be put on seed" (Lev. 11:18).

M. 1:4 He who shakes a bunch of herbs, and they [drops of water] fell from the topside to the bottom — The House of Shammai say, "[They are] under the law, 'If water be put.'" The House of Hillel say, "They are not under the law, 'If water be put.'" Said the House of Hillel to the House of Shammai, "And is it not so [that in the case of] one who shakes off the stalk [of a plant], do we take thought of whether they dropped from leaf to leaf?" Said to them the House of Shammai, "For the stalk is one, but the bunch [of vegetables] is [made up of] many stalks." Said to them the House of Hillel, "Lo, he who brings up [from the river] a sack full of produce and puts it on the bank of the river-do we take thought of whether they descend from the topside to the bottom? But: If he brought up two and put them one on top of the other, the bottom one [indeed] is under the law, 'If water be put' (Lev. 11:34)."

T. 1:1 He who shakes the tree in order to bring down liquids from it — and they fell on those [pieces of fruit] which were detached, which were on it [the tree] and on those [vegetables] which were attached [to the ground], which were under it [that tree] — The House of Shammai say, "It is under the law, "If water be put" (Lev. 11:34)." And the House of Hillel say, "As to those which were detached, [they are] under the law, 'If water be put' (Lev. 11:34)." "And as to those which were attached [to the ground], they are not under the law, 'If water be put' (Lev. 11:34)."

T. 1:2 Said R. Yosé b. R. Judah, "The House of Shammai and the House of Hillel did not dispute concerning the case of one who shakes the tree in order to bring down from it liquids, and they fell on the detached [pieces of fruit] which were on it, and on those which were attached to the ground which were beneath it, that they are subject to the law, 'If water be put.' [Nor did they dispute of the case in which] one detached them after they were dried off, that they are not subject to the law, 'If water be put.' Concerning what did they differ? Concerning the case of him who shakes the tree to bring down from it pieces of fruit, and they [drops of moisture] fell from one press to another, or from one *Sukkah* to another, in that very same tree — for the House of Shammai say, 'It is subject to the law, 'If water be put.'' And the House of Hillel say, 'It is not subject to the law, "If water be put."'"

T. 1:3 Said the House of Hillel to the House of Shammai, "All agree concerning one who brings up a single upright sack, and who placed it on the side of the river, that, even though the water descends from the upper side to the lower side, (that) it is not subject to the law, "If water be put."" The House of Shammai said to them, "Do you not agree concerning one who brings up two sacks which are upright and placed them on the bank, one on top of the other, and the water descends from the upper to the lower, (that) the lower is under the law, "If water be put" (Lev. 11:34)?"

T. 1:4 R. Yosé says, "All the same is the law covering one sack and two sacks: The House of Shammai say, 'It is under the law, "If water be put" (Lev. 11:34).' And the House of Hillel say, 'It is not under the law, "If water be put."'" R. Judah says, "R. Eliezer says, 'This and that are under the law, "If water be put" (Lev. 11:34).'" R. Joshua says, 'This and that are not under the law, "If water be put" (Lev. 11:34).' R. Aqiba says, 'The lower one is under the law, "If water be put" (Lev. 11:34). And the upper one is not under the law, "If water be put" (Lev. 11:34).'

T. 1:5 He who rubs off [in the wetness] of the press and of the leek, even though the water descends from the upper side to the lower side — it is not under the law, "If water be put" (Lev. 11:34). [If] they [the drops of moisture] were detached [from the leek or press], lo, this is under the law, "If water be put" (Lev. 11:34). R. Yosé says, "A Zab and a Zabah who were walking along, and rain fell on his hair and on his garment, even though the water is detached from the upper side to the lower lo, they are clean. For they [drops of water] are taken into account only after they have exuded from all of it. [Supply: Once they have exuded from all of it], lo, these are susceptible to uncleanness, and they are clean. For they are taken into account only after they have exuded."

M. 1:6 He who blows on lentils to test whether they are good — they are under the law, "If water be put" (Lev. 11:34). He who eats sesame with his [wet] finger — . liquids which are on his hand — they are under the law, "If water be put" (Lev. 11:34). He who hides away his fruit in water because of the thieves — they are not under the law, "If water be put" (Lev. 11:34). He who puts [floats] his fruit [along] in the stream of the river to bring them along with himself-they are not under the law, "If water be put" (Lev. 11:34).

The particular hermeneutics raises a secondary question at the outset: do we compose a "history" of the householder's attitude toward the liquid: at one point he approves of its wetting down his produce, at another not? Do we differentiate water affected by the power of the householder between that which he wishes to shake loose and that which he does not wish to shake loss? Do we differentiate between primary and secondary causation? So particular the hermeneutics generates a series of questions by invoking issues of causation, primary and secondary, principal and subordinate, in the setting of intentionality.

II. WATER CAPABLE OF IMPARTING SUSCEPTIBILITY MIXED WITH WATER INCAPABLE OF IMPARTING SUSCEPTIBILITY

M. 2:1 The sweat [of damp walls] of houses, pits, cisterns, and caves is clean. The sweat of man is clean. [If] one drank unclean water and sweated, his sweat is clean. [If] one entered drawn water and sweated, his sweat is unclean. [If] he dried himself off and afterward sweated, his sweat is clean.

T. 1:6 He who sets up jars in a vaulted chamber, even though they absorbed more than a log — it does not fall under the law, "If water be put" (Lev. 11:34). So far as the matter of purification-water is concerned, one does not take account of the possibility that they have absorbed [water].

M. 2:2 [If the water of] a bathhouse is unclean, its sweat is unclean. And [if the water of a bathhouse] is clean, it[s sweat] is subject to the law, "If water be put." The pool which is in the house — the [wall of the] house sweats on its account — if it [the pool] was unclean, the sweat of [the walls of] the entire house which is [produced] on account of the pool is unclean.

M. 2:3 Two pools — one clean, and one unclean — that [wall which sweats] nearer to the unclean one is unclean, and that [which sweats] near the clean one is clean. Half and half-it is unclean. Unclean iron which one smelted with clean iron, if the greater part is from the unclean, [the metal] is unclean, and if the greater part is from the clean, it is clean. Half and half-it is unclean. Pots into which Israelites and gentiles urinate — if the greater part is from the unclean [gentile source], it [the urine in the pot] is unclean, and if the greater part is from the clean [Israelite source], [the urine in the pot] is clean. Half and half-it is unclean. Dirty water on which rainwater fell — if the greater part [of the consequent mixture of water] is from the unclean [water], it is unclean. And if the greater part is from the clean, it is clean. Half and half-it is clean, When [does the foregoing rule apply]? When the dirty water came first. But if the rainwater, in whatever volume preceded the dirty water, [the consequent mixture] is unclean.

T. 1:7 They follow [the status of] the majority.

T. 1:8 He who plasters his roof and he who launders his

garment — when does he know whether or not rain-water has formed the greater part? At first it drips in gentle drops. And now it flows drop after drop [in a torrent]. [If] he found meat in it, they follow the status of the majority of the butchers. In the case of meat in strings, they follow the status of the majority of those who eat meat. [If] one found in it an abandoned [child] — half and half — they impose upon it the stringencies of both [gentiles and Israelites]. R. Judah says, "If there was a single gentile woman or a single maidservant, she is suspected of having abandoned [the baby]."

M. 2:4 He who plasters his roof [with dirty water and clay] and he who launders his garment — and rains fell on them — if the greater part is from the unclean [water], it is unclean. And if the greater part is from the clean [rain], it is clean. Half and half-it is unclean.

M. 2:5 A city in which Israelites and gentiles dwell, and in which was a bathhouse heated on the Sabbath, if the majority is gentiles, one washes in it forthwith [at the end of the Sabbath]. And if the majority was Israelite, one must wait a sufficient time for the water to be heated. Half and half-one must wait a sufficient time for the water to be heated.

M. 2:6 [If] one found in it [a town in which Israelites and gentiles dwell together] a vegetable [plucked on the Sabbath] which is sold [at the close of the Sabbath] — if the majority is gentile, one purchases forthwith. And if the majority is Israelite, one must wait [at the end of the Sabbath] sufficient time for [others] to come from a nearby place. Half and half-one must wait [at the end of the Sabbath] sufficient time for [others to] come from a nearby place. And if there is in it [the town] [a gentile of high] estate, one purchases forthwith.

M. 2:7 [If] one found in it an abandoned child, if the majority is gentile, it is deemed a gentile. And if the majority is Israelite, it is deemed an Israelite. Half and half-it is deemed an Israelite.

M. 2:8 [If] one found in it something which was lost, if the majority is gentile, one does not have to proclaim [that fact]. And if the majority was Israelite, one has to proclaim [that fact]. Half and half-one has to proclaim [that fact]. [If] one found a piece of bread in it [the city in which were both Israelites and gentiles], they follow the status of the majority of the bakers. And if it was a piece of bread made out of pure flour, [with reference to tithing] they follow the status of the majority of those who eat bread made out of pure flour.

M. 2:9 [If] one found in it meat, they follow the status of the majority of the butchers. If it was cooked, they follow the

status of the majority of those who eat cooked meat.

M. 2:10 He who finds produce by the wayside — if most people store up their produce in their house, it is clear [of the obligation to tithe], and [if it is the practice of most people] to sell their produce in the market, it is liable [for tithes]. Half and half-it is deemed Demai. A storage bin into which Israelites and gentiles put their produce — even if all of them are gentiles, but a single Israelite puts [his produce] into it [the storage bin], [the whole is deemed] Demai.

M. 2:11 Produce of the Second Year which exceeded in quantity produce of the Third Year, and produce of the Third Year which exceeded in quantity produce of the Fourth Year, and produce of the Fourth Year which exceeded in quantity produce of the Fifth Year, and produce of the Fifth Year which exceeded in quantity produce of the Sixth Year, and produce of the Sixth Year which exceeded in quantity produce of the Seventh Year, and produce of the Seventh Year which exceeded in quantity produce of the year after the Seventh Year — they follow the status of the majority. Half and half — [they decide] to impose the more strict status.

We proceed to the generic hermeneutics of mixtures, now the predictable ones involves the resolution of doubt, here, problems of mixtures of water that one wants and water that one does not want. Water produced in the course of nature as distinct from water that a person has subjected to his will, e.g., has drawn or collected mix together: does the mixture impart susceptibility to uncleanness as water of which one approves? The answer depends on which classification of water forms the larger part of the mixture. That imposes its status upon the entire mixture.

III. ABSORPTION OF WATER

M. 3:1 A sack which is full of pieces of fruit and which one placed on the side of the river, or over the mouth of the cistern, or over the steps of the cave, and they [the pieces of fruit] absorbed [water] — all [the fruit which] absorbed [water] is under the law, "If water be put" (Lev. 11:34).

M. 3:2 A jar which is full of pieces of fruit and placed into liquids, or one which is full of liquids and placed among pieces of fruit, and they absorbed (water] — whatever they absorbed is under the law, "If water be put" (Lev. 11:34). About what sort of liquids did they rule? [They ruled] about water, wine, and vinegar. But [in the case of] all other liquids, [the pieces of

fruit] are clean.

T. 2:1 "A jar which is full of pieces of fruit and placed in liquids — Under what circumstances? In the case of a jar made of earthenware. But in the case of all other utensils, they do not absorb [liquids]. And stone utensils which are soft — lo, they are deemed equivalent to earthenware utensils."

T. 2:2 A sheet which one stretched on top of the pipe of the potter to wet down grains of wheat thereby — if [the wheat is wet down] on account of the water, it is under the law If water be put on. If [the wheat is wet down] on account of the sheet, it is not under the law, If water be put on.

This small unit presents no surprises.

IV. WATER USED FOR ONE PURPOSE: ITS STATUS AS TO A SECONDARY PURPOSE

M. 3:4 He who sprinkles his house and put wheat into it, and they [the grains of wheat] became damp — if it is on account of the water, it is subject to the law, "If water be put." And if it is on account of the rock floor, it is not under the law, "If water be put." He who washes his clothing in a trough and put into it grains of wheat, and they grew moist, if it [the moisture] is on account of the water, it is subject to the law, "If water be put." And if it [the moisture] is on account of itself, it is not under the law, "If water be put." He who dampens [wheat] with sand, lo, this is under the rule, "If water be put."

T. 2:3 He who sprinkles his house with water and [afterward] put into it ears of grain and they became damp — if there is on them flowing liquid, lo, this is under the law, "If water be put" (Lev. 11:34), and if not, it is not under the law, "If water be put" (Lev. 11:34). In the case of one who wets down his threshing floor, that it is [supply: not] under the law, "If water be put" (Lev. 11:34). And in the case of one who gets up early in the morning to bring refuse — if [he did so] on account of the drops [of dew] on it, lo, this is under the law, "If water be put" (Lev. 11:34); and if it is so that he might not be disturbed in his work, it is not under the law, "If water be put" (Lev. 11:34).

M. 3:5 He who dampens [wheat] with dry clay — if there is dripping moisture in it, it is under the law, "If water be put." And if not, it is not under the law, "If water be put" (Lev. 11:34). He who sprinkles his threshing floor does not scruple lest he put in it grains of wheat and they grow damp. He who gathers blades of grass when the dew is on them to dampen wheat in them - it [the

moisture] is not under the law, "If water be put" (Lev. 11:34). If, however, he intended thus, lo, this is under the law, "If water be put" (Lev. 11:34). He who brings his grain to the mill and rain fell on them — if he was happy on that account, it is under the law, "If water be put" (Lev. 11:34).

M. 3:6 [If] his olives were located on the roof and rain fell on them, if he was happy, it is under the law, "If water be put" (Lev. 11:34).

M. 3:7 The ass drivers who were crossing the river and their sacks fell into the water — if they were happy, it is subject to the law, "If water be put." [If] one's feet were full of mud — and so the hooves of his beast — he crossed the river — if he was happy, it is subject to the law, "If water be put."

M. 3:8 He who brings down the wagon wheels and the cattle yokes to the water at the time of the east wind so that they may swell out — lo, this is under the law, "If water be put" (Lev. 11:34). He who brings down the cow to drink — the water which comes up in her mouth is under the law, "If water be put" (Lev. 11:34). And that which comes up with her hooves is not subject to the law, "If water be put." If he gave thought that her hooves should be rinsed off, then even the water which comes up with her hooves is under the law, "If water be put" (Lev. 11:34). In the time of hoof disease or threshing, [the water dripping from the hooves] invariably is unclean. [If] a deaf-mute, an imbecile, or a minor brought down [the beast], even though he gave thought that her feet should be rinsed off, it is not subject to the law, "If water be put", for they have the power of deed and do not have the power of intention.

T. 2:4 A beast that went down on its own account — water which comes up in its mouth and in its moustache is under the law, "If water be put" (Lev. 11:34). [Water which comes up] on its fore-leg and hind-leg is not under the law, "If water be put" The water which comes up on the feet of man invariably imparts susceptibility to uncleanness. Water which comes up on the hooves of the unclean beast invariably imparts susceptibility to uncleanness.

M. 4:1 He who kneels down to drink — the water which comes up on his mouth and on his moustache is under the law, "If water be put." [The water which comes up] on his nose and on [the hair of] his head and on his beard is not under the law, "If water be put" (Lev. 11:34). He who draws [water] with a jug — the water which comes up on its outer parts and on the rope wound round its neck and on the rope which is needed [in dipping it] — lo, this is under the law, "If water be put." And how much is needed [in dipping it]? [If] one put it under the waterspout, [the

water on its outer parts, etc.] is not under the law, "If water be put" (Lev. 11:34).

T. 2:5 He who draws water with a jug — the water which comes up on its outer parts and on its rope wound round its neck and on the rope which is needed lo, it is (not) subject to the law, "If water be put." As to purification-water, one does not scruple lest [the water which is drawn in respect to the afore-named parts of the jug be deemed water] which has [not] been drawn by means of a utensil.

M. 4:2 He on whom rains fell, even [if he is] a Father of uncleanness — it [the water] is not under the law, "If water be put" (Lev. 11:34). And if he shook off [the rain], it [the water which is shaken off] is under the law, "If water be put." [If] he stood under the waterspout to cool off, or to rinse off, in the case of an unclean person, [the water] is unclean, and in the case of a clean person, [the water] is under the law, "If water be put."

M. 4:4 A jug into which water leaking from the roof came down — The House of Shammai say, "It is broken." The House of Hillel say, "It is emptied out." And they agree that he puts in his hand and takes pieces of fruit from its inside, and they are insusceptible to uncleanness.

M. 4:5 A trough into which the rain dripping from the roof flowed — the drops [of water] that splashed out and those that overflowed are not under the law, "If water be put" (Lev. 11:34). But the water that is in it falls under the rubric, "If water be put" [since that water is wanted]. [If] one took it to pour it out — The House of Shammai say, "It is under the law, "If water be put" (Lev. 11:34)." The House of Hillel say, "It is not under the law, "If water be put" (Lev. 11:34)." [If] one left it out so that the rain dripping from the roof would flow into it — the drops that splashed out and those that overflowed — The House of Shammai say, "They are under the law, "If water be put" (Lev. 11:34)." The House of Hillel say, "They [the drops which splashed or over — flowed] are not under the law, "If water be put" (Lev. 11:34)." [If] one took it in order to pour it out, these and those agree that (both kinds of water] are under the law, "If water be put" (Lev. 11:34). He who dunks the utensils and he who washes his clothing in a cave — the water which comes up on his hands is under the law, "If water be put." [And the water which comes up] on his feet is not under the law, "If water be put."

T. 2:6 A trough into which water dripping from the roof has fallen — "the drops of water which splash out and those which overflow are subject to the law, If water be put on. [If] one took it in order to pour it out — "the House of Shammai say, 'It is subject to the law, "If water be put."'" "And the House of Hillel say, 'It is not subject to the law, "If water be put."'" "Under what circumstances? "In the case of a clean" [trough]." "But in the case of an unclean [trough], "all agree that it is under the law, "If water be put" (Lev. 11:34)"". The words of R. Meir. R. Yosé says, "All the same is the clean and the unclean — The House of Shammai say, 'Lo, it is under the law, "If water be put"' (Lev. 11:34)." And the House of Hillel say, 'It is not under the law, "If water be put" (Lev. 11:34)'"

M. 4:6 A basket which is full of lupines and [which] happens to be placed into an immersion pool — one puts out his hand and takes lupines from its midst, and they are insusceptible to uncleanness. [If] one took them out of the water — the ones which touch the basket are susceptible to uncleanness. And all the rest of the lupines are insusceptible to uncleanness. A radish which is in the cave [water] — a menstruant rinses it off, and it is insusceptible to uncleanness. [If] she brought it out of the water in any measure at all, it is unclean.

M. 4:7 Pieces of fruit which fell into a water channel — he whose hands were unclean reached out and took them — his hands are clean, and the pieces of fruit are insusceptible to uncleanness. And if he gave thought that his hands should be rinsed off, his hands are clean, and the pieces of fruit are under the law, "If water be put" (Lev. 11:34).

M. 4:8 A dish which is full of water and placed in an immersion pool, and into which a Father of uncleanness put his hand is unclean [but the water remains clean]. [If] he was unclean [only by reason of] contact with unclean things, it is clean. And as to all other liquids-they are unclean. For the water does not impart cleanness to other liquids.

T. 2:7 He who touches a piece of carrion which is in the midst of the immersion-pool is unclean, and he is clean when he ascends [from the water]. He who touched a bed or a chair [which is unclean] in the immersion pool is unclean, and he is clean when he ascends [from the water]. A Zab who stepped [exerted pressure] on a bed or a chair in the midst of the immersion-pool — it is unclean, and it is clean when it ascends.

T. 2:8 Pieces of fruit which fell into a water-channel, and one whose hands were unclean reached out and took them — his hands are unclean and the pieces of fruit are clean. And if he gave thought that his hands should be rinsed off, his hands are clean, and the pieces of fruit are subject to the law, "If water be put."

M. 4:9 He who draws water with a swape pipe — up to three days it [the water] imparts susceptibility to uncleanness.

T. 2:9 He who draws water with a swape-pipe — if it was dried forthwith, they are clean, and if it was not dried off, even after up to thirty days they are unclean. Under ordinary circumstances — three days.

M. 4:10 Pieces of wood on which liquids fell and on which rains fell — if [the rains] were more [than the liquids], [the pieces of wood] are insusceptible to uncleanness. [If] he took them outside so that the rains might fall on them, even though they [the rains] were more [than the liquids], they [the pieces of wood] are susceptible to uncleanness. [If] they absorbed unclean liquids, even though he took them outside so that the rains would fall on them, they are clean. But he should kindle them only with clean hands alone.

T. 2:10 Pieces of wood which absorbed unclean liquids, and rains fell on them — and they were more — they are unclean. Abba Yosé b. Dosa'i and R. Yosé b. Hammeshulam say, "[If] they were more, they are clean." He may kindle them, even with unclean hands. "[If] he took them out so that rains might fall on them, and the clean [liquids] were more, [in any event] he should kindle them only with clean hands."

M. 5:1 He who immersed in a river, and there was before him another river — [the water of] the second [river] renders insusceptible [the water of the first. [If] his fellow in drunkenness pushed him in [to the second river], and so his beast, [the water of] the second [river] renders insusceptible [the water of] the first. And if [he did so] as he was wrestling with him, lo, this is under the law, "If water be put."

T. 2:12 He who immerses in the sea or in a river even though he went out more than a mile lo, [water which is on him] is under the law, "If water be put" (Lev. 11:34). [If] he crossed another river — [if] his fellow pushed him or if rain fell on him and they were greater [in volume than the original water] — the second [infusion of water] imparts insusceptibility to the first.

M. 5:2 He who swam in the water — the water which splashed is not under the law, "If water be put" (Lev. 11:34). And if [the splashing was because] he intended to splash his fellow, lo, it is under the law, "If water be put" (Lev. 11:34). He who makes a 'bird' in the water. the water which splashes out and that which is in it are not under the law, "If water be put."

T. 2:13 The bird [conjectural] and the pestle which had unclean water in them and one immersed them — the first [drops of water on] are made clean, but [those on] the second are susceptible to uncleanness. "He who makes a bird in the water — the drops that splash out and those which remain in it are not subject to the law, If water be put," the words of R. Meir. R. Judah says, "Both this and that are subject to the law, "If water be put."" R. Yosé says, "The water which splashes out is not subject to the law, 'If water be put.' And that which is in it, lo, this is under the law, 'If water be put' (Lev. 11:34)." He who makes a channel among pieces of fruit — [the liquids which flow down it] are not under the law, "If water be put" (Lev. 11:34).

M. 5:3 Pieces of fruit into which rain dripping from the roof fell and which one mixed together for drying — it is not under the law, "If water be put" (Lev. 11:34).

M. 5:4 He who measures the cistern — [if he measured it] for depth, [the water on the measuring rod] is under the law, '"If water be put."' And [if he measured it] for breadth, [the water on the measuring rod] is not under the law, "If water be put" (Lev. 11:34).

M. 5:5 [If] one stuck his hand or his foot or a reed into the cistern to know whether there is water in it — [water which comes up on the hand, foot, or reed] is not under the law, "If water be put." [If he did so] in order to find out how much water is in it, lo, this is under the law, "If water be put." [If] one threw a stone into the cistern to find out whether there is water in the water which splashed out is not under the law, "If water be put" (Lev. 11:34). And that which is on the stone is insusceptible to uncleanness.

T. 2:14 He who measures the cistern. If he did so to measure its depth, [the water which comes up on the rod] is under the law, "If water be put" (Lev. 11:34). [If he did so to measure] its breadth, [the water which comes up on the measuring rod] is not under the law, "If water be put" (Lev. 11:34). [Water which is] on his hands and his feet is not under the law, "If water be put" (Lev. 11:34). [If] one let down the lifter to bring up with it a bucket or a ladle — [or if he let down a basket] to bring back a chicken on it — [water which comes up] is not under the law, "If water be put" (Lev. 11:34). And if he shook [it], lo, [water which is detached from the rope] is under the law, "If water be put" (Lev. 11:34).

]M. 5:6 He who beat upon [a wet] pelt — [if he beat on it] outside the water — [what is splashed from it] is subject to the law, "If water be put." [If he beat] in the water [itself], [the water which is beaten out] is not under the law, "If water be put."

M. 5:7 The water which comes up on (1) [the hull of] the ship, (2) on the bilge and (3) on the oars is not under the law, "If water be put" (Lev. 11:34). [The water which comes up] (1) on the snares, (2) on the gins, and (3) on the nets is not under the law, "If water be put" (Lev. 11:34) And if he shook [them to remove the water], it [the water which is detached] is under the law, "If water be put" (Lev. 11:34). (1) He who takes out a ship onto the

> **Great Sea in order to tighten [the seams] — (2) he who takes out a [hot] nail into the rain to temper it — (3) he who leaves the burning brand in the rain in order to extinguish it — lo, this is under the law, "If water be put" (Lev. 11:34).**
>
> T. 2:16 [If] one brought a nail out into the rain in order to extinguish it['s heat], [the rain which falls on it] is not under the law, "If water be put" (Lev. 11:34). If [he did so] in order to temper it, lo, [the rain which falls on it] is under the law, "If water be put" (Lev. 11:34). He who leaves the burning brand in the rain to extinguish it — [rain which falls on it] is not under the law, "If water be put" (Lev. 11:34). If [he did so] in order to turn it into charcoal, lo, this is under the law, "If water be put" (Lev. 11:34).
>
> **M. 5:8 A covering for tables, and matting for bricks — [rain which falls on these] is not under the law, "If water be put" (Lev. 11:34). And if he shook [these objects off], [the water which is detached] is under the law, "If water be put."**

The particular hermeneutics now directs our attention to the interplay of intentionality and causality. We differentiate water that is wanted and integral to one's purpose from water that is not wanted or not integral to one's purpose, e.g., M. 4:1, a lucid example of the difference. If water is used for one purpose, what is its status as to a secondary or collateral outcome? The general answer is, if one wanted the water for one purpose, whatever outcome that water brings about is classified thereby. If it rained and the householder was glad that it rained on his olives on the roof, that suffices. At issue, further, is whether or not one's intentionality must be confirmed by a deed, or whether attitude on its own suffices in the taxonomic transaction. Water that one has subjected to one's own deed, e.g., water that one shook off, is affective. If one disposes of water by an action indicating the water is not wanted, that water is not under the law; otherwise it is.

V. THE STREAM AS A CONNECTOR

> **M. 5:9 Any unbroken stream [of water] is clean, except for the thick honey and porridge. The House of Shammai say, "Also: one of porridge made from grits or beans, because it shrinks backwards."**
>
> **M. 5:10 He who empties (from) hot [clean water] into hot [unclean water], and (from) [clean] cold into [unclean] cold, and (from) hot into cold — it [the remaining upper, clean liquid] is clean. [He who empties] (from) cold into hot [water] — it is unclean.**

M. 5:11 The woman whose hands were clean, and who stirred the unclean cooking pot, if her hands sweated, they are unclean. [If] her hands were unclean, and she was stirring the clean cooking pot, if her hands sweated, [what is in] the pot is unclean. He who weighs grapes in a cup of a balance — the wine which is in the cup is insusceptible to uncleanness, until one will pour it out into [another] utensil. Lo, this is like baskets of olives and grapes when they drip.

The issue of connection, introduced by the generic hermeneutics, is accommodated to the category-formation before us.

VI. THE INSUSCEPTIBILITY OF LIQUIDS THAT ARE NOT USED INTENTIONALLY

M. 6:1 He who brings up his produce to the roof because of the maggots, and dew fell on it — it is not under the law, "If water be put" (Lev. 11:34). If he intended such, lo, this is under the law, "If water be put" (Lev. 11:34). [If] a deaf-mute, an imbecile, or a minor brought it up, even though he gave thought that dew should fall on it — it is not under the law, "If water be put" (Lev. 11:34), because they have the power of deed but not the power of intention.

M. 6:2 He who brings up bundles [of vegetables] and blocks [of figs] and garlic to the roof so as to keep them fresh — they are not under the law, "If water be put" (Lev. 11:34). All bundles [of vegetables] in the marketplaces are susceptible to uncleanness. All kinds of meal and flour in the marketplaces are susceptible to uncleanness. Pounded wheat and groats and grits are susceptible to uncleanness in all circumstances.

T. 3:1 He who brings up bundles of vegetables to the roof so that they will stay fresh — [Supply: It is not under the law,][f water be put]. [If he gave thought to them] to tie them up — lo, this is under the law, "If water be put" (Lev. 11:34). And R. Judah says, "It is not under the law, "If water be put" (Lev. 11:34) [until he actually does the deed]." He who brings [fruit] up to the roof to have it washed in dew and in rain, lo, this is under the law, "If water be put" (Lev. 11:34). [If] he brought them up to keep them free of maggots, and rain fell on them — if he was happy, it is under the law, "If water be put" (Lev. 11:34). R. Judah says, "It is not possible that he should not be happy. [Supply: But (it is not under the law, "If water be put" (Lev. 11:34)) until he turns it over]." While the dew or rain is still on them, if he gave thought to it, lo, it is under the law, "If water be put" (Lev. 11:34)

T. 3:2 An imbecile, a deaf-mute, and a minor who brought up their pieces of fruit to the roof to have them washed in the dew and in the rain — lo, this is under the law, "If water be put" (Lev. 11:34). [If] they brought them up to keep them free from maggots, and dew or rain fell on them, even though they gave thought to it, it is not under the law, "If water be put" (Lev. 11:34), for they have the power of deed but not the power of intention.

T. 3:7 The pieces of fruit in every place, lo, they are assumed to be insusceptible to uncleanness. All the same [is the rule which applies to the fruit of the] gentile, the Samaritan, and the Israelite. Even though they said, "A man is not permitted to impart susceptibility to uncleanness to his fruit," they permitted a householder to impart susceptibility to uncleanness to some small thing and to put it into a basket.

T. 3:8 All bundles of vegetables deriving from the villages, which come from the marketplaces, are susceptible to uncleanness.

T. 3:9 Sumac berries in every place, lo, they are in the presumption of being susceptible to uncleanness. Cucumbers and gourds which are suspended by reed-grass on the doors of stores, lo, they are deemed susceptible to uncleanness.

T. 3:10 Vegetables which are sold with whatever can be eaten raw in front of a store, lo, they are susceptible to uncleanness, because they water them when they sell them. And the *etrogs* of Caesarea, lo, they are in the assumption of being insusceptible to uncleanness.

M. 6:3 All eggs are assumed to be insusceptible to uncleanness, except for those of dealers in liquids. And if they were selling along with them dry produce, they are insusceptible to uncleanness. All kinds of fish are assumed to be susceptible to uncleanness. All kinds of brine are assumed to be susceptible to uncleanness. And in the case of all of them, an am haares is believed to testify, "They are insusceptible to uncleanness," except for that of [small] fish, because they are stored with an 'am ha'ares.

T. 3:11 All eggs are in the assumption of being insusceptible to uncleanness. And the egg paid to the bath-housekeeper is in the assumption of being susceptible to uncleanness.

T. 3:12 How do they catch fish in the assumption of insusceptibility to uncleanness? Whether one catches them with a net or whether one catches them with a cage or whether one catches them with a trap, [if] one did not shake off the trap over them, lo, they are in the assumption of being insusceptible to uncleanness. But they are always in the assumption of being susceptible to uncleanness until one will intend to catch them in a state of insusceptibility. And the *'am ha'ares* is not believed to testify, "I did not shake the snare over them."

The particular hermeneutics now completes its work, showing how liquids not used intentionally do not impart susceptibility to uncleanness.

VII. THE LIQUIDS THAT HAVE THE POWER TO IMPART SUSCEPTIBILITY TO UNCLEANNESS

M. 6:4 There are seven liquids [to which the law, "If water be put", applies]: (1) dew, (2) water, (3) wine, (4) oil, (5) blood, (6) milk, and (7) bee honey. The honey of hornets is insusceptible to uncleanness but is permitted for eating.

T. Shabbat 8:23-29

8:23 E. How do we know that blood is a drink [cf. M. Mak. 6:4]?
F. Since it says, And drinks the blood of the slain (Num. 23:24).

8:24 A. How do we know that wine is a drink?
B. Since it says, "And of the blood of the grape you drank wine" (Deut. 32: 14).

8:25 A. How do we know that honey is a drink?
B. Since it says, "And he made him suck honey out of the rock" (Deut. 32: 1 3).
C. How do we know that oil is a drink?
D. As it is said, "A feast of fat things, a feast of wine on the lees" (Is. 25:6).

8:26 A. How do we know that milk is a drink?
B. As it is said, "So she opened a skin of milk and gave him a drink" (Judges 4:19).

8:27 A. How do we know that dew is a drink?
B. As it is said, "He wrung enough dew from the fleece to fill a bowl with water" (Judges 6:38).
C. How do we know that the blood of menstruating woman is a drink?
D. As it is said, "Then she shall be clean from the fountain of her blood" (Lev. 12:7).
E. And further it says, "On that day there shall be a fountain opened for the house of David and the inhabitants of

Jerusalem to cleanse them from sin and menstrual uncleanness" (Zech. 13:1).

F. How do we know that a tear is a drink?

G. As it is said, "You have given them tears to drink in full measure" (Ps. 80:5).

8:28 A. How do we know that snot which drips from the nose is a drink?

B. As it is said, "And our eyelids gush with water" (Jer. 9:17).

8:29 A. How do we know that the arm is equivalent to the hand?

B. As it is said, "And the ropes which were on his arms became as flax that has caught fire, and his bonds melted off his hands" (Judges 15:14).

M. 6:5 [These are the kinds of liquids which are] subspecies of water: [liquids which] exude from (1) the eye, (2) the ear, (3) the nose, (4) from the mouth, (5) urine, whether of adults or children, whether [excreted] knowingly or unknowingly. [These are liquids which are] subspecies of blood: (1) blood from the slaughtering of cattle and beast and fowl that are clean, and (2) blood let out from the veins for drink. Whey is like milk. And sap is like oil, The blood of the creeping thing is like its flesh. It imparts uncleanness but does not impart susceptibility to uncleanness. And we have nothing that is like it.

M. 6:6 These impart uncleanness and impart susceptibility to uncleanness: (1) the flux of the Zab, (2) his spit, (3) his semen, and (4) his urine; (5) and the quarter-log [of blood] from the corpse; (6) and the blood of the menstruating woman.

M. 6:7 These do not become unclean and do not impart susceptibility to uncleanness: (1) sweat, (2) stinking pus, (3) excrement, (4) blood which exudes with them, and (5) liquid [which is excreted with a stillborn child] at the eighth month. (6)And [the discharge from the bowels of him who drinks Tiberian waters, even though it comes out clean; (7) blood from the slaughtering of cattle and beast and fowl which are unclean; and (8) blood from bloodletting for healing.

T. 3:13 The blood of the boil and the blister and what is squeezed out of the flesh, and fruit juice and salt which melted do not receive uncleanness and do not impart susceptibility to uncleanness The urine of cattle does not impart uncleanness and does not impart susceptibility to uncleanness.

T. 3:15 [All] liquid which exudes from the corpse is clean, except for his blood. And anything with the appearance of blood in connection with the corpse, lo, it is unclean.

M. 6:8 The milk of the woman imparts susceptibility to uncleanness whether it is subject to approval or not subject to approval. But the milk of the beast imparts susceptibility to uncleanness only [when it is detached] with approval.

The Tosefta at T. Shab. accounts for the list at M. 6:4.

IV. THE HERMENEUTICS OF MAKHSHIRIN

A. WHAT FUSES THE HALAKHIC DATA INTO A CATEGORY-FORMATION?

What fuses the Halakhic data into a category-formation is the particular hermeneutics that selects and interprets data to illustrate issues of man's intentionality. The taxonomic power of intentionality comes to expression in the capacity of man's deliberation to activate an inherent trait of liquid. The exegetical program then focuses upon issues involving man's intentionality to serve as what imparts to water the capacity to render food susceptible. Sages take as fact that if produce is wet down by man's deliberate action, that is, by an informed intentionality confirmed by a concrete deed, then it is susceptible to uncleanness. But if produce is wet down willy-nilly, naturally, on the one side, or by some action not initiated by man, on the second, or contrary to man's wishes, on the third side, then the produce is not rendered susceptible to uncleanness — even though it is wet. Then the category-formation of Makhshirin will find its data and the key to interpreting them in the nature and meaning of intentionality: confirmed by a deed or not confirmed, continuous or interrupted, affective here, not there, and other familiar issues. Consequently, problem after problem will explore the concrete implications of conflicting positions on one issue: is intentionality without action effective, or do we require a deed to confirm the attitude that we impute to a person? The shank of the category-formation holds together cogently in answering that question.

Note that the hermeneutics belongs to the Halakhah and its articulated category-formation, not to Scripture and its facts. What Scripture treats as a matter of fixed and final classification — something is either wet or dry — is transformed by the Halakhah into a matter that is relative and contingent. Consideration of whether or not something is wet down in the end is subordinated to attitude and circumstance. To state matters simply: in the present context, as in Kelim and Tohorot, for utensils and food alike, the householder has the power to precipitate the working of the system. What is wet is not necessarily susceptible to uncleanness. The matter is relative, not absolute; extrinsic and contingent, not material and inexorable; dependent on circumstance and intention, not uncontingent. It would be difficult to state more explicitly, or radically, the position that all things are relative to intentionality — embodying the Israelite's power of taxonomy — than in these rules. Take for example the Halakhah that differentiates in connection with the same bundle of leeks water that imparts susceptibility to uncleanness from water that does not. The upshot of the Halakhah may be stated very simply:

> [1] Liquids impart susceptibility to uncleanness only if they are useful to man, drawn with approval, subject to human deliberation and intention.
>
> [2] Liquids that can impart susceptibility to uncleanness do so only if they serve a person's purpose, are deliberately applied to produce, irrigate something through human deliberation and intention.

It suffices to refer to the illustrative case at the outset: adding water to the yeast and dough when making bread marks the moment at which life renews itself through the life-precipitating touch of water. That is the point that precipitates concern with the forces of death. Then, to preserve purity, Israel goes on the alert for the danger of pollution: at the moment when yeast, flour, and water ignite the processes of animation. So too for all of their counterparts: if water be put on the seed, take care. The dough congeals, the yeast ferments and yields gas, and so, life-processes having commenced, death and its surrogates threaten. Then the householder goes on the alert — if he cares, if by an act of deliberation he has made life happen. But that consideration — that the householder care — makes all the difference. Only then does the Eternal intersect with the temporal, the finite, and the transient, the life of man in on-going animate processes.

B. THE ACTIVITY OF THE CATEGORY-FORMATION

Some categories of halakhic problematics encompass diverse halakhic topics. Problems common to many topics and not distinctive to any one of them involve questions of mixtures and matters of doubt in connection with mixtures. Others fit into a variety of halakhic categories but come to expression with special clarity in one category rather than in some other, and the Halakhah of Makhshirin provides a remarkably comfortable home for one of them. Specifically, the Halakhah before us forms a sustained essay on the problematics inherent in the theme, human intentionality.

The opening question is, what happens if I change my mind? If I want something but then decide I do not want it, does that change of attitude affect the outcome? No, the Halakhah maintains, it does not. That is expressed in a simple way: Any liquid which in the beginning is acceptable, even though at the end it is not acceptable, or which at the end is acceptable, even though at the beginning it is not acceptable — lo, this is under the law, "If water be put." Concomitantly, do I have the power by an act of will to overcome a physical actuality? If liquid is unclean, can the fact that I do not want the liquid to wet down my produce prevent contamination of my produce? Predictably, since uncleanness works *ex opere operato,* uncleanness takes effect at the very moment of contact with the produce, and my will that the produce stay draw is null: Unclean liquids impart uncleanness [whether they are] acceptable or not acceptable.

Neither rule presents any surprises. Intention is temporally indivisible. Liquid gains but never loses the capacity to impart susceptibility to uncleanness and to render that on which it falls susceptible. Then if I want the liquid to fall in a given place and some of it does and some does not, then the liquid that has fallen other than where I want it is not deemed capable of imparting susceptibility to uncleanness (the Hillelite view being normative as usual). The contrary position is that all of the liquid has been subject to intentionality, while the normative view is that only part of the liquid has conformed to my intention.

The really critical and generative question asks about the relationship of action to intentionality. Do we decide on the basis of what one has done the character of his prior intention, that is, of what he intended to do? If I take up water in order to pour it out, does my ultimate action in pouring out the water govern the interpretation of my original plan for the water? If it does, then even though for a time I might have wanted the water in its present location, by my final disposition of the water, I have defined that original intention and determined that the water never was wanted; therefore, retrospectively it does not impart susceptibility to uncleanness. We have a variety of positions. The first is,

[1] intention without action is null;
[2] action is retrospectively determinative of the character of intention — we judge the intention by the result.

A further view is that prior intention plays a balancing role in the interpretation of the status of the water. We do not decide solely by what one has done, by the ultimate disposition of the water. So if one's action never was intended to bring down water, the water is not utilized intentionally and does not impart susceptibility to uncleanness. Or the deed dictates the character of the intent, and the result is paramount in interpreting the means. Or what one wanted has to be balanced against what has happened. If one wants the water to fall, that is not the end of the matter; he wants it to fall in a particular place, and it falls both there and elsewhere; then what has served his purpose imparts susceptibility, and what does not serve one's purpose does not. What is incidental to one's main purpose is not taken into account, and that is without regard to the ultimate consequence of one's deeds. And then there is the possibility of distinguishing immediate from ultimate result, primary from subordinate outcome, and so on.

In applying the principle that water drawn ("detached") and used with approval imparts susceptibility to uncleanness, the Halakhah raises these secondary issues: do various substances absorb liquid, does someone intend that the liquid be absorbed; and, of greatest interest, is intention signified solely by confirming action? Then the source of water forms a variable. If wheat absorbs water that was sprinkled, it is susceptible; but if it is moistened through the moisture of a rock-floor, then it is not. Then again, we ask about primary and subsidiary intentionality. If one gathers grass in the morning, the dew on the grass does not impart susceptibility to uncleanness to wheat. The man's primary intent was to gather not dew but grass. If he wanted the dew to dampen the wheat, then the wheat has been rendered susceptible. Further, one sage takes the view that we assess one's attitude toward a situation solely in terms of what he actually does. If rain falls on grain, he is glad to have the grain wet down. But unless he does some deed that serves to wet the grain down, that attitude alone is of no effect. An action then retrospectively indicates one's original attitude. Secondary disputes underscore that primary position. Finally, we take account of the status of sequences of "wetting down," so that water that is wanted and imparts susceptibility to uncleanness is washed away by water that is not wanted and removes susceptibility. This is expressed in the case of the two rivers: He who immersed in a river, and there was before him another river — the water of the second river renders insusceptible the water of the first. If his fellow in drunkenness pushed him in to the second river, and so his beast, the water of the second river renders insusceptible the water of the first. So too water that is incidental to the utilization of a utensil is not detached with approval and does not impart susceptibility to uncleanness.

Not all liquid has the power to impart susceptibility to uncleanness — another variable Scripture does not recognize. Blood produced in slaughtering (but not blood from a living creature) imparts susceptibility to uncleanness; so too do dew, water, wine, oil, milk, and bee-honey. Sub-species of the same do so as well. The basic trait throughout is that it is a drink. Sages find in Scripture reference to "drink" and that is the source for the liquids that produce susceptibility.

C. THE CONSISTENCY OF THE CATEGORY-FORMATION

The entire corpus of Halakhah at hand celebrates the primacy of human wishes: water that has in its history conformed to a man's wishes — at some point man has lifted it up and shown that he wants it for some purpose — has the capacity to impart susceptibility to uncleanness, and water that has not remains neutral in the system. I see no point at which the particular hermeneutics of Makhshirin, in collaboration with the generic hermeneutics of the Halakhah, cannot account for the entire articulation of the category-formation. This is one of the numerous category-formations of the Halakhah that tightly adheres to the particular hermeneutics as amplified by the generic.

D. THE GENERATIVITY OF THE CATEGORY-FORMATION

The power to encompass data beyond narrow limits and to identify areas of analysis not limited by the topic of the category-formation does not constitute the sole mark of generativity for a particular hermeneutics. The power of the particular hermeneutics to encompass category-formations in no way contiguous to the topic at hand still more strikingly indicates the generative capacity of a given hermeneutical principle. When diverse Halakhic category-formations turn out to respond to the same hermeneutics, then we may confidently impute to said hermeneutics unusual vitality within the larger system. And that is the case for the particular hermeneutics of Makhshirin, which turns out to serve equally well, *mutatis mutandis*, for Hallah, dough-offering. Since the former deals with the moment at which something becomes susceptible to uncleanness, and the other, the moment at which processes of sanctification get underway — the one dealing with death, the other, life — the generative power of the particular hermeneutics proves quite formidable.

To explain: the specific issue is, at what point does the householder incur the obligation to separate dough-offering from dough that is being prepared for bread? As we shall see, to understand why God claims a portion — dough-offering — we must identify the exact point at which the obligation to separate God's share actually is incurred. In the category-formation, Hallah, we uncover the counterpart and opposite of the category-formation, Makhshirin. Both categories take up the same problem, namely, the point at which in the natural processes by which life is sustained, life commences. That [1] when through the process of fermentation that starts when water is mixed with flour and yeast and [2] ends when the dough forms a crust. At the outset, with the deliberate addition of the water to the yeast, considerations of uncleanness take over (Makhshirin), and at the end, with the formation of the crust and the death of the enzyme, considerations of sanctification commence and the dough-offering is owing. The one — Makhshirin — then insists on the centrality of human intentionality in the inauguration of the processes with which it is concerned, the other — Hallah — accords no consequence to what man wants or does not want to happen. Man by an act of will inaugurates life, but death comes on its own.

What we have in the Halakhah of Hallah and Makhshirin together is a systematic account of how holy Israel in the Land of Israel triggers the working of life-processes, [1] protecting the natural life within the living dough from the uncleanness deriving from death, [2] protecting that same life-force for the sanctification that renews and sustains life, thus in dough-offering rendering to God his portion of the staff of life. But that is solely with dough made from flour that ferments. Only grains that leaven produce dough that is liable to dough-offering. They alone — for the same reason — also produce unleavened bread. Rice, sorghum, poppy, sesame, and pulse, which do not leaven, also do not produce dough subject to dough-offering. In all cases the operative criterion is the point at which the dough forms a crust in the oven, marking the death of the enzyme, at which point the dough is liable to dough-offering.

When is the point from which dough *may* be designated? People may snack on dough without first separating dough-offering from it until she the woman preparing the dough rolls the dough out or makes the dough into a ball, in the case of dough made from wheat, or until she forms it into a solid mass, in the case of dough made from barley. Once she rolled the dough out, in the case of dough made from wheat, or formed it into a solid mass, in the case of dough made from barley, one who eats from it without first separating dough-offering is liable to death. The point cannot be missed: the dough can be rolled out or made into a ball only once flour has been mixed with yeast and water; hence the obligation may be met at the outset of the process of working the dough, when the enzyme is activated and the fermentation process begun, but must be met at the end, when the enzyme dies and the fermentation process concludes. I cannot think of a more vivid way of linking the obligation to separate dough-offering to the fermentation-process. Such a process must be possible — hence the five species but no others — and it must be underway. Then the consideration of God's share in the dough registers. Or to put it somewhat materially, when the flour is brought to life by water and yeast, then God's claim on the bread registers. The dough, when alive and expanding, encompasses a share belonging to God. When the enzyme has died, God's share must be set aside.

Only dough owned by an Israelite in the Land of Israel is liable to the dough-offering in its conventional form. When grain is brought to the Land of

Israel, dough made from it is liable to dough-offering. The fact that Israelites own and eat that grain in the Land of Israel then makes all the difference. What registers is the presence of Israel in the Land of Israel, and that (within the present view) is the key to the liability of bread to dough-offering: grain, wherever grown, if eaten by Israel in the Land of Israel, is liable, grain grown in the land, if eaten abroad, may or may not be liable. Three principal considerations therefore intersect: [1] what constitutes bread that is liable to dough-offering, [2] when liability takes effect, and [3] where the offering is required. We start with the definition of bread: it is a baked food produce that is made of flour that, upon being moistened and kneaded and fermented, rises. What derives from flour that does not leaven is not liable to dough-offering and not classified as bread for purposes of Passover either.

Two criteria of liability coexist, one marking the beginning, the other the end, of the spell. First, people snack on dough without giving dough offering until the dough is made into a ball or is rolled out in a solid mass. But formal liability takes effect when a crust forms, which is to say, when the enzyme that brings about leavening dies. These points of demarcation — when the liability commences, when the liability must be met — correspond to the points at which the crop in the field *may* be tithed, at the outset, and *must* be tithed, at the end of the harvesting-process. So the spell of liability commences with the mixture of flour and water and the working of the two into a mass, and it is fixed with the conclusion of the same process. The upshot is, the span of susceptibility coincides with the process of fermentation: the activation of the enzyme, at the outset, then the cultivation of the fermentation process, and finally the realization of the goal of that process in the forming of a crust, the conclusion of fermentation.

And, to address the third question briefly, dough-offering must be presented out of dough made from grain that is eaten by Israel in the Land of Israel.[11] The Mishnah insists that the priests will not accept dough-offering from bread prepared overseas.

We may say that the critical criterion is [1] dough that has incurred liability within the Land of Israel and [2] that is consumed by Israelites in the Land. So there is a very specific point of intersection that dictates which dough is liable to dough-offering: [1] dough prepared from wheat and comparable flour, which, when mixed with yeast and water, has the power to ferment; [2] dough at the point at which the fermentation-process has realized its goal. The upshot is that the derivation of the grain by itself bears no consequence. But

[11] Not necessarily grown in the Land of Israel, but possibly from the interstitial territory of Syria, which is neither part of the Land of Israel nor part of the land of the gentiles.

the processing of the flour produced by the grain, and the location of the Israelites who consume the bread form the critical criteria. Israelites living in the Land of Israel separate dough-offering from the bread that they are going to eat, from the point at which the bread begins to ferment, and they are obligated to do so from the point at which the bread has ceased to ferment.

That the whole forms an exercise in thinking about the fermentation process — in Hallah as much as in Makhshirin — is demonstrated, moreover, by the explicit insistence that just as flour produces dough subject to dough-offering only if a fermentation process is possible, so flour produces unleavened bread valid for Passover only if a fermentation process is possible but is thwarted. So the bread that the Israelites in the Land of Israel eat to which God establishes his claim is comparable in its traits to the bread that the Israelites leaving Egypt, or commemorating their Exodus from Egypt, are required to eat — and that bread too is liable to dough-offering, as a matter of fact. At stake, then, is the fermentation-process itself: *Then God takes notice.* The process need not take place, but it must bear the potential to take place. So it may not affect the bread of the Exodus — which is liable to dough-offering — but it must affect the bread of Israel in the Land of Israel — also liable.

Having come this far, we may readily perceive the broad outlines of a simple message: bread in which God takes an interest is bread in which inhere the living processes of nature: the life of the enzyme (as we should express matters). Leavening then is the key to the definition of bread. Taken as a natural process, leavening is animate, or is perceived as animate. It comes about "through the action of gas bubbles developed naturally or folded in from the atmosphere. Leavening may result from yeast or bacterial fermentation, from chemical reactions or from the distribution in the batter of atmospheric or injected gases."[12] Fermentation, required for wine or beer as much as for bread involves a process of frothing brought about by micro-organisms growing in the absence of air.

How then draw conclusions from natural processes of fermentation, perceived as the animation of the food? The calculus then is readily discerned: Israel's life in the Land of Israel is nourished through the transformation of grain into bread, that is, through the life-process that takes grain and makes it edible and life-sustaining. Then and there God lays his claim to a share: when Israel renews its life, meal by meal, its action in invoking the life-process of fermentation, start to finish, provokes God's reaction. That is because God too has a share in the transaction by which life is maintained — but (as the priests clearly maintained) only the transaction that takes place between Israel and the

---

[12] Samuel A. Matz, "Baking and Bakery Products," *Encyclopaedia Britannica* 2:597.

Land of Israel, there alone.

Does Israel have a say in the inauguration of the fermentation process and the engagement of God therein? To this exchange, this transfer and renewal of Israel's life in engagement with the living processes of nature, Israel's intentionality plays no role; the processes go forward willy-nilly. Then what about intentionality, e.g., that of the baker? In fact, that point is raised explicitly, in connection with M. Hallah 1:5. There the question is raised on whether a third party imposes upon grain the status of that which has been fully processed and is liable to be tithed. One authority maintains that he has imposed liability, even though the owner of the pile of grain does not know and approve of his action, the other denies it. That is in line with M. 1:7: As regards women who gave dough to the baker to make it into leaven for them — if the dough of each woman comprises less than the prescribed minimum volume subject to dough-offering, the dough is exempt from dough-offering. If the volume of all the women all together does meet the requisite amount to impose liability to dough-offering, the dough will be exempt, because it was the baker, not the woman, who owned the dough, who imposed liability. But contrary opinion registers as well.

Israel becomes responsible for the cultic cleanness of the produce only by an act of intentionality, but Israel becomes liable to hand over God's share of the produce willy-nilly. So it is with life. Let me explain, beginning with the question of why intentionality plays no role in the liability of the dough to dough-offering. The reason becomes clear when we recall the critical role human intentionality plays in the Halakhah of Makhshirin, the counterpart and opposite of the Halakhah of Hallah. There, what is deliberately wet down is subject to uncleanness, but what is accidentally wet down is not. Here, by contrast, the mixing of the flour, salt, yeast, and water inaugurates a process through which, at the end, liability to the offering is incurred — whether the process came about deliberately or accidentally. A simple formulation involves a concrete case. A householder takes flour, which is dry and has not been deliberately wet down. Why not? Because once wet down, the flour moulders. The householder further takes yeast. And, putting the two together, the householder adds water. At that moment, when the process of kneading dough to bake bread commences with the irrigation of the yeast and the dough, the moment at which the dough congeals and the yeast buds and ferments, producing its sugar, its carbon dioxide, and its ethanol — at that exact moment, the instant of animation, at which the bread begins to live, the householder goes on the alert for dangers to the bread — and so throughout.

That explains why the householder goes on the alert at the point at which he or she intentionally puts water on the dough. Then the flour, now dough, is susceptible to uncleanness. So in a cuisine based on bread (not potatoes, not rice, for example) what is at stake in "wetting down seed," based on the analogy of adding water to dry flour and yeast, is the point at which vegetation begins the process by which it becomes maximally edible and useful to the householder. Then — life bubbling away in the process of fermentation, deliberately inaugurated — the state of sanctification comes under threat from the source of uncleanness, such as corpse-uncleanness and its analogues, that the Torah has identified.

Now the particular hermeneutics of Makhshirin engages with the particular hermeneutics of Hallah, each a measure of the generativity of the other. The moment of wetting grain down defines the hour of conflict between life and death, yielding sanctification or uncleanness — and this in concrete ways. Then, at the very time, the act done with deliberation precipitates the conflict. But that is only if the householder cares. If the householder does not intend the dough to congeal and the yeast to rise, in regard to susceptibility to uncleanness nothing of consequence happens. It is the Israelite's will and intention and the act that realizes them that endow with consequence what by nature happens willy-nilly. But so far as the process itself, it does not depend upon the householder's intentionality. The fermentation process that animates the flour and produces bread goes forward whether or not the householder intended it to. Nothing he does can stop it once it has started, and no call upon his alertness to prevent uncleanness is issued. That is why God's claim on the dough, for the dough-offering for the priesthood, does not depend upon man's intentionality — irrelevant to the process of animation, of bringing life to the inert flour — but upon God's own reason for engagement. That has to do with the maintenance of the processes of life, man's and nature's.

Makhshirin and Hallah meet at the moment of adding water to the yeast and dough when making bread: when life renews itself through the life-precipitating touch of water to the flour and the yeast. Here considerations of uncleanness and those of sanctification intersect, while the life bubbles, until the enzyme dies. That is the point that precipitates concern with the forces of death, prime source of cultic uncleanness. Then, to preserve purity, Israel goes on the alert for the danger of pollution: at the moment when yeast, flour, and water ignite the processes of animation. So too for all of their counterparts: "if water be put on the seed," take care. Now we see the other half of the story. Unclean or otherwise, the dough congeals, the yeast ferments and yields gas, and so, life-processes having commenced, though death and its surrogates threaten. Then the householder goes on the alert — if he cares, if by an act of deliberation he has made life happen. And there too, by sharing the outcome of the fermentation with God, the householder acknowledges the opposite of death, which is life, embodied in the living processes by which the bread comes into being, and resulting in the presence, within the dough, of a portion subject to sanctification: donation to the priest in the present instance. Wine and beer ferment, but no counterpart offering from wine, over and above the heave-offering and tithes to which all produce is liable, is demanded, nor from beer. In the wine-olive-oil-wheat-culture of the Land of Israel, it is only wheat, in the course of its later processing, that becomes subject to a further offering, one linked to its life-cycle. And that is because bread from the earth like Mana from heaven stands for life. Therefore it is the processing of flour into bread to sustain life where fermentation represents life that particularly registers. That marks the occasion for the affirmation of God's presence in all life-forms and processes.

5.
TRACTATE TEBUL YOM

I. THE DEFINITION OF THE CATEGORY-FORMATION

The Tebul Yom ("one who has immersed on that very day" or "that which...") is a person or object that for purposes of purification from uncleanness has been immersed in an immersion pool, not in flowing water, and now awaits sunset for the restoration of the natural condition of cleanness. He, she, or it (hereinafter: he) remains unclean, but (without regard to the virulence of the original source of uncleanness) at a diminished status of uncleanness: in the second remove. He is not so unclean as he was prior to immersion, nor so clean as he will be at sunset. Why does uncleanness persist beyond immersion? The reason is that when the Torah refers to washing, bathing, and laundering in the context of attaining cleanness from uncleanness in particular, it ordinarily specifies that the object remains unclean until sunset. Then the purification-process is prepared for by the immersion in the still water of the immersion-pool but effected by sunset.

To account for the articulation of the category-formation, Tebul Yom, we once more undertake a hypothetical recapitulation of the thought process that through the hermeneutics of comparison and contrast yielded the program in hand. That, as before, requires that we treat our category-formation as a species, along with another, of a common genus. What we seek is guidance on identifying and explaining the selection of the data and the mode of interpreting them. I refer, then, to how we know what is the critical issue, the variable, the source of the problematics of the exegesis, that the hermeneutics defines. That will identify for us the principle of selection and interpretation of data.

To accomplish our task, therefore, we have to identify the variable and its indicative traits. These are the pertinent questions: is the variable

[1] the source of the uncleanness,
[2] the traits of that which is subject to uncleanness, or
[3] the medium of purification, — the three familiar foci of hermeneutical reflection?

For analytical contrastive analysis, we begin with the known: the traits of the species in hand. Our species by definition is interstitial: not clean, but no longer so unclean as before. That status ends at sunset, at which point the person or object is clean. The status of that person or object in Scripture is unambiguous; Scripture is explicit: that person or object having been immersed in still water is unclean until sunset, then he or she or it is clean. But sages take the view that the immersion has affected the uncleanness, removed some of its virulence, even while not wholly effecting cleanness. So what defines the status of the person or object who is a Tebul Yom? The criterion is not the source of the uncleanness — its virulence, the removes from the Father of uncleanness — that affects him. Nor is it the traits of that which is subject to uncleanness, whether a person or a thing. Rather, the variable emerges in the character of the purification-process itself: water that conforms to certain indicative traits, as indicated.

That fact emerges when we identify the species that share the traits, water that purifies. Running water, still water, blood, and fire, the modes of cultic purification set forth in the Torah, effect purification. Of these, the one in the same genus as the water that produces the status of the Tebul Yom — water that purifies — is flowing water. Living or flowing water by itself purifies the one who has had a discharge. So still water in an immersion pool is comparable to, but distinguished from, spring or living (flowing) water. Still water, unlike running water, is not understood as a substance that purifies something from uncleanness. What accomplishes the purification, the rite having commenced in immersion, is sunset. Then wherein the contrastive component of the analytical process? Scripture shows the way. When Scripture speaks of putting into water — immersing — an unclean person or garment, it further specifies, "and it shall be unclean until evening, then it will be clean." But when Scripture speaks of running water, it makes no such qualification.

In these facts we find our two species for comparison and contrast and identify the common genus that encompasses them.[13] Now to account for the

---

[13] Admittedly, a different mode of argument would compare running water with sunset as media of purification. But we have no category-formation for either, therefore no occasion to raise the hermeneutical question of comparison and contrast that is undertaken in this project. Our given is the category-formations of the Halakhah as we know them, not the category-formations that might have been or that we might invent on our own. That is not to suggest that the Mishnah is the only great construction of the halakhah into Halakhic composites, part of a complete system. But the others came about after the formative age and in *Auseinandersetzung* with the Halakhic system of the formative age, Mishnah-Tosefta-Yerushalmi-Bavli. They are to be dealt with in their own context, both intellectual and cultural and political — a synchronic context. True, some future generation, with ample analytical results in hand, can contemplate a diachronic study of the successive composites of halakhah into encompassing category-formations, whole and complete. But this generation cannot.

governing hermeneutics of Tebul Yom presents no difficulty. The genus is water that purifies, the two species can only be

[1] water that purifies forthwith
[2] water that purifies only in conjunction with sunset.

Then the question is, how to correlate — compare, contrast — the power of the two species of the genus, purification of running water and that of immersion in an immersion pool? It is by the familiar act of hierarchization. Which is the higher of the two? That question is answered through appeal to the status of the Tebul Yom, one who has immersed in still water of requisite volume, but on whom the sun has not yet set. Such a one is not yet clean but not so unclean as before, rather falling into an intermediate stage. Where living (flowing) water serves, by contrast, it is mixed with blood for the purification of the person afflicted with the skin ailment, or with ashes and blood for the preparation of purification-water for removing corpse-uncleanness. So the hierarchization works itself out: the mixture of water and ash or blood works immediately to purify, the sequence of water and sunset works only over a span of time. Then running water with its ingredients (as the Halakhah requires) takes a higher position than still water. We find ourselves following the model defined by Miqvaot with its six gradations and indeed formulated in detail in the comparison of two of the six.

So what? To revert to the question with which we started: the classification as to uncleanness of the Tebul Yom then finds its indicative traits in the medium of purification from uncleanness, rather than the source of the uncleanness or the character of what is purified. The point of contrast is clear: complete versus partial purification, mixed versus unmixed water. Then does the contrast yield insight into the particular hermeneutics of the category-formation? I find difficult a positive answer, for, by definition, our category-formation takes up a problem of categorical interstitiality: no longer unclean as before, not yet clean. But time and again, issues of interstitiality are resolved not by appeal to a hermeneutics particular to the category-formation but by reference to the generic hermeneutics that governs throughout.

Then, it goes without saying, we should discern no marks of a particular hermeneutics, but only the adaptation to the category-formation of the generic hermeneutics. When we examine the program of the category-formation, we see the focus on problems of generic hermeneutics of the Halakhah, connection and mixtures:

I. CONNECTION IN THE CASE OF THE TEBUL YOM

A. The Governing Principle
B. Liquids and Connection in the Case of the Tebul Yom
C. Solids and Connection in the Case of the Tebul Yom

II. THE INTERSTITIAL UNCLEANNESS OF THE TEBUL YOM

The elements of the generic hermeneutics involve, first, mixtures or connections in the case of the Tebul Yom as against mixtures or connections in the case of all other sources of uncleanness, and second, firm connectives as against dubious ones. The upshot is, as we surmised, there is no indication in the topical program of the category-formation of a particular hermeneutics. Then, the upshot of our exercise of hierarchical classification, the formation turns out to depend upon the hermeneutics of Miqvaot for what is particular to the hermeneutics of Tebul Yom, that is to say, the gradation of six types of water.

That yields an unanticipated result. Once we invoke for the present category-formation the particular hermeneutics of its model, Miqvaot, we should further expect that other aspects of the particular hermeneutics of Miqvaot — involving as it does considerations of intentionality and attitude — should enter into the program of Tebul Yom. In a moment, I shall spell out how that, in fact, is the case. And that will yield the not-to-be-predicted result: while the attitude of an unclean person has no bearing upon his status as to uncleanness, which comes about willy-nilly, nor does his attitude make an impact upon that which is susceptible to uncleanness that he touches or otherwise affects, the attitude of the Tebul Yom does register in just the ways it does in the setting of Miqvaot. That produces an anomaly: the presence, in the very heart of the generic hermeneutics, of the variable of intentionality that is particular to the category-formation before us. Let me spell out this somewhat murky allegation.

Provision is made within the articulation of this category-formation for the Tebul Yom's own attitude, something that plays no role in the classification of definitively-unclean persons. Intention enters in at M. 1:1 in this way. The man — a Tebul Yom — planned to separate pieces of dough offering but they stuck together. The Halakhah takes account of his intention; since he did not mean to connect the bits of dough, they are not deemed connected. But where there is a clear and firm connection between two parts of a given composite, no taxonomic power is exercised by the Tebul Yom, and the touch of the Tebul Yom onto one part effects the contamination of the other part, so M. 1:2-3.

Intentionality further enters the picture when we deal with liquids that impart susceptibility to uncleanness; we recall from Makhshirin that that is so only if the liquid is deliberately mixed with the produce. That issue is drawn at M. 3:6: A clean person who chewed on food, and it fell on his clothing and on a loaf of bread of heave offering — it is insusceptible to receive uncleanness. If he was eating crushed olives, and wet dates — anything on the pit of which he wishes to suck — and it fell on his clothing and on a loaf of bread of heave offering — it is susceptible to receive uncleanness. If he was eating dried olives and dry dates — anything on the pit of which he does not wish to suck — and it fell on his garments and on a loaf of bread of heave offering — it is insusceptible to receive uncleanness. All the same is the rule which applies to the clean person and to the Tebul Yom in these matters.

When a person is unclean, his power to impart uncleanness to other things that he touches does not depend upon his attitude. He contaminates willy-nilly. A person afflicted with corpse-uncleanness is a Father of uncleanness and contaminates what he touches whatever his attitude toward his status. When a person is clean, his attitude fully controls the susceptibility to uncleanness of objects, e.g., that he deems useful. So in general, intentionality has no bearing upon the status as to uncleanness of an unclean person, and for the clean person matters are quite the opposite. What about the Tebul Yom: how does intentionality register? Before immersion, as is the rule for any other *unclean* person, his intentionality did not affect his capacity, by reason of his own uncleanness, to impart uncleanness. Afterward, like any other *clean* person, his intentionality forms a critical component in determining outcomes of contamination. Between immersion and sunset he is accorded the power of intentionality in the process of contamination, which he did not have before immersion, and which he will not require after sunset. In this transitional moment he climbs up the ladder toward the exercise of the fully consequential will, preparing for the moment of a new beginning that sunset will mark.

And that carries us to the center of the hermeneutical situation at hand: to explain in the context of the Halakhah the role of sunset and why intentionality forms an effective variable in the uncleanness of the Tebul Yom.[14] What difference does sunset make? How the Torah responds to that question — whether sunset is deemed palpably and tangibly to change the character of the

---

[14] "In the context of the Halakhah" excludes reference, for the moment, [1] to the fact that Scripture has established sunset as the point at which the process of purification is complete, or, to put it differently, the setting of the sun is part of that process; and it excludes reference [2] to my linkage of Tebul Yom to Miqvaot and the particular hermeneutics thereof. What I seek is not an exegetical or a formal explanation but a substantive one.

object that has been wet down and thus dries in the sun's heat, or whether it serves merely to mark a formal span of time — hardly puzzles. The Torah explicitly calls the person or garment unclean until sunset. But for its part the Halakhah makes the unmistakable statement that sunset constitutes a formality, it does not measure a substantive change in the character of things. That is shown as follows:

> A flagon which is in the status of that which had been immersed on the selfsame day and which had been filled from a jar containing first tithe which was yet untithed — if he said, "Lo, this will be heave offering of tithe once it gets dark," lo, this is heave offering of tithe once the sun sets.
>
> M. 4:4

Nothing has changed in the character of the untithed food in the status of first tithe, which requires a further tithing — only the sun has set. Now what prevented the act of tithing from taking effect prior to sunset is the status of the food, and if sunset changes that status such that, while the food is still in the flagon that was immersed that day could not be tithed before sunset, now it can, then no physical modification has taken place. The same food in the same flagon, once marginally unclean, now is deemed clean and available to give effect to the man's conditional statement earlier in the day. Accordingly, we deal with questions of relative status, not absolute condition.

Sunset proves the critical center of the category-formation, the point of differentiation of the species from the other species of its genus, the key taxonomic indicator. Then what does the sun do in setting? It marks time, which is to say, it indicates the status of a given interval of the day divided by light from darkness and by the character of light at one point from that at some other, all in sequence. The Halakhah of the status, not condition, of the Tebul Yom alerts the householder that if he wishes to know the condition as to cleanness for use for food preserved in the condition of cultic cleanness, of his property and possessions, he must pay attention to sunset. So his intentionality will now register if and when he pays attention to the turning of the day. That is in two aspects. Until sunset he not only is not to use, for purposes of preparation of food in conditions of cleanness, what has just been immersed, he has also to notice the relationships between what has just been immersed and what not. The matter of connection brings about the same heightened consciousness as the matter of removal from uncleanness on the inner side of immersion, before the rinsing. Just as removes from the source of uncleanness require us to know not only the condition of an unclean object but also the subsequent history, from the moment of contamination, of that same object, so connection in the differentiation by reason of immersion imposes alertness not only as to the primary but also the secondary and peripheral contacts of the object that has been immersed.

The matter is made explicit at M. Ber. 1:1, the famous passage that designates the time for reciting the *Shema'* in the evening — sunset — by reference to the point at which the priests, having immersed, may eat their supper of priestly rations:

A. From what time may they recite the *Shema'* in the evening?
B. From the hour that the priests enter [their homes] to eat their heave offering,

M. Berakhot 1:1

Within the idiom of the law, therefore, sunset marks the point at which people eat their supper in a state of cleanness. Having immersed prior to that moment and so removed the uncleanness that has accumulated over the day now concluding, they change in status from unclean to clean, and supper in the new day, in renewed cleanness, follows. Sunset marks the new day, closing down the uncleanness of the passing one, just as the account of creation at Gen. 1 says.

So the first point in the day of immersing unclean utensils that can be rinsed and purified at which the householder may then make use of those utensils is at suppertime. And requiring the householder to wait until then, in line with the Torah's rule, produces with the setting of the sun the result of raising his consciousness of the status of the pots and pans that he will use for supper as well as the status of the persons of his household, wives, children, domestics, to whom he will feed the meal. Sunset then triggers a whole new moment of alertness: a fresh start. At sunset the system of cultic cleanness in the home renews itself, marking the commencement of a new span of time in the ongoing process, the beginning of a new day. In the moment marked by sunset, then, the religious meaning of the Halakhah inheres: that is the point at which ambiguities are clarified, interstitialities resolved. So the intermediate status of the Tebul Yom, between immersion and sunset, accords the opportunity for intentionality to register once more, a chance to prepare for the high alert that momentarily sounds with the sun's subsidence.

Sunset marks the creation of the new day, hence the commencement of a new span of time that tells the story of the struggle of Israel, naturally clean, to remain clean from the sources of uncleanness round about. Uncleanness does not accumulate, but, when the householder determines by the act of immersion to bring uncleanness to closure, terminates at sunset, the end of the old day. That same consideration comes to mind at M. Nid. 1:1, where the passage of twenty-four hours forms the measure of one cycle of uncleanness, the last prior inspection, the other: The woman is held to have been unclean only during [the preceding twenty-four hours when this lessens the period from the examination to the [last] examination, and she is held to have been unclean only during the period from examination to examination when this lessens the period of twenty-four hours. But there sunset does not register. Here, with immersion in an immersion-pool, the relativities of twenty-four hour periods give way to the determinate time of sunset, a decisive indicator of the end of one cycle and commencement of another.

And herein we find the meaning of the matter: what sunset indicates is that Israel, having removed the uncleanness in the immersion pool but having remained subject to its affect, now returns to its natural condition, which is that of cleanness. That is the case if Israel has so acted as to accord with its nature by immersing, earlier in the day, to that end. Whatever the condition of persons or objects as to uncleanness, once the process of cleanness has properly commenced with the act of immersion, the result is inexorable: Israel becomes clean as surely, as reliably, as the sun sets. No wonder, archaeology now shows, people wanted immersion-pools in their houses, signaling as they do the authentic condition of Israel; then, with immersion just before sunset, followed by sunset, the recitation of the Shema‘, and supper in a state of cleanness as though eaten by priests in the Temple, the day in the life of holy Israel commences, first evening, then morning, as with Creation.

Perhaps sages grasped that Moses had had that very thing in mind when in the Torah he specified, “it must be put into water and it shall be unclean until evening, then it shall be clean.” For, in line with the Creation of the world, the new day starts at sunset: “and there was evening, and there was morning, one day.” Then the line demarcated by sunset in the history of the passage from uncleanness to cleanness is indeed one of classification: the spell of uncleanness has ended not with the immersion, which changes the condition but not the status of the contaminated person or object, but with sunset. Then what marks the condition is not natural to Israel. Only what indicates the status speaks of Israel by nature. So time, not circumstance, makes all the difference. When the priests of M. Ber. 1:1, having earlier immersed, now with the setting of the sun complete the restoration of their proper condition of cleanness, Israel notes the sunset by proclaiming God’s unity. Then, the Israelite who eats his food at home as if he were a priest in the Temple, accepting God’s dominion, then eats supper in the condition of the priests eating their priestly rations. That is how life is to be sustained, and why cleanness makes a difference — at sunset.

II. THE SCRIPTURAL FOUNDATIONS OF THE HALAKHIC CATEGORY-FORMATION

The upshot is simple and brings us to the present classification of the Halakhah, the status as to uncleanness of one who has immersed on the self-same day and awaits sunset for completion of the purification-rite. Pertinent verses of Scripture include the following:

> Lev. 11:31-2: "Any anything upon which any of them [dead creeping things] falls when they are dead shall be unclean...it must be put into water and it shall be unclean until evening, then it shall be clean."
>
> Lev. 15:13: "And when he who has a discharge is cleansed of his discharge, then he shall count for himself seven clean days for his cleansing and wash his clothes and he shall bathe his body in running water and shall be clean."
>
> Lev. 11:32: "What is touched by a dead creeping thing must be put in water and it shall be unclean until evening; then it shall be clean."
>
> Lev. 11:40: "He also who carries the carcass shall wash his clothes and be unclean until evening."
>
> Lev. 14:8: "And he who is to be cleansed shall wash his clothes and shave off all his hair and bathe himself in water and he shall be clean."
>
> Lev. 15:5: "And any one who touches the Zab's bed shall wash his clothes and bathe himself in water, and he shall be unclean until evening."
>
> Lev. 15:16: "And if a man has a discharge of semen, he shall bathe his whole body in water and be unclean until evening."
>
> Lev. 15:21: "And whoever touches her bed shall wash his clothes and bathe himself in water and be unclean until evening.:"
>
> Lev. 15:27: "And whoever touches these things shall be unclean and shall wash his clothes and bathe himself in water and be unclean until evening."
>
> Lev. 16:28: "And he who burns them shall wash his clothes and bathe his body and afterward he may come into the camp."
>
> Lev.17:15: "And every person that eats what dies of itself...shall wash his clothes in water and be unclean until evening. Then he shall be clean."
>
> Lev. 22:6-7: "The person who touches any such shall be unclean until evening and shall not eat of the holy things unless he has bathed his body in water. When the sun is down, he shall be clean."
>
> Num. 10:7: "Then the priest shall wash his clothes and bathe his body in water and afterwards he shall come into the camp. And

the priest shall be unclean until evening."

Num. 17:17: "And the clean person shall sprinkle upon the unclean...and he shall wash his clothes and bathe himself in water and at evening he shall be clean."

Dt. 23:11:12: "If there is among you any man who is not clean, but when evening comes, he shall bathe himself in water, and when the sun is down, he may come into the camp."

Scripture's persistent reference to the status of the Tebul Yom invites the Halakhah to ask: in what way is the Tebul Yom clean and in what way is he unclean? Is he essentially clean, but unclean in some minor aspect, or is he essentially unclean, but in a lesser status of uncleanness than before immersion? The deeper question, the power of sunset, is not addressed in the Halakhah, only taken for granted. But it is there that the Halakhah finds its animating convictions, and only there that we grasp the source from which emanates the intangibles of relationship and circumstance, which is, the turning of the light.

III. THE EXPOSITION OF THE COMPONENTS OF THE GIVEN CATEGORY-FORMATION BY THE MISHNAH-TOSEFTA

I. CONNECTION IN THE CASE OF THE TEBUL YOM

A. *THE GOVERNING PRINCIPLE OF CONNECTION FOR THE TEBUL YOM*

M. 1:1 He who collects pieces of dough offering with the intention to separate [them], but they stuck together — it is not deemed connected in the case of a Tebul Yom. Pieces of dough sticking one to the other, and loaves sticking to one another, he who bakes a cake on top of [another] cake before they have formed a crust in the oven, and a blown-up skin of froth on the water, and the first scum to rise in boiling bean grits, and the scum of new wine — it is not a connector.

T. 1:1 He who puts pieces of dough-offering [into a basket, collecting them from door to door], whether intending to separate them from one another or not intending to separate them from one another — [if] they stuck together, they are made unfit by counting [the sequence of removes of uncleanness]. In addition to them: rice, and pounded barley when not husked. They are clean [when touched] by a Tebul Yom and it is not necessary to say, [by] all other sources of uncleanness.

M. 1:2 He who collects pieces of dough offering not with the intention to separate [them] — he who bakes a cake on top of [another] cake after they have formed a crust in the oven, and a

skin of froth on water that was not blown up, and the second scum to rise in boiling bean grits, and the scum of old wine, and of oil under all circumstances, and of [boiled] lentils, are made unclean by a Tebul Yom. And it is not necessary to say, By all [other] sources of uncleanness.

M. 1:3 The knob [of dough] which is behind the loaf, and a small lump of salt, and the burned crust less than a finger's breadth are made unclean by a Tebul Yom. And it is not necessary to say, By all [other] sources of uncleanness.

M. 1:4 The pebble which is in the loaf, and a large lump of salt, and the lupine, and the burned crust larger than a finger's breadth — are clean [when touched] by a Father of Uncleanness, and it is not necessary to say, By a Tebul Yom.

M. 1:5 "Barley and spelt, when they are not husked, crowfoot root, asafoetida, and silphium — are clean [when touched] by a Tebul Yom and unclean [when touched] by all [other] sources of uncleanness." Barley and spelt when they are husked, and wheat, whether it is husked or un-husked, black cumin, sesame, and pepper — are unclean [when touched] by a Tebul Yom, and it is not necessary to say, By all [other] sources of uncleanness.

T. 1:2 In addition to them: rice and pounded vetchlings when husked.

The interstitiality as to status intersects with the consideration of intentionality. If the Tebul Yom intends to separate the pieces of dough-offering but they stuck together, they are not deemed to form a whole.

B. *LIQUIDS AND CONNECTION IN THE CASE OF THE TEBUL YOM*

M. 2:1 The liquids [which exude from] the Tebul Yom are like the liquids that he touches: these and those are not susceptible to uncleanness. And all other sources of uncleanness, whether minor or major the liquids which exude from them are like liquids which he touches: these and those are in the first remove of uncleanness, except for the liquid which [itself] is a Father of Uncleanness.

T. 1:3 All the same are liquid which is made unclean by a Father of uncleanness and liquid which is made unclean by an Offspring of uncleanness — lo, it is always deemed unclean in the first remove. It imparts uncleanness to its fellow, and its fellow to its fellow, even though they are one hundred [sequences of contact]. [This rule applies] except to liquid of the Tebul Yom, which is unfit and does not impart uncleanness.

M. 2:2 A cooking pot which is full of liquids, and which a Tebul Yom touched, if it was liquid of heave offering, the liquids are unfit, but the pot is clean. And if it was liquid of unconsecrated food, all is clean. And if his hands were dirty, all is unclean. This rule is more stringent in the case of hands than in the case of the Tebul Yom. And more stringent is the rule pertaining to the Tebul Yom than that pertaining to hands: For a matter of doubt in connection with the Tebul Yom spoils heave offering, but as to hands, a matter of doubt concerning them is deemed to be clean.

T. 1:4 More strict is the rule which applies to hands than that which applies to the Tebul Yom: For the hands are in the first remove of uncleanness in respect to unconsecrated food; they impart uncleanness at one remove and impart unfitness at one [further] remove in respect to Holy Things; and they render heave-offering unfit; and they impart uncleanness to liquid, putting it in the first remove of uncleanness, as if it was water. And anything which is not deemed connected in the case of the Tebul Yom is (not) deemed connected in the case of hands.

T. 1:5 More strict is the rule pertaining to foods than that pertaining to liquids, and more strict is the rule pertaining to liquids than that pertaining to foods. For foods have handles; and they do not require intention to be used as foods; and they impart uncleanness to liquid to put it into the first remove of uncleanness, while liquid imparting uncleanness to foods, puts them into the second remove of uncleanness. And a matter of doubt pertaining to it, in so far as it results in imparting uncleanness to other things, is deemed unclean. They cannot be made clean of uncleanness, which [rule] does not apply to liquid.

T. 1:6 More strict is the rule pertaining to liquid: For liquid [which is made unclean] is always deemed to be unclean in the first remove of uncleanness. It imparts uncleanness in any amount at all. And there are some [sorts] of them which are made unclean as a Father of uncleanness so that they impart uncleanness to clothing, impart uncleanness to man, and impart uncleanness to food. It imparts uncleanness to a utensil which is cleaned by rinsing if it touches its outer parts, and to a clay utensil if it comes into its contained airspace, which [rules] do not apply to foods.

T. 1:7 More strict is the rule applying to water than applies to [other] liquids and more strict is the rule applying to liquids than applies to water. For water becomes a Father of uncleanness so that it imparts uncleanness to man and imparts uncleanness to clothing; and it renders the immersion-pool unfit in the measure of three *logs,* and liquids in the measure of three *logs,* which is not the case for [other] liquids. And more strict is the rule concerning [other] liquids. For liquids are not made clean in the body, and they cannot be made clean of uncleanness, and they are not made clean along with the body; and they render the immersion-pool unfit if they change its color; which is not the case for water.

T. 1:8 The outer parts of utensils which are made unclean by liquids — They render liquids unclean but do not render food unfit.

M. 2:3 The porridge [made from] heave offering, and the garlic and the oil of unconsecrated food, part of which a Tebul Yom touched — he has rendered the whole unfit. The porridge [which is made] from unconsecrated food, and the garlic and the oil of heave offering, part of which a Tebul Yom touched — he has rendered unfit only the place which he touched. And if the garlic formed the greater part, they follow the greater part. And [so is the rule in the case of] all other things which are crushed, which one crushed together with liquids. But as to that which is usually crushed with liquids, and which one crushed not with liquids, and which forms a single mass in the dish, lo, they are [treated] as [if they were] a ring of figs.

M. 2:4 The porridge and the cake which were made of unconsecrated food, and oil of heave offering floats on their surface, and a Tebul Yom touched the oil — he has rendered unfit only the oil. And if he stirred [them all together], any place in which the oil ran is unfit.

T. 2:1 A piece of dough, the dough-offering of which one designated at the northern corner, and so too: a cucumber, the heave-offering of which one designated at its southern corner — lo, this is (not) deemed connected [to the remainder of the mass of the food]. If one removed its dough-offering from within it and returned it, lo, this is [not] deemed connected.

T. 2:2 The porridge [and] the cake of unconsecrated food, and the garlic and the oil of heave-offering float over them, [and] a Tebul Yom touched the oil — he has spoiled only the oil. Meat of Holy Things on which a layer of jelly formed, and so too oil which floated on the surface of wine, It is not connected [when touched] by a Tebul Yom.

M. 2:5 The meat of Holy Things on which a layer of jelly formed a crust, and a Tebul Yom touched the jelly — the pieces of meat are permitted. [If] he touched a piece of meat, the piece of meat and whatever comes up with it form a connector to one another. And so in the case of pulse which formed a crust over pieces of bread. And that which is cooked in the cooking pot and pulse, when they are Separate from one another, [are] not [deemed] connected. When they form a single mass, [they are

deemed] connected. If there were many masses [of pulse], lo, they are counted. Oil which is floating on the surface of wine, and a Tebul Yom touched the oil — he has rendered unfit only the oil.

M. 2:6 A jar which sunk into a cistern of wine, and a Tebul Yom touched it — [if he touched it] from the rim and inward, it is deemed connected. [If he touched it] from the rim and outward, it is not deemed connected.

T. 2:3 A Tebul Yom who raised up the heave-offering [wine] out of the cistern, and a jar of heave-offering [wine] fell from him and sunk down into the cistern of wine, [if it lands] from the rim and inward, it is deemed connected. From the rim and outward, it is not deemed connected. And if it was a pithos-jar, even a jar which contains a hundred kor, the entire thing forms a single connector.

M. 2:7 A jar [containing heave offering wine] which was perforated, whether at its rim or its bottom or at its sides, and which a Tebul Yom touched — it is unclean. He who pours from jar to jar, and a Tebul Yom touched the stream [of liquid], if there is in it [the jar, any wine], it is neutralized in one hundred and one.

T. 2:4 A jar which was perforated, whether at its rim or at its bottom or at its side, and which a Tebul Yom touched, is unclean.

M. 2:8 A bubble which is in a [clay] jar, which was perforated, whether on the inner side or the outer side, whether at the top or at the bottom, opposite one another — [it] is made unclean by a Father of Uncleanness and is made unclean in the Tent of the corpse. [If] the [hole on] the inside was at the bottom, and the [one on the] outside [was] at the top, it is made unclean by a Father of Uncleanness, and it is made unclean in the Tent of the corpse. [If the hole on] the inside was at the top, and the [one on the] outside was at the bottom, it is clean [if touched by] a Father of Uncleanness, but it is made unclean in the Tent of the corpse.

T. 2:5 A bubble which is in a [clay] jar which was perforated directly through from inside to outside — In the case of all of them, [if the hole is] at the sides, it is neutralized in a hundred and one.

The Tebul Yom is in a diminished remove of uncleanness by comparison with other sources of uncleanness. These latter sources impart to liquids uncleanness in the first remove (from themselves). T. 1:3 clarifies M. 2:1: the liquid of the Tebul Yom is unfit (=the second remove) but does not impart uncleanness to that which it touches (in the hypothetical third remove). Once more the interstitial situation of the Tebul Yom registers. The Tosefta then undertakes a systematic exercise of hierarchical classification of the uncleanness imparts by the Tebul Yom, the hands, foods and liquids, water and other liquids — an encompassing and brilliant realization of the hermeneutics of analogy and contrast. M. 2:3ff. proceed to differentiate primary from subsidiary components of a mixture in the context of connection, a familiar exercise indeed.

C. *SOLIDS AND CONNECTION IN THE CASE OF THE TEBUL YOM*

M. 3:1 All [stalks serving as] handles to produce which are deemed connected in the case of uncleanness imparted by a Father of Uncleanness are deemed connected in the case of [the touch of] a Tebul Yom. Produce which was severed but which is attached in part — If one holds the smaller part and the larger is pulled up with it, lo, it is deemed equivalent to it. [This estimation is made of the part that is] unclean. And as to all other produce: That which is usually held by the leaf — one holds it by the leaf. [And as to that which is usually held] by the stalk, they hold it by the stalk.

T. 2:6 Produce which was severed but which was attached in part — if it has a handle, they hold it by the handle. [If it has] a leaf, they hold it by the leaf. [If] it has both this and that, they hold it with both this and that. [If] it has neither this nor that — "They take it by the part that is] unclean." Under what circumstances? In the case of the Tebul Yom. But in the case of all other sources of uncleanness, lo, this is deemed connected.

M. 3:2 A vegetable which is of heave offering, and a beaten egg is placed on top of it — and a Tebul Yom touched the egg — he has rendered unfit only the stalk which is over against it. If it was like a cap, it is not connected.

M. 3:3 The streak of an egg which formed a crust on the sides of a pan, and which a Tebul Yom touched — [if he touched it] from the rim and inward, it is deemed connected. [If he touched it] from the rim and outward, it is not connected. And so in the case of pulse which formed a crust on the lip of the pot.

T. 2:10 The streak of an egg which formed a crust on the side of a pan and which a Tebul Yom touched — [if he touched it] from the lip and outward, it is not connected.

M. 3:4 Dough [of unconsecrated flour] which was mixed [with heave offering dough], or which was leavened with heave offering yeast, is not made unfit by a Tebul Yom. Dough which was rendered susceptible to uncleanness by liquid and kneaded with fruit juice, and which a Tebul Yom touched — he has rendered unfit only the place which he [actually] touched.

M. 3:5 An unconsecrated vegetable which one boiled in heave offering oil, and which a Tebul Yom touched — he has ren-

dered unfit only the place which he touched.

T. 2:11 Eggs which were cracked open into a dish, lo, this [mass] is not deemed connected. [When] one began to beat [them], it [still] is not connected [If] one beat them with liquids, it is deemed connected. Eggs which one cracked open into the pitcher, lo, they are not connected. [If] one began to beat them, it is not connected. [If] one beat them with liquids, it is connected. [If] one beat them with their own water, they are made susceptible to uncleanness. Lo, they are comparable to the ring of dried figs.

T. 2:12 Rings of dried figs, on part of which liquids fell — one removes from it only the place on which the liquid fell alone.

We turn from liquids to solids and from mixtures to connection. Throughout the generic hermeneutics governs.

II. THE UNCLEANNESS OF THE TEBUL YOM

M. 3:6 A clean person who chewed on food, and it fell on his clothing and on a loaf of bread of heave offering — it is subject to uncleanness. [If] he was eating crushed olives, and wet dates — anything on the pit of which he wishes to suck — and it fell on his clothing and on a loaf of bread of heave offering — it is subject to receive uncleanness. [If] he was eating dried olives and dry dates — anything on the pit of which he does not wish to suck — and it fell on his garments and on a loaf of bread of heave offering — it is insusceptible to receive uncleanness. All the same is the rule which applies to the clean person and to the Tebul Yom in these matters. The Tebul Yom is not regarded as unclean.

T. 2:13 The liquid of a Tebul Yom is like that of a clean person.

M. 4:1 Produce of tithe which was rendered susceptible to uncleanness by liquid and which a Tebul Yom touched, or dirty hands [=unclean in the second remove] — they separate from it heave offering of tithe in a state of cleanness, because it is in the third remove, and the third remove is clean so far as unconsecrated food is concerned.

M. 4:2 The woman who is a Tebul Yom kneads dough and cuts off dough offering for it, and sets it apart, and puts it in an Egyptian basket or on a board, and brings it near and designates it by name, because it is in the third remove of uncleanness, and the third remove is clean so far as unconsecrated food is concerned.

M. 4:3 A kneading trough which is in the status of that which has been immersed on the selfsame day — they knead

dough in it, and cut off dough offering from it, and she brings it near, and designates it by name, because it is in the third remove, and that which is in the third remove is clean for unconsecrated food.

M. 4:4 A flagon which is in the status of that which had been immersed on the selfsame day and which had been filled from a jar containing [first] tithe which was yet untithed — if he said, "Lo, this will be heave offering of tithe once it gets dark," lo, this is heave offering of tithe once the sun sets. If he said, "Lo, this is an 'erub," he has said nothing. [If] the jar broke, what is in the flagon continues in its status of being untithed. [If] the flagon broke, the jar remains in its status of being untithed.

M. 4:5 At first they would rule: They exchange [second-tithe money in Jerusalem] for the produce of an 'am ha'ares. They reverted to rule: Even for his coins. At first they would rule: He who goes forth in fetters and stated, "Write a writ of divorce for my wife" — lo, they are to write and deliver [the writ of divorce to his wife]. They reverted to rule: [That is the rule] even in the case of one who went out on a voyage or set forth with a caravan.

M. 4:6 The Askelon grappling irons which were broken and the hook of which remains — lo, these are unclean. The pitchfork, the winnowing fork, and the rake, and so, too, a hair-comb, one of the teeth of which was removed and [the wooden tooth of] which one repaired with a metal one — lo, these are unclean.

M. 4:7 He who gives heave offering from the cistern, and said, "Lo, this is heave offering on condition that it come up in safety" — [his condition is understood to mean], safe from breakage and from spillage, but not from uncleanness. [If the jar] broke, it does not count as heave offering. To what extent is it broken and not counted as heave offering? Only so far that it rolls back and reaches the cistern.

T. 2:14 The woman who is a Tebul[at] Yom kneads dough, and cuts off a piece as dough-offering, and sets it aside, and leaves it in a basket or on a board, and brings it near and designates it by name — because it is in the third remove, and that which is in the third remove is clean so far as unconsecrated food is concerned. A kneading trough which is in the status of that which has been immersed on the selfsame day — they knead dough in it, and cut off from it dough-offering, bring it near, and designate it by name, because it is in the third remove, and the third remove is clean so far as unconsecrated food is concerned.

T. 2:15 He who raises up heave-offering from the cistern and set it in a place from which it would roll down and reach the cistern,

> and [then] went and put it in a place from which it would not roll down and reach the cistern [if] it spilled, lo, this is deemed [to have been removed from the cistern] in safety. [If] he was raising up heave-offering from the cistern and the jar cracked or poured out, if a sufficient volume of it to be considered heave-offering trickled down from it [back into the pit], lo, this [not] deemed [to have been removed from the cistern] in safety, and if not, this is (not) deemed [to have been removed from the cistern] in safety.
>
> T. 2:16 [If] he was raising up as heave-offering four or five jars, even though a sufficient amount of each one of them did not trickle back [into the cistern] to be deemed heave-offering, lo, this is deemed [to have been raised from the cistern] in safety, because it is deemed that he made a condition to govern each one of them. Under what circumstances? In the case of heave-offering of the first [vintage] of wine or oil, for :he heave-offering of the first [vintage] is taken only from that which is nearby. But in the case of heave-offering of all other produce, this is not deemed [to have been taken up] in safety.
>
> T. 2:17 [If] one separated heave-offering and Heave-offering of tithe simultaneously — in the case of all other produce, lo, this is deemed [to have been raised up] in safety.

M. 4:1 goes over the basic rule that what is unclean in the second remove has no affect upon unconsecrated food, and the liquid produced by the Tebul Yom is unclean in the second remove, therefore of no affect upon unconsecrated food that it touches. This same consideration governs at M. 4:2ff.

IV. THE HERMENEUTICS OF TEBUL YOM

A. WHAT FUSES THE HALAKHIC DATA INTO A CATEGORY-FORMATION?

For an essay on interstitiality and mixture, the Halakhah of Tebul Yom provides an ideal setting. And that defines what fuses the category-formation, its active hermeneutics Scripture leaves no doubt that what has been washed in water is unclean until the evening, then when the sun has set, it is clean. The Halakhah registers that the Tebul Yom is in the second remove of uncleanness, imparting unfitness to heave offering. These two facts produce the hermeneutics — principle of selection and interpretation of data — of the category-formation, which I have already characterized as fundamentally generic, with elements particular to the category-formation.

The generic hermeneutics emerges from the two facts stated at the outset, which yield the logical next question: What are the parameters of interstitiality? Does that mean what has been immersed is really unclean until evening, therefore falling into the same status as all other sources of uncleanness? Or is what has been immersed really clean, therefore imparting unfitness to heave offering in accord with the distinction between what is primary and what is secondary? As we have noted, the generic issue, that of classification, is addressed at the point of acute interstitiality, which is connection. There we want to know whether the object affects the status of what is attached to it, whether the attachment (the stem to the fruit) is deemed detached therefrom. So we shift the analysis of the intermediate status of the Tebul Yom to the status of what is intermediate in the object of uncleanness. And there we further ask yet another relativizing question: what is primary and what is subordinate in a mixture, what is essential and what is peripheral in a composite. And, we note at the very outset, for the first and only time in considering the sources of cultic uncleanness that contaminate the Israelite household, we even introduce the variable of intentionality..

B. THE ACTIVITY OF THE CATEGORY-FORMATION

Only through sorting out the interstitialities triggered by immersion, waiting, and then resolved by sunset, can sages say what they wish to declare. So we must identify the main lines of halakhic thinking and then determine where they lead us: how the Tebul Yom is essentially unclean, but in some ways clean; how he is essentially clean, but in some ways, unclean.

THE ESSENTIAL UNCLEANNESS OF THE TEBUL YOM: The Tebul Yom is unclean so far as priestly rations or heave offering is concerned and clean for unconsecrated food. He cannot eat food that is preserved in conditions of cleanness. But he does not impart uncleanness to unconsecrated food. So the immersion does affect his status as to uncleanness. He functions as an unclean person or object so far as the heave offering (all the more so, Holy Things) is concerned but having immersed, is less unclean than are other unclean persons or objects prior to immersion. So he imparts uncleanness in diminished ways. What is touched by a person in the status of the Tebul Yom therefore falls into the third remove of uncleanness, and what is in the third remove in the case of unconsecrated food is clean. This is expressed at M. 4:1: Produce of tithe which was rendered susceptible to uncleanness by liquid and which a Tebul Yom touched, or dirty hands [=unclean in the second remove] — they separate from it heave offering of tithe in a state of cleanness, because it is in the third remove, and the third remove is clean so far as unconsecrated food is concerned.

In its own terms, the uncleanness of the Tebul Yom is then both explicit in the Torah and carefully circumscribed in the Halakhah. But sages wish to clarify the ambiguity of that status by classifying it is interstitial, for which purpose the ideal medium is the notion of connection: how one component — primary or subordinate — of a composite affects the status of other components. The ambiguous status of the Tebul Yom in regard to uncleanness comes to concrete expression in the matter of connection. The recurrent issue of the Halakhah is whether the Tebul Yom imparts uncleanness through certain substances to the objects to which they are connected. Some Rabbinic opinion declines to distinguish connection in the case of the Tebul Yom from connection in the case of all other sources of uncleanness. But the normative position is that the Tebul Yom is in a separate category from all other sources of uncleanness, and therefore where there is a dubious connection, in the case of the Tebul Yom but no other source of uncleanness, connection is null.

Where we have a mixture of food in the status of heave offering and unconsecrated food, the issue of connection further arises. At M. 2:3 the matter is worked out in terms of what is primary to a mixture as against what is secondary. If the porridge is heave offering and the Tebul Yom has touched it, he renders unfit also garlic and oil in the mixture. If the porridge is unconsecrated and the garlic and oil are in the status of heave offering, then the Tebul Yom renders unfit only the place that he touches. So what touching what is secondary does not affect what is primary in the mixture, and that distinction reaches even Holy Things, not only heave offering. If we have egg that is unconsecrated and a vegetable beneath, then what is connected to the egg? It is only the stalk. If the egg is beaten and forms a little cap over the vegetable without touching, then there is no connection; touching the egg is not like touching the vegetable.

THE ESSENTIAL CLEANNESS OF THE TEBUL YOM is expressed in connection with excretions and liquids that he touches. Liquid that he produces is in the status of the Tebul Yom himself; his spit or urine does not impart uncleanness, but if it touches heave offering, it renders the heave offering unfit. But liquid produced by all other sources of uncleanness, minor or major, is equivalent to liquid touched by said sources of uncleanness, but not equal in uncleanness to the sources themselves. The liquid is unclean in the first remove; the exception is liquid that itself is a Father of uncleanness, e.g., the spit or urine of the Zab. Then if there is liquid in the status of heave offering in a pot and a Tebul Yom touched it, the liquid is unfit, but the pot clean. If the liquid is unconsecrated, the touch of the Tebul Yom has no effect: A cooking pot which is full of liquids, and which a Tebul Yom touched, if it was liquid of heave offering, the liquids are unfit, but the pot is clean. And if it was liquid of unconsecrated food, all is clean. But if the hands of the Tebul Yom — which by definition are in the second remove of uncleanness, and what is in the second remove of uncleanness places liquid into the first remove — have not been washed in the manner specified in the Halakhah of Yadayim, they — and they alone of all his body — impart uncleanness to the liquid.

STATUS VERSUS SUBSTANCE: That the entire construction of the Halakhah forms an exercise in immaterial, impalpable relationships emerges in the illustration of what it means to be "unclean until sunset, then it will be clean." That is provided at M. 4:4. The flagon has been immersed on the same day and is in the second remove of uncleanness. There is a jar that has tithe from which heave offering of tithe has not yet been removed. If the man has said that, once sun sets, concluding the process of purification of the flagon and rendering the flagon suitable even for heave offering, what is in the jar is regarded as heave offering of tithe, what he has said is valid. That is because there is no reason not to use the flagon for heave offering; the flagon is clean. If he said, when it gets dark, it will be deemed an ''erub-meal, the statement is null, because the meal must be available for use while it is still daylight, and at that time, what is in the flagon is still in the status of tithe from which heave offering tithe has not been removed. If before sunset the jar broke, the tithe goes to waste; what is in the flagon is untithed, because, once it got dark, at the time when it was necessary to designate heave offering tithe, we do not have the tithe, that is, we don't have what was in the broken jar.

The upshot is, the statement that the man makes takes effect at the specified time; nothing has changed in the character of the produce in the flagon, except that the sun has set and the man's declaration has taken effect. So uncleanness and cleanness are treated here as not substantive but contingent, and they depend upon circumstance and declared intentionality. Everything then depends on sunset, and the religious significance of the sun's setting provides the key to the interpretation of what is at stake in the Halakhah that is before us.

C. THE CONSISTENCY OF THE CATEGORY-FORMATION

We can explain each component of the category-formation within our general theory of the hermeneutics, generic and particular but principally generic. All the data that are chosen and the entire program of interpreting those data, realized within the exegetical agenda of the category-formation, are founded upon the category-formation as defined at section I.

D. THE GENERATIVITY OF THE CATEGORY-FORMATION

I see no marks of the power to extend the boundaries to new territory, to generate new problems and to solve them. We deal with a secondary development of Miqvaot, not a primary category-formation capable of precipitating thought in new directions.

6.
TRACTATE YADAYIM

I. THE DEFINITION OF THE CATEGORY-FORMATION

The category-formation devoted to the uncleanness and purification of the hands encompasses issues usually not joined in a single such formation: [1] a source of uncleanness, [2] a medium of purification. That represents an anomaly, for the category-formations Zabim-Niddah and Ohalot do not join together with Miqvaot and Parah, respectively. In the present case, by contrast, we deal with a distinct source of uncleanness and the particular medium of removing uncleanness therefrom. The outline shows the layout:

MODES OF PURIFICATION OF THE HANDS

I. WASHING HANDS. A REPERTOIRE OF RULES

II. WASHING HANDS. THE STATUS AND CONDITION OF THE WATER. FIRST AND SECOND POURINGS OF WATER

THE HANDS AS A SOURCE OF UNCLEANNESS

III. THE STATUS OF UNCLEANNESS IMPUTED TO HANDS

AN ANALOGUE

IV. THE UNCLEANNESS OF SACRED SCRIPTURES

Clearly, units I-II concern themselves with the purification of hands, viewed as a distinct domain of uncleanness and purification, and unit iii takes up the uncleanness of hands: at what remove, with what consequence? While, obviously, we cannot treat the two components of the category formation in isolation from one another, to remain consistent with the modes of analysis that we have followed throughout, we have also to ask our hermeneutical question to each part on its own, in sequence.[15] Then, as usual, the decisive, contrastive

[15] It may seem more natural to proceed in the order of the category-formation, purification, then source of uncleanness. I reverse the order because the result of the

issues emerge as soon as we articulate the analogical process.

ANALOGICAL-CONTRASTIVE ANALYSIS OF THE HANDS' UNCLEANNESS: An animate source of uncleanness, the hands are like the body in that they contract and transmit uncleanness. But they are unlike the rest of the body in one fundamental trait: they are active, and one is not always aware of what his hands are doing. Intentionality need not apply. So while one may bear the intent to preserve cleanness and so take note of possible sources of uncleanness he may touch, when it comes to the hands, alertness does not suffice; the hands ultimately fall beyond man's responsible control. By reason of the contrast to the rest of the body, which is reasonably subjected to sentient intentionality, the hands form a distinct realm of uncleanness, distinct from the body. Fingertips to wrist subject to different rules, they are deemed perpetually unclean. That marks the hands as a distinct among the animate sources of uncleanness. They are deemed under all circumstances unclean in the second remove.

ANALOGICAL-CONTRASTIVE ANALYSIS OF THE PURIFICATION-PROCESS OF HANDS: The contrast to the rest of the body carries over to the purification process. The body is purified by immersion in an immersion pool of still water, unaffected by man's power and intentionality. What of the hands? Subject to their own rite of purification, the area from the wrists to the fingertips forms a separate area not only for contracting uncleanness but also for removing it.

The analogical-contrastive process is readily worked out. Purifying the body and the hands by water self-evidently defines the analogical component. The contrast begins in the now-established premise that, willy-nilly, known or unknown, as a matter of certainty, not as a matter of doubt, the hands have contracted uncleanness (in the second remove, to be sure). That is because the hands act without regard to man's will. Then in respect to purifying the hands we invoke the opposite of the rule governing the situation that is entirely beyond man's control. Purifying the hands requires a supreme act of will, confirmed by human intervention, to counteract the utter absence of intentionality. That explains why the immersion pool will not serve, and water collected and applied without human intervention will not do; water that lies still, into which man descends, will not purify. Water man has collected and by force of his own hand used for rinsing the hand is what purifies. So, we see, thinking along the analogical-contrastive path, we devise a contrasting mode of purifica-

---

analogical-contrastive analysis of the species of uncleanness of hands in the genus, bodily uncleanness, prepares the way for the work on the purification-process. The result of both analyses is uniform, as, by this point, we should expect of the Halakhic system. But in a moment I shall account for the received order of sub-divisions, and the prevailing theory of the ordering of matters will be shown to account for matters here too.

tion, one that is congruent with, therefore responds to, the conditions under which, in the case of the distinct domain of the hands, uncleanness is contracted.

In hermeneutical terms, what we want is the opposite of the hermeneutics of Miqvaot, which excludes human intervention in the purification-process. We seek a hermeneutics — a principle of selection and interpretation of data — of intense human engagement with the preparation and delivery of the medium of purification, water. What category-formation provides the model? The opposite of Miqvaot is Parah. Then the hermeneutics of Parah must govern: water subject to human intervention, delivered in a utensil, by the force of a man's own power. So the analogical-contrastive analysis of the species of a common genus does its work: while the genus is, water that purifies, the species contrast at the critical point of the role of man in bringing into existence and in utilizing the medium of purification. And we can explain both elements of the complex category-formation, Yadayim, the uncleanness of hands, distinct from the body, the purification of hands by a distinctive process of purification. To state the hermeneutical principle that generates the exegetical program of the category-formation, Yadayim: *uncleanness contracted by utter disengagement of man's will is removed by water totally subject to man's intentionality and physical power.*

DEFINING THE CATEGORY-FORMATION, YADAYIM, THE MEDIUM OF PURIFICATION, THE CHARACTER OF THE BODY-UNCLEANNESS: First, are we able to explain the sequence of topics, the medium of purification, then the character of the uncleanness? Having accounted by a hypothetical reconstruction of the analogical-contrastive reasoning process for the hermeneutics of the category-formation, we realize, the key point of contrastive analysis pertains to the character of the purification-process, the water. There the contrast of Parah and Miqvaot proved blatant. And the particular hermeneutics of the category-formation turns out to take first place in the exegetical program thereof — as, we have found, defines the priority of matters throughout: first comes the particular hermeneutics of the category-formation, then the generic hermeneutics of the Halakhah.

Second, are we able to identify the key-points of the particular hermeneutics that trigger the exegetical program of the category-formation? Indeed we are. They are these. Water used for purification of the hands involves human agency and intentionality, and water used for purification of the body from uncleanness does not — a huge difference signaled by a small distinction. Since the hands are not immersed in water, but rather water is poured out by the force of a man's action onto the hands, human agency is required in the use, not only the preparation of the water. Human agency would spoil the water for the immersion-pool, which must be collected naturally; by contrast, human agency is demanded for water used for the purification-rite. Then the exegetical program of the Halakhah will want to know the exact rules governing human intervention, the collecting and the pouring of the water by the intentional act of man, and the like.

Third, with Parah as the model, what statement emerges from the facts now adduced? These facts establish

[1] that the hands are deemed always just one remove away from corpse-contamination, and

[2] that it is through water analogous to that used for preparing purification-water for the removal of corpse-uncleanness that the hands are sanctified (not merely cleansed of uncleanness, with sunset required to complete the process of purification) even for eating food in the status of priestly rations?

What I hear from the Halakhah is the statement, death is ever-present, if not in what is touched, then in what has touched what is touched. So the hands are always in the second remove of uncleanness, meaning, death is always just a step or two away from contact with what is meant to be kept holy, clear of death. And that is — in the context of the hands and when they are sanctified — food for the nourishment of Israel. But death and all that death overspreads can be kept beyond the boundary of the household table by deliberate action defined by perpetual concern: the right intention, especially for the meal. So with that first bite of bread at the meal, the stakes are very high indeed.

"SANCTIFYING THE HANDS" IN THE CONTINUOUS ENCOUNTER WITH DEATH: The vocabulary of the category-formation makes a distinction in purification-rites, between "sanctifying" the hands (in Scripture's language, as we shall see) and "rinsing/washing" persons or garments in an immersion pool. And that difference between "sanctifying" hands and "rinsing/washing" persons or garments leads to the question, What about the contrast between uncleanness of hands and sanctification of hands? That too is drawn explicitly. The Halakhah expresses the contrast between death and sanctification, as we now understand, by a statement of the match of opposites. A single complex component of the category-formation bears the entire message: the contrast between [1] the character of the utensil used in connection with water for sanctifying hands as against water for rinsing, and [2] the preparation of the water used for sanctification of hands as against that used for removing uncleanness of the rest of the body.

[1] As to the utensil, here is how: "For they draw, and they mix water with the ash of the red cow, and they sprinkle purification water, and they pour [water] for hands only with a utensil ." Matters could not be made

more explicit. As usual, the exegetical program of the category-formation flows directly from its particular hermeneutics. Thus a utensil that cannot be used for drawing water for hand-washing does not require a tightly-sealed cover to serve to interpose against uncleanness, and one that does also requires a tightly sealed cover in the Tent of a corpse. So the areas of Halakhah are deemed corresponding and opposite. The contrastive force of death and sanctification renews itself in the present matter.

[2] The same rules govern water for mixing with ashes to make purification-water for the removal of corpse-uncleanness and water for use in sanctifying the hands. The gathering of the water used for sanctifying the hands conforms in the definition of the required attitudes and actions to the requirements for collecting the water used for mixing with the ashes of the red cow (Num. 19:1ff.) in preparing purification-water for the removal of corpse-uncleanness.

As we saw at the Halakhah of Parah, the collection of the water for combining with the ashes, not only the appropriate utensil for use in that connection, involve strict and rigid rules. These same rules govern here as well, so far as sages can apply them. The act must be purposive, the water gathered deliberately, by human action, in a valid utensil. Water for the immersion pool must collect naturally, unaffected by human action, and may not be collected in a utensil. It follows that uncleanness of hands is removed by water, and preparation of the water accords with the rules pertinent to purification-water utilized for mixing with the ashes of the red cow, Num. 19:14ff. That governing analogy is made explicit, e.g., they draw, and they mix water with the ash of the red cow, and they sprinkle purification water, and they pour water for hands only with a utensil. The analogy of the immersion pool and its water is rejected. Deliberate human action effected through a whole, useful utensil is required. I do not know how the Halakhah could have stated more blatantly than it does the contrast between death and sanctification, and the identification of the hands as the principal media, the arena where that contrast is acted out.

INTENTIONALITY: MOST STRICTLY REQUIRED WHERE NATURALLY ABSENT: And to underline the difference between the sanctification of the hands and the purification of utensils or the greater part of persons, intentionality is insisted upon: the collection of water by intention for sanctifying hands would invalidate water for immersing persons and utensils in an immersion pool. That is to say, by contrast, deliberate human action that collects water in a utensil spoils water for use in an immersion pool. So the special standing of the hands and their sanctification comes to expression in the halakhic invocation of the metaphor of the rite for removing corpse-uncleanness rather than the rite for moving uncleanness in general. So sanctification and corpse-uncleanness are explicitly juxtaposed as opposites in the details of the Halakhah, which turns out to set forth a uniform message by saying the same thing about many things, but not about everything.

II. THE SCRIPTURAL FOUNDATIONS OF THE HALAKHIC CATEGORY-FORMATION

Scripture is explicit that priests in the tabernacle "sanctify" (wash) their hands and feet before performing priestly functions at the altar (Ex. 30:19-21, 40:12, 31-32): "Command the priests that they wash their hands and feet lest they die" (Ex. 30:21). Hand-washings punctuate the high priest's conduct of the rite on the Day of Atonement (Lev. 16). The word-choice bears heavy implications, but in the category-formation the data of Scripture play no role that I am able to identify.

III. THE EXPOSITION OF THE COMPONENTS OF THE GIVEN CATEGORY-FORMATION BY THE MISHNAH-TOSEFTA

I. WASHING HANDS. A REPERTOIRE OF RULES

M. 1:1 [To render hands clean] a quarter-log of water do they pour for hands, for one, also for two. A half-log [is to be used] for three or four. A log [is to be used] for five and for ten and for a hundred. They add [to the water used] for the second [pouring], but they do not add [to the water used] for the first [pouring of water over the hands].

T. 1:1 [To render hands clean], a quarter-log of water do they pour for one, but not for two. A quarter-log of water do they pour for hands, even for two, and a half a *log* for three, even for four, a *log* for five and ten and a hundred.

T. 1:2 They add to the second but they do not add to the first — How so? [If] one poured the first [water] and rubbed off [his hands] and went and poured the second, and it [the water] is not sufficient to reach the wrist, lo, this one adds to it. All the same is one who washes one of his hands and one who washes two of his hands, [all the same is] the hand of a large person and the hand of a small one — he must pour out a quarter-log [of water]. How so? [If] two people washed their two hands with a quarter-log, the second one should not go and wash his hands with what is left of the quarter-log.

T. 1:5 He who washes his hands [for unconsecrated food prepared in accord with cleanness required for] Holy Things must pour out a quarter-log of water. And as to the sanctification [washing] of hands and feet, there is no fixed measure.

M. 1:2 With all sorts of utensils do they pour [water] for hands, even with utensils made of dung, utensils made of stone, utensils made of [unbaked] clay. They do not pour [water] for hands either with the sides of [broken] utensils, or the bottom of a ladling jar, or with the plug of a barrel. Nor should a man pour [water] for his fellow with his cupped hands. For they draw, and they mix [water with the ash of the red cow], and they sprinkle purification water, and they pour [water] for hands only with a utensil. And only utensils afford protection with a tightly fitted cover, and nothing affords protection from the power of a clay utensil [in the Tent of a corpse] except utensils.

T. 1:6 A stopper which one made for a utensil — they pour out water from it for hands. The water-skin and the tub, even though they are broken down — they pour out from them water for hands. The sack and the basket, even though they hold [liquid] — they do not pour out water from them for the hands. A chest, box, and cupboard, when they hold [requisite measure to be insusceptible to uncleanness], even though they are not deemed as Tents — they do not pour out water from them for hands.

T. 1:7 Priests sanctify in the sanctuary only with a utensil. And they force the suspected wife to drink, and they purify person afflicted with the skin-ailment of Lev. 13 s [only with a utensil]. The sides of a wooden utensil and a bone utensil and glass utensil — they do not pour out from them water for hands. If one smoothed them, sanded them, and made them into utensils and they can hold a quarter-log of water, they do pour out water from them for hands.

T. 1:8 Shards of earthenware utensils which can hold a quarter-log of water — they pour out from them water for hands. Shards of metal utensils, even though they can hold a quarter-log of water — they do not pour out from them water for hands.

T. 1:9 He who hews out a water-channel and made in it a receptacle, even though the water uprooted it and attached it — they do not draw with it water for the purification-rite and they do not mix in it, and they do not sprinkle from it [purification-water onto someone made unclean by the corpse], and it does not require a tightly-sealed cover, and they do not pour out water for hands from it. [If] one uprooted it and affixed it and gave thought to it to make use of it as a utensil after its uprooting — they do draw with it, and they do mix in it, and they do sprinkle from it, and it does require a tightly sealed cover [in the Tent of the corpse], and they do pour water for hands from it.

M. 1:3 Water which was unfit for cattle to drink [when it is located] in utensils, is unfit. [When it is located] on the ground, it is fit. [If] there fell into it ink, gum, or copperas, and its color changed, it is unfit. [If] one did work with it, or if he soaked his bread in it, it is unfit.

T. 1:10 Water which has been made unfit for cattle to drink — [If] it is on the ground, they immerse [in it], but they do not pour from it water for hands. Water which is before the baker, even though its color has not changed — they do not pour from it water for hands. And when he takes it with his hands and pours it on loaves, if its color changes, it is unfit. And if not, it is fit.

M. 1:4 [If] he rinsed utensils in it, or scrubbed measures in it, it is unfit. [If] he rinsed in it vessels which had already been rinsed, or new [vessels], it is fit.

M. 1:5 The water in which the baker dips loaves of fine bread is unfit. And when he rinses his hands in it, it is fit. All are fit to pour water on hands, even a deaf-mute, an imbecile, or a minor. One places the jar between his knees and pours [out water on his hands]. One sets the jar on its side and pours [out water]. And the ape pours water for hands.

T. 1:11 Water which is before the smith, even though its color has not changed — they do not pour from it water for hands, for it is certain that work has been done in it. Water which is before the scribe, if its color has changed, is unfit, and if not, is fit.

T. 1:12 All are fit to pour out water for hands, even a person unclean by reason of corpse-contamination, even a man who has had intercourse with a menstruating woman. Whoever does not impart uncleanness to water when he carries it is fit to pour out water for hands.

T. 1:13 [If] the one who takes the water intends and the one who pours out the water does not intend [that by his act the water will clean the hands], [if] the one who pours out the water intends, and the one who takes the water does not intend [that the water should clean the hands] his hands are deemed clean.

T. 1:14 [If] one broke open the caldron and poured out water for hands from a pipe which contains a place capable of containing a quarter-log of water — his hands are clean.

The key-requirement is at M. 1:2: we must have a whole, valid utensil, just as for water for the purification-mixture. Broken utensils cannot be used. The analogy is made explicit, lest we miss the point. The Tosefta at T. 1:7 makes an explicit link between the vocabulary of Scripture ("priests sanctify" and the rite of rinsing the hands). But, M. 1:5, the intentionality of the one who pours the water on the hands is null. The power of the pouring must be human; the intent behind the pouring does not pertain. T. 1:13 makes that point explicit.

II. WASHING HANDS. THE STATUS AND CONDITION OF THE WATER. FIRST AND SECOND POURINGS OF WATER

M. 2:1 [If] one poured water for one hand with a single rinsing, his hand is clean. [If he poured water] for two hands with a single rinsing — [If] a loaf of heave offering fell [on the water a quarter-log in quantity which has been poured on the hands in a single rinsing], it is clean.

T. 1:3 One who pours water on his hands must rub his hands off. [If] he rubbed one hand on the other, it is unclean. [If he rubbed it] on his head or on the wall, it is clean. [If] he went and touched them, it is unclean.

M. 2:2 [If] one poured out the first [water] in one place and the second in another place, and a loaf of heave offering fell on the first, it is unclean. And [if it fell] on the second, it is clean. [If] he poured out the first [water] and the second in one place, and a loaf of heave offering fell [on it], it is unclean. [If] he poured out the first [water], and a splinter or pebble was found on his hands, his hands are unclean, for the second water cleans only the water which is on the hand.

T. 1:4 Whatever interposes in the case of the body interposes in the case of the hands, with reference to the sanctification of the hands and feet for the Temple House.

T. 2:3 He who pours out water on his hands, if he had proper intention, his hands are clean, and if not, his hands are unclean. But he who immerses his hands, one way or the other — his hands are clean.

T. 2:5 [If] one poured out the first water, and one of his hands was made unclean, lo, this one pours out the second water on the second hand and does not scruple in the matter. [If] he poured out the first water, and it flowed beyond the wrist, and then he poured out the second water on it, and a loaf of bread fell from the wrist and inward, it is unclean. [If it fell] from the wrist and outward, it is clean

T. 2:6 [If] he poured out the first water and the second water beyond the wrist, and a loaf of heave-offering bread fell, it is unclean. But logic requires that it be clean: Now if the (first) [rain] water, which does not impart cleanness to water which is on the hand, imparts cleanness to water which is on the ground, the second water, which does impart cleanness to the water which is on the hand, logically should impart cleanness to water which is on the ground.

M. 2:3 The hands are susceptible to uncleanness and are rendered clean up to the wrist. How so? [If] one poured the first [water] up to the wrist, and the second beyond the wrist and it went back to the hand — it is clean. [If] he poured out the first and the second [pouring of water] beyond the wrist and it went back to the hand, it is unclean. [If] he poured out the first water onto one hand, and was reminded and poured out the second [water] on to both hands, they are unclean. [If] he poured out the first water on to both hands and was reminded and poured out the second [water] on to one hand, his hand [which has been washed twice] is clean. [If] he poured out water on to one hand and rubbed it on the other, it is unclean. [If he rubbed his hand] on his head or on the wall, it is clean. They pour out [water on the hands of] four or five people side by side, or above one another, J. on condition that they [the hands] lie loosely so that the water will flow among them.

T. 2:1 The priests sanctify in the sanctuary, in regard to the hand, up to the wrist, and in regard to the foot, up to the calf. He who pours out water on his hands should not say, "Since the first [water] is unclean [anyway], lo, I shall pour out unclean [water to begin with]." If he did so, lo, he must dry off his hands. He who pours out water on his hands must dry his hands. But he who immerses his hands does not have to dry off his hands.

T. 2:2 He who pours water on his hands must raise his hands so that the water does not flow beyond the wrist and go back and render his hands unclean. But he who immerses his hands does not have to raise his hands.

T. 2:4 He who pours water on his hands — if the water goes up to the wrist, his hands are clean, and if not, his hands are unclean. [If] he poured out the first water on this [hand] by itself and changed his mind and poured out the second water on both hands simultaneously, they render one another unclean. [If] he poured out the first water on both hands and changed his mind and poured out the second [water], this on this hand by itself and that on that hand by itself, if he had proper intention in the matter, his hands are clean, and if not, his hands are unclean.

T. 2:7 They pour out water for four or five people, one beside the other, and they do not scruple on account of four things: lest it be made unclean; lest work have been done with it; lest it not be poured from a utensil; and lest a quarter-log not be poured out on a hand. But he who takes and he who pours out for his fellow with his cupped hands — his [the fellow's] hands are unclean, for in the first place the water has not been poured from a utensil.

T. 2:8 Two who poured out water for two hands, this one from [a measure of] an eighth of a *log,* and this one from an eighth of a *log,* even though it goes and is mixed together in a spout — their hands are unclean. For in the first place [the water] was not poured from a quarter-log.

M. 2:4 [If it is in] doubt that work has or has not been done with it, [if it is in] doubt that they contain or do not contain the requisite measure, [if it is in] doubt whether it is unclean or clean — a matter of doubt concerning it is clean. For they have said: A matter of doubt concerning the hands, whether [they are] unclean, or whether [they are deemed] to have imparted uncleanness, or whether [they are deemed] to have been made clean, is resolved as clean. How so? [If] his hands were clean, and before him were two unclean loaves of bread, [if it is in] doubt whether or not he touched them — [if] his hands were unclean, and before him were two clean loaves of bread, [if] one of his hands was unclean and one of his hands was clean and before him were two clean loaves of bread, [and if] he touched one of them, [if it is in] doubt whether he touched with the unclean or whether he touched with the clean [hand] — [if] his hands were clean, and before him were two loaves of bread, one of them unclean and one of them clean, [and if] he touched one of them, [if it is in] doubt whether he touched the unclean or whether he touched the clean [loaf of bread] — [if] one of his hands was unclean and one was clean, and before him were two loaves [of bread], one of them unclean and one of them clean, [if] he touched both of them, [if it is in] doubt whether the unclean [hand touched] the unclean [loaf of bread] and the clean [hand touched] the clean [loaf of bread], or [whether] the clean [hand touched] the unclean [loaf of bread] and the unclean [hand touched] the clean [loaf of bread] — the hands remain as they were before [in their former status], and the loaves of bread as they were before [in their former status].

T. 1:15 [If] there were before him two glasses [of water] — with one of them work had been done, and with one of them work had not been done — [if] he poured [water] from one of them onto both of his hands and prepared foods requiring cleanness — they are held in suspense. [If he poured out water] from the second and prepared [foods requiring cleanness], they are clean. [If he poured out water] from the first and did not prepare foods requiring cleanness, [and if he then poured out water] from the second and prepared [foods requiring cleanness], they are clean. [If he poured out water] from the first and prepared from the second and prepared [if] these and those are lying [before him] these and those are clean.

T. 1:16 [If] one poured out [water] from one of them on to one of his hands and prepared foods requiring cleanness, they are held in suspense. [If he did so] from the second and prepared [foods requiring cleanness], they are clean. [If he did so] from the first and did not prepare from the second and did prepare [foods requiring cleanness], they are clean. [If he poured out water] from the first and prepared from the second and prepared [if] these and those are lying [before him], these and those are clean.

T. 1:17 [If] there were before him two glasses [of water], one unclean and one clean. and he poured out [water] from one of them for one of his hands and prepared foods requiring cleanness they are held in suspense. [If he did so] from the second and prepared [foods requiring cleanness], they are clean. [If he did so] from the first and did not prepare from the second and prepared [they are clean. (If he did so) from the first and prepared, from the second and prepared] — [if] these and those are lying before him lo, they determine [the status of one another]. [If] he ate the first [foods which he prepared], or they were made unclean, or they were lost, before the second [foods requiring cleanness] were prepared, they are clean. [If this took place] after the second were prepared, the second are kept in a state of suspense. [If] he poured out water from one of them on to one of his hands and prepared things requiring foods requiring cleanness, they are kept in suspense. [If he poured out] the second and prepared [foods requiring cleanness], they are clean. [If he did so] with the first and did not prepare, with the second and did prepare, [if] these and those are lying [before him], [supply: lo, they determine (the status of one another).]

T. 1:18 [If] one of his hands was unclean, and one of his hands was clean, and before him were two glasses, one unclean and one clean, and he poured out water from one of them on to both his hands and prepared foods requiring cleanness, they are kept in a state of suspense. [If] one of his hands was unclean, and one was clean, and before him were two loaves of bread, one unclean and one clean, and [if] his two hands touched one loaf, whether simultaneously or in succession, or one of his hands touched both of the loaves, in succession the hands and the loaves are kept in a state of suspense. [If] one of his hands touched the two loaves simultaneously, the hands remain as they were, and the loaves of bread are to be burned.

The generic hermeneutics takes over, now with a series of interstitial cases and cases of doubt. We have specified the correct volume of water to be used, so now we want to know the result of using the correct volume on a single hand, instead of on both hands. Then again, two rinsings are required, M. 2:2-3. Why is that the case? If hands are washed only once, one may not touch heave offering, because the water with which the hands were washed the first time around is unclean in the first remove; the man washes his hands a second time to remove the uncleanness of the water that has touched his hands and was thereby made unclean.

III. THE STATUS OF UNCLEANNESS IMPUTED TO HANDS

M. 3:1 He who pokes his hands into a house afflicted with nega' his hands are in the second remove of uncleanness. Whoever imparts uncleanness to clothing, when in contact [with them], imparts uncleanness to the hands — so that they are in the second remove of uncleanness. That which is made unclean by a Father of Uncleanness imparts uncleanness to the hands. [That which has been made unclean] by an Offspring of Uncleanness does not impart uncleanness to the hands. That which has been made unclean by a Father of Uncleanness imparts uncleanness to the hands. [That which has been made unclean] by an Offspring of Uncleanness does not impart uncleanness to the hands.

T. 2:9 These spoil [heave-offering]: hands, food in the first remove, maddaf-objects, and liquids.

M. 3:2 That which is unclean in the second remove does not put [something else into uncleanness at] the second remove.

The key is simple: whatever the source of uncleanness, it affects the hands only if it is in the first remove (or more unclean than that), and then the hands are unclean in the second remove.

IV. THE UNCLEANNESS OF SACRED SCRIPTURES

M. 3:3 The straps of tefillin [while they are still attached] to the tefillin impart uncleanness to hands.

M. 3:4 The blank spaces in a scroll, whether above or below or at the beginning or at the end impart uncleanness to hands.

T. 2:11 The blank space which is at the beginning of the scroll and is of the breadth of the entire [scroll] imparts uncleanness to the hands. He who writes *Hallel* and the *Shema'* for child's practice — even if it is not permitted to do so — it imparts uncleanness to hands.

M. 3:5 A scroll which was erased and in which remain eighty — five letters — such as the paragraph, "And it came to pass when the ark set forward" [Num. 10:35f.], imparts uncleanness to hands. A scroll in which eighty — five letters are written,

such as the paragraph, And it came to pass when the ark set forward, imparts uncleanness to hands. All sacred scriptures impart uncleanness to hands. The Song of Songs and Qohelet impart uncleanness to hands.

T. 2:10 A scroll which wore out, if one can gather from it eighty-five letters, such as the paragraph, "And it came to pass when the ark set forward" [Num. 10:35f.], imparts uncleanness to hands. A scroll in which are written eighty-five letters, such as the paragraph, "And it came to pass when the ark set forward," does (not) impart uncleanness to hands. [If] one attached to it other sheets, it imparts uncleanness to hands. But the remainder does not impart uncleanness to hands.

T. 2:12 The thongs and straps which one sewed onto a scroll, even though it is not permitted to keep them, impart uncleanness to hands. The container of a scroll and the box of a scroll and the wrappings of scrolls, when they are clean, impart uncleanness to hands. The [segments used for] blessings, even though they contain letters of the divine name and of many passages which occur in the Torah, do not impart uncleanness to hands.

T. 2:13 The Gospels [better: the leaves of parchment at the beginning and end of a scroll, without writing] and the books of heretics do not impart uncleanness to hands. And the books of Ben Sira and all books written thenceforward do not impart uncleanness to hands.

M. 4:1 On that day did they vote and decide concerning a foot-bath — which holds from two logs to nine qabs and which was cracked, that it is susceptible to uncleanness through midras-uncleanness.

M. 4:2 On that day they said: All sacrifices which were slaughtered not for their own name are fit. But they do not go to their owner's credit in fulfillment of an obligation, except for the Passover and the sin offering, the Passover at its season, and the sin offering at all times.

M. 4:5 The Aramaic [passages] which are in Ezra and Daniel impart uncleanness to hands. The Aramaic [passages contained in Scriptures) written in Hebrew, or a Hebrew [version] written in Aramaic or [passages written in archaic] Hebrew script do not impart uncleanness to hands. [Holy Scriptures] impart uncleanness to hands only if written in Assyrian characters, on parchment, and with ink.

M. 4:6 Say Sadducees: "We complain against you, Pharisees. For you say, 'Holy Scriptures impart uncleanness to hands, but the books of Homer do not impart uncleanness to hands.'" Said Rabban Yohanan b. Zakkai, "And do we have against the

> **Pharisees only this matter alone? Lo, they say, 'The bones of an ass are clean, but the bones of Yohanan, high priest, are unclean.'" They said to him, "According to their preciousness is their uncleanness. So that a man should not make the bones of his father and mother into spoons." He said to them, "So too Holy Scriptures: According to their preciousness is their uncleanness. But the books of Homer, which are not precious, do not impart uncleanness to hands."**
>
> T. 2:19 Said to them Rabban Yohanan b. Zakkai, "The preciousness of Holy Scriptures accounts for their uncleanness, so that a man should not make them into bedding for his cattle."

The inclusion of the composition marks the generative power of the hermeneutics, as I shall explain presently.

IV. THE HERMENEUTICS OF YADAYIM

A. WHAT FUSES THE HALAKHIC DATA INTO A CATEGORY-FORMATION?

What fuses the Halakhic data into a category-formation are two complementary principles: the hands form a distinct domain, separate from the body, and a special rite of purification is required for them.

The hands as a distinct domain of uncleanness, separate from the body: The hands are deemed constantly active, whether or not the person pays attention, and so are assigned a perpetual position in the second remove of uncleanness. That is to say, even though the person may know what he or she may or may not have touched, the person cannot know with what the things the hands have touched themselves have had contact — thus the second remove. Accordingly, the hands form a distinct realm of uncleanness and require their own rite of purification. The hands form a distinct entity because of their perpetual motion. That is why they precipitate doubt that cannot be resolved; we simply cannot trace their "history," — the story of the objects that they touch through the day — in the way in which we can trace the "history" of the rest of the body, which, in the course of a day, can have entered into contact with a source of uncleanness in some affective remove from a corpse or uncleanness of equivalent character. That is why, in addition to immersion of the body for known encounters with uncleanness that have taken place during the day, handwashing is required for cultic cleanness prior to eating a meal; and that has no bearing on whether or not the sun has set or when the meal takes place.

Like persons or objects in the status of the Tebul Yom, the hands are in the second remove of uncleanness. Sages maintain that even though a person does not contract uncleanness from an Offspring, but only from a Father, of uncleanness, the hands are in a different category. If the hands have touched something unclean in the first remove of uncleanness, even though the person's body is not made unclean, his hands are deemed in the second remove. They then spoil priestly rations that they touch, even though they do not make it unclean. Along these same lines Sacred Scriptures impart uncleanness to the hands that touch them. Finally, even if someone does not know whether or not his hands have touched an Offspring of uncleanness, they are deemed by definition to be unclean in the second remove: "the hands keep themselves busy." Then, if someone wishes to protect the cleanness of priestly rations or to eat his ordinary food in a state of cultic cleanness, he must properly, cultically wash the hands.

THE SPECIAL RITES OF PURIFICATION OF HANDS: To wash hands one must make use of a utensil, just as for the purification-rite one draws water with a utensil. For immersion pools one does not make use of water drawn in a utensil. To wash hands, one must make use of water that has never been used before. Further, an act of labor extraneous to the rite itself spoils the water used for washing hands. The same rule applies to the water for use in preparing purification water. An act of labor extraneous to the rite spoils that water that is to be mixed with the ashes of the red cow in the making of purification water. But the water of an immersion pool may be used again and again, and that is not so for the water used for washing hands. Thus the rules of washing hands clearly depend on the analogy drawn to rules of water used for purification water. The rite of the red cow depends upon cleanness established and attained outside of the Temple, and the rite of washing hands leads to cleanness for eating food outside of the cult, so in both cases, human agency, guided by an alert human being, is required, by contrast to rain-water, which is collected naturally upon the ground and would be spoiled for an immersion pool if human action intrudes.

DISTINCTIONS THAT MAKE A DIFFERENCE, UNCLEANNESS AND PURIFICATION OF HANDS: The difference between the uncleanness of the hands and of the rest of the body and removing that uncleanness through a process guided by its own distinctive rules derives from the Torah, which identifies the hands (and feet) as a realm of uncleanness unto themselves and specifies a process of removing that uncleanness distinct from the process that pertains to the rest of the body. And it uses its own language for the one and for the other. The key-language derives from Scripture, using the word "sanctify" to refer to the cultic rinsing of hands and feet. Take, for instance, the very vocabulary at hand. The word for wash for purposes of cultic cleanness used in the Halakhah of Yadayim is "sanctify," as at T. 1:7: Priests sanctify in the sanctuary only with a utensil.

The analogous actions then involve the purification rite, sprinkling purification-water, pouring water for hand-washing. The uncleanness of hands and the purification thereof carry us deep into the halakhic theory of the interpenetration of household and sanctuary. Here the model of the cult, for both uncleanness and cleanness in the home, is most explicit. The language of Scripture for rinsing persons and objects from uncleanness for purpose of restoring cleanness is "rinse" or "wash" (rhs), and Scripture is always explicit that after such dunking in an immersion-pool, the object remains unclean until sunset. So matters could not have been made more explicit.

B. THE ACTIVITY OF THE CATEGORY-FORMATION

THE UNCLEANNESS OF THE HANDS: The hands are deemed a cogent area, so that what affects part of them affects the entirety of them. What affects the hands does not contaminate the rest of the body and vice versa (M. 3:1). The uncleanness affecting them exhibits other distinctive traits as well. The hands never enter the first remove of uncleanness. They are made unclean only by a Father of uncleanness, not by an Offspring, such as food and utensils that have been made unclean by liquids. They are deemed unclean in the second remove, affecting heave offering. The hands are susceptible to uncleanness and are rendered clean up to the wrist.

This theory of purification is constructed in the model of the one that governs in the Temple: The priests "sanctify" — that is, wash hands — in the sanctuary, in regard to the hand, up to the wrist, and in regard to the foot, up to the calf. Consequently, when pouring water on the hands for cultic cleanness, one has to hold the hands up, so that the water will not flow beyond the wrist and then flow back and render the hands unclean again. So too the analogy is explicitly drawn: Whatever interposes in the case of the body interposes in the case of the hands, with reference to the sanctification of the hands and feet for the Temple House

PURIFYING THE HANDS OF CULTIC UNCLEANNESS: The water that hits the hands affects but is affected by them, and that water too requires a rinsing — hence a cultic purification through a repeated act of rinsing. Then, in the two washings, water may touch one part of the hands at the first, another at the second, and the process is fully valid. This conception is expressed in the following language: If one poured out the first water, and one of his hands was made unclean, lo, this one pours out the second water on the second hand and does not scruple in the matter. The result is as follows: If one poured out the first water in one place and the second in another place, and a loaf of heave offering fell on the first, it is unclean. And if it fell on the second, it is clean.

But if the first and second rinsings fall on the ground together, a loaf of bread in the status of heave offering that afterward falls on the puddle is unclean; the second water cleans the first water — only when the first water is located on the hands, but first water situated elsewhere than on the hands is not cleaned by the second water. What interposes on the hands prevents them from being cleaned: for the second water cleans only the water which is on the hand. Interposition involves uncleanness of the first water removed by the second water. The second water does not clean the interposing object or the first water that is located on it.

I have already explained the requirement of two rinsings. A quarter-log of water accomplishes the first washing, any small amount of water, the second. The water to be used the second time around may be augmented. It is going to be poured on hands made clean the first time around, so if we add water, it will not be made unclean. Accordingly, the hands are washed in two stages, first, a washing that removes uncleanness but renders unclean the water that is used, second, a washing that removes the unclean water of the first and so completes the process.

The action must be done purposively, effected by human intervention. Utensils are to be used for the purpose. These must be whole and useful, underscoring the purposive quality of the action. The rule once more corresponds to the one governing mixing water and the ashes of the red cow. Water that has been used in connection with an act of labor may not be used for washing the hands. An act of labor spoils water for use in the purification-rite. A deliberate action is required, whether the action is primary or secondary to the actual pouring out of water. The hands are to be washed up to the wrist, which demarcates the locus of uncleanness and purification pertaining to the hands in particular.

INTENTIONALITY: Intentionality enters in to the process of purifying the hands. He who pours out water on his hands, if he had proper intention, his hands are clean, and if not, his hands are unclean. But he who immerses his hands, one way or the other — his hands are clean. Thus intentionality is not required for immersion but it is required for the particular process that removes the uncleanness affecting the hands alone. If he poured out the first water on this hand by itself and changed his mind and poured out the second water on both hands simultaneously, they render one another unclean. If he poured out the first water on both hands and changed his mind and poured out the second water, this on this hand by itself and that on that hand by itself, if he had proper intention in the matter, his hands are clean, and if not, his hands are unclean. But in the following — a standard problem for the generic hermeneutics — the consideration of intentionality is subjected to limitations:

A. If the one who takes the water intends and the one who pours out the water does not intend that by his act the water will clean the hands,

B. if the one who pours out the water intends, and the one who takes the water does not intend that the water should clean the hands

C. his hands are deemed clean.

T. 1:13

But the main point is, the intentionality that defines the purpose of washing the hands also dictates the effect of doing so.

The matter of the status of sanctified documents, e.g., tefillin, Sacred Scripture, and the like, is subordinate. If the hands touch holy Scriptures, they are made unclean. That protects Scriptures from mishandling.

C. THE CONSISTENCY OF THE CATEGORY-FORMATION

Remarkable consistency in hermeneutics marks the two parts of the category-formation.

D. THE GENERATIVITY OF THE CATEGORY-FORMATION

The generativity of the hermeneutics of the category-formation emerges in the inclusion of the uncleanness of sacred Scriptures — but particularly in the Aggadic extension of the matter. There the analogical power of the hermeneutics is made explicit. What is implicit in the Halakhah — the invocation of Parah as the model for Yadayim, yielding (in my reading of matters) the contrast of sanctification and death — is made explicit in the exchange at M. 3:6:

> "According to their preciousness is their uncleanness. So that a man should not make the bones of his father and mother into spoons...So too Holy Scriptures: according to their preciousness is their uncleanness."

What begins in the uncleanness of the ever-active hands comes to its climax in the — to us, not surprising! — explicit comparison of the uncleanness of the corpse and of holy Scriptures, all according to its hierarchical classification, the more unclean, the more holy.

7.
TRACTATE UQSIN

I. THE DEFINITION OF THE CATEGORY-FORMATION

Uqsin complements the category-formation, Tohorot, the former saying about fruit and vegetables what the latter says about meat. If the two category-formations form species of a common genus — household food and its susceptibility to uncleanness — I see only analogy, and no contrast. The same hypothetical process of reasoning that produced the particular hermeneutics of Tohorot is to be replicated here. The only differences between the two category-formations is that Tohorot applies the same principles to a broader range of problems, deals with the matter of removes of uncleanness as these affect edibles and, further, addresses issues of doubt affecting the status, as to uncleanness, of food. But such a contrast pertains not to hermeneutics but to topical imperatives alone.

Concerned with fruit and vegetables Uqsin systematically expounds two matters: connection and intentionality. The Halakhah of the category-formation in response to the generic hermeneutics takes up the husks or handles of pieces of fruit or vegetables, how these are deemed distinct from one another, and how they join together reciprocally to affect the status of one another, e.g., to form a volume of food sufficient to contract uncleanness or to impart uncleanness. Stressing intentionality, the Halakhah takes shape within that particular hermeneutics when it deals with preparation of produce for eating, at which point the produce enters the system of contamination as food; a key point throughout is that produce that a person deems suitable for food enters the system, and that deemed inedible does not, so here, intentionality plays an explicit role.

In the matter of meat Tohorot takes up these same matters within the same hermeneutics. Because the particular hermeneutics in both cases focuses on intentionality, what has been stated at Chapter Five in explanation of the analogical-contrastive analysis that has defined the selection and interpretation of data need not be repeated. The generic hermeneutics is equally familiar. Here is the program of the category-formation:

I. FOOD: HANDLES, HUSKS
   - A. SUSCEPTIBILITY TO UNCLEANNESS
   - B. JOINING TOGETHER

II. FOOD: CONNECTION

III. FOOD: PREPARATION TO BRING ABOUT SUSCEPTIBILITY TO UNCLEANNESS

As to the particular hermeneutics, we address the question of the volume of food that is required for susceptibility to affect a given bit of edible material, and that is defined by the attitude of a person toward the stated volume. If he would take it into account, it registers, and if not, not. A second, still more paramount, issue concerns whether or not intentionality is required to classify edible material as food; issues of connection; and the like. As to generic hermeneutics, connection is the key. Uqsin concerns the status of parts of produce connected with but not integral to the fruit that is eaten, the other. A brief reprise of the particular and the generic hermeneutics suffices.

INTENTIONALITY: The primacy of intentionality over material actualities in the status of the components of produce — are they integral or extrinsic, connected or deemed distinct? — comes to expression explicitly. Here is one such statement:

> Olives which one pickled with their leaves — the leaves are insusceptible to uncleanness, for one pickled them only for appearance sake. If one changes the physical form of produce, chopping it up for cooking, it is deemed not connected; its form has changed. But if one had the intention not to cook the produce but to pickle or seethe or place it on the table, it remains connected.

The form is the same; the intention is what changes the matter. But intentionality can change, and sages want an action to confirm the intention. A simple case suffices. If one wants the marrow of a bone, that does not change the status of the marrow — it is connected to the bone. Only when one has crushed the bone to get at the marrow has the intention of taking the marrow been confirmed; then it is not connected.

CONNECTION: The issue of connection sorts out the relationship of parts of a utensil or a piece of produce that man values from the parts he does not value. What is classified as "connected" is a component of the fruit or vegetable, extraneous to the edible portion itself, that is deemed part of the edible portion of the fruit or vegetable. What difference does that fact make? At issue is whether or not the volume of the edible portion of fruit or vegetable is of sufficient size to contract or convey uncleanness to begin with. If it is too small, it is inconsequential. If the piece of the produce is connected, then that component adds to the volume of the edible portion to attain for the whole sufficient size to contract uncleanness or to convey uncleanness, and, moreover, that same component, if made unclean, transmits the uncleanness to the essential, edible portion of the fruit or vegetable, and, if the edible part is made unclean, that component contracts uncleanness as well. Now what dictates the status of "connection"? It is the value placed by man upon the distinct, but attached component, e.g., the twig or the husk. What man values enters the system of sanctification (effected through the human will) and uncleanness, and what man treats as null neither can be sanctified nor can contract uncleanness.

II. THE SCRIPTURAL FOUNDATIONS OF THE HALAKHIC CATEGORY-FORMATION

There is none. To the present corpus of Halakhah — Uqsin and Tohorot equally — Scripture makes no explicit contribution whatsoever, and the framers of the Halakhah do not pretend that it does.

III. THE EXPOSITION OF THE COMPONENTS OF THE GIVEN CATEGORY-FORMATION BY THE MISHNAH-TOSEFTA

I. FOOD: HANDLES, HUSKS

A. *SUSCEPTIBILITY TO UNCLEANNESS*

M. 1:1 Whatever is a handle but not a protector contracts uncleanness and imparts uncleanness but does not join together [to form the requisite volume of food to enter the system of contamination to begin with] . [If] it protects even though it is not a handle, it contracts uncleanness and imparts uncleanness and joins together. [If] it is not a protector and not a handle, it does not contract uncleanness and does not impart uncleanness.

M. 1:2 The roots of garlic, onions, and leeks, when they are wet, and the nipple end thereof, whether wet or dry, and the scape that is close to the bulb, the roots of the mint and of the rue, and wild herbs and garden herbs which one uprooted to transplant, and the spine of an ear [of corn] and its husk, lo, these contract uncleanness and impart uncleanness and join together.

T. 1:2 The roots of all things which are uprooted are not made unclean and do not impart uncleanness and do not join together. [If] one bound a sheaf, whether within the limit or beyond the limit — unclean is only that which is up to the limit alone.

T. 1:1 The prick of the grape imparts uncleanness and is made unclean and joins together. The leaves of garlic [and of] onions and the leeks when wet are made unclean and impart uncleanness and join together. [When they are] dry, they are not made unclean and do not impart uncleanness and do not join together. The roots of the dill do not impart uncleanness and are not made unclean and do not join together. The roots of the lettuce and the parsnip and the long radish and the round radish impart uncleanness and are made unclean and join together.

T. 1:3 He who plucks ripe ears to bring them into his house — their measure is a handbreadth. The handle of the stem of the brush of the palm-tree on which one left a single date is susceptible to uncleanness. And the entire handle is joined to it. And the fruit-stalks are not connected to one another.

M. 1:3 These contract uncleanness and impart uncleanness but do not join together: The roots of the garlic and onions and leeks when they are dry, and the scape that is not close to the bulb; and the branch [handle] from which the grape cluster hangs, a handbreadth on either side, and the stem of the grape cluster, whatever its length, and the tail of the grape cluster that is stripped [of grapes]; and the stem of the brush of the palm tree to a length of four handbreadths; and the stalk of an ear [of corn] to a length of three handbreadths; and the stalks of anything that is reaped, three [handbreadths]; and as to that which is not usually reaped — their stems and their roots, in any measure at all, and the outer husks of ears of corn — lo, these contract uncleanness and impart uncleanness but do not join together.

M. 1:4 These do not contract uncleanness and do not convey uncleanness and do not join together: The roots of stalks of cabbage, and shoots of beet roots, and turnips, those which it is the way to chop off but are uprooted.

T. 1:4 The handle of the broom of a palm-tree which is longer than four handbreadths, and the reed of the sheaf which is longer than three handbreadths, and all other things which are uprooted do (not) impart uncleanness and are (not) made unclean but do not join together.

T. 1:5 Grain which one threshed in the threshing floor does not impart uncleanness and is not made unclean and does not join together.

T. 1:7 A stem of [a bunch of] garlic, on one [bulb] of which liquid fell, is susceptible to uncleanness, but the [garlic] joined to it is not susceptible to uncleanness, because connection effected by man is no connection. An *etrog* which burst and which one stuck onto a spindle — this is not deemed connected, because connection effected by man is no connection.

M. 1:5 All stalks of produce which one threshed in the threshing floor are insusceptible to uncleanness. The sprig of a grape cluster which is stripped of its grapes is clean. [If] one left

on it a single grape, it is susceptible to uncleanness. The fruit stalk of a date palm which is stripped [of its dates] is insusceptible to uncleanness. [If] one left on it a single date, it is susceptible to uncleanness. And so with pulse: A stalk which is stripped is insusceptible to uncleanness. [If] one left on it a single pod, it is susceptible to uncleanness.

M. 1:6 Stalks of figs and dried figs, and acorns and carobs, lo, these contract uncleanness and impart uncleanness and join together And the stems of pears and pippins and quinces and medlars, the stem of the gourd — a handbreadth, the stem of the artichoke — a handbreadth, lo, these contract uncleanness and impart uncleanness and do not join together. And the stalks of all other [produce] do not contract uncleanness and do not impart uncleanness.

T. 1:8 Dough which was kneaded with fruit juice is insusceptible to uncleanness. You have nothing which joins together foods except seven [specified] liquids alone. The prick of a pomegranate is susceptible to uncleanness

The category-formation commences with its issue of generic hermeneutics: the parts of a piece of fruit or vegetable and how they participate in establishing the volume and the status as to cleanness or uncleanness of that piece. The criterion is set by the physical form, the traits of the part and how the part functions, not by the attitude of a person eating the produce toward the part of the produce. The correspondence to issues of Tohorot and Kelim is self-evident.

B. *JOINING TOGETHER*

M. 2:1 Olives which one pickled with their leaves — they [the leaves] are insusceptible to uncleanness, for one pickled them only for appearance sake. The fine hair on a cucumber and the sprout thereof are insusceptible to uncleanness.

M. 2:2 All pits contract uncleanness and impart uncleanness but do not join together. The pit of a soft date, even though it is detached [from the edible part] joins together, and that of the dry [date] does not join together. Therefore the skin around the pit of a dried [date] joins together, and that of the soft does not join together. A pit, part of which is detached — that which is near the edible part joins together. A bone on which is flesh — that which is near the edible part joins together. [If] it was on it [the bone] on one side — That which is near the edible part joins together. For example, the savory, marjoram, and thyme.

M. 2:3 The pomegranate or the watermelon, part of which is rotten — [what is rotten] does not join together. [If it is)

sound on one side and the other and rotten in the middle, it does not join together. The nipple of the pomegranate joins together. And its sprouting hair does not join together.

T. 2:1 The soft date, part of which is eaten, and part of which remains — [That part of the pit which is] near the food joins together. [That part which is] not near the food does not join together. [As to] a dry one, the whole is insusceptible to uncleanness.

T. 2:2 The fresh date, part of which turned rotten and part of which remains — [that part of the pit which is] near the food joins together. [That part which is] not near the food does not join together. What is the part which is near the food?

M. 2:4 All rinds contract uncleanness and impart uncleanness and join together [to make up the requisite bulk to impart uncleanness].

T. 2:3 Bundles of savory and marjoram and thyme — [that part which is] near the food joins together, [and that part which is] not near the food does not join together. Up to the empty space.

T. 2:4 A bone on which is meat, and so [marrow in] the brain which is in the head and which is in the thigh-bone — [that part which is] near the food joins together, [and that part which is] not near the food does not join together. What is the part which is near the food? If there is there empty space, it is up to the empty space. [If there] is not there empty space, unclean is only the uppermost layer of the bone alone.

T. 2:5 A thigh-bone — even though there is on it only so much as a bean, it leads the whole thing to become susceptible to uncleanness.

T. 2:6 The bones and the sinews and the horns and the hooves join together [to form the requisite bulk] to impart the uncleanness of food but not to impart the uncleanness of carrion. But they are made [serve as] handles to impart the uncleanness of carrion.

The issue of connection spills over into the matter of "joining together." We turn to parts of a piece of fruit or a vegetable that contract uncleanness or impart uncleanness and whether or not they form part of the bulk of the edible part of the produce to reach the volume that becomes susceptible to uncleanness. The interstitial issues are represented by the pit, M. 2:2, and the rind, M. 2:4.

II. FOOD: CONNECTION

M. 2:5 He who chops up [produce] to cook [it], even if he did not [wholly] cut it through — it is not connected. [If he did so] to pickle it, to seethe it, or to set it on the table, it is connected.

[If] he began to take [it] apart, the food with which he began is not deemed connected. The nuts which one strung out on a string, and the onions which one tied into a bunch — lo, they are connected. [If] he began to take the nuts apart or to peel the onions, it is not connected. The nuts and the almonds are connected until one has crushed them.

T. 2:7 The soft date which one put on top of pieces of meat to moisten them, and so [too] beans which one put on top of pieces of bread to congeal them — that which touches either the soft date or the pieces of meat, or the [congealed] bread or the beans — the whole is deemed connected. Dates and dried figs which one boiled so that they were turned into a congealed mass — [the mass] is deemed connected.

T. 2:8 Dates, nut, almond, and palm which rattle are measured just as they are. He who cuts off [produce] in order to cook it, once he has cut if off — it is not deemed connected. [If he did so] to pickle or seethe it or leave it on the table, it is deemed connected, until it will begin to fall apart. [If] he began to take it apart, this one on which he began is not deemed connected. And the remainder is deemed connected.

M. 2:6 [The shell of] a roasted egg [is connected for uncleanness] until it has been chipped. And that of a boiled egg — until it is crushed. A bone in which is marrow is connected until it will be wholly crushed. [The rind of] a pomegranate which one has cut into two is connected until one will knock it with a stick [to empty it of seeds]. Likewise: the loose stitches of the laundrymen, and the garment which is sewn with threads of mixed stuff — it is connected until one will begin to take it apart.

T. 2:9 The shells of beans and of sesame, if they contain food-matter, receive uncleanness as food. [If] they do not contain food-matter, they do not receive uncleanness as food.

T. 2:10 The shells of squash, even though they contain food, do not receive uncleanness as food. The pits of olives and the pits of dates which one boiled do not receive uncleanness as food. [If] one mixed them together with food, they do receive uncleanness as food. Pits of carobs, even though one boiled them, do receive uncleanness as food. Grape-pits and grape-skins, even though one mixed them up with food — his intention is null.

M. 2:7 The outer leaves of produce — when green, join together; and when white, do not join together.

M. 2:8 The leaves of onions and the shoots of onions — if there is sap in them, are measured as they are. If there is empty space in them, one presses down on their empty space. A spongy piece of bread is measured as it is. If there is an empty space in it, one presses down on its empty space. Calf meat which is swol-

len, and old meat which is shrunken, are measured as they are.

M. 2:9 A cucumber which one planted in a pot and which grew and [the root of which] went outside of the pot is insusceptible to uncleanness.

M. 2:10 Utensils of dung and utensils of [unbaked] clay, through which roots can penetrate, do not render seeds [contained therein] susceptible to uncleanness. A pot with a hole does not render seeds susceptible to uncleanness. One without a hole renders seeds susceptible to uncleanness. How large is the measure of the hole? Sufficiently large so that a small root can go out. [If] one filled it up with dirt to its brim, lo, it is like a tray which does not have a rim.

T. 2:11 Vegetables which dried up in their roots, for example, carob and gourd which dried up in their roots [while still attached to the ground-root], do not receive uncleanness as food. [If] one gathered them, and they then dried out, they do (not) receive uncleanness as food.

T. 2:12 A piece of wood which became soft, half of which is rotten, and half of which remains — lo, this is not connected. [If] the middle part became soft and the sides remain, the sides are not deemed connected to one another. A pomegranate, part of which turned rotten and part of which remains, lo, this is not connected. [If] the middle turned rotten and the sides remain, the sides are not deemed connected to one another. A tree which was cut down and on which were pieces of fruit — lo, they are as if they were detached. [If] the tree dried up, and pieces of fruit are on it, lo, they are is if they were attached to it.

T. 2:13 [If] one began to take nuts and to strip off the onions, even though there are before him a hundred kor — [once] he began with a single one of them, [the whole] is not deemed connected. [If] there were two or three and he began with one of them, this one with which he began is not deemed connected, but the remainder are deemed connected.

T. 2:14 A melon which one cut and put on the table is deemed connected until one will begin to take it apart. [Once] one has begun to take it apart, the segment and everything that is pulled up with it are (not) deemed connected, but the remainder is [not] deemed connected. The lower knob is connected with its own, but it is not deemed connected to the segments. [If] there were two or three, and one began with one of them, this one with which he began is not deemed connected, but the remainder is deemed connected.

T. 2:15 Nuts and almonds, even though one has crushed them are deemed connected, until one will begin to separate them. A boiled egg and an egg baked down to the size of a pill are deemed connected until one will begin to scale off the shell.

T. 2:16 An egg which was spiced in its shell, lo, this is deemed connected. Wool which is on the head of sheep and on the beard of goats, even though one scorched it in fire, is deemed connected, until one will begin to pull it up.

Issues of connection between and among parts of food — an egg and its shell — unfold, now with reference to transmission of uncleanness. We follow the "history" of the piece of food, which at one point exhibits one set of indicative trait s, at another, a different set, with the obvious consequences. The shell of the egg is connected, e.g., to transmit uncleanness, until chipped or crushed, as the case may be, and so throughout. But issues of measuring the volume of the fruit or vegetable to establish whether it meets the minimum standard arise as well.

III. FOOD: PREPARATION TO BRING ABOUT SUSCEPTIBILITY TO UNCLEANNESS

M. 3:1 There are [things] which require preparation [to be made susceptible to uncleanness] but do not require intention, intention and preparation, intention and no preparation, neither intention nor preparation. All edible foods designated for use by man require preparation but do not require intention.

M. 3:2 He who cuts off [flesh] from man and from beast and from a wild animal and from fowl, from the carrion of an unclean bird, and fat in the villages, and all other produce of the field, except for truffles and fungus — lo, these require intention and preparation.

M. 3:3 The carrion of an unclean beast located anywhere, and the carrion of clean fowl in the villages require intention but do not require preparation. The carrion of a clean beast located anywhere, and the carrion of clean fowl, and fat in the markets do not require intention or preparation.

M. 3:4 The dill, once it has imparted its flavor in the cooking pot, is no longer subject to heave offering and does not receive uncleanness as food. The sprouts of the service tree and of candytuft and leaves of arum do not receive uncleanness as food until they are sweetened.

M. 3:5 Costus, and amomum, and the principal spices, crowfoot, and asafoetida, and black pepper, and lozenges of safflower are purchased with money of [second] tithe, but do not receive uncleanness as food. When is that the case? If they are purchased with money of [second] tithe, then why do they not receive uncleanness as food? If they do not receive uncleanness as food, then they also should not be purchased with the money of [second] tithe.

M. 3:6 Unripe figs and grapes are susceptible to uncleanness as food when they reach the time of liability to tithes. Olives and grapes which have turned hard are insusceptible to uncleanness. Black cumin is declare susceptible.

T. 3:6 What are olives and grapes which have turned hard? They are those which exude from under the beam and the peat and the grape-skins. [If] one gave thought to them for food, they [nonetheless] do not receive uncleanness as food. [If] one gathered them for food, his intention is null. Grape pits and skins, even though one has gathered them [for food] — his intention is null.

T. 3:7 Hard pears, Crustumenian pears, quinces, crab-apples [follow] their season for tithes and do not receive uncleanness as food earlier than that [time]. And [if] one seethed them, they do receive uncleanness as food.

M. 3:7 The palm sprout — lo, it is like wood in every respect, except that it is purchased with money of [second] tithe. Unripened dates are food, but are free of tithes.

T. 3:10 Palm-sprout is purchased with money of [second] tithe, but it does not receive uncleanness as food. Unripened dates are not purchased with money of [second] tithe and do not receive uncleanness as food.

T. 3:11 Palm-sprout — lo, it is like wood in every respect, but it is purchased with money of [second] tithe. Lo, they are like fruit in every respect but they are free of tithes.

T. 3:9 The sprouts of the service-tree and of carobs, before they have turned sweet, do not receive uncleanness as food. Once they have turned sweet, they do receive uncleanness as food. But arum, mustard, and lupines, and all other things which are pickled, whether or not they have turned sweet, do receive uncleanness as food.

M. 3:8 Fish — from what point do they receive uncleanness? When they die. [That is the point at which by all parties they are deemed edible, e.g., even raw, as in sushi.] The branch of a fig tree which was broken off but was still attached by its bark — if it can live. Grain which was uprooted and is attached

even by a small root is insusceptible to uncleanness.

T. 3:1 Clean fish and clean locusts in every location unclean fish and unclean locusts in the villages require preparation but do not require intention. The fat of a dead [beast] in every place requires intention and does not require preparation, because it is like [or: from] its body. Fat of a slaughtered beast in the villages requires intention and preparation.

M. 3:9 Fat of [the carrion of] a clean beast is not unclean with the uncleanness of carrion. Therefore it requires preparation. Fat [of the carrion of] an unclean beast is unclean with the uncleanness of carrion. Therefore it does not require preparation. Unclean fish and unclean locusts require intention in the villages.

T. 3:3 The fat of an unclean beast is unclean. The fat of a wild animal, whether it is unclean or whether it is clean, lo, it is equivalent to its body. The fat of carrion and the fat of an animal improperly slaughtered is clean, as it is said, "The fat of an animal that dies of itself and the fat of one that is torn by beasts may be put to any other use, but on no account shall you eat it" [Lev. 7:24].

T. 3:4 He who tears meat off a limb of a living creature and gave thought to it — it does not require preparation. [If] he gave thought to it and afterward tore it off, it requires preparation.

M. 3:10 A beehive — It is (1) not like the ground; 2. and they do not write a prosbol depending on it; 3. and it does receive uncleanness [when standing] in its place; 4. and he who scrapes honey from it on the Sabbath is free.

M. 3:11 Honeycombs — from what point are they susceptible to uncleanness as liquid? When one will have broken [the honeycombs to remove the honey] .

T. 2:17 A perforated pot which one set on top of two pegs, even if they are a cubit above the ground, does not render seeds susceptible to uncleanness. Under what circumstances? When [the hole] is below. But if it is at the side [of the pot], it [the pot] does render the seeds susceptible to uncleanness. If there is on the hole [in the pot] any amount of dirt at all, it does not render the seeds susceptible to uncleanness.

T. 2:18 A tray on which is a rim and which one tipped on its side does not impart susceptibility to seeds. [If] there was liquid in the pot which is not perforated [If] liquids fell on top of a cucumber [in the pot] and it was made susceptible to uncleanness, [and if a root then] grew large and went outside the pot it is insusceptible to uncleanness.

T. 3:12 Mixed seeds of the vineyard and the ox which is to be stoned to death and the heifer whose neck is to be broken and the bird-offerings of the mesora and the hair of the Nazir and the first-

> born of the ass receive uncleanness as food.
>
> T. 3:14 As to fenugreek, all agree that it does not receive uncleanness as food. Vetch does not receive uncleanness as food. Palm-sprout which one seethed or fried does receive uncleanness as food. Dates and dried figs which one put into the pot as spices do receive uncleanness as food until they cease to be edible by man.

The particular hermeneutics defines the program of the concluding component of the category-formation, with the distinction announced at the outset, M. 3:1. As I explained at the beginning, some types of fruit or vegetables are inedible without preparation; they then are not susceptible as food until prepared. Some types of fruit or vegetables are not ordinarily used by man. Then a particular act of intentionality is required to subject them to the system of cleanness and uncleanness as food. And these two criteria intersect and yield four categories, spelled out below. The way in which the categories work is elegantly instantiated, in one of the great exercises of the Halakhah.

IV. THE HERMENEUTICS OF UQSIN

A. WHAT FUSES THE HALAKHIC DATA INTO A CATEGORY-FORMATION?

The Halakhah makes judgments about the effect of man's intentionality. It further classifies causes into diverse classifications, e.g., primary and derivative, efficient and secondary. The particular hermeneutics responds to the question, how do we sort out the intentions of man as Heaven responds to those intentions. The generic hermeneutics addresses the issue, how do we classify types of causality, efficient versus secondary and derivative. The position of the Halakhah about the character of man cannot be missed: intentionality is to be confirmed by deed. Whatever man may intend or say, wait to see what he does.

Certainly the most fecund statement of intentionality comes at the end of the Halakhic repertoire. To understand the statement, we recall that what requires intention is food not usually consumed by human beings, and what does not is food people naturally eat. If food is not ordinarily eaten by people, then a particular intentionality of an individual to eat that food is what is required to render the food susceptible to uncleanness. Further, produce in one status is not food, when the status is revised, it is, e.g., things too hard to eat have to be boiled. This yields two rules and four points of intersection: preparation, no preparation; intentionality, no intentionality. Now, there are things which require preparation to be made susceptible to uncleanness but do not require intention, intention and preparation, intention and no preparation, neither intention nor preparation. That familiar mode of schematization of matters yields profound judgments.

First comes the main one: All edible foods which are designated for use by man require preparation but do not require intention. "Do not require intention" means, these are foods that the generality of humanity deems edible. They therefore fall into the class of food for purposes of contracting uncleanness, whatever a given individual may have in mind. But they have to be prepared as food for the generality of intentionality to take effect. By contrast to what? Meat. To be classified as food, meat must be prepared for eating. Not only so, but whatever its source, whatever its status, to be deemed food man must intend that it serve as food; we do not take for granted that meat is food unless man means to eat it (and then by deed confirms that intentionality). Placing perfectly valid meat, from a beast or fowl, in the same class with meat that Israelites cannot meat, e.g., carrion, fat that may be forbidden, carrion and the like makes a striking statement. It is that eating meat is not done by nature, in the way in which eating fruits and vegetables is — there, intentionality is not required, we recall! — but always subject to a particular decision on man's part.

The matter of intentionality carries with it the on-going reflection on when action is required to confirm intention. It is raised at the concluding pericope, M. 3:12, of which, in my repertoire of the Halakhah, I cite only the normative position. Here are the contending views:

A. Honeycombs — from what point are they [is the honey-liquid] susceptible to uncleanness as liquid?

B. The House of Shammai say, "When one will smoke out [the bees therefrom]."

C. And the House of Hillel say, "When one will have broken [the honeycombs to remove the honey]."

Liquid is susceptible to uncleanness when it is wanted, that is, when it serves man's purposes, and it is not susceptible to uncleanness when man does not regard it as bearing consequence.

What is at stake here? The important distinction is, is liquid deliberately applied to produce? Then dry produce, insusceptible to uncleanness, has been deliberately wet down, and because of man's deliberate action has been brought into the system of uncleanness and rendered susceptible, just as at Makhshirin. The subsidiary point that is clarified here concerns when man's intentionality takes effect. When the bee-keeper smokes out the bees from the honey-combs, he exhibits his intentionality of taking and using the honey. So that is the point at which susceptibility to receive uncleanness affects the liquid honey, or, in the correct context, it is the point at which the honey if applied to dry produce imparts to the produce that puissant moisture that imparts susceptibility — that is to say, liquid deliberately put onto the produce. So far as the House of Shammai are concerned, therefore, a secondary cause (smoking out the bees) serves as readily as a primary cause (actually breaking the honeycombs). But the House of Hillel insists, and the Halakhah with them, that one actually must have carried out an action that directly confirms the intentionality. Secondary causation does not suffice; primary causation is required.

CONNECTION: Through the detailed exposition of connection the Halakhah concerns itself with the definition of connections within the components of food. food. Three issues inhere.

First, what part of a vegetable or fruit contracts uncleanness as, or in the category of, food?

Second, what part of a vegetable or fruit interposes between the edible part of the fruit or vegetable and a source of uncleanness, so that, if something unclean touches that component of the fruit, the edible portion of the fruit is unaffected?

Third, what part of a vegetable or fruit is deemed intrinsic to the vegetable or fruit so as to form the requisite volume of edible material to be able to contract uncleanness — there being a minimal measure, less than which the vegetable or fruit is deemed null?

The upshot is a detailed analysis of the issue of connection. So, throughout, we explore the definition of that which falls into the category of what sustains life: the vegetable or fruit that serves, not the husks or leaves of the plant or tree that do not. What can be eaten is classified as food. What is attached to the edible part — a handle — is classified as food for the purposes of uncleanness. What serves to protect the fruit interposes against uncleanness. What is useless to the fruit, either as a handle or as a protector, is not reckoned with the fruit ("does not join together") to form the requisite volume to contract uncleanness.

B. THE ACTIVITY OF THE CATEGORY-FORMATION

CONNECTION: As is commonly the case, the Halakhah takes for granted a set of premises and turns immediately to interstitial cases and problems. That is why it commences with the distinction that is subsidiary to the basic principle of connection, the distinction between serving as a handle to a piece of fruit or a vegetable (thus: the stem), and serving as a protector for the fruit or edible vegetable itself. What is a handle but does not shield the edible part of the produce is connected for purposes of uncleanness but not connected for purposes of forming the requisite volume of food to enter the system of contamination.

What protects but is not a handle is wholly connected. What does not protect and is not a handle does not contract from the produce or transmit to the produce uncleanness. So the Halakhah finds three classifications.

RECEIVE/TRANSMIT	JOINS TOGETHER	UNCLEANNESS
Handle & protector	+	+
Handle, not protector	+	-
Protector, not handle	-	(-)

Then the key consideration is what serves as a handle; the step is part of the fruit or vegetable for all purposes, the husk with the stem for some, the husk without the stem for none.

With that pattern in mind, the detailed rulings are self-evident, and knowledge of the classification-scheme yielded by an inductive examination of the detailed rulings can have yielded the opening generalization. Not only so, but with the generalization in hand, we can explain the traits imputed to varieties of fruit and vegetables, e.g., why do the roots of garlic and onions contract and impart uncleanness from and to the garlic or onion itself but do not join together to form part of its volume? Because they are deemed handles, not protectors, and so throughout. There is nothing arbitrary about the rulings before us, and, beyond the problematics of the law itself, that seems to me what the Halakhah in the aggregate demonstrates in every line.

The matter of "joining together" to form the requisite volume to constitute food of which people take account deals not only with attachments to the produce but also inner parts. Pits, for example, are taken into account. They are deemed intrinsic for purposes of uncleanness but extrinsic for purposes of joining together. At the end result they enter the class of "handle, not protector," presumably because they hold the edible mass together but are protected by that mass. In the case of the soft date, the meat of the date adheres, so the pit forms part of the mass; in the case of a dry date, the meat does not adhere to the pit, so the pit does not join together. Rinds are classed as handles and protectors; by them the fruit is held; by them the fruit is shielded. Not only so, but the rotten part of a melon does not contribute to the volume of the melon to bring it to the size requisite to contract uncleanness.

INTENTION AND PREPARATION OF PRODUCE FOR USE AS FOOD: The rule at M. 3:3 deserves attention here: The carrion of an unclean beast located anywhere, and the carrion of clean fowl in the villages require intention but do not require preparation. The carrion of a clean beast located anywhere, and the carrion of clean fowl, and fat in the markets do not require intention or preparation. Carrion of unclean beasts is not usually eaten, whether in villages or in the market places. An olive's bulk of carrion of an unclean beast does not require intention to impart uncleanness, because it itself imparts the uncleanness of carrion. Then the meaning of the opening sentence is, even less than an olive's bulk of carrion (the requisite volume) does not impart the uncleanness of carrion if one gives thought to it for food, it does join together with less than an egg's bulk of unclean food to impart uncleanness as food. The items do not require preparation because they impart uncleanness of food on their own and so make other food unclean. What about the carrion of clean beasts? That is eat; that of clean fowl and fat in the markets is eaten. Someone in the vast population of the markets will eat it, though in the villages with a smaller sample of the population that may not take place; so the carrion of clean beasts is deemed always ready for human consumption. Preparation is not required. Carrion imparts uncleanness on its own; less than an olive's bulk of carrion of a clean beast joins together with less than an egg's bulk of unclean food to impart uncleanness. As to fat, it is susceptible to uncleanness by reason of the blood of the slaughtering; it does not require intention. If something unclean touched the fat that has not been made ready to receive uncleanness, the fat in any event is made unclean.

How about preparation in the process of entering the system of uncleanness. M. 3:9 deserves a closer reading. Fat of the carrion of a clean beast is not unclean with the uncleanness of carrion. Therefore it requires preparation. Fat of the carrion of an unclean beast is unclean with the uncleanness of carrion. Therefore it does not require preparation. Unclean fish and unclean locusts require intention in the villages. If intention is not required, then what needs preparation but not intention? Fat of the carrion of a clean beast, for the reason stated. We assume people in the villages will not eat unclean fish or locusts, but in the market towns, there will be people to do so, so intentionality is not an issue. We assume the villages are entirely Israelite, the market towns not.

The issue of the susceptibility to uncleanness of vegetation encompasses questions not only of function and intentionality but also form. If the stalks are threshed in the threshing floor, whatever their status when attached to the produce, once removed, they are insusceptible. That form takes over is explicit: The sprig of a grape cluster which is stripped of its grapes is clean. If one left on it a single grape, it is susceptible to uncleanness. The fruit stalk of a date palm which is stripped of its dates is insusceptible to uncleanness. If one left on it a single date, it is susceptible to uncleanness.

C. THE CONSISTENCY OF THE CATEGORY-FORMATION

The brief category-formation adheres tightly to its two, intertwined hermeneutical programs.

D. THE GENERATIVITY OF THE CATEGORY-FORMATION

The category-formation, Uqsin, does not exhibit traits of generativity, but the hermeneutics in play here does — remarkably so. We see the close bond between the Halakhah of Kelim and that of Uqsin and Tohorot. Utensils, meat, and produce bear much in common. Since it is man's attitude that subjects a utensil to susceptibility to uncleanness as a useful tool, or a piece of produce to susceptibility to uncleanness as food, the sages differentiate what man deems of value from what he dismisses. Specifically, the law treats as distinct from one another the parts of a tool man utilizes from those not essential in utilization of the object, parts of produce man deems edible from the parts he dismisses as null. Sages conceive that an object (in the case of Kelim) or a piece of fruit or a vegetable (in the case of food, as in the present category) contracts uncleanness by reason of its utility (in the case of Kelim) or edibility (in the case of food). Uncleanness is conceived to pertain, therefore, only to that part of a utensil or a piece of fruit or a vegetable that a human being considers useful, on the one side, or deems edible and plans to eat, on the other.

In the three category-formations at hand, the particular hermeneutics intersects with the generic hermeneutics of connection and yields category-formations of diverse size but single character: each of the three leaves no doubt as to the principles of selection and interpretation of data. Then what we must characterize as highly generative is the hermeneutics, both particular and generic. It remains to investigate how substantial a proportion of the Halakhah takes shape — selects data and interprets them — in the workings of the apparently limited repertoire of particular and generic hermeneutics that we have identified.